THE NEW POLITICS OF SEX
The Sexual Revolution, Civil Liberties,
and the Growth of Governmental Power

THE NEW
POLITICS OF SEX

*The Sexual Revolution, Civil Liberties,
and the Growth of Governmental Power*

by

Stephen Baskerville

 Angelico Press

First published in the USA
by Angelico Press 2017
© Stephen Baskerville 2017

For information, address:
Angelico Press
4709 Briar Knoll Dr.
Kettering, OH 45429
www.angelicopress.com
info@angelicopress.com

pbk: 978-1-62138-287-4
cloth: 978-1-62138-289-8
ebook: 978-1-62138-288-1

Cover design: Michael Schrauzer

CONTENTS

"As political and economic freedom diminishes,
sexual freedom tends compensatingly to increase."
—Aldous Huxley, *Brave New World*

"To be able to destroy with good conscience, to be able
to behave badly and call your bad behavior 'righteous
indignation'—this is the height of psychological luxury,
the most delicious of moral treats."
—Aldous Huxley, *Crome Yellow*

Introduction

"Any man of genius is paralyzed immediately by the thought
that his efforts will win him punishment rather than rewards."
　　　　　　　　　—Evariste Huc, Christian missionary[1]

"Frankly, it is irritating that anybody would be distracted by
which statistics are accurate."
　　　　　　　　　—US Senator Claire McCaskill[2]

WITH ASTONISHING SPEED the public agenda of the Western world and beyond has come to be dominated by what *Newsweek* magazine calls "the politics of sex."[3] Demands to recognize same-sex marriage, liberalize abortion laws, and open military units to women and homosexuals are only the most salient manifestations of a much larger trend, whose full dimensions we do not yet understand. The extraordinary spectacle we have seen over five decades is the emergence of a political agenda and ideology that derives political power from demands to control and change the terms of sexuality.

Few people today need to be told about the sexualization of culture. Images of sex surround us, and they are deplored by many across the spectrum. Less noticed, and very poorly understood, is how the demand for unlimited sexual freedom is being politicized by radical ideologies and exploited by governments, whose operatives are able to greatly increase their power as a result. One can welcome this development or deplore it, but there can be no doubt that it is taking place, even though scholars and journalists across the spectrum seem determined to avert their eyes.

---

1. Quoted in David Landes, *The Wealth and Poverty of Nations* (London: Norton, 1999), 342.

2. Ashe Schow, "Claire McCaskill: Statistics? We Don't Need No Stinkin' Statistics!" *Washington Examiner*, 26 December 2014, http://www.washingtonexaminer.com/claire-mccaskill-statistics-we-dont-need-no-stinkin-statistics/article/2557887.

3. See http://prattcomd.com/blog/2012/2/profs-dan-covert-andre-andreev-create-newsweek-cover/.

For decades, sophisticated people have chortled as an assortment of moralists, reactionaries, and religious zealots warned that unrestricted sexual indulgence would lead to social turmoil, tyranny, and civilizational decline. The argument of this book is that matters turned out to be not so simple as the sophisticates thought and that the moralists, reactionaries, and religious zealots have turned out to be broadly correct, but that this process is unfolding in ways somewhat different from what they too expected, to the point that these Cassandras have often been strangely blind to the fulfillment of their own prophecies. Indeed, many of those most vocal in warning about the dangers of the Sexual Revolution have not only failed to understand its full dynamic; some of their direst warnings are being fulfilled with little opposition in part because even the Cassandras themselves have sometimes been made unwitting accomplices in advancing the very trend they deplore.

This book is an attempt to step back and gain a perspective on the larger phenomenon of how not only our society but particularly our politics has been pervaded by sexual ideology and the impact of almost unlimited sexual freedom on our political culture, public policy, and government machinery.

It does not claim to be exhaustive. A thorough critique of this phenomenon is too large for one book, and each subject deserves more focused treatment. The aim here is to show the larger pattern created by sexual political ideology and the similarities that emerge from its divers manifestations. It is necessarily an overview, therefore, and not all points are treated as thoroughly as I would like. Some topics have been researched by qualified scholars, and I have drawn freely upon their work. Elsewhere, the necessary research has not yet been undertaken, often because the right questions have not been asked. Partly for this reason, the few scholars and journalists who write critically about some manifestations of sexual radicalism are usually unaware of parallels to their findings elsewhere, and so even they do not see that what they have discovered is only one piece of a larger puzzle: the arrival of a new political ideology.

A major reason is fear. One feature of sexual politics is the almost complete absence of critical scholarship that approaches it from any viewpoint other than enthusiastic advocacy. Ostensibly objective scholars are often active participants and promoters of the phenomenon they should be studying and understanding critically. Scholars who refrain from endorsing sexual liberation and insist on analyzing these subjects from a detached perspective find it almost impossible to publish their work and are quickly driven from the universities. "Some subjects are not only undebatable; they are unresearchable," writes Phyllis Schlafly, "because they don't want the public to know the facts that research might uncover."[4]

The fact is that the Western academic world today is not an "open society" of free inquiry and critical thinking. It is largely closed, inbred, and controlled by heresy-hunters who vet scholarship according to a litmus test of political doctrine and punish heterodoxy with ostracism. Contrary to the accepted wisdom of conservative critics, this is not driven primarily by the soft targets toward which those conservatives usually direct their complaint: Marxism, racial militancy, multiculturalism. These are now relatively passé academic fashions, and few risks are incurred by criticizing them. Of all the radical ideologies that seek to control the institutions of learning today, wrote the late Robert Bork, "feminism is by far the strongest and most imperialistic, its influence suffusing the most traditional academic departments and university administrations."[5] The vanguard of academic bolshevism today—like the vanguard of leftist politics generally—is sexual.

Certainly no shortage of academic attention is lavished on sexual matters; quite the contrary. Like all ideologies, sexual radicalism is spread by cadres of academic ideologues. Novel disciplines like "women's studies," "gender studies," and "queer studies" recast all knowledge as sexual-political grievances, and sexual activists have colonized other disciplines, where they exert a veto power over what others may write and say. This is true foremost in the social sciences and humanities but even extends to the natural sciences.[6]

While these topics now dominate academic "discourse," the clearest indication of an unhealthy environment is that scholars refuse or fear to ask the awkward questions. "Among false statistics the hardest of all to slay are those promoted by feminist professors," writes Christina Hoff Sommers. "One reason . . . is that reasonable, evidence-backed criticism is regarded as a personal attack."[7]

And the counter-attack is always savage. Despite this massive academic enterprise claiming to subject all knowledge to the scrutiny of

---

4. Phyllis Schlafly, *Who Killed the American Family?* (Washington: WND Books, 2014), 180.

5. Robert H. Bork, *Slouching Towards Gomorrah*, ch. 11, 193–225, excerpted at http://fathersforlife.org/feminism/borkch11.htm.

6. "Feds Paid $709,000 to Academic Who Studies How Glaciers Are Sexist," *Daily Caller*, 7 March 2016, http://dailycaller.com/2016/03/07/feds-paid-709000-to-academic-who-studies-how-glaciers-are-sexist/#ixzz42ddMacvj.

7. "Persistent Myths in Feminist Scholarship," *Chronicle of Higher Education*, 29 June 2009 (http://www.aei.org/article/100695).

"gender analysis," glaring is the determination with which this vast scholarly industry avoids precisely the questions raised in this book. "Gender analysis is not a scientific study of the relative influence of biology and culture in the creation of the differences between men and women," observes Dale O'Leary. "Indeed, gender feminists vigorously oppose serious research into biological differences between men and women."[8] The scholars are advocates and activists, and no attempt to approach their subject matter from a detached or critical viewpoint is tolerated.

The evidence is very plain: no scholar at any university in the Western world today focuses his or her research on a critical analysis or detached appraisal of sexual ideology. "In 2014, there were more than 200 chairs for gender/queer studies, nearly all held by women, and around thirty interdisciplinary gender institutes."[9] But no academic scholar has produced any systematic critique that fundamentally challenges the truth or integrity of these ideologically defined fields. In other words, we are being asked to believe that there is 100% unanimity in academia that feminist and homosexual political agendas are simply matters of factual knowledge, equivalent to medieval history or organic chemistry. Recent scholars who argue otherwise are almost all forced to work and publish outside the universities, where a string of recent critiques indicates that something at least is wrong with the dogma that the academies refuse to confront: Gabriele Kuby, *The Global Sexual Revolution: Destruction of Freedom in the Name of Freedom* (2015); Phyllis Schlafly, *Who Killed the American Family* (2014); Jennifer Roback Morse, *The Sexual Revolution and Its Victims* (2015); Wendy McElroy, *Rape Culture Hysteria: Fixing the Damage Done to Men and Women* (2016); Helen Smith, *Men on Strike: Why Men Are Boycotting Marriage, Fatherhood, and the American Dream—and Why It Matters* (2013); and K.C. Johnson and Stuart Taylor, *The Campus Rape Frenzy: The Attack on Due Process at America's Universities* (2017). (A partial exception that proves the rule is Laura Kipnis, *Unwanted Advances: Sexual Paranoia Comes to Campus*, 2017.) Within the academies, everyone knows that such dissent is career suicide. "Professors watch as colleagues are terminated," observes McElroy.

8. Dale O'Leary, *The Gender Agenda* (Lafayette, Louisiana: Vital Issues Press, 1997), 120.

9. Gabriele Kuby, *The Global Sexual Revolution: Destruction of Freedom in the Name of Freedom* (Kettering, OH: LifeSite, 2015), 101. Steven Rhoads, now retired from the University of Virginia and author of the 2005 book, *Taking Sex Differences Seriously,* may be a partial exception.

"They self-censor to avoid a similar fate. . . . Professors do not listen to logic but to the inner voice of caution about their own job security."[10]

One confirmation is that even mild criticism of sexualized politics, no matter glaring its injustices or deadly its consequences, must be presented according to the formula that "it's bad for feminism." "The power of feminism as an orthodoxy is made evident every time someone limits a critique of feminism to this argument," writes Daphne Patai, "for this reveals how illegitimate it is thought to be to attack feminism for the harm it is doing to men and to non-feminist women."[11] Similar immunity from criticism is now being achieved by homosexual political ideology. This very absence and intolerance of disagreement or dissent brings predictable consequences, as the exceptions demonstrate.

When award-winning child development psychologist Jay Belsky of Pennsylvania State University began to dissent from feminist orthodoxy over day care, he was quickly shunned by the same colleagues who had previously showered him with honors. "It was rather amazing how quickly former supporters and admirers demonized me almost overnight," he writes. "I had violated what I have come to regard as the eleventh commandment of the field of child development: 'Thou shalt not speak ill of day care.'"[12] Belsky left his university and the United States for employment abroad.

Edward Green of the Harvard School of Health and his colleagues received similar treatment in a different field. Green recounts how he himself was treated like a superstar by his colleagues in academia and the media, feted, featured in media reports, well-paid and promoted, and his research well-funded—but only so long as he followed the party line that condoms are the panacea for AIDS. All this collapsed when he transgressed the AIDS establishment's orthodoxy by demonstrating that condoms have proven much less effective than campaigns encouraging sexual restraint. He himself explains the treatment ideologically: "The quickest way to kill criticism of condoms has been to suggest that religious belief, conservatism, bigotry, patriarchy, homophobia, or sexism has polluted the dissenter's thinking."[13]

---

10. McElroy, *Rape Culture Hysteria* (Vulgus, n.p., 2016), 2. I am grateful to the author for an advance copy.

11. Daphne Patai, *Heterophobia: Sexual Harassment and the Future of Feminism* (Lanham, Maryland: Rowman and Littlefield, 1998), Kindle locations 2149–51.

12. Jay Belsky, "The Politicized Science of Day Care," *Family Policy Review*, vol. 1, no. 2 (Fall 2003), 26.

13. Edward Green, *Broken Promises: How the AIDS Establishment Has Betrayed the Developing World* (Sausalito, California: PoliPoint Press, 2011), 25, 35, 91–92 (see also 62). See below, page 299, "Politicizing AIDS."

The exceptions starkly demonstrate the rule, because the few scholars or journalists bold enough to challenge or even analyze any single item on the sexual agenda feel they must first register their party affiliation and ideologically correct opinions on all the others, so toxic is it for any career to become visible on the wrong side.

"I am a feminist," states one dissenter, who obviously would not have been published even in a conservative newspaper without declaring this essential credential. "I have marched at the barricades, subscribed to *Ms.* magazine, and knocked on many a door in support of progressive candidates committed to women's rights." She then narrates how her son was declared guilty of trumped-up rape accusations by a feminist university tribunal.[14]

"The author fully supports gender equality in all aspects of life," announces a scholar in introducing his critique of the sexual assault industry in an ostensibly dispassionate academic journal, imploring that his findings "not be confused with a lack of concern for the feminist ideals." He pleads for understanding, knowing how likely his work is to be vetted ideologically: "Those who might be inclined to dismiss the author's viewpoint or the remedy he advocates as insensitive to the needs of rape survivors or somehow anti-feminist should keep an open mind as they read."[15]

It is not difficult to see why he must kowtow to the party in order to publish his findings. Caroline Kitchens found herself receiving accusations by campus radicals following her exposé of their dishonest statistics in *US News*. "Hardline gender activists ... prefer to shout 'victim blamer!' and 'rape apologist!' whenever they encounter a perspective that does not further their victim agenda," she writes. "Many social scientists hesitate to broach the topic at all because of the moral fervor and stridency of the activists." When the popular columnist George Will became one of the few bold enough to question the "rape epidemic" hysteria, the *Saint Louis Post-Dispatch* stopped publishing his column. "If a person dares to suggest that there is another aspect to the sexual-assault story, one that goes beyond rape hysteria, that person is viciously attacked and accused of being an apologist for rape," according to Sherry Warner-Seefeld, whose son became a poster child for false rape

14. Judith Grossman, "A Mother, a Feminist, Aghast," *Wall Street Journal*, 16 April 2013, http://online.wsj.com/article/SB10001424127887324600704578405280211043510.html.

15. Stephen Henrick, "A Hostile Environment for Student Defendants: Title IX and Sexual Assault on College Campuses," *Northern Kentucky Law Review*, vol. 40, no. 1 (2013), 49–50.

accusations. "I know this from personal experience."[16] This resembles the Salem witch accusations (also initiated by girls and young women): "It took much courage . . . to speak out . . . because the outspoken often quickly joined the accused."[17]

In no other field of inquiry must scholars proclaim, at the outset of supposedly detached and apolitical works of scientific research, that they hold certain political opinions or subscribe to a particular political ideology in order to publish their professional research. "For the record, I am a lifelong, outspoken liberal-progressive leftist," writes Green in his critique of gay- and feminist-dominated AIDS policy. "I have always supported reproductive rights and sexual freedom, and I spent many years working in contraception, family planning, and condom marketing. I am not an active adherent of any sect, denomination, or religion." Green is appropriately ashamed for this verbal self-flagellation and admits that "I shouldn't have to say these things, but such is the level of argument that some people judge one's findings by one's politics and vice versa." And as he goes on to show, "some people" are the people that control academic funding and hiring and publications and thus whose findings and whose careers are permitted to survive.[18]

In short, sexual ideology has already largely curtailed academic freedom in Western universities. When Patai and Noretta Koertge interviewed academics scholars for their critique of women's studies programs, "Nearly every woman . . . requested that her name, affiliation, and other identifying features be disguised."[19]

Fields like "women's studies," "gender studies," and "queer studies" are not disinterested scholarship or pedagogy. They are government-funded political advocacy, and their aim is to advance a political agenda that rationalizes government measures of intervention into the private lives of non-criminal people who have no comparable platform to defend themselves from the measures being advocated against them by government-funded scholars, institutions, and publications. These government-bankrolled scholars are (and readily describe themselves as being) players in a competitive game of power. In fact, these fields make

16. Caroline Kitchens, "Mothers for Due Process," *National Review Online,* 7 August 2014, http://www.nationalreview.com/corner/384780/mothers-due-process-caroline-kitchens.

17. Paul R. McHugh, *Try to Remember: Psychiatry's Clash Over Meaning, Memory, and Mind* (New York: Dana Press, 2008), Kindle locations 2319–20.

18. Green, *Broken Promises,* xviii–xix.

19. Patai, *Heterophobia,* Kindle locations 1027–28; Daphne Patai and Noretta Koertge, *Professing Feminism: Cautionary Tales from the Strange World of Women's Studies* (New York: Basic Books, 1994), xxv.

little pretense at detached scholarship. "The explicit objective of Women's Studies is political," according to one practitioner. "The ideology is to be propagated as widely as possible, with the ultimate goal of achieving social change."[20] While frequently criticized for overt bias against men and masculinity,[21] equally serious is how they have commandeered scholarship in the service of ideology and use the classroom for advocacy and activism. According to its website, "The National Women's Studies Association leads the field of Women's Studies in educational and social transformation."[22] There is no pretense that it is other than political advocacy: "Women's studies ... is equipping women to transform the world to one that will be free of all oppression ... a force which furthers the realization of feminist aims." Subjects addressed at its conferences include "Feminist Activism from the Inside Out: Connecting Campus to Community," "'You Say You Want a Revolution?': Paving New Paths in Feminist Mentorship," and "Drive a Mind Wild: How Feminist Pedagogy can Teach Resistance."[23]

Christine Stolba surveyed the leading women's-studies textbooks, which she describes as propaganda rather than scholarship, and found that they "encourage students to embrace aggrievement, not knowledge." She found "a large number of factual inaccuracies" and "deliberately misleading sisterly sophistries." These textbooks make no pretense of objective pedagogy or scholarship but openly advertise their "transformative" power as political ideology, and Stolba observes the "authors' unwillingness to engage with critics." "Antifeminist, antiwoman forces on the right have whittled away at our demands for human parity, for reproductive autonomy, and for economic justice, and today they promise continued assault," declares one textbook. "Antifeminism supports the present abusive gender system.... It opposes women's freedom and it denigrates our selfhood." While they describe the world as "antiwoman" when it does not grant their "demands," their own literature—propagated in the name of education—launches aggressive screeds against people most of whom have no platform to defend themselves: "Who creates weapons and marches off to war? Who hunts and kills liv-

20. Quoted in O'Leary, *Gender Agenda*, 34.

21. Paul Nathanson and Katherine K. Young, *Legalizing Misandry: From Public Shame to Systemic Discrimination against Men* (Montreal: McGill-Queen's University Press, 2006), 465–70.

22. Website of the National Women's Studies Association: http://www.nwsa.org/about/index.php, accessed 29 November 2008.

23. Karin Agness, "Illegitimate Political Agenda," *TownHall.com*, 25 June 2008, http://www.townhall.com/columnists/KarinAgness/2008/06/25/illegitimate_political_agenda&Comments=true; Patai and Koertge, *Professing Feminism*, 4.

ing creatures for fun? Who fights for kicks? Who pillages the earth for profit? Who colonizes and exploits? What destruction could [women] have wrought that even nearly compares?"[24]

Patai and Koertge describe the "sea of propaganda" that overwhelms the contemporary feminist classroom. They found that both students and faculty feel "silenced" and "ostracized" by militants posturing to outshine one another in their zealotry. The dynamic is reminiscent of China's Cultural Revolution, with militant students publicly denouncing professors who lack sufficient ideological zeal. "The theories as well as the practices of feminist pedagogy are explicitly intended to change students' political attitudes." Patai and Koertge describe this as a "form of brainwashing." "Feminist research demands loyalty to an ideological agenda rather than empirical adequacy and logical consistency," they write. "And if one raises this as a criticism, the defense is that feminism prides itself on subverting and challenging the norms of academic inquiry."[25]

The real-world consequences are seen in the peculiar logic of politically influential academics like Catherine MacKinnon: "Intimate violation of women by men is sufficiently pervasive in American society as to be nearly invisible."[26] Aside from constituting an open admission that no evidence exists for what (as we shall see) is the most determined juggernaut in the sexual machinery—measures against supposedly widespread "violence against women"—such pretense at scholarship would not (yet) be tolerated in any other academic field.

Like the new gender crimes which (as we shall see) are created in the feminist academies and adjudicated in the feminist courtrooms, the academic thought crime of "sexism" is one which permits no defense, because it is vague beyond any possible definition. Cases like that of the tenured full professor who was dismissed not because he himself committed any ethical transgression but because he refused to submit to anti-"sexist" indoctrination sessions demonstrate that heresy and heterodoxy are the ultimate gender crimes. "To believe in the reality of sexual differences is to be a 'sexist,' and 'sexism' comes next to racism in the litany of crimes," writes Roger Scruton. "There is no defense, since the charge is too vague and too all-encompassing to permit one. As a result, few people will take the risk, in an American university, of questioning

24. Christine Stolba, *Lying in a Room of One's Own: How Women's Studies Textbooks Miseducate Students* (Arlington, Virginia: Independent Women's Forum, 2002), 6, 8, 25, 27, 32.
25. Patai and Koertge, *Professing Feminism*, 13–15, 366.
26. Quoted in Patai, *Heterophobia*, Kindle Location 338.

the fundamental tenets of feminism, even if these tenets are . . . transparently false."[27]

Recent years have witnessed numerous dismissals of scholars, journalists, and others for ideologically incorrect utterances about sexual relations. The resignation of Harvard President Lawrence Summers for a comment about women in science is only the most famous in the ongoing purge. In 2015, the University of North Carolina fired wrestling coach C. D. Mock, not because he himself committed any legal offense, but because he criticized the unjust methods of adjudicating rape accusations at US universities.

Also in 2015, Sir Tim Hunt, a Nobel Prize winning scientist, was forced to resign his academic post for saying at an informal gathering that it is difficult to criticize female scientists or hold them responsible: "You fall in love with them, they fall in love with you and when you criticize them, they cry." No one denied the factual accuracy of his utterance; its ideological inconsistency with their own political beliefs was the sole complaint. As they stripped him of his honors, the Royal Society tweeted that "Tim Hunt's comments don't reflect our views." Apparently consistency with the Royal Society's political doctrines is a requirement for scientific recognition. Even his defenders treated the comments as "off-hand," but Sir Tim insisted that it is "terribly important" to be able to criticize scientists without them bursting into tears. As some pointed out, the university that found his comments intolerable regularly hosts speakers advocating Islamist terrorism by invoking "academic freedom."[28]

Sexual radicals today are open about their commitment to censorship in universities and claim the authority of all women and other sexual "minorities" to support silencing others. "More women then [sic] men think universities should safeguard people of a particular gender, race or sexuality against offensive views," one feminist notes approvingly.

---

27. "Sacrilege and Sacrament," in *The Meaning of Marriage*, ed. R. P. George and J. B. Elshtain (Dallas: Spence, 2006), 27.

28. "U. of North Carolina Wrestling Coach, an Advocate for Men Accused of Rape, Is Fired," *Chronicle of Higher Education*, 12 June 2015 (http://chronicle.com/blogs/ticker/u-of-north-carolina-wrestling-coach-an-advocate-for-men-accused-of-rape-is-fired/1006 17); Boris Johnson, "Male and Female are Different. . . ." *Daily Telegraph*, 14 June 2015 (http://www.telegraph.co.uk/news/society/11674257/Male-and-female-are-different-hardly-earth-shattering-news.html); Charles Moore, "Sexist Jokes are Graver than Terror Preachers," *Daily Telegraph*, 22 June 2015 (http://www.telegraph.co.uk/news/society/116 90094/Sexist-jokes-are-graver-than-terror-preachers.html).

"Students with privilege . . . have the opportunity to learn . . . that after centuries of being in charge, it's someone else's turn."[29]

As the academic culture filters down to the media we see the debasement of intellectual inquiry that discards any pretense of the detachment and critical inquiry that is essential to the integrity of both academics and journalism. Witness the outpouring of triumphalist articles in prestigious journals gloating over the new feminine power. Often written as first-person accounts, these articles trumpet the radicals' acquisition of power ("empowerment") as a virtue for its own sake, complain indignantly about the obstacles to acquiring more as quickly as they would like, and announce their intention nonetheless to obtain it regardless of the consequences. In "A Woman's World," on the cover of the *Wilson Quarterly*, Sara Sklaroff proclaims that "women are taking over." In *Foreign Policy*, Reihan Salam announces "The Death of Macho" and of "the macho men's club" (of which he himself is presumably not a member), and David Rothkopf tells us that it is "The End of an Era . . . for White Males" (but "not fast enough"). In "The End of Men" on the cover of the *Atlantic Monthly*, Hanna Rosin describes "how women are taking control of everything."

These are highbrow journals, read by educated people, including academics. Yet none of these articles makes the slightest effort to justify the trend, to analyze its implications, approach it with critical detachment, describe any complexities, or entertain the possibility that it may entail any negative aspects or injustices of its own. On the contrary, the only point apparently worth making—and it is hardly more subtle than this—is that women (really feminist women) are the new ruling class, and everyone else must get used to it. "The Richer Sex" proclaims the cover of *Newsweek*, with no apology or any intention of probing the reasons. Much of this bravado seems inspired by *The Shriver Report: A Woman's Nation Changes Everything*, which boasted that it is now a "woman's world," and "emergent economic power gives women a new seat at the table—at the head of the table."[30]

Needless to say, did such trends favor men we would hear calls for studies, investigations, affirmative action, and other corrective govern-

---

29. Kaite Welsh, "Universities Have Always Been a Safe Space for Straight, White Men—'Censorship' Just Evens the Playing Field," *Daily Telegraph*, 23 May 2016, http://www.telegraph.co.uk/women/life/universities-have-always-been-a-safe-space-for-straight-white-me/.

30. Heather Boushey and Ann O'Leary (eds.), "The Shriver Report: A Woman's Nation Changes Everything" (Washington: Center for American Progress, 2009, http://www.americanprogress.org/issues/women/report/2009/10/16/6789/the-shriver-report/).

ment measures to "redress the balance," end the "discrimination," and engineer gender equality.

In sum, no book like this one now exists because it is not safe for any academically employed scholar to write one. Its existence is the exception that proves the rule of its argument, and I can raise these questions because I am employed in a college that does not depend on government funding. Otherwise, I would quickly be dismissed from my employment as I was from a government-funded university when I began to write about these issues almost two decades ago. This book attempts to ask these unasked questions and begin a broader and more open discussion about the impact of unrestrained sexuality on our public life. It is my hope that it will help other scholars to summon the resolve to undertake further investigations and supply more definitive answers where I can mostly pose questions and suggest hypotheses.

I am grateful to my colleagues and students, to editors and many others who have read, heard, and provided feedback on earlier versions of various sections of this book and who have supplied me with information. Above all, I am indebted to my wife, Ioana Baskerville, whose support and ideas have made this a better book.

I

Politicizing Sex
—and Sexualizing Politics

"All politics is on one level sexual politics."
—George Gilder[1]

FIVE DECADES INTO the boldest social experiment ever undertaken in the Western democracies, the full impact of what was once quaintly known as "women's liberation" is at last becoming clear. Politicians of both the left and right have colluded to limit the discussion to a series of apparently innocuous controversies superficially reminiscent of America's troubled racial politics: job discrimination, equal pay, affirmative action. Only abortion indicates deeper issues, and that debate has been mired in stalemate.

Meanwhile, from beneath the media radar screen, the more profound consequences are finally emerging: a fundamental restructuring of the social order, demographic trends that threaten the very survival of some nations, and—least noticed of all—an exponential increase in the size and reach of the state, the state at its most bureaucratic and intrusive.

The Sexual Revolution, it is now apparent, has been about much more than simply discarding sexual inhibitions and restrictions. Like all revolutions, it has been driven from the start by revolutionaries seeking power. Feminists and more recently homosexual political activists (sometimes termed "homosexual-*ism*") have now positioned themselves at the vanguard of left-wing politics, shifting the political discourse from the economic and racial to the social and increasingly the sexual. What was once a socialist campaign against private enterprise and private property has expanded into a social and sexual confrontation with the private family, marriage, masculinity, and religion. This marks a

---

1. *Men and Marriage* (Gretna, Louisiana: Pelican, 1986), 112.

truly new kind of politics, the most personal and thus potentially the most total politics ever devised: the politics of sexual and family life.

No sexual ideology has ever before appeared, and its unprecedented power is at once obvious and disguised. Obvious, because it is not difficult to see that politicizing sexual intimacy permeates far deeper into the human psyche, unleashes energies and emotions, and disrupts relationships and institutions far more fundamental than those attacked by radical ideologies of the past. Daphne Patai and Noretta Koertge point out "feminism's explicit assault not only on hierarchies generally but also on the boundaries between the public and private."[2] The capacity for intrusion into the private sphere of life is unrivalled since the bureaucratic dictatorships of the last century and potentially surpasses even them. "Radical feminism is the most destructive and fanatical movement to come down to us from the sixties," writes Robert Bork. "This is a revolutionary, not a reformist, movement. . . . Totalitarian in spirit, it is deeply antagonistic to traditional Western culture and proposes the complete restructuring of society, morality, and human nature."[3]

Yet how precisely the scenario is unfolding is far less clear and, indeed, has escaped most observers. Even conservatives like Bork who are quick to label feminism as "totalitarian" seem strangely unable to comprehend of dynamic of their own warnings. The grip that sexually innovative politics already commands over our political culture is so profound that its most disruptive implications remain misunderstood, even by critics. Apart from its advocates, few scholars or journalists have even singled out sexual politics as a subject for focused critical examination. Conservatives bemoan it as simply another facet of leftist politics, like socialism or multiculturalism. But it is much more. "Feminism, today, is the most utopian project around," wrote one supporter (and later critic) at its inception. "It demands the most radical and truly revolutionary transformation of society, and it is going on in an extraordinary variety of ways."[4] Feminists today believe that "it is necessary to change the whole existing social structure in order to achieve women's liberation."[5] They are correct.

2. Daphne Patai and Noretta Koertge, *Professing Feminism: Cautionary Tales from the Strange World of Women's Studies* (New York: Basic Books, 1994), 112.

3. Robert Bork, *Slouching Towards Gomorrah*, ch. 11, 193, excerpted at http://www.tldm.org/news5/bork_feminism.htm.

4. Daphne Patai, *Heterophobia: Sexual Harassment and the Future of Feminism* (Lanham, Maryland: Rowman and Littlefield, 1998), Kindle locations 105–6, quoting herself.

5. Alison Jagger, "Political Philosophies of Women's Liberation," in *Feminism and Philosophy*, 9, quoted in Dale O'Leary, *The Gender Agenda* (Lafayette, Louisiana: Vital Issues Press, 1997), 100.

Here as elsewhere, homosexualists have piggybacked on the feminists' agenda and adopted their methods. As Wyndham Lewis and Bryce Christensen have pointed out, "Homosexuals inevitably form alliances with feminists against masculine authority."[6] In both cases the "salami tactics" are strikingly reminiscent of methods pioneered by their Bolshevik mentors. "The means . . . included street actions . . . marches, picket lines, political lobbying . . . and a constant in-your-face presentation of the fact that gay is good," declares activist Marc Rubin. "Its goals were revolutionary in that it sought, through these means, to restructure society."[7]

Both feminism and the newer homosexualist ideology began with apparently modest demands: feminists to legal equality with men; homosexuals to be left alone in private life. It is now apparent that these agendas encompass far more than meets the eye and that we have opened a Pandora's Box of demands and urges that, like sex itself (and political power), are insatiable.

On one level, of course, sex has been integral to politics since Potiphar's wife. Exchanging sexual favors for political influence is probably universal. Nor is today's "sexual politics" limited to explicitly sexual controversies, though that is a major part of it. "Sexual politics" (as the term's originators made clear) is an *ideology* that uses sexuality as an instrument to satisfy the human craving for power. One sympathetic scholar calls it "the ideology of the erotic":[8] the claims of feminists, homosexualists, and others to base not only the goals of their political agenda but also the means and methods of achieving those goals on sexual leverage and sexual power.

Helen Alvare has termed this "sexualityism," which she describes as "a commitment to uncommitted, unencumbered, inconsequential sex." "There has been a massive expansion of 'sexual liberty' on a nationwide scale," she writes. "The federal government is seeking to expand sexualityism . . . claiming that . . . religion and marital sexual intimacy

---

6. Bryce Christensen, "The End of Gender Sanity in American Public Life," *Modern Age*, vol. 49, no. 4 (Fall 2007), 411.

7. "GAA Must be Restored to History," Gay Today website (n. d.): http://www.gaytoday.com/garchive/viewpoint/071999vi.htm.

8. Richard G. Parker, *Bodies, Pleasures, and Passions: Sexual Culture in Contemporary Brazil* (Nashville: Vanderbilt University Press, 2009), 111. Parker reveals (135) how using sexual deviancy to elicit disgust serves as a weapon of rebellion: "Within this ideology of the erotic, then, the *bunda* can become a focus for sexual pleasure. Because of its . . . negative . . . associations with *excremento* (excrement), with *bosta* or *merda* (shit)—it . . . is especially well suited to the undermining of social norms and proper decorum that is fundamental to the constitution of erotic experience."

are irrational and unscientific."[9] Perhaps the first to name this phenomenon was the inimitable Ralph Nader, who sneered at what he called "gonad politics."

"Sex is always political," we are told by the scholar-advocates, because some are perpetrating "sexual oppression" that denies others their "sexual rights." But the oppressed are now organizing "movements of resistance." This "sexual rights movement" will secure "sexual citizenship" and "sexual self-determination." Sexual rights "are inextricable from economic, social, cultural, and political rights," including "the right to pursue a satisfying, safe, and pleasurable sexual life"—apparently "rights that are protected by the state." Sexual oppressors use "hierarchies of sexual value" such as religion and traditional values that "function in much the same ways as do ideological systems of racism." This sexual agitprop demands much more than the right to be left alone. "Sexual politics has expanded," and "feminists and other sexual politics actors have expanded, deepened, and intensified their engagements with the state," including the police and prison system, which must be used to punish oppressors for their "crimes." Moreover, "an increasing number of sexual politics actors have started to engage in global policy arenas," and so "sexuality theory, research, and political activism have been sustained, renewed, and diversified across national and cultural boundaries." The result of this activism: "'Sex' and gender norms were extensively reconfigured in most countries. . . ." Yet still needed is "a more radical sexual politics" to articulate "a vision of sexual self-determination and freedom" and a full-scale "cultural revolution."[10]

We have heard this before. With updated grievances, it is driven by a hatred of restraint and authority and a thirst for unrestricted freedom and revenge reminiscent of the ideologies of the recent past. Palpable in these manifestos is the emotion that feeds all violent political movements: resentment. The resentment is directed not at named individuals—who could be formally charged and tried for specific and recognized crimes using established procedures and tangible evidence—but against groups of unnamed political transgressors *en masse*, against whom new crimes and new justifications for punishment must

---

9. Helen Alvare, "The White House and Sexualityism," *Public Discourse*, 16 July 2012, http://www.thepublicdiscourse.com/2012/07/5757/. The term "sexual ideology" has been adopted by other scholars: e.g., Mary Rice Hasson on hook-up culture (see below, ch. III), Douglas Sylva in analyzing UNICEF (ch. IV), and Edward Green on AIDS (ch. IV).

10. Sonia Corrêa, Rosalind Petchesky, and Richard Parker, *Sexuality, Health, and Human Rights* (Abingdon: Routledge, 2008), 4–5, 24, 26–27, 29–30, 93; Richard Parker, Rosalind Petchesky and Robert Sember (eds.) *Sex Politics: Reports from the Front Lines* (n.p.: Sexuality Policy Watch, n.d.), 9, 20.

be devised. For the resentment rationalizes the desire "to restructure society": to rebel, to overthrow the existing order and institute a new order with themselves in command, and to use their new power to punish their political opponents, who in this case—even more than in the past—are ordinary people minding their own business.

Sexual ideologues are explicit that their ideology is consciously devoted to using sex as an instrument of rebellion; one militant observes "the ebullient glee with which [they] kick over the pedestal of female virtue."[11] This ranges from the level of adolescent popular culture to professional scholarship, with a sometimes thin line delineating the difference. The female chairperson of a major university Women's Studies department writes in a government-funded (and presumably peer-reviewed) paper how she visited a nightclub to not only watch drag queens "grope and fondle men and women, use foul language, and mimic sex acts on stage," but participated herself and felt "powerful disguised as a man dressing as a woman."[12] Sexual radicals openly celebrate their right to "pleasure," but among these is the pleasure of desecrating other people's values and beliefs and the existing social order, and feeling "powerful" in the process. Richard Parker explains how effectively sex operates as a weapon to overturn social and political hierarchies, offend sensibilities, and glorify rebellion as a virtue for its own sake:

> The erotic . . . is linked to the structures of power. . . . The relationship between power and eroticism can only be understood . . . by situating the erotic . . . as a kind of alternative to these other systems. . . . Breaking down the separations of daily life in the fleeting moments of desire, pleasure, and passion, the erotic offers an anarchic alternative to the established order of the sexual universe: an alternative in which the only absolute rule is the transgression of prohibitions. . . .
>
> Transgressing the established order of daily life . . . even the structures of power can themselves be eroticized within this frame of reference. . . . No less than same-sex interactions, extramarital affairs, masturbation, or anal intercourse, they become especially erotic because they destroy the hierarchical values of the everyday world. . . . The workings of power must be understood through the cultural forms and meanings of the erotic, and the symbolism of the erotic must be interpreted through the structures of power and its capacity to transform them.
>
> Organized around a distinct cultural logic and possessing its own

---

11. Rita Felski, quoted in Anne Barbeau Gardiner, "Feminist Literary Criticism: From Anti-Patriarchy to Decadence," *Modern Age*, vol. 49, no. 4 (Fall 2007), 398.

12. Leila Rupp, quoted in Gardiner, "Feminist Literary Criticism," 399.

particular relation to power, then, this ideology of the erotic can be situated in relation to the systems of gender and sexuality.[13]

We will see this theme reappear in different contexts: the sex and the politics are inseparable, not simply because political activism offers a means to the end of sexual freedom, as liberalism superficially understands it, but because (as any parent of an adolescent might testify) sexual freedom is itself a form of rebellion and one easily politicized. Breaking sexual restraints and "taboos" is an end in itself because it defies convention and authority and therefore provides "power." "Your abortion can be a rebellious and empowering act," declares one feminist.

> It is an act through which you can assert yourself.... It is a surgical operation with a mission.... My hope is that... you will use your abortion to connect with women everywhere. You will connect your very special personal with the very important political, and you will begin to know your own power.[14]

Homosexuals, especially males, do not necessarily understand their sexuality in expressly political terms. Yet homosexuality too has itself become a political statement, and it is likely that today's political revolt originates in and expresses the sexual drive itself, which is often a revolt against parents.[15] Lesbianism is more obviously political and for many constitutes the personal dimension of feminist ideology: "Feminism is the theory, lesbianism is the practice," in words attributed to Ti-Grace Atkinson. "For many of today's feminists, lesbianism is far more than a sexual orientation.... It is, as students in higher education learn, 'an ideological, political, and philosophical means of liberation of all women from heterosexual tyranny.'"[16] For sexual activists, sex itself is not a personal but a political act. Recalling Henry Adams's definition of politics as the "systematic organization of hatreds," it requires little imagination to see that this rebellion against "sexual tyranny" has politicized and transformed sex, an act associated at its most sublime with love, into what may yet prove history's purest distillation of hate.

Many have discerned an affinity with older ideologies like Marxism, but few appreciate how far sexual radicalism expands socialist logic and

---

13. Parker, *Bodies, Pleasures, and Passions*, 151–52.

14. Rebecca Walker, "She's Come for An Abortion. What Do You Say?" *Harper's Magazine*, November 1992, 51, quoted in Charmaine Crouse Yoest, "The New Feminist at 50: Women Alone," *The Family in America*, vol. 27, no. 1 (Winter 2013), 18.

15. See chapter II, under "Homosexualism."

16. Rene Denfeld, *The New Victorians* (London: Simon and Schuster, 1995), 45, quoting Cheryl Clarke, *This Bridge Called My Back*.

intrusiveness. "Women's liberation ... the most influential neo-Marxist movement in America, has done to the American home what communism did to the Russian economy, and most of the ruin is irreversible," writes Ruth Wisse. "By defining relations between men and women in terms of power and competition instead of reciprocity and cooperation, the movement tore apart the most basic and fragile contract in human society, the unit from which all other social institutions draw their strength."[17] Sexual radicals acknowledge their camaraderie with past revolutionaries. "The great value of Engels' contribution to the Sexual Revolution lay in his analysis of patriarchal marriage and family," wrote Kate Millett in her seminal *Sexual Politics*.[18] Engels himself confirmed that socialist logic leads to sexualist ideology. "The first division of labor is that between man and woman for the propagation of children," he wrote. "The first class opposition that appears in history coincides with the development of the antagonism between man and woman in monogamous marriage, and ... with that of the female sex by the male."[19]

Anyone who doubts the similarly repressive logic of today's ideologies need only listen to the aspirations of the sisterhood. "A world where men and women would be equal is easy to visualize, for that precisely is what the Soviet Revolution promised," wrote Simone de Beauvoir.[20] As with the Soviet and other socialism in its day, feminism (and increasingly homosexualism) stands largely unchallenged and unchallengeable, even as it re-creates the familiar combination of political corruption, economic stagnation, swollen prison populations, and politicized criminal justice that the elites refuse to face. Arnold Beichman's lament over the previous opiate of the intellectuals might describe where we currently stand with this one:

> How could so many intelligent people have been so wrong, so damnably wrong about Communism, about Stalin, about the Russian Revolution, so oblivious of the human price being paid in the name of revolution? ... Why would such people (and there were thousands of them of otherwise high intellectual achievement) have willingly, even enthusiastically, written and published Soviet propaganda and offered it up as truth in books, academic journals, op-eds, monographs?[21]

17. Quoted in Arnold Beichman, "Undercurrents in the Conservative Tide," *Washington Times*, 11 February 1997, A17.

18. New York: Avon, 1971, 167, quoted in O'Leary, *Gender Agenda*, 98.

19. *Origins of the Family, Private Property, and the State* (1884), online: http://www.marxists.org/archive/marx/works/1884/origin-family/cho2d.htm.

20. Simone de Beauvoir, *The Second Sex* (New York: Random House, 1952), 806.

21. Arnold Beichman, "Tyrant's Death Recalled," *Washington Times*, 5 March 2003, A17.

E. Michael Jones has shown how sexual radicalism has coincided historically with political radicalism, including the most violent upheavals such as the French and Russian revolutions. "Sexual revolution is, if not synonymous with revolution in the modern sense of the word," he observes, "then certainly it is contemporaneous."[22] Feminists have long had intimate associations with Bolshevism and before them with Jacobinism. Likewise, homosexualists have longstanding involvement in Fascism, including Nazism. "Gay men have been at the heart of every major fascist movement . . .—including the gay-gassing, homicidal Third Reich," writes Johann Hari. "Many of the mainstream elements of gay culture—body worship, the lauding of the strong, a fetish for authority figures and cruelty—provide a swamp in which the fascist virus can thrive."[23] Yet even as they perceive the logic unfolding, some of the Sexual Revolution's most severe critics still insist that "the women's movement has produced no gulags—not yet, anyway."[24] I shall demonstrate that some of the Sexual Revolution's most severe critics are not well informed.

Yet politicizing sex takes the logic of class conflict a great leap forward. The old leftist cry of "social justice" has been extended to demands for "erotic justice":[25] "erotic justice may be . . . integrated within, broader struggles for social justice."[26] Here the charge of "oppressor" is extended from impersonal social classes to intimate personal relationships. The oppressor is not the entrepreneurial class but the most intimate relations: the husband (or "intimate partner"), the father, even the son. "A mother may love her son dearly, but he is nevertheless a member of a class that has controlled and oppressed her," writes Anne Schaef. "As a result, she cannot help but feel rage and hostility toward him."[27]

22. E. Michael Jones, *Libido Dominandi: Sexual Liberation and Political Control* (South Bend, IN: St. Augustine's Press, 2000), 20.

23. Johann Hari, "The Strange, Strange Story of the Gay Fascists," *Huffington Post*, 21 October 2008, http://www.huffingtonpost.com/johann-hari/the-strange-strange-story_ b_136697.html. See also Scott Lively and Kevin Abrams, *The Pink Swastika: Homosexuality in the Nazi Party* (Keizer, Oregon: Founders Publishing Corp., 1995).

24. Carol Iannone, "The 'Good Feminism' Delusion," *Modern Age*, vol. 49, no. 4 (Fall 2007), 383. Mary Eberstadt has highlighted the similarity of these two opiates. *Adam and Eve After the Pill: Paradoxes of the Sexual Revolution* (San Francisco: Ignatius Press, 2012), ch. 1. She too cautions that her argument "is not to say that the sexual revolution has caused anything like the Gulag archipelago" (24), but see chapter III, below.

25. Corrêa, et al., *Sexuality*, 4–5.

26. Ibid.

27. Anne Schaef, *Women's Reality: An Emerging Female System in a White Male Society* (Minneapolis: Winston Press, 1985), 80.

To relieve the oppressed, the all-powerful state nationalizes not only the private firm but the private family. Romantic and family intimacy— the individual's last refuge from state power—is not merely a collateral casualty but the targeted enemy. "The Soviet system controlled the political and economic structures," observes one scholar; "the feminists want control of intimate and family relationships."[28]

The innovation comes less from the assault on political freedom (which traditional tyrannies also curtail) but from the attack on private life, especially family life (which traditional dictatorships usually left alone). "Radical feminism is totalitarian because it denies the individual a private space; every private thought and action is public and, there- fore, political," writes Bork. "The party or the movement claims the right to control every aspect of life."[29] Likewise Patai: "Feminism today, in its erasure of the boundaries between public and private, is writing a new chapter in the dystopian tradition of surveillance and unfreedom ... whereby one's every gesture, every thought, is exposed to the judge- ment of one's fellow citizens."[30]

This attack on privacy is especially elusive, because those who once extolled and defended private life—conservatives, who constitute femi- nism's natural opposition—themselves do not always value privacy and civil liberties today. By a perverse irony, feminists have co-opted "pri- vacy" to rationalize unrestricted abortion, leading conservatives to abandon the concept itself. Many conservatives also dismiss due process protections as a pretext for acquitting criminals, leaving radicals as sole guardians of civil liberties. Doubtless some guilty do go unpunished, but partly because the politicization of the criminal justice system incarcerates the innocent in their place. As we shall see, the principal ideological force driving the incarceration of the innocent today is sex- ual.[31]

"Revolutions are very hard indeed on privacy," observed a leading sociologist of revolution.[32] That the totalitarian governments of the last century intruded themselves into the intimate corners of personal life, politicized the private, and sabotaged much of family life is well

---

28. O'Leary, *Gender Agenda*, 123.

29. Bork, *Slouching*.

30. Patai, *Heterophobia*, 199. Patai continues (212): "To conflate much of what today is labeled 'sexual harassment' with serious forms of sexual assault and abuse is to invite authoritarianism into our lives—the hand of the state everywhere in the private sphere, until there is virtually no private sphere left."

31. See chapter III.

32. Crane Brinton, *Anatomy of Revolution* (New York: Vintage, 1965), 181.

known.[33] But even they did not make the destruction of private life their priority. Arguably it was inherent in their agenda, but it was not usually explicit and for many may not even have been a conscious aim.

Modern sexual politics, by contrast, makes the denial of privacy—specifically family privacy—the specific goal of its advocates. The fundamental feminist slogan—that "the personal is political"—is so obviously totalitarian that historian Eugene Genovese has termed it "Stalinist."[34] Less appreciated is how far this potential has already been realized. "Radical feminists must regard it as unfortunate that they lack the power and mechanisms of the state to enforce their control over thoughts as well as behavior," mused Bork, who like many conservatives was more eloquent in his principles than current in his facts. "However, the movement is gradually gaining that coercive power in both private and public institutions."[35] Actually, in many spheres they possess it now and are discarding any reservations about saying so. "We want to transform the most intimate and private relations between women and men," says Katherine Rake, then the British Labour government's spokesperson on the family. "We want to change not just who holds power in international conglomerations, but who controls the household budget. We want to change not just what child care the state provides, but who changes the nappies at home."[36]

The corollary to all this is the absence of dissent. More than any other ideology, sexual radicalism neuters, literally emasculates its opposition. "It is hard to imagine any other group of people in the United States today who could be so crassly maligned in a public setting without arousing immediate protest," writes Patai. "Somehow men seem to have been cowed into silence."[37] In important respects feminism especially possesses a strange status to be above criticism and even scrutiny—at least from non-feminists.[38] Women themselves are not off-limits, since like Jacobins or Bolsheviks, feminists aim to liberate the oppressed from their false consciousness, whether or not they wish to be liberated. Women's "existing desires and preferences may be corrupted or mis-

---

33. Allan Carlson, "Standing For Liberty: Marriage, Virtue, and the Political State," lecture delivered at the Family Research Council, Washington, DC, 16 June 2004 (http://www.profam.org/docs/acc/thc_acc_frc_sfl_040616.htm).

34. Interview with *National Review*, 24 February 1997, 55(3).

35. Bork, *Slouching*, loc. cit.

36. "Feminist Who Thinks Men Should Bring Up Babies Is New Labour Family Guru," *Daily Mail*, 13 August 2009, http://www.dailymail.co.uk/news/article-1192720/Feminist-thinks-men-bring-babies-new-Labour-family-guru.html.

37. Patai, *Heterophobia*, Kindle locations 153–55.

38. See the Introduction.

taken when they are adapted to unjust social circumstances," insists one feminist; "for example, women may sometimes fail to recognize that they are oppressed."[39]

While militants are challenged on specific issues like abortion and same-sex marriage, no longer questioned is the larger assumption that private relationships are legitimate matters for state regulation. This ideology is therefore transforming our public life into sexualized confrontations and private lives into political battlegrounds.

The result is its strikingly relentless advance. Horror stories brought to light do little to halt the juggernaut, which rolls on despite clear revelations of injustice. Exposés of feminist social workers confiscating the children of patently innocent parents trigger no systematic investigations of the child protection gendarmerie. Sensational "rape" accusations in universities and the military repeatedly exposed as hoaxes and revelations of innocent men prosecuted and sentenced to decades in prison for rapes that everyone knows never happened result in no investigations into, or controls over, the rape industry. Revelations of innocent fathers separated from their children at gunpoint and incarcerated without trial simply for trying to see their children stimulate no investigations or controls over the divorce machinery. Opinion polls and referenda clearly demonstrating that most people oppose same-sex marriage do little to slow the legal institutionalization of same-sex marriage. The tortured excuses and convoluted weasel words—mouthed less by the radicals than by the conservatives—usually consist of expressions of helplessness before the inexorable march of "progress," though the reality probably has more do to with collective diffidence and the inability to articulate a coherent response to ever-expanding sexual freedom.

This too follows a familiar trajectory. Extremist ideologies break out of the margins to assume power when they create a new politics that existing elites fail to understand, when they can make an end run around society's defenses and the clash of established interests, or when they can deceive enough of the elites into believing that their agenda is compatible with existing values. This is usually accomplished not by the most extreme ideologues but by those who manage to co-opt, appropriate, and distort the respectable values of the mainstream and use them to camouflage their innovations.

Today we have constructed a Maginot Line against the ideologies of yesteryear—communism and fascism—and consequently are ill-pre-

---

39. Alison M. Jaggar, "'Saving Amina': Global Justice for Women and Intercultural Dialogue," in *Ethics and International Affairs: A Reader*, ed. Joel H. Rosenthal and Christian Barry (Washington DC: Georgetown University Press, 2009), 209.

pared to meet the challenge from sexual radicalism, whose operatives effortlessly circumvent our archaic defenses. The key to its runaway success is to grasp that it is due to not the extremism of the radicals but the misapprehension, gullibility, and fear of others. While I have cast this issue in terms of the sexual ideologies of feminism and homosexualism, these ideologies have achieved their spectacular success largely owing to the acquiescence, unwitting complicity, and even active collusion of people who see themselves as conservatives. Indeed, the key to understanding the success of the Sexual Revolution is to understand that it is not radicals but conservatives who have not only allowed it to triumph unopposed but in some instances facilitated its rise to power.

Paradoxically but critically, radical sexual ideologues have preempted opposition largely by invoking conservative values. While radicals and conservatives do clash over abortion and same-sex marriage, these are not the issues on which sexual activists are building a repressive state machinery. As always, the serious loss of freedom comes from unexpected quarters: the threats most people (including political elites) ignore; issues on which they are afraid to challenge feminists or inclined to give them the benefit of the doubt or even credulously agree with them; or those which conservatives will concede to radicals in the hope of restraint elsewhere. These machinations are therefore not usually visible on the mainstream political radar screen. Feminist political temptresses frame these issues in terms that elicit outrage from the credulous and self-righteous ("child abuse," "violence against women"), seduce us all into the soothing, self-indulgent pleasures of moral posturing, and place opponents to their agenda on the side of unnamed "sex offenders" that no one dares to defend.

The triumph of sexualityism therefore has not arrived through its most extreme ideologues. Rather, much as Stalinism inherited and transformed the practices of czarist absolutism and Russian nationalism, the triumphal phase of the new feminist and gay politics comes by politicizing the very institutions that earlier, ideologically pure feminists renounced: motherhood, marriage, the family, the church, the state. Feminism's neo-puritanism "should not be mistaken for a nostalgic return to Victorianism," insists Patai. "On the contrary, its best fit is with the dismaying history of twentieth-century totalitarianisms."[40]

Today, even as the purists are relegated to the margins of a "post-feminist" society, sexual ideology is nonetheless wheedling its way into the mainstream and even conservative culture by appropriating traditional

---

40. Patai, *Heterophobia*, Kindle locations 2119–20.

morality—including, as we will see shortly, the very feminine "stereotypes" against which it initially rebelled.

Both feminism and homosexualism in their earliest stages attained a foothold in the mainstream culture with demands for "equality" and "rights" and other language taken largely from the American civil rights movement. The language of "discrimination," "inequality," "stereotypes," and other agitprop buzzwords taken from the 1960s is the mainstay of these champions of "sexual, gender, and bodily minorities."[41] This disarming tactic tends to silence critics as equivalent to racial "bigots."

This succeeds because our political culture has lost the ability to distinguish or (if the term is permissible) discriminate. Ideologues treat as morally equal all practices they choose to label "oppression." This not only debases that important word but insults its true victims. The notion that an equivalency in suffering connects the victims of slavery and segregation with upper middle-class women or affluent homosexuals in North America and Western Europe during the twenty-first century—among the most privileged and comfortable groups in human history—is often perceived as highly insulting to those whose forebears endured serious oppression.

What distinguishes true civil rights movements from today's sexual militancy is that the sexual agenda is open-ended. It demands a liberation from sexual restraint that is limitless—not only from specific, legally imposed barriers like chattel slavery or segregation statutes but from any moral disapproval arising from the traditional values, religious faith, or political opinions of private citizens who disagree. Thus the emphasis is not on removing specific legal restrictions but on "pride" as a weapon to disparage other people and their values. The result turns the political tables on their critics by wielding a political power that is also without bounds. "Liberty, when men act in bodies," wrote Edmund Burke, "is power." Demands for "liberation" from "stereotypes," "inequality," and "oppression" have shifted almost imperceptibly, through the dynamics of collectivist ideology, into unabashed claims to "power" or "empowerment" over others—words now ubiquitous in the literature—revealing an ambition to regulate others' beliefs and lives. Whereas homosexual politics once appeared to be limited to the liberal demands to be left alone to lead lives in private, homosexualists made a rapid leap of logic to enter the revolutionary world of sexual

---

41. Council of the European Union, "Guidelines to Promote and Protect the Enjoyment of all Human Rights by Lesbian, Gay, Bisexual, Transgendered, and Intersex (LGBTI) Persons," 24 June 2013, 4.

politics by demanding the right to display their sexual desires and acts in public, to use government propaganda machinery such as public schools and the diplomatic corps to disseminate their politics to children and overseas populations, to make sexual proclivities a claim to political privilege, to claim immunity from criticism, and to stop the mouths of dissenters.

"Power is the alpha and the omega of contemporary Communism," wrote Milovan Djilas during the repressions of the 1950s. "Ideas, philosophical principles, and moral considerations ... all can be changed and sacrificed. But not power."[42] Sexual radicalism shows a similar absence of fixed principles and adopts irreconcilably contradictory positions as needed: all gender differences are social constructions, but women have special "needs." Women are oppressed by artificial gender roles, but those same roles make women more "caring" and "compassionate." Men and women must be treated identically, except when men must be excluded from certain competitions so that women can win. Fathers should assume equal responsibility for rearing children, but custody (along with the power and money that accompany it) must go to mothers. Alison Jaggar, author of *Living with Contradictions*, proclaims unashamedly that feminists should insist on having it both ways: "Feminists should embrace both horns of this dilemma," she writes. "They should use the rhetoric of equality in situations where women's interests clearly are being damaged by being treated either differently from or identically with men."[43] So principles are merely "rhetoric" in the cynical sense. As with Humpty Dumpty, words like "equality" change meanings as necessary; "interests" alone endure. As Jaggar admits, it proceeds from no principles other than power: to increase the power not of women, but of those women who claim to speak on behalf of all. Thus the fashionable euphemism used to disguise it: "empowerment."[44]

---

42. Milovan Djilas, *The New Class* (New York: Praeger, 1958), 170. "Everything happened differently in the USSR and other Communist countries from what the leaders ... anticipated," Djilas added. "The Communist revolution, conducted in the name of doing away with classes, has resulted in the most complete authority of any single new class." Op. cit., 36–37.

43. Alison Jaggar, "Sexual Difference and Sexual Equality," in Alison Jaggar ed., *Living with Contradictions* (Boulder: Westview Press, 1994, 25–26, http://chisimba.umu. ac.ug:8081/xmlui/bitstream/handle/123456789/72/EDSAlison%20M.pdf?sequence=1).

44. "The incoherence of the two positions (social constructionism when that is most useful; biological essentialism the rest of the time) seems not to have produced any terminal discomfort among feminists, since they are able to shift from one position to the other without difficulty." Patai, *Heterophobia*, Kindle locations 1974–75.

Feminist and homosexualist literature today is saturated with this demand. "The feminist approach to female sexuality . . . has . . . completely transformed our feelings about ourselves . . . giving women a new sense of autonomy and power."[45] Here too, then, power is the bottom line. "The so-called women's movement has never been about equal rights for women," write Suzanne Venker and Phyllis Schlafly. "It's about power for the female left."[46]

In true dialectical fashion, the very attributes that feminists once claimed were "oppressing" women are now increasingly exploited as sources of power: sex, children, physical infirmity, tears, fear. Once renounced by purists on the principle that women should compete on equal terms with men and not resort to feminine guile, today these traditional sources of feminine power are more likely to be politicized and exploited as weapons to achieve gender dominance. "On the one hand, [we]'re told women are equal," observes Kathleen Parker; "on the other, [we]'re told women get special privileges because they're women." One feminist now considers "a gender-neutral notion of power" to be "a serious departure from feminism" and worries about a "sex-blind universal application."[47] The formula provides for infinite empowerment: the more power feminists wield through specifically feminine weapons, the more they can claim to be "oppressed" by them.

The quest for "power" is precisely what today's critics have missed. Conservatives see only the libertinism and individual license. Their failure to understand the collective lust for power leaves them impotent—lamenting and bemoaning the hedonistic debauchery but helpless to check the militants' consolidation of government power. Their all-purpose excuse is helplessness before a nebulous deterioration in the "culture" that is endlessly and pointlessly bewailed.

We long ago moved beyond cultural decay to enter a contest for political supremacy. The will to political power means commandeering the state machinery against opponents: the power to create criminals. This is what conservatives (some of whom also like to create criminals) cannot see because they will not see. And so they allow themselves to become a part of the process.

The creation of sexual criminals has two broad stages, only one of which receives any critical attention. The first expresses the natural

45. Quoted in Melanie Phillips, *The Sex-Change Society* (London: Social Market Foundation, 1999), 131–32.

46. *The Flipside of Feminism*, quoted on the promotional website: http://www.the-flipsideoffeminism.com/.

47. Patai, *Heterophobia*, Kindle locations 1508–09, 1578.

human longing for sex without restraint. Shulamith Firestone long ago outlined her scheme for "pansexuality."[48] Firestone's views, once considered extreme, have now essentially been realized in current public policy. Gerard Bradley notes the demand "that women will and should have lots more sexual intercourse than they have interest in conceiving children" and that it is among "the government's responsibilities to establish conditions that make this life achievable for all with ease."[49]

But sexual ideology is more than libertinism. The inseparable corollary is authoritarian—what one scholar calls "punitive feminism" and describes as "the vigilante atmosphere promoted in the name of feminism."[50] This has been almost wholly neglected, even by feminism's severest critics, some of whom credulously even endorse its most vindictive measures: the seemingly paradoxical juxtaposition of libertinism and puritanism, demanding unrestricted sexual freedom and celebrating the right to "be sexual," combined with draconian sexual regulation and hysterical demands to punish a host of new sexual crimes and sexual criminals who either partake of the new freedom or obstruct it. These two facets of sexual radicalism are neither contradictory nor accidental: they are the essence of its grab for power.

There is no need to invoke conspiracy theories. Sexual license cannot help but produce moral chaos and social anomie. Consciously or spontaneously, the sexual revolutionaries are simply reaping the rewards of the disorder they themselves engender. "Since sexual 'liberation' has social chaos as one of its inevitable sequelae," writes E. Michael Jones, "sexual liberation begets almost from the moment of its inception the need for social control." Having eroded or eliminated the voluntary, apolitical controls provided by religion and traditional morality, the revolutionaries are positioned to substitute their own sexual regulations, rationalized by their own secular theology and backed by the criminal enforcement machinery. This is why, as Jones insists, "Sexual revolution is a form of political control."[51]

Jones's key insight has yet to be adequately explored, though already it explains far-reaching legal changes throughout our society: "The absence of self-control in matters sexual invariably means the presence

---

48. O'Leary, *Gender Agenda*, 106.

49. Gerard Bradley, "What's Behind the HHS Mandate?" *Public Discourse*, 5 June 2012, http://www.thepublicdiscourse.com/2012/06/5562/. "This orthodoxy commands the cultural heights and has achieved ascendancy in the academy," he adds.

50. Patai, *Heterophobia*, Kindle locations 1406, 499.

51. Jones, *Libido*, 2, 5.

of instruments of political control which fill the moral vacuum created by immoral action."[52]

The paradox of sexual ideology is that each newly demanded sexual freedom comes with a corresponding criminal punishment. The new license has brought with it a panoply of new crimes and new definitions of crime—all involving sexual and family relations: "rape," "sexual assault," "sexual harassment," "domestic violence," "stalking," "child abuse," "bullying," "sexual slavery," "hate crimes," "hate speech," and much more. These new, loosely-defined and loosely-adjudicated crimes have politicized law enforcement and criminal justice, rendered the law vague and subjective, by-passed and eroded due process protections for the accused, and criminalized and incarcerated vast numbers of men and some women who could not possibly have understood that they were committing a crime.

Compounding the authoritarianism is that, because of the collusion of conservatives, no one dares to speak for the accused. Helpless to halt the groundswell of sexual decadence and power, conservative pundits seem determined to alleviate their impotence by jumping on the bandwagon of punishment, adding their voices to the radical mob baying for the blood of unnamed and unproven "rapists," "abusers," "batterers," "harassers," "stalkers," "bullies," "deadbeats," "pedophiles," "traffickers," "misogynists," and more. Only now, when "bigots," "haters," and "homophobes" are being added, do some conservatives show signs of opening their eyes to the threat this hysteria poses to everyone's freedom.

The potential of sexual politics therefore is not the extremists, but the steady erosion of family integrity, personal privacy, critical thought, and civic freedom, through the relentless politicization of private life by an ideology to which we are now so acculturated that we are largely immune from realizing its effects. Feminist and more recently homosexualist tenets have now permeated the mainstream and thrive largely unchallenged and unchallengeable on the left, the center, and even the right. Politicized slogans have been absorbed unquestioningly into the daily lives of vast numbers of people—including well-educated people—who cannot understand the full implications of the jargon they mouth. Politicized buzzwords like "gender," "gender equality," "sexual orientation," "sex discrimination," "sexual harassment," and "domestic abuse," have been accepted into our vocabulary and are employed uncritically by people who—because these terms are intentionally fluid and elusive in their meanings—cannot possibly be fully cognizant of the

52. Ibid., 531.

implications they can carry. We have already passed the point where we accept unquestioningly changes that alter the social foundations of our civilization, find formulaic excuses for routine violations of constitutional government, use personal attacks to demonize and ostracize dissenters, and studiously look the other way as patently innocent persons (formerly known as men) are led away in handcuffs.

For indeed, the consequences are not diminished because the zealots cannot immediately realize the entirety of their utopian fantasies. The effect of ideologies results from the way they eventually go wrong, as the power they confer is used by other people for other purposes; zealots themselves become victims as the revolution "devours its own children." And while the zealots never fully realize their dreams, they do change us all. Even if we do not consider ourselves comrades, few of us have entirely withstood the temptation to avail ourselves, at one time or another, of both the exciting new sexual freedom and the equally exhilarating sexual power. As Daphne Patai writes in this context, "No social group selflessly refrains from using whatever weapons its historical moment makes available in order to gain money, position, fame . . . and retribution, all in the name of equity and righteousness."[53] Few today have not had at least the opportunity to taste the delights of sexual freedom, and more and more people are now discovering the intoxicating "empowerment" it also confers. Even those who consider themselves abstemious and traditionalist are tempted to take advantage of the new weapons. One need only observe the zeal with which conservative political operatives abandon traditional stigmas against quaint, old-fashioned concepts like adultery or fornication and adopt sexualized agitprop jargon, whose full implications they do not and cannot comprehend, when they opportunistically accuse President Bill Clinton of "sexual harassment" or Muslims of "homophobia."

Virtually every item on the public agenda is now feminized. Every issue, both domestic and foreign, is now cast in terms of its impact on women or "women and children" or "sexual minorities": health, taxation, welfare, immigration, development, war—all, we are told, involve some "special hardship." "Women would suffer most from congressional budget cuts," reports *The Hill*, where such headlines are frequent.[54] (As satirized in *The Onion*: "World Ends—Women, Minorities Hardest Hit.") Here too, homosexuals are following the playbook. "It

---

53. Patai, *Heterophobia*, Kindle locations 499–500.
54. 29 July 2011. See the letter at http://thehill.com/opinion/letters/175141-politicians-attitude-leaves-dc-ripe-for-third-party.

seems that just about everything in Britain is now run according to the gay agenda," writes Melanie Phillips: "gay-friendly hotels, gay adoption, and gay mathematics, now . . . gay drugs policy."[55]

Even issues with no apparent connection to sex and "gender" are now being sexualized and feminized. Economic crises are addressed according to their allegedly special impact on women, though the vast majority of those left unemployed are men. War and foreign policy are transformed by debates about women and homosexuals in the military and evaluated for their impact on women, though casualties are overwhelmingly heterosexual men. The environment is a women's issue, we are told, and so is climate change.

But in every case the alleged hardship exists, if it exists at all, only because women and children have first been separated from, and set in opposition to, the families and men that traditionally protected and provided for them—as demanded by sexual radicals themselves. Solutions restoring the roles of families and men are never an option, and any such suggestion is quickly purged from the discussion. The only ideologically acceptable response is to devise new powers for state functionaries and gendarmes, whose interest is to further weaken and marginalize the families and men. In this way, the ideology relentlessly expands government power at the expense of private life.

The result—when every source of fear becomes a source of power, when every claim of oppression is a claim for more police and prisons—is predictable: everything oppresses, because every grievance is "empowering." Even problems and hardships created by militants themselves oppress "sexual minorities." "Utopians are actually multiplying the social problems they claim to be solving," observes Bryce Christensen. "Gender-neutering utopians adroitly turn the social problems they cause into a justification for seizing yet more power."[56]

The vulnerability of women and children, which every society recognizes, must be attributed to some social injustice remediable only through ever-more extensive government power. "Feminists think they're fighting a society that has wronged them," write Venker and Schlafly. "In reality they are fighting human nature."[57] Marshaling society's entire political machinery to alter human nature is, as the Com-

---

55. "Yes, Gays Have Often been the Victims of Prejudice. . . ." *Daily Mail*, 24 January 2011, http://www.dailymail.co.uk/debate/article-1349951/Gayness-mandatory-schools-Gay -victims-prejudice-new-McCarthyites.html#ixzz2jgCA79uy.

56. "The End of Gender Sanity in American Public Life," *Modern Age*, vol. 49, no. 4 (Fall 2007), 412.

57. *Flipside of Feminism*, loc. cit.

munist regimes discovered, a formula for open-ended and total "empowerment."

All of this is so wildly successful because it exploits and politicizes the natural concern of every society to protect and provide for women and children. The one condition every civilized society demands in return for this protection and provision is sexual restraint: the restriction of sex and childbearing to married families. But this sexual restraint and its religious regimen are precisely what politicized Western women—along with adolescents and homosexuals—are now in open revolt against, and it is no accident that the principal threats to religious freedom in the Western world almost all come from demands for sexual liberation.[58] What has changed is not that these groups are any less protected or provided for—on the contrary, they are the safest, least restrained, and most affluent people in history—but precisely that they have achieved unprecedented levels of economic, political, and sexual freedom that allow them to demand indefinite "empowerment" while still exploiting the privileges and deference afforded to women. Both feminists and homosexualists demand the prerogative to pick and choose between male or female behavior as it suits their advantage. The myth of "gender"—the theory that the privileges and responsibilities specific to men or women are constructed artificially and may be eliminated—allows affluent feminists to select and enjoy the privileges and the power specific to both sexes without having to assume the responsibilities specific to either. Men do not have this prerogative unless they become homosexuals. This is why all sexual radicalism is power-seeking.

The obsession with power has transformed the means as well as the ends of our politics, resurrecting the relentless "salami tactics" familiar from neo-Bolshevik movements in post-war Eastern Europe. "Instead of trying to convince the public and working through elected representatives, they often bypass the legislatures and work instead behind closed doors ... through the courts and within the bureaucracies," observe two scholars. "The revolution could be achieved quietly, in committee chambers, and without resistance."[59]

Indeed, sexual radicalism has helped transform the very nature and purpose of civil government. The most basic state functions—external defense, border security, and punishing criminals—have been weakened or altered, with the diminution of state sovereignty. Sovereignty is

---

58. See chapter III, under "Religious Belief."

59. Paul Nathanson and Katherine K. Young, *Legalizing Misandry: From Public Shame to Systemic Discrimination against Men* (Montreal: McGill-Queen's University Press, 2006), 402.

threatened internally by warlords, insurgencies, cartels, gangs, and militias of violent (mostly fatherless) youth and externally by supranational organizations like the European Union and the United Nations.

At the same time that governments relinquish these traditional functions, they are increasingly taking on new ones that few in the past considered appropriate: care of children and the aged, education, medical care. This open-ended project is now bankrupting wealthy societies, both governments and families, while creating growing public-sector constituencies with a vested interest in looting productive households to finance their salaries and benefits.

Sexual radicalism is not responsible for all of this. But it is tempting to point out that the traditional functions being surrendered by the state are masculine, whereas the new roles are feminine. Governments have forsaken their traditional roles as the men who conducted them have been marginalized, and they have taken on new tasks that were previously performed privately in the home by women because women now refuse or cannot afford to perform them without compensation. Here, as we shall see elsewhere, gender roles are not eliminated but merely politicized. The face of the modern state is less the male soldier or policeman and more the female social worker and civil servant.

And yet critically, the new feminized functionaries are no less police, and they command force that is no less coercive. They simply do not wear uniforms, do not risk physical danger, and they are not similarly restrained from the authorization to enter and control the private lives of citizens who are not criminals.

Correspondingly, the most basic internal function of any government—punishing criminals—has also been dramatically redefined. On the one hand, the criminal justice system has long been adapting itself to be more humane and "caring," with lighter sentences, alternatives to incarceration, and special procedures for youth and others deemed not fully responsible for their actions. Yet alongside this feminization of criminal justice, as we will see further, have emerged the new sexual crimes defined and enforced by the new feminine and feminized gendarmeries.

By a similarly subtle sleight-of-hand, the older liberal demands for unisex "equality" have given way to claims of a positively superior feminine ethic characterized by greater "caring" and "sensitivity" than traditional masculine power politics. What some naively regard as a moderating compromise with traditional gender roles is in reality a modest sacrifice of ideological purity in exchange for power. Both sexes are equal, Orwell might say, but one sex is more equal than the other.

One consequence is the politicization of children. As politics becomes feminized and marriage weakens, children have become pawns and weapons in the competition for power. This is true in several policy areas we will explore: divorce, welfare, child protection, and schooling. But it has spread beyond family policy to a vast array of other policies and programs, from seat-belt laws to tobacco and gun lawsuits and even international treaties, all now justified "for the children." Decisions previously left to parents are now taken by officials, which not only transfers control over children from parents to the state, but also rationalizes limiting adult freedom.

Political theorist Kathy Ferguson envisions a world where male-dominated power politics will be replaced with a superior feminine politics of empowerment. Male power brokers will be replaced by quasi-Platonic female "caretakers" whose claim to leadership will be their compassion. In this feminist utopia the only remaining problem will be who will minister to the needs of these saintly souls. "For a feminist community, then, Plato's question 'Who will guard the guardians?' might be rephrased as, 'Who will care for the caretakers?'"[60]

But the real question might be, "Who will guard the caretakers?" For her dream of a syndicalism of caretakers is now the reality, and the caretakers have run amok. "Caretakers routinely drug foster children" runs a headline in the *Los Angeles Times*. "Children under state protection in California group and foster homes are being drugged with potent, dangerous psychiatric medications, at times just to keep them obedient and docile for their overburdened caretakers."[61]

The new feminized power may not appear at first glance so different from the old version. What is new is its political role: instead of serving within the family as a private source of power that checks and limits that of the state, it is now part of the government power structure, with a stake in its expansion. It is no accident that feminists want to erase the distinction between public and private, for they are politicizing precisely those spheres of life that women have always dominated and that until now we have been careful to protect from calculations of power politics: the family, marriage, children, the household, private life in general—as well as the criminal justice system.

It is to these that we now turn.

---

60. Kathy E. Ferguson, "Male-Ordered Politics: Feminism and Political Science," in *Idioms of Inquiry*, ed. Terrence Ball (Albany: SUNY, 1987), 222.
61. *Los Angeles Times*, 17 May 1998.

II

Liberating Sex:
The Politics of the Family

"The marriage-tie, the marriage bond . . . is the fundamental connecting link in Christian society. Break it, and you will have to go back to the overwhelming dominance of the state, which existed before the Christian era."
—D. H. Lawrence

THE DECLINE OF THE FAMILY is the most urgent crisis of our age. What sophisticated people dismiss as fundamentalist "hang-ups" over sex now reflects trends whose far-reaching consequences are still poorly understood. It is a cliché of the right—now grudgingly acknowledged by the left—that the family is the "building block" of civil society. Yet seldom is this truism pursued to its logical conclusion: the dissolution of the family threatens not only social order but civic freedom. Moreover, it does so in ways that are not easy to perceive, and have not been clearly perceived, even by those who see themselves as the family's defenders.

Some of the most eminent sociological minds have suggested that sexual decadence and family decline threaten civilizational survival.[1] Scholars like J. D. Unwin, Carl Wilson, Pitirim Sorokin, and Carle Zimmerman long ago predicted the epidemics of divorce and unwed childbearing and the birthrate decline, and they saw these as the signs of the same civilizational decline they studied in ancient history. What they could not foresee was the precise forms these would take and in particular the authoritarian role of the state machinery.

Today's family crisis must be understood politically, and this is precisely where self-described family advocates have failed. Until now, the

---

1. See chapter III, under "Rape and Sexual Assault."

leading voices sounding the alarm on family decline have portrayed it as a crisis of social norms and "culture" and point to decadent popular culture, pornography, and sexual promiscuity.

Cultural threats to family solvency should not be dismissed, as they often are by the educated, as the obsession of ignorant reactionaries. But the problem has now advanced well beyond that stage. To limit the focus to impersonal forces, personal comportment, or a nebulous "culture" while neglecting new political ideologies and the growing power of the state machinery is to invite paralysis. The words of a prominent conservative political scientist (ironically) illustrate the despair: "If you believe, as I do, in the power of culture," wrote the late James Q. Wilson of family decline, "you will realize that there is very little one can do."[2]

Our concern is with government policy, where tangible and effective measures are available and need discussion. The full dimensions of the family crisis can only be understood politically, because the family is the pivotal intermediary between the individual and the state. Many basic questions raised by political philosophy are pointless without accounting for the family, which is why most major philosophers address it. Family decline therefore carries serious implications for civic freedom in ways that likewise are not always obvious.

Sexual radicals often profess that they do not wish to destroy the family, only to redefine it. But this amounts to the same thing. While today most feminists and homosexualists avoid attacking the family directly, their definitions do not generally include the married, two-parent family (and almost never include the heterosexual father, their foremost enemy), or they consider it one of many possible family configurations. In the long run, the married, two-parent heterosexual family is the only family configuration that is compatible with a stable, prosperous, and free society, because it is the only one that checks and diminishes the state's monopoly on power; all others necessarily increase it. For the same reason, it is the only one targeted by state officials.

The direct attack on marriage and the family by early feminists is now largely forgotten, but it is still alive in current public policy. "We can't destroy the inequities between men and women until we destroy marriage," *Ms.* magazine editor Robin Morgan wrote in her 1970 book, *Sisterhood is Powerful.*[3] Sheila Cronin, then head of the National Organization for Women, wrote in 1973 that "Freedom for women cannot be

2. "Why We Don't Marry," *City Journal*, Winter 2002 (http://www.city-journal.org/html/12_1_why_we.html).

3. Quoted in Carrie Lukas, *The Politically Incorrect Guide to Women, Sex, and Feminism* (Washington: Regnery, 2006), 76.

won without the abolition of marriage."[4] Linda Gordon elaborated in a famous 1969 article. "The nuclear family must be destroyed," she declared:

> The break-up of families now is an objectively revolutionary process. . . . Families have supported oppression by separating people into small, isolated units, unable to join together to fight for common interests. . . . Families make possible the super-exploitation of women by training them to look upon their work outside the home as peripheral to their "true" role. . . . Families will be finally destroyed only when a revolutionary social and economic organization permits people's needs for love and security to be met in ways that do not impose divisions of labor, or any external roles, at all.[5]

Academic feminists voice similar aspirations today. Judith Stacey bids "good riddance to the traditional family."[6] More to the point, a glance at the state of marriage and the family today reveals that this is precisely what feminists, along with their homosexualist allies, have now achieved. But they achieved it in ways much more subtle than these screeds indicate. While Germaine Greer famously urged women to refuse to marry, and Shulamith Firestone suggested that they should refuse to have children, such strategies could change little. It was by participating in marriage and the family that feminist-inspired women undermined them.

Homosexual activists have followed the feminists' lead. Homosexuality today is more than a private personal preference; for militant activists, it is a political ideology that aims to use sex to transform society in the homosexual image. "Being queer is more than setting up house, sleeping with a person of the same gender, and seeking state approval for doing so," says the former legal director of the Lambda Legal Defense and Education Fund. "Being queer means pushing the parameters of sex, sexuality, and family, and in the process transforming the very fabric of society."[7]

The 1978 Gay Liberation Front *Manifesto* stated that "We must aim at the abolition of the family, so that the sexist, male supremacist system

---

4. Sheila Cronan, "Marriage," in Anne Koedt, Ellen Levine, and Ania Rapone (eds.), *Radical Feminism* (New York: Quadrangle, 1973), 219.

5. "Functions of the Family," WOMEN: *A Journal of Liberation* (Fall 1969).

6. Judith Stacey, "The New Conservative Feminism," *Feminist Studies* 9 (1983), 570, quoted in Bryce Christensen, "The End of Gender Sanity in American Public Life," *Modern Age*, vol. 49, no. 4 (Fall 2007), 409.

7. Michael L. Brown, *A Queer Thing Happened to America* (Concord, NC: Equal-Time Books, 2011), 37.

can no longer be nurtured there."[8] Despite disclaimers similar to the feminists', there can be no doubt that the homosexualist agenda remains fundamentally hostile to the family, to heterosexuality in general, and above all to traditional masculinity. "The oppression of gay people starts in the most basic unit of society, the family, consisting of the man in charge, a slave as his wife, and their children on whom they force themselves as the ideal models. The very form of the family works against homosexuality."

These people are not asking merely to be left alone. Hostility toward parents and parental authority, especially fathers, is palpable in homosexualist literature, and the aspiration to eradicate them is undisguised. This hostility extends beyond what any particular parents *did* to encompass what parents in general *are*: married, heterosexual couples who acknowledge differences between men and women. "At some point nearly all gay people have found it difficult to cope with having the restricting images of man or woman pushed on them by their parents. It may have been from very early on, when the pressures to play with the 'right' toys, and thus prove boyishness or girlishness, drove against the child's inclinations." By the very fact of accepting sex differences, parents and especially fathers are "oppressors" and therefore the targets of political campaigns: "This is certainly a problem by the time of adolescence, when we are expected to prove ourselves socially to our parents as members of the right sex . . . and to start being a 'real' (oppressive) young man or a 'real' (oppressed) young woman." This hatred of the family starts from "the fact that gay people notice they are different from other men and women in the family situation": "How many of us have been pressured into marriage, sent to psychiatrists, frightened into sexual inertia, ostracized, banned, emotionally destroyed—all by our parents?" But the radicals are not content with renouncing the two-parent family for themselves; it must be eliminated for everyone: "It is because of the patriarchal family that reforms are not enough. Freedom for gay people will never be permanently won until everyone is freed from sexist role-playing and the straightjacket of sexist rules about our sexuality. And we will not be freed from these so long as each succeeding generation is brought up in the same old sexist way in the patriarchal family." Citing those with traditional values as "the enemy," the sexual radicals call for their elimination: "Any reforms we might painfully exact from our rulers would only be fragile and vulnerable; that is why we, along with the women's movement, must fight for something

8. Fordham University internet site: http://www.fordham.edu/halsall/pwh/glf-london.html.

more than reform. We must aim at the abolition of the family, so that the sexist, male supremacist system can no longer be nurtured there."

Hatred of parents and especially fathers is thus not only the starting point for homosexuality itself (as psychologists have long argued);[9] it also drives the homosexualist political agenda. Here as elsewhere, the political goals and the methods of achieving them both proceed directly and inseparably from the sexual drive.

Feminism and homosexualism thus target not simply men and masculinity but fathers above all, the embodiments of the hated "patriarchy" and the "system" by which "men dominate, oppress, and exploit women."[10] It follows that the destruction of the family—and the corresponding rise in feminist power (and even homosexualist)—has come largely through the control and manipulation of children. This is enabled by the weakening of parental and especially paternal authority, with demands for a "democratic revolution in the family" where children are given a "choice about whether to accept their parents' power."[11]

While the politicization of children has been promoted at the expense of both parents, fathers are usually the first targets. This owes its inspiration directly to feminists, many of whom "look at children as comrades in suffering at the hands of an oppressive patriarchy."[12] Children, like women, are designated an oppressed minority and enlisted as political comrades, and their natural rebellious impulses become politicized as a force for "social change."

Hostility to the family in general and fathers in particular is manifest in feminist writings. "Patriarchy's chief institution is the family, within which men hold the power to determine the privileges, statuses, and roles of women and children," write Esther Ngan-ling Chow and Catherine White Berheide. "Traditional gender-role ideology . . . is further institutionalized and reproduced in gendered power relationships throughout society."[13] This elaborates on an older Marxist contempt for family relations. "The family is often the site of hideous violence, abuse, and oppression," writes Colin MacLeod in a Marxist academic journal. "A child's earliest lessons in bigotry often begin at home. . . . Patriarchy

---

9. See below, under "Homosexualism."

10. Sylvia Walby, quoted in Anne Barbeau Gardiner, "Feminist Literary Criticism: From Anti-Patriarchy to Decadence," *Modern Age*, vol. 49, no. 4 (Fall 2007), 393.

11. Shere Hite, *The Hite Report on the Family* (New York: Grove Press, 1995), 345, 26.

12. Quoted in Kay S. Hymowitz, *Ready or Not: Why Treating Children As Small Adults Endangers Their Future—and Ours* (New York: Free Press, 1999), 43, from a pamphlet by the organization Women Against Rape (WAR).

13. Esther Ngan-ling Chow and Catherine White Berheide (eds.), *Women, the Family, and Policy: A Global Perspective* (Albany: SUNY Press, 1994), introduction, 15.

and misogyny are frequently nourished and perpetuated in the traditional family."[14] Amy Gutman believes state officials should monitor and intervene against parents who do not inculcate in their children the political doctrines she advocates or "bias the choices of [their own] children."[15]

Feminist academics openly disdain family privacy and a private sphere of life free from state interference. Chow and Berheide deride "the ideology of the family as a bastion of privacy." Political theorist Carol Pateman asserts that denying "the dichotomy between the public and the private . . . is, ultimately, what the feminist movement is about." Political theorist Susan Okin describes the "artificial nature of the dichotomy between the sphere of private, domestic life and that of the state." "The separation of private from public is largely an ideological construct," Okin believes. "Public policies must respect people's views and choices . . . only insofar as it can be ensured that . . . *for those who choose it*, the division of labor between the sexes does not result in injustice. . . . The protection of the privacy of a domestic sphere in which inequality exists is the protection of the right of the strong to exploit and abuse the weak."[16] So even those who voluntarily choose traditional families have no right to be left alone.[17]

While such screeds garner little active support beyond committed ideologues, they do highlight what the ideologues have in fact already achieved and what acculturation blinds us from realizing. For here too, sexual ideologues have dismantled family life not by proscribing it but by politicizing it.

This emerges clearly in feminist campaigns to appropriate motherhood. Whereas fatherhood is a targeted enemy, motherhood offers the opportunity to cynically exploit the pieties of traditional morality and conservative people. Feminists like Ann Crittenden have learned to pose

14. Colin MacLeod, "Conceptions of Parental Autonomy," *Politics and Society*, vol. 25, no. 1 (March 1997), 118.

15. Amy Gutman, *Democratic Education* (Princeton: Princeton University Press, 1987), 34.

16. Chow and Berheide, *Women, the Family, and Policy*, 18; Carol Pateman, "Feminist Critiques of the Public/Private Dichotomy," in Stanley Benn and Gerald Gaus (eds.), *Private and Public in Social Life* (London: Croom Helm, 1983); Okin, *Justice, Gender, and the Family*, 23, 172–74, 179, and ch. 6 *passim* (emphasis added).

17. Compare the Nazi writers: "In the struggle for self-preservation which the German people are waging there are no longer any aspects of life which are non-political," they wrote. "The so-called 'private sphere' is only relatively private; it is at the same time potentially political." Quoted in Mark Mazower, *Dark Continent: Europe's Twentieth Century* (New York: Vintage, 1998), chapter 1, note 57.

as victims and gain sympathy from the public and even from conservatives. Waving the banner of motherhood, feminists leave the patriarchy little defense.

But feminists are not defending motherhood; they are politicizing it. "The feminists . . . want to thoroughly politicize the last bastion of personal life in our society: families," writes Wendy McElroy. "They want to wrest motherhood from its traditional right-wing associations and make it a left/liberal issue, with 'Mothers Are Victims' writ-large on its banner." The sleight-of-hand is subtle but profound. Motherhood is no longer a private role but a claim to political power and to marshal the coercive state apparatus against those depicted as the oppressors of mothers.

The feminization of issues having no obvious connection with sexuality produces what one newspaper calls "the radicalization of America's mothers": "Some commentators argue that the whole agenda in the US is shifting towards 'the politics of maternity.'"[18] Not only Code Pink, mobilized to oppose the Iraq war, but Mothers Against Drunk Driving, the Million Mom March (advocating gun control), and the militant Moms Rising, are all influential variations on the theme.

Moms Rising seeks to "build a more family-friendly America." Yet every item on their agenda would increase the power of the state over the family: day care and after-school programs (including television), universal government health insurance, wage regulation. Citing Crittenden's book, Moms Rising works with feminist groups, unions, social workers' organizations, medical pressure groups, and others with a vested interesting in expanding government authority over children and families.[19] "These 'pro-family' women wish to 'harness' what [Naomi] Wolf calls the 'pissed-offedness' of mothers in order to play 'hardball politics,'" writes McElroy. Many are deceived into believing that feminists have become the champions of traditional motherhood and families, when their actual agenda is to wrest them from fathers and make them dependents of the state. "Crittenden indicts not feminism, but capitalism, and argues for government to 'economically recognize' motherhood so that women will not be dependent upon husbands."[20]

The deception succeeds because motherhood is always an easy claim to privilege. Crittenden's book title, *The Price of Motherhood: Why the*

---

18. Viv Groskop, "The Mother of All Battles," *The Guardian*, 7 March 2007 (http://www.guardian.co.uk/g2/story/0,,2027979,00.html).

19. Moms Rising internet site: http://momsrising.org/aboutmomsrising.

20. Wendy McElroy, "Feminists Claim Motherhood as Liberal Cause," *Foxnews.com*, 21 May 2002, http://www.wendymcelroy.com/ifeminists/2002/0521.html.

Most Important Job in the World Is Still the Least Valued, is itself a revealing sleight-of-hand. If anyone has devalued motherhood, of course, it is feminists. Susan Douglas and Meredith Michaels demonstrate with their own book title, registering precisely the opposite gripe: *The Mommy Myth: The Idealization of Motherhood and How It Has Undermined Women*. Regardless of what these authors think of one another's arguments, they all share the conviction that mothers are oppressed by *something*, and the state must rescue them. The two titles succinctly convey feminism's determination to depict everything pertaining specifically to women as "oppression" and highlight feminist complaints as a strategy to "have it all" without regard for consistency or logic. This trait feminism shares with other radical ideologies but carries much further: the capacity to expand its power exponentially by creating the very problems about which it complains. "Mothers do not receive sufficient respect from society," McElroy paraphrases Crittenden, "as if feminism weren't largely to blame."

The Welfare State

The political manipulation of motherhood points to feminism's most institutionalized achievement: not eliminating gender roles, which it has not done and can never do, but politicizing and bureaucratizing feminine ones.

By trying to eliminate the sexual division of labor that was the basis for family life, feminists have not created a gender-neutral utopia, with men and women interchangeably caring for children and earning wages. Instead, they have merely placed women as well as men on the employment treadmill. By flooding the workforce with new workers, they have driven down male wages, intensifying pressures on families to send the woman into the workforce and for the man to work longer hours, giving him *less* involvement with his family.[21] The result is "big business socialism," where every adult must work and provide tax revenue for the growing state machinery. Meanwhile children are institutionalized in day care and extended school days and activities for ever-longer hours at ever-younger ages, their childhoods regimented in preparation for similar lives as worker bees and suppliers of state revenue.[22]

Pushing women into the workforce has hugely expanded government power. While elite feminists proudly pursued high-status, traditional

21. Allan Carlson, "The Wages of Kin: Building a Secular Family-Wage Regime," in *Third Ways* (Wilmington: ISI Books, 2007), 37–38.

22. Brian Robertson, *Day Care Deception: What the Child Care Establishment Isn't Telling Us* (San Francisco: Encounter, 2003), 161.

male occupations, many more women entered the workforce at functions resembling the traditional domestic roles with which they were
comfortable. "Women in Sweden have not been employed as substitutes
for male workers in industry and commerce, but have been the benefi-
ciaries of the expansion of welfare services," writes Patricia Morgan. "By
1985 women accounted for 87% of total health/education/welfare
employment." Thus rather than caring for their own children within
their own families, women began leaving the home to care for other
women's children as part of the public economy: day care, early education, professionalized nursing, and ever-more "social services."[23] "Out
went unpaid domestic work, and in came the state as provider *and*
employer." In Denmark from 1960 to 1982, female homemakers declined
by over half a million while employees *in the public sector* increased by
almost the same number.[24] "Women have . . . developed a large and
important relationship to the welfare state as the employees of [its] programs," observes Frances Fox Piven.[25] Rather than accepting that these
are the tasks to which many women naturally gravitate, some of Fox
Piven's fellow feminists see this as yet another oppression, complaining,
"The power and capriciousness of husbands is being replaced by the
arbitrariness, bureaucracy, and power of . . . the very state that has
upheld patriarchal power," and welfare states (designed and operated by
feminists) "channel women in disproportionate numbers into feminine
occupational niches," such as child care, elder care, nursing, and elementary education.[26]

Yet other feminists see the resulting matriarchy as a victory. "The US
economy is in some ways becoming a kind of traveling sisterhood,"
declares Hanna Rosin triumphantly. "Upper-class women leave home
and enter the workforce, creating domestic jobs for other women to
fill."[27] But this illusory experiment has not generated an "economy" in
any productive sense. "If Swedish women take care of each other's children in exchange for others taking care of theirs," asks Morgan, "how

---

23. Documented in Allan Carlson, "The Last March of the Swedish Social House-
wives," in *Third Ways*.

24. Patricia Morgan, *Family Policy, Family Changes: Sweden, Italy, and Britain Compared* (London: Civitas, 2006), 55, 36.

25. Quoted in Allan Carlson, "The Natural Family Dimly Seen Through Feminist
Eyes," *Modern Age*, vol. 49, no. 4 (Fall 2007), 427. She adds: "As early as 1980, American
women held 70% of the jobs at all levels of government concerned with social service."

26. Hadas Mandel and Moshe Semgonov, "A Welfare State Paradox: State Interventions and Women's Employment Opportunities in 22 Countries," *American Journal of
Sociology*, vol. 111 (May 2006), 1913, 1916, 1933, quoted in ibid., 428.

27. Hanna Rosin, "The End of Men," *Atlantic*, July–August 2010.

much additional output can come out of this?"[28] This false "economy" is precisely the economic bubble about which G.K. Chesterton warned a century ago. "If people cannot mind their own business, it cannot possibly be made economical to pay them to mind each other's business; and still less to mind each other's babies," he observed:

> The whole really rests on a plutocratic illusion of an infinite supply of servants. When we offer any other system as a "career for women," we are really proposing that an infinite number of them should become servants, of a plutocratic or bureaucratic sort. Ultimately, we are arguing that a woman should not be a mother to her own baby, but a nursemaid to somebody else's baby. But it will not work, even on paper. We cannot all live by taking in each other's washing, especially in the form of pinafores. In the last resort, the only people who either can or will give individual care, to each of the individual children, are their individual parents.[29]

The only benefit this change can give to women is to increase not their affluence (though this may have been part of the short-term temptation), and certainly not their leisure, but their power—the power against their husbands that accrues from a separate paycheck and with it the ability and willingness to divorce. (In the US, single mothers are the main constituency demanding comprehensive government health care.)[30]

But the real beneficiary is the state. For this trend has transformed child-rearing from a private family matter into a public communal and taxable activity, expanding the tax base and with it the size and power of the state, while the elite sisters in traditional male occupations drive down male wages, lower productivity, and fuel inflation.[31] Likewise, a political class paid from those taxes has taken command positions over vastly expanded public education and social services bureaucracies, where they supervise other women who look after other people's chil-

---

28. Morgan, *Family Policy*, 37.

29. *The Superstition of Divorce* (1920, http://www.gkc.org.uk/gkc/books/divorce.txt). The complement to the welfare state was the regulatory state, in both its quasi-socialist and environmentalist phases. Research is still needed to determine how far this hastened the demise of the mostly male manufacturing sector, while likewise creating vast numbers of government jobs for mostly female clerical workers and regulators.

30. See *Unmarried Women on Health Care: Unmarried Women Driving Change on Leading Domestic Issue*, Greenberg Quinlan Rosner internet site: http://www.greenbergresearch.com/articles/2066/3853_wvwv%20_health%20care%20memo_%200807m9_FINAL_.pdf, 8 August 2007.

31. As Communists like Karl Kautsky recognized. Carlson, "Wages of Kin," 37–38, also 50–51.

dren, further expanding the size and scope of the state into what had been private life.

Despite feminist claims, this trend renders the dream of a more "caring" public sphere naïvely utopian.[32] For as feminists correctly pointed out, the feminine roles were traditionally private. Politicizing and bureaucratizing feminine duties has therefore meant politicizing and bureaucratizing private life. This is how the "totalitarian" potential conservatives perceive is already being realized in ways even they may have yet to grasp.

Far from softening the hard edges of power politics, feminism has merely inserted calculations of power into the private corners of life by subjecting family life to increasing political and bureaucratic control. It has decimated families through twin processes whose direct connection with feminism have not been fully appreciated: weakening parents and politicizing children.

The most obvious example (where some opposition has arisen) is in

---

32. Professionalizing feminine functions appears to have made the "caring professions" less caring. In modern nursing, writes Melanie Phillips, "the presumption of care has been systematically eroded—by modern feminism." As a government report recounts hideous abuse of patients in Britain's hospitals, Phillips explains how feminism has turned nursing into a bureaucratic fiefdom:

...during the Eighties, nursing underwent a revolution. Under the influence of feminist thinking, its leaders decided that "caring" was demeaning because it meant that nurses—who were overwhelmingly women—were treated like skivvies by doctors, who were mostly men.

To achieve equality, therefore, nursing had to gain the same status as medicine. This directly contradicted an explicit warning given by Florence Nightingale that nurses should steer clear of the "jargon" about the "rights" of women "which urges women to do all that men do, including the medical and other professions, merely because men do it, and without regard to whether this is the best that women can do."

That prescient warning has been ignored by the modern nursing establishment. To achieve professional equality with doctors, nurse training was taken away from the hospitals and turned into an academic university subject.

Since caring for patients was demeaning to women, it could no longer be the cardinal principle of nursing. Instead, the primary goal became to realise the potential of the nurse to achieve equality with men. (The great irony is that more women than men are now training to be doctors in British medical schools, thus making this ideology out of date.)...

Student nurses now studied sociology, politics, psychology, microbiology and management, and were assessed for their communication, management and analytical skills. "Specific clinical nursing skills were not mentioned," she wrote.

Melanie Phillips, "How Feminism Made So Many Nurses Too Grand to Care," *Daily Mail*, October 17, 2011 (http://www.dailymail.co.uk/debate/article-2049906/How-feminism-nurses-grand-care.html). See also Cristina Odone, "Nursing is No Longer the Caring Profession," *Daily Telegraph*, August 28, 2011 (http://www.telegraph.co.uk/news/health/8728849/Nursing-is-no-longer-the-caring-profession.html).

the politics of schooling. Public schools were the earliest triumph of socialism and the first "social service" to usurp parental roles within the liberal democracies. The ideological foundation of public education in weakening parental authority and justifying communal child rearing emerges in the words of a political scientist:

> Children are owed as a matter of justice the capacity to choose to lead lives—adopt values and beliefs, pursue an occupation, endorse new traditions—that are different from those of their parents. Because the child cannot him or herself ensure the acquisition of such capacities and the parents may be opposed to such acquisition, the state must ensure it for them. The state must guarantee that children are educated for minimal autonomy.[33]

What has not been made explicit—even by critics such as private school and homeschool advocates—is that the schools were the first triumph of not simply the welfare state but the welfare state *matriarchy*.

Connected to this matriarchy is another that has become even more powerful and authoritarian because it has grown up upon less resistant low-income communities and, until recently, was largely hidden from the middle class: the massive and expanding political underworld of the "social services" bureaucracies.

Ironically, two leftist authors have perceived the danger more readily than most conservatives. They even adopt Milovan Djilas's Communist-era term, describing "a new class of professionals—social workers, therapists, foster care providers, family court lawyers—who have a vested interest in taking over parental function." "If children are the clients, parents can quite easily become the adversaries," write Sylvia Ann Hewlett and Cornel West, "—the people who threaten to take business away."[34] What Hewlett and West do not tell us is that this new class is driven—in addition to bureaucratic aggrandizement—largely by feminist ideology.

The power of this bureaucratic underworld is derived almost entirely from children. It is the world of social work, child psychology, child and family counseling, child care, child protection, foster care, child support enforcement, and juvenile and family courts. Overwhelmingly, it is feminist-dominated. This is not always obvious, because its matriarchs are

33. Rob Reich, "Testing the Boundaries of Parental Authority over Education: The Case of Homeschooling," paper prepared for delivery at the 2001 Annual Meeting of the American Political Science Association, San Francisco, 2001, 33.

34. Sylvia Ann Hewlett and Cornel West, *The War Against Parents: What We Can Do for America's Beleaguered Moms and Dads* (New York: Houghton Mifflin, 1998), 109 (emphasis added). Cp. Milovan Djilas, *The New Class* (New York: Praeger, 1958).

not necessarily Vassar women's studies majors indulging in tedious dormitory debates about whether feminists may wear lipstick. But what it lacks in ideological purity it more than makes up for in coercive power. Its operatives are quasi-police functionaries with a political agenda, and they are concerned less with ideological consistency than with coercive power.

These feminists created and control the vast and impenetrable social services industries that most journalists and scholars find too dreary to scrutinize. In the US they dominate the $53 billion federal Administration for Children and Families, itself part of the gargantuan trillion dollar Department of Health and Human Services. They are both dispensers and recipients of its $350 billion grant program ("larger than all other federal agencies combined," according to HHS) funding local "human services" or "social services" bureaucracies—by far the largest patronage machine ever created, reaching into almost every household in the land and making the Soviet *nomenklatura* look ramshackle. They created and control the "family law sections" of the bar associations and family courts, which they modified into their image from an earlier incarnation as juvenile courts (rationalized by "caring" and "compassion"). And they dominate the forensic psychotherapy industry, with its close ties to the courts, social service agencies, and public schools. By no means are they all doctrinaire *devotées* of *The Feminine Mystique* or *The Female Eunuch*. But when push comes to shove, they understand that their power comes from being female. And again, their most potent source of power is other people's children.

These are the operatives and functionaries of the welfare state, that great experiment in open-ended social engineering and government expansion that continues to evolve and wheedle its way into ever more intimate corners of private life, increasingly by bankrupting the most prosperous societies in human history.[35]

Though the sexual revolution has recently tried to distance itself from the class struggle, their origins are similar. As with previous episodes in the destruction of freedom, the politicization of the Sexual Revolution was built upon appeals to help "the poor." The earliest institution of sexual warfare was the welfare state.

The welfare state has been regarded as the triumph of class politics

---

35. The welfare state has been incisively critiqued on economic grounds, but not on social. See Tom Palmer (ed.), *After the Welfare State* (Ottawa, IL: Jameson Books, 2012). For a critique in terms of its cost, destruction of the family, and inability to relieve poverty, see Phyllis Schlafly, *Who Killed the American Family?* (Washington: WND Books, 2014), ch. 5.

within the liberal democracies—the one successful achievement of socialism or "social democracy" that has grown and survived even in countries, like the United States, which avoided these terms. Yet in retrospect, the welfare state stands as the first salvo of gender politics, following directly from the enfranchisement of doctrinaire feminists.[36] Simultaneously, the professionalization of social work and its nationalization by government agencies led quickly to government control over the family.

From its inception, each stage of US welfare state expansion was justified not simply for the poor but specifically for poor *children*. The interests of these children could also be gradually divorced from their parents, though in practice they tended to be identified with the mothers who claimed to be the guardians of those interests: increasingly, single mothers. The proliferation of single-mother homes lent superficial plausibility to the new rallying cry, the "feminization of poverty," that shifted poor relief from a socialist to a feminist crusade.[37]

But the feminization of poverty was a deception from the start—a creation of ideology rather than an objective social reality and a textbook example of ideology creating its own grievances. Originally justified to provide for the families of men who had been laid off during economic downturns or eliminated by war, the welfare state quickly became a subsidy on single-mother homes and fatherless children. In good bureaucratic fashion, that is, it immediately set in to vastly expand and effectively to create precisely the problem of poverty it claimed to be alleviating.

To justify this sleight-of-hand, the welfare state engineers needed a rationale, and they found it in one of the most potent and destructive falsehoods ever foisted on a well-meaning but gullible public, one that has served, directly or indirectly, to justify the exponential expansion of not only the welfare state but the scope and power of government in many areas. This is the falsehood that government must provide for massive numbers of women and children whose men are abandoning them. With the abrupt reversal of an airbrushed Kremlin photograph, the welfare state's rationalizing figure was demoted from a hero to a

36. John Lott and Larry Kenny, "How Dramatically Did Women's Suffrage Change the Size and Scope of Government?" University of Chicago Law School, John M. Olin Law and Economics Working Paper No. 60, 5–6. See also John Lott, "Women's Suffrage Over Time, *Washington Times*, 27 November 2007, A19 (http://www.washingtontimes.com/article/20071127/EDITORIAL/111270007/1013).

37. Barbara Ehrenreich and Frances Fox Piven, "The Persistence of Poverty. 1: The Feminization of Poverty When the 'Family-Wage System' Breaks Down," *Dissent*, vol. 31, no. 2 (1984), 162–70.

villain. The same working men who, we were previously told, had been valiantly sacrificing themselves in imperialism's wars or laid off as innocent victims of heartless capitalism were suddenly and ignominiously absconding from the bastards they had sired.

Both the lucrative potential and the destructive force of this untruth are incalculable. It instantly legitimized the entire welfare state behemoth. Accept it, and virtually every expansion of both social welfare spending and law-enforcement authority is readily justified and, indeed, unanswerable. It thus prompted a spontaneous collusion of the left and the right: leftists loved it and conservatives feared it. Women and children are being abandoned by irresponsible men: no politician could resist that appeal.

Significantly, the most eminent peddler of the falsehood was a radical leftist who skillfully began marketing himself as a family-values conservative. In his hugely influential 1995 book, *Fatherless America*, David Blankenhorn provided a superb description of the destructive social consequences resulting from the sudden appearance of tens of millions of fatherless children. But to make his case broadly palatable, he predicated it all on one fundamental, massive untruth: "Never before in this country have so many children been voluntarily abandoned by their fathers," he declared. "Today, the principal cause of fatherlessness is paternal choice . . . the rising rate of paternal abandonment."[38] Blankenhorn provided no documentation for this libel against millions of innocent men who had no platform to speak in their own defense, and he has not done so subsequently when challenged to verify these statements.[39]

But the truth was very different. While examples can be found of anything, no evidence indicates that the ongoing crisis of fatherless children is caused primarily or even significantly by fathers abandoning their children.[40] It is now very clear that it has been driven throughout by policies and agencies rooted in feminist ideology. Single mothers are not being, and never have been, thrown into poverty by absconding men; they are choosing it because it offers precisely the "sexual freedom" that is feminism's seminal urge, regardless of the consequences for their children and society. Single motherhood is feminism's most potent and

38. David Blankenhorn, *Fatherless America* (New York: Basic Books, 1995), 1, 22–23.

39. See Stephen Baskerville, "The Failure of Fatherhood Policy," LewRockwell.com, 3 September 2004 (http://www.lewrockwell.com/orig2/baskerville5.html). Blankenhorn is —in words on his website—"a Saul Alinsky-inspired community organizer."

40. Stephen Baskerville, *Taken Into Custody: The War Against Fathers, Marriage, and the Family* (Nashville: Cumberland House, 2007), 13–16, 35–44.

most destructive achievement, and before the right audience feminists not only concede but boast about it. Single Mothers By Choice expresses this boast organizationally, and when pressed, most single mothers will insist that that is precisely what they are. "This is the life I chose," declares one, and we are told by the sisters themselves that this is typical. Best-selling books now extol the practice and the "freedom" it confers, and they are celebrated in the media. "When you're a single mom," writes one promoter, "you don't have to deal with unrealized expectations about your partner, nor do you have to cope with a partner's preconceptions or expectations."[41] In other words, it means sexual freedom and, above all, sexual power—with monopoly control over the children and, through the children, the father. While feminists readily pose as the champions of children when it comes to perpetuating welfare dependency, it is clear that, beneath the rhetorical fluff, the exhilarating power is more than adequate compensation for pulling their children into poverty. The very feminist intellectuals who popularized the term "feminization of poverty" defiantly declare as much: "Independence, *even in straitened and penurious forms*," proclaim Barbara Ehrenreich and her colleagues, "still offers more sexual freedom than affluence gained through marriage and dependence on one man."[42]

Indeed, the great hoax of paternal abandonment is an optical illusion, for today it is not fathers who are abandoning both their marriages and also their children *en masse*. A glance at both the law and social infrastructure reveals that, under feminist prompting, it is quite clearly mothers. A panoply of mechanisms and institutions now allows liberated mothers to rid themselves, temporarily or permanently, of inconvenient children: "safe havens" legalize cost-free child abandonment by mothers; day care is tailored to the convenience of mothers (and employers), not the needs of children; foster care relieves single mothers who cannot provide their children basic care and protection; "CHINS" petitions ("Child in Need of Services") allow single mothers to unload unruly adolescent boys to the custody of social workers; "SIDS" and in some countries infanticide laws have now made even the murder of children by mothers semi-legal. And then of course there is abortion.

When one adds the massive growth and proliferation of institutions

41. Peggy Drexler, *Raising Boys Without Men* (n.p.: Rodale, 2005), 133. Drexler goes on to describe how single mothers engineer the genetic composition of their children according to what one calls "the plan": choosing the sperm donor according to his physical characteristics to create the mail-order child of their dreams.

42. Barbara Ehrenreich, Elizabeth Hess, and Gloria Jacobs, *Re-Making Love: The Feminization of Sex* (Garden City and New York: Anchor Press/Doubleday, 1986), 197 (emphasis added).

not normally associated with welfare but whose purpose is clearly to relieve parents in general and mothers in particular of what had previously been their childrearing responsibilities—public schools, "early childhood education," organized after-school activities, convenience food and fast food, psychotropic drugs to control undisciplined boys—we can begin to see how massively the society and economy have been gearing up for decades to facilitate single motherhood, marginalize fathers, collectivize childrearing, and generally render parents and families redundant.[43]

Day Care

Foremost among these institutions is institutionalized child care. It was "radical feminism of the late 1960s, which began to agitate for universal day care as a way of liberating women from the drudgery of the home."[44] Instead it substituted the drudgery of the workplace and, for the children, the drudgery and danger and loneliness of institutional care.

Despite media determination to depict day care as yet another benefit "for the children," the clear aim is not the welfare of children but the convenience and power of working women and employers. "As long as the private sphere remains largely women's concern, they will be much less available than men for positions of responsibility in economic and political life," writes the former president of Iceland, who proposes "greater availability of childcare facilities, care for the old, and encouragement for men to participate in housework."[45] In United Nations documents, day care consistently tops the list of measures that governments are required to provide in order to eradicate "discrimination against women."[46]

Yet serious questions have been raised about the impact of consigning young children to institutions. Indeed, irrefutable scientific evidence collected by Brian Robertson and other researchers clearly connects institutional care directly with an assortment of severe problem behaviors in children, foremost aggression, disruption, and bullying.[47]

The response of day care apologists to ideologically unwelcome research results has generally been to punish the researcher. When the respected child development psychologist and day care supporter Jay

---

43. Carle Zimmerman pointed out this trend decades ago in *Family and Civilization* (orig. 1947; abridged edn., Wilmington: ISI Books, 2008).

44. Robertson, *Day Care Deception*, 5.

45. Quoted in ibid., 156.

46. See chapter IV.

47. The literature is summarized in Robertson, *Day Care Deception*, 48–55.

Belsky of Pennsylvania State University began raising awkward questions about its detrimental effects on children, not only his research but he himself was personally attacked in the media and academy and effectively ostracized from his profession.[48]

As we will see elsewhere with sexually politicized scholarship, evidence and reasoned arguments are replaced with weasel words in the service of political positions. The principal argument used by apologists was that institutionalized care is a *fait accompli* that is here to stay, regardless of whether it is good for children or not. "It isn't a question of whether there's going to be day care," according to Janellen Huttenlocher, "because people's lives today require it. The question is one of how good day care is going to be."[49] How far day care serves a political agenda—in which children become pawns in a game of power played by grown-ups—is clearly revealed when feminists dismiss peer-reviewed research findings as "backlash against the women's movement."[50]

Day care also serves the needs of expanding government power. Not only does it place children under the control of officials; it also frees their mothers to serve the expanding welfare machinery. The extensive welfare benefits demanded foremost by feminists themselves "can be financed only by taxes from a labor market in which almost everyone is working and paying taxes," according to the Swedish government.[51] So the welfare state, which already funds family breakup and then justifies itself as providing for those same broken families, drives the process of family dissolution in yet another way, by demanding that mothers leave the home for the workplace in order to pay the taxes that finance the machinery. Despite demands that fathers "participate in housework" and childrearing, they too must work more, since their wages are depressed by the addition of lower-paid women into the labor force.

An equally questionable rationalization for "quality" day care is its supposed educational value. Despite enormous media attention lavished on studies claiming to find enhanced "cognitive development" among children in care, the reputable academic studies in fact demon-

---

48. Robertson, *Day Care Deception*, 42–57; Jay Belsky, "The Politicized Science of Day Care: A Personal and Professional Odyssey," *Family Policy Review*, vol. 1, no. 6 (Fall 2003), 23–40.

49. Quoted in Robertson, *Day Care Deception*, 59.

50. Thomas Ricks, "Day Care for Infants is Challenged by Research on Psychological Risks," *Wall Street Journal*, 3 March 1987, 37, quoted in Bryce Christensen, "A Schoolhouse Built by Hobbes: The Hidden Agenda of Day Care Education," *Family Policy Review*, vol. 1, no. 2 (Fall 2003), 119.

51. Quoted in Robertson, *Day Care Deception*, 151.

strate the opposite: the more hours they were placed in care, the poorer the children's academic performance.[52] Yet these findings have received none of the attention devoted to government-funded studies extolling the educational value of institutional care. Indeed, they are seldom reported in the media at all. "There's gatekeeping going on," says Belsky. "The intelligentsia has decided that we don't want mothers to feel bad about their decisions."[53]

What the feminist media mean by "enhanced cognitive development" may also be indoctrination into feminist ideology, facilitated by institutionalizing children, as the chairman of the Swedish People's Party puts it very plainly: "The parental monopoly cannot be broken solely by indirect measures—the State must intervene directly, by, for example, taking the children from the parents during part of their growing up years.... It is best for the children and society that a universal and compulsory preschool program become clearly indoctrinating, thus enabling society to intervene more directly when it comes to the children's values and attitudes."[54]

So government child care offers yet another opportunity, much like the government schools for which it prepares them, to indoctrinate children in officially approved ideology. Government schools and other institutions already function effectively as extended day care, with mandatory programs for preschoolers, lower ages for kindergarten, longer school days and school years, and mandatory summer schools. This institutionalization of children, in both day care and schooling, contributes to what some have described as the "regimentation" and "bureaucratization" of children's lives.[55] The re-education process becomes complete as parents too must submit to bureaucratic instruction on how to raise their children. "Every home and family should be taught, through parenting education and family visitation by social service intermediaries, how to raise children," said then-Senator Hillary Clinton.[56]

What appears as a difference of social science findings between researchers and feminists may in fact be a difference of ideological semantics, since the imputed educational value and the heightened

---

52. Christensen, "Schoolhouse," 115–16.
53. Quoted in ibid., 117.
54. Quoted in Robertson, *Day Care Deception*, 151.
55. Ibid., 156; Dana Mack, *The Assault on Parenthood* (New York: Simon and Schuster, 1997), 21.
56. Quoted in Robertson, *Day Care Deception*, 156–57.

aggressiveness, both attributed to day care, may in fact be the same thing. There may be no need to sort out the clinical data on the aggressiveness and rebelliousness of children who are not permitted to form secure and loving attachments with their parents; here as elsewhere, the point—and the political consequences—are highlighted very clearly by feminists themselves. A *Los Angeles Times* reporter indulges in armchair psychology to explain that children become aggressive not because they are institutionalized for eight to ten hours a day with minimal supervision and no parental love and authority but because their mothers cannot leave them there guilt-free: "Society still views working mothers with ambivalence," and therefore the mothers' "guilt and anxiety—even resentment—is absorbed by their children and manifested as aggression." Children will therefore be helped not by the attention of their mothers but by "society" giving working mothers more "support, appreciation, and reassurance" when leaving their children in institutions.[57] Huttenlocher is less resourceful but more forthright when she concedes that institutionalized children tend to become "less polite, less agreeable, less respectful of others' rights, more irritable, more rebellious [and] more aggressive with their peers." She then suggests that such traits are precisely the ones needed for the next generation of sexual revolutionaries. "Children who have been in day care," she writes, "think for themselves [and] want their own way. . . . They are not willing to comply with adults' arbitrary rules."[58] This is not the last time we will see how the virtues of adolescent rebellion are extolled and enlisted—and frequently also exhibited—by feminist academics. What researchers call aggression Huttenlocher prefers to see as "self-assertion." "Kids who've spent time in day care certainly learn how to cope socially, and they're certainly much more sturdy little interactors" than those raised at home. Time magazine likewise sees irritable, rebellious, and aggressive children as "spunky and independent."[59]

Bryce Christensen has detected rather less positive implications of raising children according to the principles of *Lord of the Flies*. Christensen suggests that this Hobbesian state of nature encouraged in the day care setting, where every child must survive by looking out for himself, leads logically to the Hobbesian leviathan state, with day care engineers demanding ever-more authority through an "increase in centralized planning and quality control." Collectivized childrearing is

---

57. Quoted in Christensen, "Schoolhouse," 118.
58. Quoted in Maggie Gallagher, "Day Careless," *National Review*, 26 January 1998 (http://www.nationalreview.com/article/223060/day-careless-williumrex).
59. Christensen, "Schoolhouse," 119.

of course the logical conclusion of day care, impeded only by the politically unacceptable "premise that children are the responsibility of individual families."[60]

A final question is how far day care deprives children of fathers as well as mothers by facilitating divorce. This has not been explored even by critical researchers, but the potential is obvious and the results testified by myriad fathers. Despite perfunctory feminist demands for fathers to share childrearing equally, such involvement seems to be what few divorcing mothers in fact desire, and day care provides yet another tool to ensure that children have minimal contact with their fathers. Day care providers (now a formidable financial lobby) certainly have no incentive to involve fathers. Over their objections that they are willing to care for their children themselves, fathers are routinely ordered by divorce courts to place their children in day care at their own expense, in addition to their regular child support.

Obesity

The increasing problem of obese people and especially obese children has captured international attention. Some argue that it has been elevated, largely by government officials, to the level of hysteria. "Listening to Mrs. Obama, officials in her husband's administration, and other would-be nutrition gurus, one might be justified in thinking childhood obesity to be a disaster of gargantuan proportions," observes one writer. "The former head of the Centers for Disease Control and Prevention, Julie Gerberding, even compared obesity to a worldwide pandemic, saying: 'If you looked at any epidemic—whether it's influenza or plague from the Middle Ages—they are not as serious as the epidemic of obesity in terms of the health impact.'"[61]

Yet, while the problem should not be dismissed, childhood obesity and diabetes may be directly correlated to broken families, as single parents resort to convenience and fast food or leave children to select their own diet. Research from the Centers for Disease Control show that children living in low-income households (i.e., single-parent households) suffered from obesity in far greater numbers than children living in high-income households (two-parent families),[62] and independent research confirms that teens in one-parent families and children of

60. Quoted in ibid., 121.

61. Julie Gunlock, "Three Squares a Day, Courtesy of the Federal Government," *National Review*, 17 January 2011 (http://www.iwf.org/news/show/24127.html).

62. Julie Gunlock, "Children, Parents, and Obesity," Independent Women's Forum website: http://www.iwf.org/news/2432814/Children-Parents-and-Obesity.

divorced parents are much more likely to be obese than those in intact homes.[63]

If confirmed, then the problem is connected to the Sexual Revolution. There is no doubt from the research that obese children have resulted from the proliferation of single-parent homes and the inability or refusal of working mothers to cook regular healthy meals for their families.[64] Noting that "the statistical analysis . . . identifies family structure as a strong predictor of adolescent weight problems [and] compared to peers in two-parent families, teens in one-parent families are far more likely to be overweight or obese," one editor adds facetiously: "Who would ever have guessed that divorce lawyers had struck a sweetheart deal with diet promoters?"[65] (Likewise concerning other health problems: "If divorce lawyers are not already receiving a kickback from cigarette makers, they should be!")[66]

Here once again, the radicals' solution to the problem they themselves created is expanded government power. Blaming "advertising" and the "market," radicals demand lucrative new taxes. "New interest in the use of taxes on foods rich in fat and sugar," is approved by the Organization for Economic Cooperation and Development in Europe, which notes that governments are unlikely to pass up an opportunity to fill their coffers and expand their reach: "They may generate important revenues, which must have contributed to governments' attraction to these measures at a time of tight fiscal constraints." Hungary expects to raise over 70 million and France 280 million, courtesy of unhealthy children.[67]

But there is nothing new about advertising or fat and sugar. Rather

---

63. K.A. Thulitha Wickrama, K.A.S. Wickrama, and Chalandra M. Bryant, "Community Influence on Adolescent Obesity: Race/Ethnic Differences," *Journal of Youth and Adolescence* 35 (2006), 647–56; Anna Biehl et al, "Parental Marital Status and Childhood Overweight and Obesity in Norway: A Nationally Representative Cross-Sectional Study," *BMJ Open*, vol. 4, no. 6 (2014), http://bmjopen.bmj.com/content/4/6/e004502.full.

64. Taryn W. Morrissey, Rachel E. Dunifon, and Ariel Kalil, "Maternal Employment, Work Schedules, and Children's Body Mass Index," *Child Development*, vol. 82, no. 1 (January–February 2011), 66–81 (http://onlinelibrary.wiley.com/doi/10.1111/j.1467-8624.2010.01541.x/full).

65. "Fat Chance," *The Family in America*, vol. 21, no. 9 (September–October 2007), 3.
66. Ibid., 4.
67. "OECD Obesity Update 2012," http://www.oecd.org/health/health-systems/49716427.pdf. Compare Czarist Russia's vodka tax: "The state deliberately took advantage of these habits to augment its income—which meant in turn that it came to have a stake in popular drunkenness." Geoffrey Hosking, *Russia: People and Empire, 1552–1917* (Cambridge, MA: Harvard, 1997), 104.

than face the politically incorrect truth, the US government proposes to federalize the feeding of children in its entirety, three meals a day, 365 days a year.[68] Here yet again, ideology first creates the problem by undermining the proven utility of the traditional family and then offers solutions that increase state power, in turn further eclipsing family autonomy. As Julie Gunlock notes: "The real impact of this bill is much larger than nutrition. It represents an enormous growth in government. Not in the way we've seen it lately—into the financial and business sectors—but into our personal lives and the lives of our children. It tells parents to cease their most basic role—to feed your child. Because . . . schools now feed children three squares a day."[69]

And having weakened parental responsibility and authority, the state puts itself in a position to curtail parental rights. Proposals are now afoot to confiscate obese children from their parents.[70]

Divorce

The hoax of the absconding father rationalized and leveraged a massive expansion of state power through emotional blackmail. It was nothing less than a declaration of judicial and bureaucratic war against the first and foremost feminist enemy, the literal embodiment of the hated "patriarchy": fathers. "Women are lone parents in 84% of cases not because men abandon their children," writes John Waters, "but because . . . the fathers have been constructively banished, with the collusion of the state, which encourages women to abuse the grotesque power we have conferred on them."[71] Social science research confirms unequivocally that Waters is correct.[72]

So long as the principal engine for creating single-mother homes was welfare, the abandonment myth was only implied. Everyone knew that welfare was subsidizing and proliferating single-mother homes, but until money became contentious no one was greatly bothered with assigning blame. Most couples producing fatherless children were never married in the first place, so no documentation attested to who was breaking up a "family" that had often never really existed in intact form.

---

68. Gunlock, "Three Square Meals." Some evidence suggests that school meals may be contributing to obesity. Gunlock, "Children, Parents, and Obesity."

69. Julie Gunlock, "Fatter Government Will Not Shrink Kids," *National Review*, 15 December 2010 (http://www.iwf.org/news/show/23999.html).

70. Lindsey Tanner, "Parents Would Lose Custody of Obese Kids," *Washington Times*, 12 July 2011 (http://www.washingtontimes.com/news/2011/jul/12/parents-would-lose-custody-of-obese-kids/).

71. "Women Who Banish Fathers Seen as Heroines," *Irish Times*, 6 October 1998.

72. Baskerville, *Taken Into Custody*, 18.

As the problem spread to the middle class (which today is the fastest-growing sector of unwed childbearing), this changed dramatically. Here the implicit became explicit with an open media and academic assault on two inextricably interrelated institutions that had quietly ceased to exist in the welfare underclass but which were still thriving in the middle class: fathers and marriage.

The matriarchal logic of the welfare state became more aggressive as it expanded, perhaps inexorably, into the middle class. This was effected through the most subtle and potent weapon ever devised for sexual warfare, the device that destroyed "patriarchy" once and for all by quite literally criminalizing fatherhood itself: divorce.

Divorce has seldom been analyzed politically.[73] Not generally perceived as a political issue or a gender battleground, and never one they wished to advertise (largely because they won an instant and unopposed victory), divorce became in fact the most devastating weapon in the arsenal of gender warriors, because it brought the gender war into every household in the Western world and beyond.

Feminists long recognized its political power. As early as the American Revolution, divorce was associated with female rebellion and power. "The association of divorce with women's freedom and prerogatives, established in those early days, remained an enduring and important feature of American divorce," writes Barbara Whitehead. Into the nineteenth century, "divorce became an increasingly important measure of women's political freedom as well as an expression of feminine initiative and independence."[74]

But it was in the twentieth century that feminists teamed up with trial lawyers and other legal entrepreneurs to institutionalize not simply divorce by mutual consent but unilateral divorce-on-demand and involuntary divorce. The National Association of Women Lawyers (NAWL) claims credit for pioneering "no-fault" divorce as early as the 1940s, which it describes as "the greatest project NAWL has ever undertaken." Once the laws began to be enacted at the height of the Sexual Revolution in California in 1969, they swept through the legislatures of the United States and the entire Western world with lightning speed and virtually no public debate or organized opposition. By 1977, "the ideal of

---

73. Maggie Gallagher, *The Abolition of Marriage* (Washington: Regnery, 1996); Baskerville, *Taken Into Custody.*

74. Barbara Dafoe Whitehead, *The Divorce Culture* (New York: Vintage, 1998), 15–16, 26. Divorce was soon to be institutionalized in the French and, later, Russian revolutions, as Louis de Bonald described in his 1805 book, *On Divorce.*

no-fault divorce became the guiding principle for reform of divorce laws in the majority of states."[75]

Today, divorce stands as the proudest celebration of feminine power. "Exactly the thing that people tear their hair out about is exactly the thing I am very proud of," says Germaine Greer.[76] Contrary to popular belief, the overwhelming majority of divorces—and virtually all involving children—are filed by women. Few involve specific grounds, such as desertion, adultery, or violence. The most frequent reasons given are nebulous and subjective: "growing apart," "not feeling loved or appreciated."[77]

Journalists, scholars, and other supposed government watchdogs trade in clichés about "ugly divorce" and "nasty custody battle," but they have failed (or refused) to investigate in any depth. No legislative enactment has spread more turmoil throughout the social order, transferred more power to the state, or done more to debase the legal machinery from a dispenser of justice into a weapon of plunder and aggrandizement of power. For the first time, a legally unimpeachable citizen ("no-fault"), sitting in his own home and minding his own business—without any finding of legal culpability for anything—could be summoned to a court and find himself summarily evicted from his home, permanently separated from his children, confiscated of all his property and income,

75. Selma Moidel Smith, "A Century of Achievement: The Centennial of the National Association of Women Lawyers," *Experience* (Fall 1998 and Winter 1999), reprinted in the *Women Lawyers Journal*, vol. 85, no. 2 (Summer 1999), and at http://wlh.law.stanford.edu/wp-content/uploads/2011/01/smith-a-century-of-achievement.pdf, 10–11.

Here too feminists unabashedly pose as victims of the divorce revolution they themselves created and which is administered by their operatives: "It is in families," writes Martha Nussbaum, "...that the cruelest discrimination against women takes place."

> [T]he patterns of family life limit their opportunities in many ways: by assigning them to unpaid work with low prestige; by denying them equal opportunities to outside jobs and education; by insisting they do most or all of the housework and child care even when they are also earning wages. Especially troubling are ways that women may suffer from the altruism of marriage itself. . . . [A] woman who accepts the traditional tasks of housekeeping and provides support for her husband's work is *not likely to be well prepared to look after herself and her family in the event (which is increasingly likely) of a divorce* or an accident that leaves her alone.

Martha Nussbaum, "Justice for Women," *New York Review of Books*, October 8, 1992, 43 (emphasis added). In short, the hardship and "cruelty" is entirely emotional blackmail created by radical ideology.

76. Amanda Banks, "Greer Cheers Divorcing Women," *The Australian*, 8 September 2004.

77. Braver, *Divorced Dads*, chap. 7 and *passim*. See also figures quoted from the National Center for Health Statistics in Farrell, *Father and Child Reunion*, 169, 278 note 1.

and incarcerated without trial. Banal as it has been made to appear by euphemisms and platitudes, it has been clearly documented that the divorce epidemic is driven by a deadly, authoritarian ideology that sets aside virtually every legal protection afforded to citizens in democratic countries and has sent massive numbers of innocent people into a legal nightmare that frequently ends in poverty, prison, and death.[78]

Conservative moralizers have completely misunderstood the significance of the divorce revolution. While they bemoan mass divorce, they actively resist confronting its political causes. One conservative pundit (who later came to a highly sophisticated understanding) could even gratuitously defend divorce when no one in public life was attacking it.[79]

Maggie Gallagher once attributed this silence to "political cowardice": "Opposing gay marriage or gays in the military is for Republicans an easy, juicy, risk-free issue," she complained. "The message [is] that at all costs we should keep divorce off the political agenda." No American politician of national stature has ever seriously challenged involuntary divorce. "Democrats did not want to anger their large constituency among women who saw easy divorce as a hard-won freedom and prerogative," writes Whitehead. "Republicans did not want to alienate their upscale constituents or their libertarian wing, both of whom tended to favor easy divorce, nor did they want to call attention to the divorces among their own leadership."[80] Vice President Dan Quayle was careful to qualify his famous denunciation of single parenthood, saying, "I am not talking about a situation where there is a divorce."[81] The exception proves the rule. When Pope John Paul II spoke out against divorce, he was viciously attacked from the right as well as the left.[82]

This omission is especially puzzling and paradoxical among Christian conservatives whose "pro-family" advocacy is the centerpiece of their self-identification. "Instead of following a fixed and enduring moral compass on divorce," observes a perplexed scholar, "religious groups in America . . . gradually accommodated a cultural trend that gained widespread acceptance." So glaring is the anomaly that it has even attracted scholarly investigation from secular political science:

---

78. Baskerville, *Taken Into Custody*.

79. Dennis Prager, "Being More Compassionate on Divorce," Dennis Prager Show website: http://www.dennisprager.com/columns.aspx?g=706de827-b726-408d-bf79-c77f e297cab1&url=being_more_compassionate_on_divorce, 12 November 2002. But see also "Smoke and Lose Your Son," *World Net Daily*, 26 March 2002.

80. Whitehead, *Divorce Culture*, 7.

81. Gallagher, *Abolition of Marriage*, 245.

82. Tunku Varadarajan, "Clash With the Titans," *Wall Street Journal* online edition, 30 January 2002, http://opinionjournal.com/columnists/tvaradarajan/?id=95001795.

One might suspect that being "pro-traditional family" would have led the Moral Majority to take a strong stand against the easy availability of divorce. After all, it is difficult to identify a greater threat to the traditional family than breaking it apart through divorce. During the 10 years of its existence, [Jerry] Falwell's organization mobilized and lobbied on many political issues, including abortion, pornography, gay rights, school prayer, the Equal Rights Amendment, and sex education in schools. Divorce failed to achieve that exalted status, ranking so low on the group's agenda that books on the Moral Majority do not even give the issue an entry in the index. In the 1980 presidential election, the Moral Majority used voter registration drives to promote the candidacy of Ronald Reagan, himself a divorced and remarried man who had signed the nation's first no-fault divorce law as governor of California in 1969. One could hardly imagine a stronger signal that the issue of divorce would not receive the Moral Majority's attention.

Likewise the Christian Coalition: "The subject of divorce was noticeably absent from the list of issues on which the group spent large amounts of time."

More recent groups whose names explicitly signal devotion to family preservation like Focus on the Family and the Family Research Council (FRC) also ignore divorce as a political issue. FRC "has stated that 'we will not relent in our insistence to reform divorce laws,' but that abstract support has not been matched by a sustained commitment to spending time or resources on the issue." Such groups actively lobby on many issues that are hardly as directly relevant to family preservation as divorce:

> FRC staff also published editorials that criticized wasteful government spending, warned against universal health care, and challenged the science behind global warming. Certainly no one could deny that government spending, health care, and global warming are important subjects for American citizens and political leaders to consider. For an organization whose self-definition holds that it "champions marriage and the family," however, these issues are considerably removed from its core mission.

When confronted, the rationalizations provided by such groups are profoundly unconvincing. Our political scientist's observations confirm the personal experiences of those who advocate divorce reform:

> The FRC has stated that constraints of budget, time, and staff prevent it from engaging questions surrounding same-sex marriage and heterosexual divorce at the same time, but it managed to allocate its scarce resources to addressing many other issues of current interest. Even if one could justify on practical or biblical grounds prioritizing gay mar-

riage over divorce, such a view could hardly justify pushing divorce all the way to the bottom of the pecking order, below issues with only a tenuous connection to marriage and the family.

Unlike feminists, Christian conservatives, like conservatives generally, have treated divorce as a moral failing to be lamented, rather than as a public policy issue to be debated and reformed. "Leading organizations representing Christian conservatives have treated divorce as a private matter to be handled by individuals, families, and churches rather than a political question requiring legislative, executive, or judicial action."[83]

This anomaly is simply too glaring and bizarre not to be indicative of some larger problem. FRC director Tony Perkins led the campaign against divorce in Louisiana. "Because Perkins has established his credibility on the subject of divorce, the relative silence of his organization on the matter cannot be attributed to an absence of caring on the part of its leadership," Mark Smith observes. "The FRC's priorities instead appear to reflect straightforward political calculations." Smith continues, "Their leaders seem to recognize how much a strong push to limit divorce would alienate their own members and supporters." As we will see, this has discredited their claim to be "pro-family" and "pro-marriage" and rendered their campaign against same-sex marriage ineffectual.

To the extent that conservatives mention divorce at all, their approach has consists of moralizing and scolding. Rather than confronting the law with constructive reforms, they bemoan the "culture" and scold people with the hackneyed feminist party line that divorce is caused by philandering men who abandon their families for "trophy wives."[84] As we have seen, current divorce laws were devised by feminists, and divorces involving children are driven almost entirely by women.[85]

As cover for their timidity over divorce, conservatives during the Bush administration endorsed "marriage education" programs—essen-

---

83. Mark H. Smith, "Religion, Divorce, and the Missing Culture War in America," *Political Science Quarterly*, vol. 125, no. 1 (Spring 2010), 59, 74–75, 77–78, 81, 83, 85.

84. "Middle-aged men, at the peak of their careers and earning capacities, frequently trade in the wives of their youth . . . for young and sleeker models—so-called 'trophy wives.'" Robert George, "Marriage, Morality, and Rationality," in *The Meaning of Marriage*, ed. R.P. George and J.B. Elshtain (Dallas: Spence, 2006), 148. George's only evidence is a quotation from fellow political scientist James Q. Wilson: "If divorce becomes easier, a lot of prosperous men will leave their spouses and marry a trophy wife." *The Marriage Problem*, 15, where likewise no evidence is provided. Such, from two of America's most brilliant and influential intellectuals, is the state of conservative scholarship on divorce. (As we will see, quoting one another's unsupported clichés is a favorite technique among feminist scholars.)

85. Baskerville, *Taken Into Custody*, 35–44.

tially government psychotherapy ostensibly designed to (somehow) "strengthen" or "promote" marriage. Essentially repackaging similar fatherhood promotion schemes from the Clinton years, these were justified on the principle that marriage is a "public" institution, with public benefits extending beyond private individuals. "The time has come to recognize that marriage is a public social good," writes Matt Daniels of the Alliance for Marriage. "The health of American families—built upon marriage—affects us all."[86] Conservatives like Daniels insist that the family is the building block of civil society and that weakening marriage could therefore threaten the social basis of civilization itself. "No one would argue that crime and child poverty in America are not the business of government," he wrote. "And no one wants to see the government turn a blind eye to the social trends that are doing the most damage to American children." Daniels' facts are compelling and borne out by social science research:

> Therein lies the problem with the fantasy that the health of the legal and social institution of marriage is an exclusively private matter. The reality is that our government is permanently in the business of dealing with the social fallout from marital and family decline. . . . Decades of social-science studies have proven that most of our nation's most daunting social problems are driven more by family breakdown than any other social variable—including race and economics.[87]

Yet to declare marriage a "public" institution, and use that principle to justify involving the state machinery in citizens' private lives and even to define (and potentially redefine) marriage, would seem self-defeating. Both conservatives and liberals have questioned how government officials can strengthen anyone's marriage. Moreover, some predicted (accurately) that government therapy would become feminist therapy under a less conservative administration, since therapy programs open the question of spousal behavior to discussion and therefore invite feminist therapists to assume control of a process that allows them to dictate, with the quasi-authority of quasi-science, how citizens must comport themselves in their own homes.[88] Daniels never distinguishes

---

86. Matt Daniels, "Marriage, Society," *Washington Times*, 15 April 2004, online at http://www.washingtontimes.com/op-ed/20040414-090033-8998r.htm.

87. Daniels, "Marriage, Society."

88. Jonah Goldberg, "No Angels," *National Review Online*, 23 July 2004, http://www.nationalreview.com/goldberg/goldberg200407230847.asp; Stephen Baskerville, "Wedded to the State," LewRockwell.com, 21 October 2005, http://www.ejfi.org/family/family-8.htm.

the public's interest from the government's. Government is not a neutral player, and it is impossible to assess the weakening of family structure without understanding the state machinery that already circumscribes marriage and family life.[89]

Just how ineffectual these programs were fated to be is rendered clear by the testimonies of men who refuse to marry because they have become aware of how easily divorce can be inflicted upon them unilaterally. Helen Smith and others have demonstrated that divorce laws have driven men to a marriage "strike."[90] No man in his right mind will marry and have children knowing that, through literally "no fault" of his own, he can lose his children, home, and savings and be jailed without trial. "I could not in good conscience urge any young man . . . today to marry, or even to date," confesses one strong advocate of marriage. "There is simply no point in continuing to play by the old rules with women who openly despise those rules." One begins to wonder what these "pro-family" and "pro-marriage" groups are thinking when they promote these pointless programs as a solution to the crisis of marriage. "The conservative commentariat is clueless as usual about these realities," Roger Devlin continues. "All they have to offer is empty sermonizing about the sacredness of the marriage vow."[91] But no amount of nagging by sanctimonious apostles of marriage professing to know the benefits of marriage for other people is going to persuade men to commit their lives to an agreement that offers them no protection against the confiscation of their children and can send them straight to jail. "Preaching hasn't worked," writes Laura Wood. "As long as our government sustains single mothers, as long as family courts continue to strip spouses of their assets and children when they have done no wrong, preaching is an exercise in fatuous denial."[92]

In ironic contrast to marriage, divorce is often defended as a "private" matter and therefore immune from public scrutiny; some even claim it is a "civil liberty."[93] Yet it is among government's most intrusive acts. Divorce raises fundamental questions about the government's reach

89. Stephen Baskerville, "The Politics of Fatherhood," *PS: Political Science and Politics*, vol. 35, no. 4 (December 2002).

90. Helen Smith, *Men on Strike* (New York: Encounter, 2013), ch. 1. Also Baskerville, *Taken Into Custody*, ch. 1.

91. F. Roger Devlin, *Sexual Utopia in Power* (San Francisco: Counter-Currents, 2015), 52, 54.

92. Quoted in Schlafly, *Who Killed*, 144.

93. Glenda Riley, *Divorce: An American Tradition* (New York: Oxford University Press, 1991), 6.

into private life that have never been confronted. Far more than marriage, divorce by its nature requires active and almost incessant government intervention into private life. Marriage creates a private household, which may or may not necessitate signing some legal documents. Divorce dissolves not only a marriage, but also the private household formed by it, usually against the wishes of one spouse. It inevitably involves state functionaries—including police and prisons—to enforce the post-marriage order. Otherwise, one spouse might continue to claim the protections and prerogatives of private life: the right to live in the common home, to possess the common property, or—most vexing of all—to parent the common children.

The truism that marriage is a public institution therefore requires some qualification. The legal systems of the Common Law countries have long recognized the married family as a zone of privacy that is off-limits to the state—what Supreme Court Justice Byron White called a "realm of family life which the state cannot enter."[94]

Family inviolability was never absolute, but the basic principle governed what traditionalists themselves insist is the unique and foremost purpose of marriage and family: raising children. The private family creates a legal bond between parent and child that allows parents (within reasonable limits) to raise their children according to their own principles, free from government interference. "Whatever else it may accomplish, marriage acknowledges and secures the relation between a child and a particular set of parents," writes Susan Shell. "The right to one's own children . . . is perhaps the most basic individual right—so basic we hardly think of it."[95]

This right has long been recognized as fundamental by the Supreme Court and other federal courts, as well as by centuries of Common Law practice. Numerous decisions have reaffirmed that parenthood is an "essential" right, "far more precious than property rights," that "undeniably warrants deference, and, absent a powerful countervailing interest, protection."[96] "The liberty interest and the integrity of the family encompass an interest in retaining custody of one's children," according to one decision.[97] Parental rights have been characterized by the courts

---

94. *Prince v. Massachusetts*, 321 U.S. 158, 166 (1944).

95. Susan Shell, "The Liberal Case Against Gay Marriage," *The Public Interest* 156 (Summer 2004), 7.

96. *May v. Anderson*, 345 U.S. 528, 533 (1953); *Meyer v. Nebraska*, 262 U.S. 390, 399 (1923); *Stanley v. Illinois*, 405 U.S. 645 (1971). See Donald C. Hubin, "Parental Rights and Due Process," *Journal of Law and Family Studies*, vol. 1, no. 2 (1999), 123 and *passim*.

97. *Langton v. Maloney*, 527 F. Supp. 538, D.C. Conn. (1981).

as "sacred" and "inherent, natural right[s], for the protection of which ... our government is formed."[98]

For this reason, the married family, and particularly parenthood, is the guarantor of freedom for the entire society—a conservative cliché whose basis is seldom explored thoroughly. It creates a zone of privacy that is off-limits to the state and creates an authority that is the only exception to the government's monopoly on coercive force.

Parenthood after all is politically unique. It is the one relationship, other than the state, where some may legally exercise coercive authority over others, which is why governments often try to undermine it and why state officials—social workers, family court judges, divorce lawyers, forensic psychotherapists, public school administrators—seek to prohibit or curtail activities by which parents instruct, protect, and provide for their own children without dependence on the state. Without parental authority, government's reach is total.[99]

This principle has become largely a fiction, and the cutting edge is divorce. Shell summarizes principles that, until recently, were so universal as to be unstated among free societies: "No known society treats the question of who may properly call a child his or her own as simply ... a matter to be decided entirely politically."

> No known government, however brutal or tyrannical, has ever denied ... the fundamental claim of parents to their children.... A government that distributed children randomly ... could not be other than tyrannical.... A government that paid no regard to the claims of biological parenthood would be unacceptable to all but the most fanatical of egalitarian or communitarian zealots.[100]

As a statement of society's moral consensus, Shell's points are unexceptionable. Yet they also provide an unintended commentary on the ignorance that pervades today's debates. For divorce law in the Western democracies has rendered these statements both prescient as principles and factually false. What she regards as a dystopian nightmare into which "no known government" has ever ventured has today become precisely the routine practice of governments throughout the Western democracies. It is having precisely the consequences she predicts.

Shell observes the obligatory gender neutrality, but her principles

98. Quoted in Bruce C. Hafen, "Children's Liberation and the New Egalitarianism: Some Reservations about Abandoning Youth to Their 'Rights,'" *Brigham Young University Law Review* (1976), 615–16.

99. Mike Donnelly, "Religious Freedom in Education," *International Journal for Religious Freedom*, vol. 4, no. 2 (2011).

100. Shell, "Liberal Case," 5–6.

concerning marriage pertain to one parent far more than the other. The reasons for this go to the heart of current controversies over marriage. They also pinpoint and explain the ineffectiveness and futility of conservative campaigns on marriage, and why their failure to understand and confront divorce is fatal to any pretense about saving marriage. Indeed, this explains why, when it comes to family decline, conservative armchair moralists are probably doing more harm than good.

For all their eloquence over the virtues and benefits of marriage, conservative advocates have singularly failed to elucidate why the institution exists.[101] Their main argument, usually directed at advocates for same-sex marriage, is that the purpose of marriage is procreation.[102] But millions of single mothers attest that procreation is perfectly possible without marriage. This fallacious platitude is easily refuted by the homosexualists, who point out that fruitlessness of many heterosexual marriages.

The purpose of marriage is not procreation but fatherhood: marriage allows children to have fathers.[103] Marriage turns a man from a sperm donor into a parent and thus creates paternal authority, allowing a man to exercise the authority over children that otherwise would be exercised by the mother alone. Feminists understand this when they renounce marriage as an institution of "patriarchy" and promote single motherhood and divorce as positive goods for their own sake.[104] Instead of recognizing this truth, conservative sentimentalists labor the cliché that marriage exists to civilize men and control their promiscuity.[105] If so, that is part of a larger function: to protect the father-child bond and with it the intact family. This point, potentially the strongest in their

101. The best effort is Sherif Girgis, Robert P. George, and Ryan T. Anderson, "What Is Marriage?" *Harvard Journal of Law and Public Policy*, vol. 34, no. 1 (Winter 2010), 245–87. Of course, all these arguments are directed against same-sex marriage.

102. The best formulation is Allan Carlson, "The End of Marriage," *Touchstone*, September 2006.

103. Once this is recognized, it is clear that gender-neutral marriage is a contradiction in terms. Moreover, the homosexualists can have no answer, because even fruitless marriages can adopt, and the children will still have a father. Other benefits are rightly claimed for marriage by its advocates. But in the end, the central one is this, to establish fatherhood. Once this is understood, everything else about the current problems of marriage and the family falls into place. And once this is understood, same-sex marriage is revealed as not simply an absurdity, but an ideological attack on civilization's most basic institution.

104. Jyl Josephson, "Citizenship, Same-Sex Marriage, and Feminist Critiques of Marriage," *Perspectives on Politics*, vol. 3, no. 2 (June 2005), 275.

105. E.g., Leon R. Kass, "The End of Courtship," *The Public Interest* 126 (Winter 1997).

case, is overlooked by traditionalists who argue that marriage under-girds civilization. For it is the presence of the father that creates both the intact family and, by the same measure, the civil institution itself. Thomas Hobbes attributed to married fatherhood a central role in the process of moving from chaos to civilization. In nature, Hobbes argued, "the dominion is in the mother": "For in the condition of mere nature, *where there are no matrimonial laws*, it cannot be known who is the father, unless it be declared by the mother. And therefore the right of dominion over the child dependeth on her will and is consequently hers."[106] Only in civilized society, where "matrimonial laws" do operate, is authority over children shared with the father. It fact, for all the ink spilled over delineating the proper role of the state in marriage, the role of tax incentives, and so forth, it is probably fair to say that the only truly essential role of the state in marriage (and this shows why it does have an essential role, pace some libertarian advocates for complete privatization) is to guarantee the rights and authority of the parents, and especially the father.

Our legal system has long insisted that marriage, not sperm, designates the father. The legal standard was Lord Mansfield's Rule, stipulating that a child born within wedlock is presumed to be that of the husband, because it enabled a marriage to survive the wife's adultery.[107] (Earlier ages had perhaps a more balanced assessment of the female and male tendencies toward promiscuity.)

The role of marriage in creating paternity is also seen in its absence. Today, the weakening of marriage produces fatherless, not usually motherless, homes. (Motherlessness often follows, but fatherlessness begins the process.) As out-of-wedlock births explode, governments have developed elaborate bureaucratic substitutes for marriage in their efforts to "establish paternity" for purposes of collecting child support and (it is claimed, usually disingenuously) re-connecting fathers with their children.

This helps us understand why the divorce revolution is much more subversive of the social order than a matter of excessive individualism. Here as elsewhere, a provision rationalized in the name of greater freedom is in reality a highly authoritarian attack on an institution that provides for freedom, an attack that permits sexual ideologues and gov-

---

106. Thomas Hobbes, *Leviathan*, part II, ch. 20 (Harmondsworth: Penguin, 1982), 254 (emphasis added).

107. Frederick Pollack and Frederic William Maitland, *The History of English Law* (2d edn., 1968), 398–99. For the feminist manipulation of this principle, see O'Leary, *Gender Agenda*, 32.

ernment functionaries to rationalize the most intrusive and repressive government machinery ever erected in the English-speaking democracies.

"No-fault" divorce was a deception from the start. What lawmakers and the public were told would permit divorce by mutual consent in fact allowed unilateral and involuntary divorce: divorce that was not only without the consent or over the objections of an innocent spouse, but that forced the innocent spouse to bear the burden of the costs and consequences. In retrospect, it was nothing less than the boldest social and legal experiment ever undertaken in the Western democracies: the end of marriage as a legally enforceable contract, or what Maggie Gallagher called the "abolition of marriage."[108] Today it is not possible to form a binding agreement to create a family. Regardless of the terms by which it is created, government officials can and will, at the sole request of one spouse, automatically dissolve a marriage over the objection of the other. Then follows the inescapable authoritarian logic that no one will acknowledge or confront: government functionaries will then assume total control over the entire household—including the children and all property—and distribute them as they choose, to whom they choose.

Under no-fault, the spouse that divorces without recognized grounds or breaks the marriage contract through adultery or desertion incurs no liability for the costs or consequences. "In all other areas of contract law those who break a contract are expected to compensate their partner or partners," writes Robert Whelan, "but under a system of 'no fault' divorce, this essential element of contract law is abrogated."[109] As critics pointed out, no sound judicial system can possibly operate on such a principle, because it undermines the very principle of justice itself. "There is fault on both sides in every human relationship," Fred Hanson acknowledged when the new divorce laws were drafted. "The faults, however, are far from equal. No secular society can be operated on the theory that all faults are equal." Hanson was the dissenting member of the National Conference of Commissioners of Uniform State Laws, which presented "no-fault" laws to the states. "To do justice between parties without regard to fault is an impossibility," he warned. "I wonder what's to become of the maxim that no man shall profit by his own wrong—or woman either, for that matter."[110] Today we have the answer

---

108. Gallagher, *Abolition of Marriage.*

109. Robert Whelan (ed.), *Just a Piece of Paper?* (London: Institute of Economic Affairs, 1995), introduction, 3.

110. Quoted in Judy Parejko, *Stolen Vows: The Illusion of No-Fault Divorce and the Rise of the American Divorce Industry* (Collierville, Tennessee: InstantPublisher, 2002), 52.

to that question: when courts stop dispensing justice, they start dispensing injustice.

Few stopped to consider the implications of laws that shifted the dissolution of private households from a voluntary to an involuntary process. Unilateral divorce inescapably involves government agents forcibly removing legally innocent people from their homes, seizing their property, and separating them from their children. It inherently denies not only the inviolability of marriage but the very existence of a private sphere of life.

The implications were not debated at the time and have never been debated in the decades it has taken for the logic to work itself out to its nightmare conclusions. The result gave government officials—armed with no evidence of any legal wrongdoing and nothing more than a piece of paper and a spouse with a private grievance—the power to summarily force legally innocent people out of their homes, seize all their property, assume permanent and absolute control over their children, permanently separate them from their children, and—if they fail or refuse to cooperate in any way—to incarcerate them indefinitely without charge or trial. Through literally "no fault" of their own, legally innocent citizens found themselves turned into outlaws in ways they were powerless to avoid. No-fault divorce allowed the modern state to achieve its most coveted ambition: to control the private lives of its citizens.

Divorce today is very unlikely to be a mutual decision. It is usually a power grab by one parent, assisted by lawyers, judges, and other officials. By extending the reach of the state over the children and the forcibly divorced parent, unilateral divorce has turned children into weapons of not only parental but governmental power.

"No-fault" divorce introduced radical new legal concepts—including, ironically, unproven guilt. "According to therapeutic precepts, the fault for marital breakup must be shared, even when one spouse unilaterally seeks a divorce," observes Whitehead. "Many husbands and wives who did not seek or want divorce [and who had committed no legally recognized infraction] were stunned to learn . . . that they were equally 'at fault' in the dissolution of their marriages."[111] So the "fault" that was ostensibly thrown out the front door of divorce proceedings re-entered through the back, but with no precise definition. The judiciary expanded its traditional role of punishing crime or redressing tort to

111. Whitehead, *Divorce Culture*, 70–71.

punishing personal faults and private differences: suddenly, one could be summoned to court without having committed any legal infraction; the verdict was pre-determined without any evidence being examined; and one could be found culpable for things that were not illegal. "No other court process is so devoid of recourse for a defendant," writes Judy Parejko. "When one spouse files for divorce, his/her spouse is automatically found 'guilty' of irreconcilable differences and is not allowed a defense."[112]

Though marriage ostensibly falls under civil law, the new logic quickly extended matters into the criminal realm. What Parejko calls the "automatic outcome" effectively became a presumption of guilt against the "defendant." Yet the due process protections of criminal proceedings do not apply in family courts, where formal criminal charges seldom arise. So involuntary litigants can now be criminalized and incarcerated without any action on their part and in ways they are powerless to avoid. In some jurisdictions, the "defendant" in a divorce case is the only party in the courtroom without legal immunity.[113]

No-fault divorce does much more than allow families to self-destruct. It permits the state in the person of a single judge to assume jurisdiction over the private lives of citizens who are minding their own business and turn otherwise lawful private behavior into punishable offenses. Previously, a citizen could be incarcerated only following conviction by a jury for willfully violating a specific statute, passed with citizen input and after deliberation by elected legislators, that applied equally to all. Suddenly, a citizen could be arrested and jailed without trial for failing to live in conformity with an order, formulated in a matter of minutes from limited information by an unelected judge, that applied to no one but himself, and whose provisions might well be beyond his ability to obey.[114] In effect, a personalized criminal code is legislated ad hoc around each divorced spouse, subjecting him or her to arrest for doing what anyone else may lawfully do.

Unilateral divorce thus places the family in a legal-political status precisely the opposite of the original purpose of marriage. Far from preserving a private sphere of life immune from state intervention, involuntary divorce opens private lives to unprecedented state control.

The logic reached its conclusion in measures devised by the Ameri-

---

112. Judy Parejko, "No Fair Process in Divorce Laws," *Middletown Journal*, 27 January 2004.

113. *McLarnon v. Jokisch*, 431 Mass. 343 (2000).

114. Hubin, "Parental Rights," 136.

can Law Institute (ALI).[115] This influential practitioners' group announced—on what authority other than their own will it was unclear—that the scope of family law would be extended to encompass jurisdiction over non-marital private arrangements such as cohabiting couples, both heterosexual and homosexual, and indeed all private homes.

Marriage defenders protested, but again they misunderstood the full implications. As they now argue with respect to same-sex marriage, traditionalists charged that ALI was undermining marriage by blurring the distinction between traditional marriage and cohabitation.[116]

But ALI was doing much more than this. Family law practitioners were using the toehold they had established in married households through divorce law to extend state jurisdiction into every household entailing an "intimate relationship," regardless of whether that household was created through marriage. Divorce operatives were declaring that no home was too private to be beyond the reach of official government scrutiny. With breathtaking irony, an "intimate relationship" (which officials reserved for themselves to define) became not a status which is off-limits to government supervision, but precisely the opposite, one that gives government an entrée to exert virtually unlimited power over personal life. The "abolition of marriage" led straight to the abolition of private life.

ALI then went on to demand recognition of co-parenting agreements giving parental rights to the same-sex partners of custodial mothers, despite objections by the fathers.

The feminist-driven divorce machinery thus intertwines the personal and the political as nothing before, and its personal dimension is what disguises the intrusiveness of its political power. Divorce injects state power—including the penal apparatus with its police and prisons—directly into private households and private lives. "The personal is political" is no longer a theoretical slogan but a codified reality institutionally enforced by new and correspondingly feminist tribunals: the "family" courts. Through these feminist-controlled pseudo-courts men are subjected to punishments, including wholesale expropriation and

115. *Principles of the Law of Family Dissolution: Analysis and Recommendations* (Philadelphia: American Law Institute, 2002). Josephson's contention ("Citizenship," 270) that the privacy of marriage is "not accorded to those who do not or may not marry," while theoretically logical, is therefore diametrically wrong. Cohabiting couples have enjoyed privacy denied by divorce law to the married, which is precisely the freedom ALI seeks to curtail.

116. *The Future of Family Law: Law and the Marriage Crisis in North America* (New York: Institute for American Values, 2005).

summary incarceration, based entirely on the conduct of their private lives, without having to be charged with any actionable offense for which they could be tried in a criminal court.

Family courts are thus unquestionably the arm of the state that routinely reaches farthest into the private lives of individuals and families. The very concept of a "family" court—whose rulings are enforced by plainclothes officials who amount to family police—should alert us to danger. Roscoe Pound once observed that "the powers of the Star Chamber were a trifle in comparison with those of our ... courts of domestic relations."[117] Family courts routinely separate children from parents who have done nothing legally wrong, ignore due process of law, and even silence political dissent. Unambiguous documentation proves that parents jailed without trial in divorce cases have been violently killed in prison.[118]

Family courts usually operate behind closed doors and do not record their proceedings. Ostensibly this secrecy is to protect litigants' privacy, though it has precisely the opposite effect: it provides a cloak to invade family privacy with impunity. Intimate personal information coerced from involuntary litigants is then made available to anyone, including the media, where it can be used to defame or blackmail anyone who is tempted to criticize the courts.

Courts are only the centerpiece of the divorce industry, a massive and largely hidden political underworld consisting of judges, lawyers, psychologists and psychiatrists, social workers, child protective services, child support enforcement agents, mediators, counselors, and feminist groups, plus an extensive host of economic interests, such as divorce planners, forensic accountants, real estate appraisers, and many others. These officials and professionals profess concern for the "best interest" of other people's children.[119] Yet their services are activated only with the dissolution of families, the removal of parents, and the seizure of children and property by the government. Whatever pieties they mouth therefore, the hard reality is that they have a concrete interest in facilitating family break-up and punishing anyone who stands in the way. Virtually all their power and earnings derive from the harm that divorce inflicts on children. "Fights over control of the children," reports one divorce insider, "are where most of the billable hours in family court are

---

117. David Heleniak, "The New Star Chamber," *Rutgers Law Review*, vol. 57, no. 3 (Spring 2005), 1009.

118. Baskerville, *Taken Into Custody*, 157–58.

119. For critiques of "the best interest of the child," see Baskerville, *Taken Into Custody*, ch. 1, and Schlafly, *Who Killed*, ch. 4.

consumed."[120] Harsh as it sounds, it is undeniable that these officials are united by one overriding interest: having children separated from their parents. Without the power to remove children from their parents—and first and foremost their fathers—this industry cannot thrive, and these officials will have no business. And so it must declare that the parents are criminals and that the fathers have "abandoned" their children, even when this is plainly not true. The first principle of the divorce industry, the basic premise without which it has no reason to exist and without which its operatives derive no earnings or power, the first item of business and the first measure taken when a divorce is filed and before anything is discussed is: remove the father.

Divorce instantly destroys fatherhood and, by extension, parenthood. The moment one spouse files for divorce, even if it is literally for "no fault" of the other spouse, the innocent parent enters the penal system: to raise his children as he sees fit according to his own values—to even be with his children without government authorization—is henceforth a crime for which he can be arrested and incarcerated indefinitely without trial. And there will be no record of the incarceration.

Few enterprises have forged so intimate and elaborate a public-private symbiosis. More than four decades of unrestrained divorce has created a vast industry with a stake in maximizing it. David Schramm cautiously estimated that divorce cost the public $33.3 billion annually in 2003.[121] As one divorce lawyer forthrightly reveals,

> Speaking as a lawyer, I am unalterably opposed to any change in our divorce act. Our divorce act has greatly increased divorces, crime, bankruptcy, and juvenile caseloads. Any change in our no-fault system would be a financial disaster for the bar and for me personally, as these type of cases comprise a majority of my practice.[122]

Divorce and custody are the cash cow of the judiciary, constituting some 35–50% of civil litigation,[123] and also bring employment and

---

120. Parejko, *Stolen Vows*, 99.

121. David G. Schramm, "Counting the Cost of Divorce: What Those Who Know Better Rarely Acknowledge," *The Family in America* (Fall, 2009) http://familyinamerica.org/journals/fall-2009/counting-cost-divorce-what-those-who-know-better-rarely-acknowledge/#.WBSfnSorL3h.

122. Quoted in Alex J. Harris, "Why Divorce is Missing from the Political Agenda in America: A Comprehensive Treatment of the Obstacles to Reform," *George Wyeth Review*, vol. 4, no. 1 (Fall 2012), 34, and Mike McManus, *How to Cut America's Divorce Rate in Half* (Potomac, MD: Marriage Savers, 2008), 38–39.

123. Helen Alvare, "Types and Styles of Family Proceedings," *Report of the United States to the XII World Congress*, International Association of Procedural Law, 2003, 1, cautiously cites the lower figure.

earnings to a host of executive and legislative officials, plus private hangers-on. Divorce litigation fuels well-known lines of political and judicial patronage.[124] "The judge occupies a vital position . . . because of his control over lucrative patronage positions," according to Herbert Jacob, where appointments "are generally passed out to the judge's political cronies or to persons who can help his private practice."[125] Divorce also fills state and local government coffers with federal money for a host of divorce-related social problems. So entrenched has divorce become within our political economy and political culture that even perfunctory critics seem to have developed a vested interest in having something to criticize. Hardly anyone has an incentive to bring it under control.

To recognize the power of these interests is not to engage in conspiracy theories. It is to recognize that the family is not only an institution that is integral to our social order (as the conservative platitude has it); it is also one that can only function in this role if we protect it from calculations of political power. By politicizing the family and inviting the state to assume control over the household through involuntary divorce, feminists opened a Pandora's Box of opportunities for numerous interests to weaken parents, grab power, exploit children, and plunder and criminalize fathers.

Dickens' observation "the one great principle of the . . . law is to make business for itself" is strikingly validated. Nothing requires a judge to honor the divorcing parent's initial request to forcibly separate the other parent from his children. A judge could rule that the father has committed no infraction that justifies being forcibly separated, even temporarily, that he has a recognized constitutional right not to be separated, and that neither the mother nor the court has any legal grounds to separate them. Such rulings never happen. Judges who refused to reward divorce would be rendering themselves redundant and denying earnings to a huge entourage of hangers-on, who have a strong say in the appointment and promotion of judges. So the judges have little choice but to channel litigants' money to the lawyers and others by maximizing litigation. "*Boni judicis est ampliare jurisdictionem*, went the old saying," observed Walter Bagehot; "'It is the mark of a good judge to augment

---

124. Jerome R. Corsi, *Judicial Politics* (Englewood Cliffs, NJ: Prentice-Hall, 1984), 107–14, and Richard Watson and Rondal Downing, *The Politics of the Bench and the Bar* (New York: John Wiley and Sons, 1969), 98, 336.

125. Herbert Jacob, *Justice in America: Courts, Lawyers, and the Judicial Process* (4th edn., Boston and Toronto: Little Brown, 1984), 112.

the fees of his court', his own income, and the income of his subordinates."[126]

Having seized control of his children, the judge then presides over a feeding frenzy in which everything the father has and earns is doled out to cronies and clients of the court: attorneys' fees, fees for guardians *ad litem*, child support, various psychological and custody evaluations, therapists, counselors, and others who manage to get their noses in the trough. It is no exaggeration to say that the driving principle behind divorce and custody proceedings is to loot the father and the taxpayer.

One especially striking example is the practice whereby involuntary litigants are ordered, on pain of incarceration, to pay the fees of lawyers they have not hired. In a kind of judicial shakedown, judges regularly order involuntary litigants to pay the fees of attorneys, psychotherapists, and other court officials they have not hired and jail them for failing to comply.[127] What are described as "reasonable attorney's fees" are not determined by the market forces of supply and demand but are set with the backing of the penal apparatus, with the police and jails acting as the attorneys' private collection agency. There is thus effectively no limit to what can be charged.[128]

Such official thievery has become so rampant that even the feminist *New York Times* has reported on how easily "the divorce court leads to a jail cell."[129] In short, citizens completely innocent of any legal wrongdoing and simply minding their own business are ordered into court and told to write checks to officials they have not hired or they will be summarily arrested and jailed. Judges also order citizens to sell their houses and other property and turn the proceeds over to lawyers and others they have not hired.

Having successfully asserted the power to remove children from legally innocent parents, the courts then preside over other violations of basic constitutional rights and civil liberties. The entire divorce regime is nothing less than a massive assault on every major principle of the English Common Law, the United States Constitution, and centuries of Anglo-American principles of freedom and limited government.[130] The logical conclusion of the system is that fathers are routinely jailed, for as much as five years, for criticizing judges.[131]

126. *The English Constitution* (Cambridge: Cambridge University Press, 2001), 144.

127. *Graves v. Graves*, 4 Va. App. 326, 333, 357 S.E.2d 554, 558 (1987).

128. Baskerville, *Taken Into Custody*, ch. 1.

129. Paul Vitello, "When the Divorce Court Leads to a Jail Cell," *New York Times*, 15 February 2007.

130. Baskerville, *Taken Into Custody*, ch. 2.

131. Ibid., and Schlafly, *Who Killed*, 116–17.

To enforce these punishments, the divorce *apparat* has created extensive cadres of feminist police: child protective services, domestic violence operations, and child support enforcement agencies. These political police do not wear uniforms, target men almost exclusively, and operate largely free of due process protections.

The growth of this feminist gendarmerie did not follow but *preceded*—in other words, it itself generated—a series of hysterias against men and especially fathers so hideous and inflammatory that no one, left or right, dared question the accusations or defend those accused. To the abandonment hoax was added the nonpayment of "child support," whereby fathers whose children had been confiscated by the divorce courts were required to pay for it through instant "obligations" they had done nothing to incur and that could well constitute 60–100% of their income and even more. Any arrears are quickly collected by predawn raids at gunpoint. Wild and patently fabricated accusations of wife-beating, child abuse, and pedophilia turned the father into a monster and a pariah with whom no one dared associate. This government-propagated hysteria rationalized its own funding and expansion. While American family law is ostensibly the province of state and local government, Congress began subsidizing family dissolution with a panoply of lucrative federal programs to replace fathers with functionaries by doing precisely what fathers themselves were already doing in their homes before being evicted from them by the divorce judges: protect and provide for their children. Legislators invariably approve these measures by near-unanimous majorities, with no debate and without listening to any dissenting viewpoints, out of fear of being accused of being soft on "batterers," "pedophiles," and "deadbeat dads." In each case, no public demand or outcry preceded the new law-enforcement powers; they were enacted entirely under pressure from feminists and their allies. (Yet neither did they meet any challenge by "pro-family" advocates.) Each of these hysterias originated in welfare policy, each is propagated largely by feminist lawyers and feminist social workers who receive the resulting federal funding, and each expanded dramatically because of involuntary divorce and child custody.

The criminal aspects of these witch-hunts will be examined shortly. The point here is that each one has dramatically exacerbated and even created the very problem it claims to address. Child support is popularly understood to be a mechanism for forcing men to pay for the children they have sired and abandoned. Once the abandonment myth is exploded and single-motherhood is revealed as a feminist rebellion against "patriarchy," child support can be seen for what it is: a windfall subsidy on single-parent homes that pays mothers to create more of them by looting the father. Women are thus paid to have children without fathers or to divorce, ensuring precisely the explosion in fatherless children that we now see. Even more astoundingly, in the United States—the epicenter of these developments and the country where criminalization is most advanced—federal taxpayers pay into state government coffers according to the amount of child support the state collects. This gives state governments a financial incentive to create as many single-mother homes as possible. They accomplish this by first evicting fathers from their homes and then setting child support burdens at preposterously high levels, not only causing hardship for and criminalizing more fathers but increasing the incentive for more mothers to raise more children without them.[132]

Trumped-up accusations of child abuse and domestic violence have a similar effect. The myth of the perverted and violent father provides a silver bullet for eliminating fathers who have been convicted of, tried for, and charged with, no crime whatever. It is also effective for cowing lawmakers and judges into submission to feminist demands and for ensuring that no trouble is caused by ostensibly "pro-family" conservatives and Christians, who likewise live in terror of being accused of defending "sex offenders."[133]

Completely innocent fathers are now routinely accused of pedophilia and other sex offenses, purely in order to eliminate them from their homes and confiscate their children. Yet it is firmly proven in the scientific literature that a miniscule number in fact ever perpetrate these crimes.[134] Instead, through the lobbying of the same sexual radicals, the real pedophiles are becoming legal adoptive parents.

Child Support

The "deadbeat dad" is a figure almost entirely manufactured by the feminist-driven divorce machinery to encourage more divorce, expand the power of government officials, and increase profits of divorce entrepreneurs.[135] Through the child support machinery millions of fathers and some mothers who have committed no legal infraction find their family finances plundered and their lives placed under round-the-clock penal

132. Baskerville, *Taken Into Custody*, ch. 3.

133. Ibid., ch. 4.

134. Leslie Margolin and John Craft, "Child Sexual Abuse by Caretakers," *Family Relations* 38 (1989); Martin Daly and Margo Wilson, "Child Abuse and Other Risks of Not Living with Both Parents," *Journal of Ethnology and Sociobiology* 6 (1985).

135. This section summarizes Baskerville, *Taken Into Custody*, ch. 3, with additional material.

supervision. Once they have nothing left to loot they are incarcerated without trial.

Contrary to government propaganda (and Common Law tradition), child support today has nothing to do with fathers abandoning their children, deserting their marriages, or even agreeing to a divorce. It is automatically assessed on all non-custodial parents, even those involuntarily divorced without grounds (literally through "no-fault" of their own). It is an entitlement for all divorcing parents, regardless of any culpability for violating the marriage contract, and coerced from involuntarily divorced parents, regardless of their innocence—all rationalized as the "best interest of the child." The "deadbeat dad" is far less likely to have voluntarily abandoned the offspring he callously sired than to be "forced to finance the filching of his own children."[136]

No-fault divorce allows a mother to divorce for any reason or no reason and obtain automatic monopoly control of the children. Child support takes this process a step further by giving the divorcing mother a claim on her husband's income, regardless of any fault on her part (or lack of fault on his) in abrogating the marriage. A child support schedule will tell her exactly the size of the tax-free windfall she will automatically collect from him simply by filing for divorce without having to give any reason. It is collected at gunpoint, and alleged failure to pay means summary and indefinite incarceration.

Mothers are not the only ones who can profit by creating fatherless children. Governments also generate revenue from child support and therefore from the proliferation of single-parent homes.

Child support was originally rationalized (and federalized) to save taxpayers money by recovering welfare costs from allegedly absconding low-income fathers. Under feminist pressure, it became a huge federal subsidy on middle-class divorce in which taxpayers instead *subsidize* divorce through generous federal payments to states based on the amount of child support they collect.

This provides incentives to create as many single-mother households as possible by encouraging divorce and giving mothers exclusive custody over children while eliminating the father completely. This logic is carried to draconian lengths by setting child support at onerous and even impossible levels, which has the double benefit of increasing the state's windfall and encouraging more mothers to divorce. While little child support—or government revenue—can be generated from the impecunious young unmarried fathers for whom the system was osten-

---

136. Jed H. Abraham, *From Courtship to Courtroom* (New York: Bloch, 1999), 151.

sibly created, middle-class divorced fathers have deeper pockets to loot. By including middle-class divorcees, the welfare machinery has become a means not of distributing money but of collecting it. Without legislative control, state governments can raise revenue—which they can add to their general funds and use for any purpose they choose—by creating single-parent homes among the affluent. By profiting off child support at federal taxpayer expense, state governments have a financial incentive to create as many single-mother homes as possible, which they effect by offering a guaranteed, tax-free windfall—often involving arbitrary and impossible sums—to any divorcing mother.[137] In short, divorce allows everyone to plunder both the father and the taxpayer.

This marks a whole new development in the expansion of the welfare state: from distributing largesse to raising revenue and, from there, to law enforcement. A self-financing perpetual growth machine, generating operating revenue and expanding the size of state operations, is all fueled by creating single-parent homes and criminalizing parents. The combination of welfare and divorce has created, in effect, a massive, government-run child kidnapping and extortion racket.

While child support (like divorce itself) is awarded ostensibly without reference to "fault," nonpayment brings swift and severe punishments. "The advocates of ever-more-aggressive measures for collecting child support," writes Bryce Christensen of Southern Utah University, "have moved us a dangerous step closer to a police state."[138] Attorney Jed Abraham calls the machinery "Orwellian": "The government commands . . . a veritable gulag, complete with sophisticated surveillance and compliance capabilities such as computer-based tracking, license revocation, asset confiscation, and incarceration."[139]

Resembling the new gender crimes we will explore in the next section, due process protections are almost non-existent. "The burden of proof may be shifted to the defendant," according to the National Conference of State Legislatures. Like Kafka's Joseph K., the "defendant" may not even know the accusation against him, "if the court does not explicitly clarify the charge facing the [allegedly?] delinquent parent," says NCSL. Further, "not all child support contempt proceedings classified as criminal are entitled to a jury trial," and "even indigent obligors

---

137. I have described this in "Welfare and the 'Road to Serfdom,'" *Issue Brief, Institute for Policy Innovation* (15 June 2007), and in "From Welfare State to Police State," *The Independent Review* vol. 12, no. 3 (Winter 2008).

138. Bryce Christensen, "The Strange Politics of Child Support," *Society,* vol. 39, no. 1 (November–December. 2001), 63–64.

139. Abraham, *From Courtship to Courtroom,* 154–55.

are not necessarily entitled to a lawyer."[140] One could hardly imagine a system more clearly designed to railroad the innocent: the accused must prove his innocence against unspecified accusations, without counsel, and without a jury.

Assembly-line hearings last one to two minutes, during which parents are sentenced to months or years in prison. Many receive no hearing at all but are accused in an "expedited judicial process" before a black-robed lawyer bearing a title such as "judge surrogate."[141] "Most child support activities are carried out by a hearing officer who is not a judge," reports one scholar. The few judges function more like bureaucrats. "The hearing officer makes a recommendation to the judge who reviews the recommendation without a hearing."[142] Without legislative confirmation, these officials are not in any way accountable to citizens or their representatives. Unlike true judges, they may lobby to create the same laws they adjudicate, flagrantly violating the separation of powers. Often they are feminists in robes. One surrogate judge simultaneously worked "as a radical feminist lobbying on proposed legislation" on child support.[143]

Scholars have repeatedly exposed and documented horrific abuses of basic civil liberties by the child support system. Attorney Ronald Henry calls the system "an obvious sham," a "disaster," and "the most onerous form of debt collection practiced in the United States."[144] As elsewhere in family court, "the father is denied the basic rights enjoyed by criminal defendants, such as the presumption of innocence and the necessity that

140. Teresa Myers, "Case in Brief: Courts Uphold Criminal Penalties for the Failure to Pay Child Support," NCSL internet site: http://www.ncsl.org/programs/cyf/Criminal-non.htm.

141. *2004 Green Book*, House of Representatives, Ways and Means Committee Print WMCP: 108–6, U.S. Government Printing Office Online via GPO Access, section 8 (http://frwebgate.access.gpo.gov/cgi-bin/getdoc.cgi?dbname=108_green_book&docid=f:wm006_08.wais).

142. Rebecca May and Marguerite Roulet, "A Look at Arrests of Low-Income Fathers for Child Support Nonpayment: Enforcement, Court and Program Practices," Center for Family Policy and Practice (Madison, Wisconsin: January 2005; http://www.cpr-mn.org/Documents/noncompliance.pdf), 41.

143. Kevin Landrigan, "Lacking Support, Judicial Nominee Abandons Bid," *Telegraph* (Hudson, NH), 26 July 2001. See also Helen M. Alvare, "Types and Styles of Family Proceedings," Report of the United States to the XII World Congress, International Association of Procedural Law (2003), 1, 10.

144. Ronald Henry, "Child Support Policy and the Unintended Consequences of Good Intentions," *The Law and Economics of Child Support Payments*, ed. William Comanor (Cheltenham: Edward Elgar, 2004), 135.

the accuser provide proof beyond a reasonable doubt."[145] Courts have repeatedly declared that their states' guidelines "bear no relationship to the constitutional standards" and are "irrational" and "contrary both to public policy and common sense." When a court struck down Tennessee's guidelines on such grounds, the state Department of Human Services (which jails fathers for not obeying court orders), simply announced they would not obey the ruling.[146]

The mercenary features of the child support system resemble the "Absurdistan" lampooned by dissidents in the Soviet bloc:

• Child support "obligations" are arbitrarily increased by enforcement officials without any judicial proceeding or even notification to the payer.

• Fathers whose payments are current are arrested.

• Fathers are forced to pay child support not on their actual income but on what a judge declares should be their income.

• Men forced to pay for children that are not theirs and even for children that do not exist.

• Mothers collect full child support for the same child from multiple men.

• Officials routinely raid the bank accounts of innocent parties ("deadbeat accomplices") such as second wives, grandparents, and even children themselves and help themselves to what they want.

• Elderly parents are forced to pay for "children" in their 40s and 50s.

• Runaway children, even after they are grown, can sue their own parents for child support.

• Paternity testing is criminalized, so that men can be imprisoned for proving that they are not the fathers of the children they are ordered to support.[147]

• Child molesters can collect child support from the children they have criminally raped.

In short, child support turns children into cash prizes and even cash crops. "I'm going to marry a really rich guy, then divorce him," one girl

---

145. Schlafly, *Who Killed*, 114.

146. Baskerville, *Taken Into Custody*, ch. 3.

147. "Paternity Testing Ban Upheld in France," International Biosciences internet site, https://www.ibdna.com/paternity-testing-ban-upheld-in-france/, accessed 4 June 2017.

tells a Toronto newspaper. "But first I'm going to have his kids, so I get child support."[148]

Though grandstanding government officials sensationalize "round-ups" of alleged "deadbeat dads," who are jailed for months and years without trial, we do not know how many citizens are incarcerated for alleged nonpayment of child support because, contrary to federal law, no government information is available on incarcerations. We do know "there has been an increasing effort by states to criminalize the nonpayment of support," but there is a complete absence of information on arrests and incarcerations. The Bureau of Justice Statistics, which maintains detailed figures on every other category of crime, is utterly silent on child support incarcerations. Rebecca May and Marguerite Roulet of the Center for Family Policy and Practice found "ample testimony by low-income non-custodial parents of spending time in jail for the nonpayment of child support." Yet they could find no documentation of their incarceration. Government literature "yields so little information on it that one might be led to believe that arrests were used rarely if at all." Hiding or disguising information on arrests is a serious matter, but this is precisely what researchers have found on both the federal and state levels in the United States and Canada. While May and Roulet personally witnessed fathers sentenced in St. Louis, "We could find no explicit documentation of arrests in St. Louis." In Illinois, "We observed courtrooms in which fathers appeared before the judge who were serving jail sentences for nonpayment, but little information was available on arrests in Illinois."

May and Roulet also encountered the secrecy that impedes any journalist or scholar who tries to penetrate the legal underworld of family court and child support: "Although the court cases are public...it is not easy for observers who are not family members or support people to be allowed in the courtroom, despite their right to be present," they found (and family members too are regularly excluded from proceedings). "A written request from the Center for permission to monitor paternity cases was denied by a Family Court Commissioner." What the US Constitution calls "open" justice has effectively been eliminated in family law courts, which call themselves "equity" courts and even claim that this status exempts them from the provisions of the Constitution. "Child support enforcement cases that go to court are so rarely monitored that in Chicago we were first told that the cases were private," May and Roulet found. "Only when we asked to see the state law that provided for this privacy and a supervisor was consulted, was it confirmed

---

148. This is all documented, ibid. For more stores, see Schlafly, *Who Killed*, ch. 4.

that in fact the hearings were open to the public and we were allowed access to the courts. Most cases are heard without oversight from the public." Courts that summarily incarcerate citizens for indefinite periods are "private" affairs that can bar the citizens in whose name they operate and whose taxes allow them to exist.

In many ways they do operate like the private fiefdoms of the judges and their cronies, who, on various pretexts, can extort virtually any amount of money from defendants not only for child support but also for themselves. "A striking observation in several courtrooms was the apparent priority placed by different stakeholders in obtaining payment from noncustodial parents for fees related to their services," May and Roulet report, diplomatically. First and foremost are fees for attorneys, whose bar associations control the reappointment and promotion of judges. "Noncustodial parents who are intimidated by the court system are easily persuaded to use scarce financial resources to hire private attorneys," they observe. "Payment of attorney fees can cause severe hardship particularly when added to the other fees imposed during the process of contending with child support enforcement agencies." Given the fact that almost all of these litigants are there involuntarily, these additional fees reveal the child support machine to be little more than a system of government-organized looting, a mafia of cronyism and corruption. "For many parents, yet more fees are charged related to incarceration work-release privileges, jail costs, probation fees, and other locally mandated fees, the payment of which might all be a condition of probation or parole." The penal system is thus converted into a shakedown racket using children as hostages, which is hardly surprising, since that is really what the child support system is from the beginning. "Judges seemed to have the payment of court fees as a high priority."

> The presiding judge . . . made the payment of court fees by a particular date a condition of letting a noncustodial parent leave the courtroom. He repeatedly asked the parent for a date by which the court fees (not the child support payments) could be made, and stated that if the fees were not paid by that date, there would be a warrant for the parent's arrest.

This account, by two scholars who are clearly sympathetic to the child support and child welfare systems, documents and confirms what numerous litigants experience. "Judges were observed chastising clients in sometimes inappropriate ways." Sanctimonious bullying of innocent parents by family court judges is very common, as recounted in this rare documentation from these secretive courts:

In this same courtroom, one father arrived late and, when asked to explain, responded to the judge that he didn't get off work until 3:15 pm, and that he could not get to the court by the designated time of 3:00 pm. The judge responded, "Too bad. You're under arrest," and had the father move to the other side of the courtroom to be arrested. . . . This father had started a job that would allow him to begin making payments but stated that the employer would not let him off for his court date.[149]

Despite the government secrecy, we know the arrests are extensive. To relieve jail overcrowding in Georgia, a sheriff and judge propose detention camps specifically for fathers. The Pittsburgh City Planning Commission has considered a proposal "to convert a former chemical processing plant . . . into a detention center" for fathers.[150] Rendered permanently in debt by incarceration, fathers are farmed out to trash companies and similar concerns, where they work 14–16 hour days with their earnings confiscated.[151]

Any man who marries and has children opens himself to this nightmare and to the gulag where he subsequently resides, as many discover too late. Yet conservative groups that "promote marriage," while ignoring these matters, wonder why their campaigns have zero impact.

Homosexualism

It is ironic, but significant for the present argument, that conservatives rationalize their inaction over divorce by adopting a stance of chivalry and by invoking the feminist subterfuge that divorce is perpetrated by philandering men to oppress women. For the real effects of divorce are to weaken not only marriage but masculinity and fatherhood. Though seldom understood in this context, one direct consequence is the rise of homosexual militancy, including demands for same-sex marriage.

Until recently, homosexual politics was ostensibly limited largely to the demand to simply be left alone, and as such it won widespread sympathy. Yet homosexual activists entered the world of sexual radicalism

---

149. May and Roulet, "Look at Arrests," 6, 9, 11, 41, 42, 43, 44. This account further confirms the argument in Baskerville, *Taken Into Custody*, ch. 3.

150. Richard Raeke, "County Eyes Work-Release Facility for 'Deadbeat Dads,'" *Walton County Tribune*, 14 March 1999; Brian Nearing, "Facility Proposed for Deadbeat Dads," *Pittsburgh News*, 26 June 2001.

151. "ACLU Applauds Montgomery County Judge for Agreeing to Appoint Lawyers For Poor People Facing Jail Time," ACLU of Pennsylvania press release, 10 December 2003; Jan Ackerman, "Lawrence County Judges Free 37 Child-Support Offenders," *Pittsburg Post-Gazette*, 12 September 2002; interview with Jay Todd, who filed a Freedom of Information Act petition.

when they began redefining marriage. Ostensibly moderate leftists whom Stanley Kurtz calls "family radicals" have repeatedly expressed the goal of using same-sex marriage as one step in a more radical recognition of virtually any other configuration of individuals as a legitimate "marriage," effectively rendering the institution empty.[152]

It is critical to understand that they could do this only because marriage had already been effectively redefined out of existence by their feminist allies through divorce. By permitting promiscuity under cover of matrimony, divorce law rendered marriage consistent with most homosexual preferences.

Looked at in this larger perspective, it is even possible that homosexuality itself may actually be increasing as the result of weakened fatherhood and of fatherlessness. "With the breakdown of the family," E. Michael Jones suggests, "the son does not get the needed affirmation of his own masculinity from the father."[153] Lack of healthy masculine identification was the standard explanation for homosexuality before it became politically unacceptable, and, while it is difficult to prove that homosexuality itself is increasing because of widespread fatherlessness, Joseph Nicolosi cites "a number of studies [that] show that father absence in boys may result in dependency, lack of assertion, and/or weaker gender identity." One study found that "Men were more likely to enter a homosexual partnership if they had had one of the following childhood experiences: divorced parents, absent father, older mother, youngest child."[154] If these scholars and psychologists are correct in arguing that homosexuality results from a poorly developed relationship with the father and an overly prolonged identification with the mother, it is possible (though this apparently has not been directly researched) that tens of millions of children growing up without fathers over several generations now has contributed to an increase in homosexuality itself and with it the newly aggressive militancy of homosexual politics. "Homosexuality is a developmental problem that is almost always the result of problems in family relations, particularly between

152. Stanley Kurtz, "The Confession," *National Review Online*, 31 October 2006 (http://www.nationalreview.com/articles/219092/confession/stanley-kurtz), and "The Confession II," *National Review Online*, 1 November 2006 (http://www.nationalreview.com/articles/219108/confession-ii/stanley-kurtz).

153. E. Michael Jones, *Libido Dominandi: Sexual Liberation and Political Control* (South Bend, IN: St. Augustine's Press, 2000), 247.

154. Morten Frisch and Anders Hviid, "Correlates of Heterosexual and Homosexual Marriages: A National Cohort Study of Two Million Danes," *Archives of Sexual Behavior* 35 (2006), quoted in Gabriele Kuby, *The Global Sexual Revolution: Destruction of Freedom in the Name of Freedom* (Kettering, OH: LifeSite, 2015), 145.

father and son," writes Nicolosi. "As a result of failure with father, the boy does not fully internalize male gender-identity, and develops homosexually." Nicolosi argues that in homosexuals typically, "there is an overly close relationship between mother and son, with the father distant from them both."[155] This of course is precisely the domestic configuration now codified and institutionalized in the welfare and divorce regimes, and enforced by government agents.

Further, the divorce system may be responsible not simply for the failure to acquire a healthy attachment with the father but also for an intense hatred of him of a kind that is often apparent in both homosexuality itself and homosexualist politics. This hatred reaches extreme dimensions in the divorce-related phenomenon known as "parental alienation," whereby one parent, usually the mother, encourages children to hate the other. But it is also clear that the divided loyalty into which children are forced by the very process of divorce itself cannot help but create a measure of this animosity toward one if not both parents. As child psychologist Joan Kelly writes:

> Because it is anti-instinctual to hate and reject a parent, the child must develop an elaborate delusional system consisting of spurious, frivolous, and absurd rationalizations to justify the hatred and rejection. Eventually, the child comes to believe all the absurdity. The double-bind situation of being unable to have, love, and to be loved by both parents can lead to psychosis. Remaining with hatred and anger is not healthy under any circumstances, let alone for a parent.[156]

Kelly words it in politically correct gender-neutral terms, but given not only the proclivity of judges to grant sole custody to mothers but also the natural early attachment of children to the mother, the object of this hatred is almost invariably the father. Nicolosi's and others' argument, that children's default identification is with the mother and that "masculinity is an achievement" requiring positive encouragement, is consistent with this possibility.[157]

This hatred toward the father in the children of divorce is remarkably

155. Mostly older studies, since the hypothesis is now too unacceptable ideologically to be investigated. *Reparative Therapy of Male Homosexuality* (Northvale, NJ: Jason Aronson, 1991), 32, 27–28.

156. Quoted in Michelle Jones, "Parental Alienation: Understanding It—Strategies to Fight It," website of National Parents Organization, https://nationalparentsorganization.org/component/content/article/16-latest-news/21661-parental-alienation-understanding-it-strategies-to-fight-it, 10 April 2014.

157. Therapies based on theories such as that of Nicolosi (again, at one time accepted as standard by most psychologists) are now being legally banned, and non-profit groups offering them are sued for millions of dollars by leftist lawyers (with assets of some $340

similar to what is expressed in both homosexuality itself and homosexual politics. It is likely, though here no one appears to have researched it, that the hostility of both male and female homosexuals toward their fathers constitutes the beginning of the political mobilization and ideological militancy that many now exhibit. We have already observed the intense anger expressed by the homosexual political movement toward parents in general and fathers in particular (as well as the role of traditional heterosexual marriage in providing children with fathers). Male homosexuality (and probably female as well) clearly involves hostility and resentment—sexual and emotional, but also potentially political—toward male authority, beginning with the father. "As a consequence of his early sense of rejection by father and resulting defensive detachment from masculinity," writes Nicolosi,

> The homosexual carries a sense of weakness and incompetence with regard to those attributes associated with masculinity, that is, power, assertion, and strength. He is attracted to masculine strength out of an unconscious striving toward his own masculinity. At the same time, because of his hurtful experience with father, *he is suspicious of men in power.* Homosexual contact . . . is a way of finding masculine acceptance—not through personal strength, but vicariously *through erotic power.* Since the homosexual is particularly inclined to see *relationships with men in terms of power,* there is sometimes an overcompensation in power drive.

In homosexual relationships, Nicolosi adds, "*power issues* are very common."[158] Nicolosi is not at all concerned with politics, so his choice of words is especially significant. He finds hatred of fathers combined with craving for their power: "When homosexual clients report what they are attracted to in other men, the masculine qualities that would have been conveyed in the healthy father-son relationship are mentioned over and over: assertiveness, self-confidence, control of one's life, leadership, decisiveness, and *power.*" Moreover, while heterosexuals might express

---

million) in the name of "consumer fraud," even when the groups receive no money for trying to help those with same-sex attraction. One trial ongoing (at present) for three years is characterized by the defendants' lawyer as "a contrived lawsuit put on by gay activists" to punish their political opponents. The plaintiffs' lawyers are demanding some $4 million in legal fees from the non-profit. As with divorce, the courts become instruments of plunder. Austin Ruse, "Powerful Leftist Group Sues to Close Jewish Counseling Service for Gays," *Breitbart,* 29 May 2015, http://www.breitbart.com/big-government/2015/05/29/powerful-leftist-group-sues-to-close-jewish-counseling-service-for-gays/.

158. Ibid., 103 (emphases added).

disappointment with their fathers, homosexuals harbor "a grudge, an axe to grind" or a "festering *resentment*, hurt, disappointment, and an inability to understand what the father is about." Homosexuals express "frustration, bitterness, and *smouldering sense of victimization*"—precisely the emotions that feed radical political ideology.[159]

Not for the first time in this study, and not for the last, we can see that mobilizing politically is not simply a means to the end of greater sexual liberation; the sexuality itself is inseparable from the content of the political ideology. As with the aggressive behavior of children raised in day care, one might hesitate to accept without scrutiny the findings of clinical "experts." But here again we can see that the psychology ultimately reveals its inseparability from the political agenda. In this case, hatred of paternal authority, and the desire to eradicate it, appears to be the starting point for both.[160]

It is worth posing the question of whether we are now caught in a vicious cycle, whereby dysfunctional families are the breeding ground and mechanism for recruiting children into radical ideologies, which in turn demand measures that further weaken families. We have certainly reached the point where sexual confusion is codified in law, and citizens now face legal punishment for failure to choose words consistent with the most extreme manifestations of sexual ideology.[161]

Same-Sex Marriage

Same-sex marriage illustrates how the Sexual Revolution propagates itself in ever more extreme forms. The media debate has been characterized by superficial clichés on both sides, which need no further repeating. What does need emphasizing, and what many opponents of same-sex marriage have trouble accepting, is its inextricable connection to the larger issues already examined.

159. Ibid., 36–37 (emphases added). See also: Kenneth Zucker and Susan Bradley, *Gender Identity Disorder and Psychosexual Problems in Children and Adolescents* (New York: Guilford Press, 1995), 281; Linda Nicolosi and Joseph Nicolosi, "Masculinity is an Achievement," *Bulletin* of the Deutsches Institut fuer Jungen und Gesellschaft, no. 5 (2003, http://www.dijg.de/english/masculinity-traits-identity-gender/), 24–32.

160. Perhaps this explains the virulence in the current campaign to criminalize reparative therapy: Greg Quinlan, "Why Homosexual 'Marriage' Signals the End of Heterosexual Rights," *LifeSite News* (2013), http://www.sovereignindependentuk.co.uk/2013/03/08/why-homosexual-marriage-signals-the-end-of-heterosexual-rights/.

161. "NYC Will Fine Employers...." *LifeSite News*, 23 December 2015, https://www.lifesitenews.com/news/nyc-will-fine-employers-up-to-250000-for-referring-to-transsexuals-by-their. "Refusal to use a transgender employee's preferred name, pronoun, or title (e.g., Ms./Mrs.) may constitute unlawful gender-based harassment," in New York City.

Whether or not family dissolution actually encourages or increases homosexuality and homosexual political militancy, the divorce revolution has certainly ushered in same-sex marriage, which would not be an issue today if marriage had not already been devalued by divorce. "The weakening of marriage has been heterosexuals' doing, not gays', for it is their infidelity, divorce rates, and single-parent families that have wrought social damage," observes *The Economist*.[162] Marriage advocate Maggie Gallagher (who once accused other conservatives of cowardice for refusing to confront divorce) dismisses this argument as a "lawyer's trick,"[163] but it is a powerful and legitimate argument. "The problem today is not gay couples wanting to get married," writes Jonathan Rauch. "The threat to marriage is straight couples not wanting to get married or straight couples not staying married."[164] While these advocates conveniently neglect to mention that this "social damage" has been wrought by their own feminist allies, who devised the new divorce laws and encourage unwed motherhood, traditionalists' attempts to take the moral high ground have clearly been seriously undermined, even among potential sympathizers, by their inability to answer this point effectively. "People who won't censure divorce carry no special weight as defenders of marriage," writes columnist Froma Harrop. "Moral authority doesn't come cheap."[165] Some marriage advocates, like Michael McManus of Marriage Savers, do forthrightly insist that "divorce is a far more grievous blow to marriage than today's challenge by gays," but their voices are drowned out by the sound bites of high-profile media figures.[166]

Though same-sex marriage advocates have exploited this myopia,[167] its implications cut both ways. For the logical corollary is that the push for same-sex marriage is entirely a symptom of how debased marriage has already become for other reasons and would not have arisen otherwise. "Commentators miss the point when they oppose homosexual marriage on the grounds that it would undermine traditional under-

---

162. "The Case for Gay Marriage," *The Economist*, 26 February 2004.

163. Maggie Gallagher, "The Divorce Thing," *National Review Online*, 13 August 2003 (http://www.nationalreview.com/comment/ comment-gallagher081303.asp).

164. Jonathan Rauch, "What I Learned at AEI," *The Public Interest* 156 (Summer 2004), 19.

165. Froma Harrop, "What God Has Joined, Let No Man…" *Providence Journal*, 26 November 2003. For a scholarly statement, see Smith, "Religion."

166. Michael McManus, "Is Gay Marriage Next?" 12 July 2003 (http://www.marriage-savers.org/Columns/C1141.htm).

167. Frederick Liu and Stephen Macedo, "The Federal Marriage Amendment and the Strange Evolution of the Conservative Case Against Gay Marriage," *PS: Political Science and Politics*, vol. 38, no. 2 (April 2005), 212–13.

standings of marriage," writes Bryce Christensen. "It is only because traditional understandings of marriage have already been severely undermined that homosexuals are now laying claim to it."[168] Though gay activists cite their very desire to marry as evidence that their sexuality is not inherently promiscuous, they also acknowledge that that desire arises only by the promiscuity permitted in today's marriage terms. "The world of no-strings heterosexual hookups and 50% divorce rates preceded gay marriage," Andrew Sullivan points out. "All homosexuals are saying . . . is that, *under the current definition*, there's no reason to exclude us. If you want to return straight marriage to the 1950s, go ahead. *But until you do*, the exclusion of gays is simply an anomaly—and a denial of basic civil equality." Homosexuals are entirely correct that it was not they but heterosexuals who first devalued marriage, but they then use that fact to rationalize devaluing it further. Feminist Stephanie Coontz notes that gays are attracted to marriage only in the form adulterated by heterosexual divorce: "Gays and lesbians simply looked at the revolution heterosexuals had wrought and noticed that, *with its new norms*, marriage could work for them, too."[169]

This hardly constitutes a commitment to the health of the institution. "I'd be for marriage if I thought gay people would challenge and change the institution and not buy into the traditional meaning of 'till death do us part' and monogamy forever," says Mitchel Raphael, editor of *Fab*, a popular gay magazine.[170] Numerous such admissions could be quoted:

> It's a no-brainer that [homosexual activists] should have the right to marry, but I also think equally that it's a no-brainer that the institution of marriage should not exist. . . . Fighting for gay marriage generally involves lying about what we are going to do with marriage when we get there—because we lie that the institution of marriage is not going to change, and that is a lie. The institution of marriage is going to change, and it should change.[171]

Further, existing divorce practice rationalizes not only same-sex marriage, but whatever repressive state measures may be felt "necessary" to

168. Bryce Christensen, "Why Homosexuals Want What Marriage Has Now Become," *The Family in America*, vol. 18, no. 4 (April 2004).

169. Andrew Sullivan, "Unveiled: The Case Against Same-Sex Marriage Crumbles," *New Republic*, 13 August 2001 (http://www.andrewsullivan.com/homosexuality.php?artnum=20010813, emphasis added); Stephanie Coontz, "The Heterosexual Revolution," *New York Times*, 5 July 2005 (emphases added).

170. "Free to Marry, Canada's Gays Say, 'Do I?'" *New York Times*, 31 August 2003 (http://www.nytimes.com/2003/08/31/international/americas/31CANA.html).

171. Lesbian journalist Masha Gessen, quoted in Schlafly, *Who Killed*, 58.

enforce it. Political scientist Jyl Josephson revealingly pushes the ideological envelope to justify the increased state control over private life that same-sex marriage entails. Having blamed marriage deterioration (accurately) on heterosexual divorce, she then invokes the divorce machinery's most authoritarian features to rationalize marshalling state power to undermine it further through same-sex marriage. "The *state-created* institution of marriage has historically been altered . . . to serve new or newly recognized *state interests*," she argues, citing the most intrusive and invasive policy innovations: "no-fault divorce" and "heightened enforcement of child support."[172] Having already mobilized a family gendarmerie to dissolve the marriages and households of legally innocent people, confiscate their children and property, forcibly remove them from their own homes, and incarcerate them without trial, assigning those same police to implement same-sex marriage is comparatively easy to justify.

As if to prove the point, one satirist even started a petition to ban divorce, playing on the "hypocrisy" of family defenders who refuse to confront it. Gay marriage advocates exploited the polemical value of the petition (but significantly, refused to endorse it), while the few embattled groups with the boldness to challenge involuntary divorce openly responded by trying to take it seriously: "It's a worthwhile conversation to have."[173] Yet mainstream marriage and family defenders, at whom the satire was of course directed, passed up the opportunity to take the moral high ground and turn the tables on their critics, so once again they were humiliated and made to look like hypocrites.

Here again then, feminist and homosexualist purists who at one time decidedly rejected family and marriage as "patriarchal" institutions achieved little. It was by appealing to conservative values that feminists undermined marriage, to the point where homosexuals can move in to mock the institution.

Ironically too, the "freedom" that homosexuals hope to derive from having their marriages recognized by the state may come back to haunt them, since it opens their private lives to the increasingly conspicuous tribulations of family law proceedings—as we have seen, the most invasive sector of not only the law but government power overall. Here too the implications are seen not in marriage itself but in its official dissolution through divorce. A California bill legalizing same-sex marriage

172. Josephson, "Citizenship," 271 (emphasis added).
173. "California Man Looks to Ban Divorce, Ruffle Conservative Feathers," *Personal Liberty Digest*, 30 December 2009, http://www.personalliberty.com/news/california-man-looks-to-ban-divorce-ruffle-conservative-feathers-19490845/.

was nicknamed the "gay divorce law," because it would force individuals simply wishing to part company into court proceedings and to spend money on lawyers.[174] Previously, in the eyes of the law, such a couple was simply two individuals in a dwelling, whose sexual "intimacy" was a matter of official indifference. With marriage or civil unions, they become spouses or "intimate partners" into whose private lives the state may claim an interest to insert its coercive power at the mere invitation of either, rationalized by any grievance or none. But this consideration has prompted no discussion, because it clearly reveals why homosexuals really have little interest in marriage and why the few who choose to avail themselves of the option do so mostly to provoke legal cases and political measures. Same-sex marriage has not arisen to improve life for homosexuals. It is another weapon in the ongoing political campaign to destroy "patriarchy."

Applying the litmus test that the strength of marriage is measured by the terms of its dissolution, same-sex marriage must, by its nature, complete the descent into legal nihilism begun by "no-fault" divorce. Same-sex marriage must by necessity exist without any reference to fault—which is the basis for all justice not only in family law but throughout the legal system—because with same-sex marriage it is all-but-impossible to define legal grounds like non-consummation and adultery.[175] Same-sex marriage—and therefore marriage generally—can have no substance or meaning because there are no possible grounds for abrogating it other than the whim of one or both parties. Henceforth, anyone can marry anyone to procure whatever legal or economic perquisites the state chooses to dangle before them. Here again, the real "abolition of marriage" was affected long ago by "no-fault" divorce.

Homosexual Parenting

Once again it is the role of marriage in creating parents that demonstrates most glaringly the dysfunctionality of same-sex marriage. Opponents argue that marriage is foremost an institution for bearing and raising children, but once again even those who insist that it must be limited to "one man and one woman" seem oblivious to the clearest and most compelling evidence: the critical role of marriage in creating

174. Maggie Gallagher, "(How) Will Gay Marriage Weaken Marriage as a Social Institution," *University of St. Thomas Law Journal*, vol. 2, no. 1 (Fall 2004), 41–42.

175. Charles Moore, "David Cameron Would Like to Forget Gay Marriage, But it Will Haunt Him," *Daily Telegraph*, 10 May 2013 (http://www.telegraph.co.uk/news/religion/10049451/David-Cameron-would-like-to-forget-gay-marriage-but-it-will-haunt-him.html).

fatherhood. Not only is marriage not a "gender neutral" institution; it is not a gender symmetrical one and exists to reconcile one of the most basic differences between the sexes: the fact that one sex has an indisputable biological connection to her offspring whereas the other must have his bond to his children deliberately established by social convention and legal guarantee. This is why "The trends toward non-marriage and toward same-sex marriage are a direct attack on fathers."[176]

Here is where same-sex marriage can be seen as not merely absurd but corrosive of the most socially stabilizing feature of marriage. Judge Vaughn Walker's finding of "fact" in the California Proposition 8 case that "Gender no longer forms an essential part of marriage" is rendered preposterous, because "gender" is quite clearly the central reason for marriage. Marriage between two men or two women simply mocks the purpose of marriage. It attempts to apply gender interchangeability at precisely the point where sex difference demands that biological fact (motherhood) be reconciled to social necessity (fatherhood). But far from establishing paternity, and therefore a settled and stable family, same-sex marriage compounds the problem of who precisely are the parents of a given child. A presumption of "parenthood" confers parent status on any individual (or individuals) recognized as "married" to another individual who acquires a child by whatever means. Maggie Gallagher calls this the problem of "too many parents."[177] A California proposal to legalize multiple parents (in the children's "best interest" of course) "would not have protected any children," according to Phyllis Schlafly, who perceives the logic far more clearly than most conservatives:

> The primary purpose was to let lesbians interfere with natural parents and wipe out the rights of fathers. A divorced mom could get a lesbian spouse, and soon the dad is just one of three or four parents under the law. . . . Lesbian marriage is all about forcing kids to grow up without their fathers. They talk about equality and rights, but they are dead set against equalizing moms and dads in family law, and dead set against the rights of kids to have fathers.[178]

Once marriage becomes detached from procreation, the entire system of domestic and social stability created by marriage unravels. Marriage then is no longer an autonomous and self-renewing institution, mediating the generational interface between public and private, and therefore checking government power. Instead, it becomes merely a

---

176. Schlafly, *Who Killed*, 196.
177. Gallagher, "(How) Will Gay Marriage Weaken Marriage," 56–57.
178. Schlafly, *Who Killed*, 72–73.

prize in the political competition, to be doled out by the very state it once served to control, a form of government patronage handed out to favored groups based on their relative power, like jobs or contracts. This is the meaning of Josephson's claim that access to marriage constitutes a badge of "citizenship" and mark of "equality." With this kind of marriage, the family no longer even renews itself naturally—its unique advantage over the state, according to G. K. Chesterton[179]—since it cannot produce children of its own. Instead this pseudo-family can have children only by taking them from others.

Indeed, what is true of marriage is also true of its product: children. Just as the divorce revolution led directly to same-sex marriage, so the divorce-dominated child abuse machinery now allows same-sex couples to, effectively, confiscate the children of heterosexuals.

Most critiques of homosexual parenting have focused on the therapeutic question of whether it is developmentally healthy for children to be raised by two homosexuals.[180] So much has been written on this that there is no need to labor it here, except to note that, by conducting the discussion on the therapists' terms, half the argument has been conceded, since subjective assessments of mental health can be debated *ad infinitum*.

What few have stopped to ask is the far more momentous political question of where homosexual "parents" get children in the first place. This question does not require esoteric child-development theories or psychological jargon from putative "experts." It can readily be understood by any parent who has been interrogated by social workers after a playground injury or one who has gone through divorce court. The answer is that homosexuals get other people's children, and they get them from the same courts and social service bureaucracies that—operated by their feminist allies—are confiscating them from their real fathers and sometimes mothers, whose marriages still other feminist operatives in the divorce system are dissolving without any grounds. While attention has focused on sperm donors and surrogate mothers, thus far most of the children sought by aspiring homosexual parents are existing children whose ties to one or both of their real parents have been severed. Most often, this happens through divorce or cohabitation.[181]

---

179. *The Superstition of Divorce* (1920), V, "The Story of the Family," http://www.basilica.org/pages/ebooks/G.K.Chesterton-The%20Superstition%20of%20Divorce.pdf.

180. Eric Zorn and Allan Carlson, "A Primer on the 'Gay Marriage' Debate," *The Family in America*, vol. 17, no. 8 (August 2003).

181. I have argued this in "The Real Danger of Same-Sex Marriage," *The Family in America*, vol. 20, nos. 5–6 (May–June 2006).

The question then arises whether the original parent or parents ever agreed to part with their children or committed some offense to warrant forcible separation. As we have seen and will see further, current law governing divorce and child custody renders the answer to this question, "not necessarily." The explosion of foster care and the assumed but unexamined need to find permanent homes for allegedly abused children has provided perhaps the strongest argument in favor of gay marriage and gay parenting.[182] Yet the politics of child abuse and divorce indicate that this assumption is far from valid.[183]

The government-generated child abuse panic, and the mushrooming foster care business it feeds, have already allowed government social-work agencies to operate what amounts to a traffic in children. A San Diego Grand Jury reports "a widely held perception within the community and even within some areas of the Department [of Social Services] that the Department is in the 'baby brokering' business."[184] Introducing same-sex marriage and adoption into this political dynamic will almost certainly increase the demand for adoptable children, thus intensifying pressure on social service agencies and biological parents to supply more children. While sperm donors and surrogate mothers supply some children for gay parents, in practice the vast majority are already taken from their natural parents because of divorce, unwed childbearing, child abuse accusations, or connected reasons. Massachusetts feminist Senator Therese Murray, claiming that 40% of adoptions have gone to gay and lesbian couples, urges sympathy for "children who have been neglected, abandoned, abused by their own families."[185] But we will see that false and exaggerated abuse accusations against not only fathers but mothers too make it far from self-evident that these children are in fact victims of their own parents. It is far more likely that they are the victims of baby trafficking by feminist welfare agencies. This needs more research, but the bottom line is that the very issue of gay parenting has arisen as the direct and perhaps inevitable consequence once government functionaries got into the business—which began largely with divorce—of distributing other people's children.

182. See Lethimstay.com, ACLU Lesbian and Gay Rights Project, https://www.aclu.org/news/aclu-launches-special-web-site-fight-floridas-gay-adoption-ban-protect-families, accessed December 2016.

183. See chapter II, under "Divorce," and chapter III, under "Child Abuse."

184. "Families in Crisis," 9.

185. "The Debate on Gay Marriage, Pro and Con," *Boston Globe* online edition, 12 March 2004 http://www.boston.com/news/specials/gay_marriage/articles/2004/03/12/the_debate_on_gay_marriage_pro_and_con/.

So thoroughly has the therapeutic mentality displaced the ethic of family integrity and parental responsibility that the debate has become mired in what must inevitably be esoteric and insoluble psychological debates over the therapeutic value of homosexual childrearing rather than asking the more straightforward and urgent question of what right homosexuals (or feminists, or social workers, or judges, or anybody) have to take children away from legally unimpeachable natural parents in the first place, regardless of how good for them the therapists' claim it is.

In short, the demand to legitimize same-sex marriage and homosexual parenting is the direct and probably inevitable fallout of the divorce revolution. As recent events confirm, marriage advocates who challenge same-sex marriage and homosexual parenting without confronting the dramatic explosion of government power through divorce and child custody are fighting a pointless and losing battle.

And the loss will be significant indeed, since same-sex marriage is of course only the beginning. A manifesto entitled "Beyond Same-Sex Marriage," issued by prominent "lesbian, gay, bisexual, and transgender (LGBT), and allied activists, scholars, educators, writers, artists, lawyers, journalists, and community organizers," demands "legal recognition for a wide range of relationships, households, and families, and for the children in all of those households and families." Despite professions by "moderate" advocates that monogamous same-sex marriage is all they seek to legitimize, Stanley Kurtz argues, this document demonstrates that the real agenda is "to dissolve marriage, not through formal abolition, but by gradually extending the hitherto unique notion of marriage to every conceivable family type."[186]

Yet here again, there is more than meets even the critic's eye, and what is being overlooked is the role of the state in marriage. The radicals demand "government recognition" and "legal recognition" for "a wide range of relationships, households and families—regardless of kinship or conjugal status." The state must recognize them as it now does marriage.

Why precisely? Obviously anyone may conduct a ceremony, cohabit, and call it marriage. What is critical about state recognition? The answer is welfare.

State recognition of marriage, we have suggested, traditionally exists to ensure that children have effective fathers by guaranteeing the father-child bond. With fathers to provide for their own children, each house-

---

186. Stanley Kurtz, "The Confession," *National Review Online*, 31 October 2006, http://www.nationalreview.com/articles/219092/confession/stanley-kurtz.

hold is financially viable and self-sufficient and contributes to the general prosperity of society. But the state recognition demanded here for "a wide range of relationships" has precisely the opposite effect. Rather than permitting and requiring each father to provide for his own children, this allows any combination of individuals to form private conspiracies ("relationships, households, and families") to loot the public purse and the rest of society by demanding welfare services. (And note the essential addition of state recognition "for the children in all of those households and families…")

This is why state recognition is necessary. The radicals demand not only "freedom from state regulation of our sexual lives and gender choices, identities and expression," which of course was granted long ago. The state (meaning the rest of the population) must also support these "households": "access for all to vital government support programs, including but not limited to: affordable and adequate health care, affordable housing, a secure and enhanced Social Security system, genuine disaster recovery assistance, welfare for the poor…"

In other words, prosperous two-parent homes (people, that is, who practice sexual restraint) will be plundered with taxation to finance dysfunctional, government-dependent, and fatherless homes. Because taxation is collected through the penal system and ultimately at gunpoint, this effectively enslaves the sexually restrained to the sexually liberated. The model for this slavery is child-support enforcement, which originated in welfare and then expanded to the middle class through divorce.[187] Two-parent families will be looted through taxation and welfare much the way fathers are already being looted through divorce and child support.

The manifesto's ideological subtext presents the homosexual-led dissolution of the family as the method for realizing the radical agenda of the 1960s: eliminate private property and business; weaken the military; subsidize dysfunctional households.

> Poverty and economic hardship are widespread and increasing. Corporate greed, draconian tax cuts and breaks for the wealthy, and the increasing shift of public funds from human needs into militarism, policing, and prison construction are producing ever-greater wealth and income gaps between the rich and the poor.… More and more individuals and families (disproportionately people of color and single-parent families headed by women) are experiencing the violence of poverty.

187. Baskerville, "From Welfare State to Police State."

Extending the quasi-Marxist vision of the New Left, it is now homosexuality that is presented as the basis for a utopian scheme to eliminate "the structural violence of poverty, racism, misogyny, war, and repression, and to build an unshakable foundation of social and economic justice for all, from which authentic peace and recognition of global human rights can at long last emerge." But now the utopia adds the promise of sexual paradise, not only socialism but "communities in which we are encouraged to explore the widest range of non-exploitive, non-abusive possibilities in love, gender, desire, and sex."

And as always (and as we will see shortly), all that is required to realize this paradise is for the police to remove anyone who becomes an obstacle.

The Family and Criminality

The state's reconfiguration of the family has consequences well beyond the family itself. As is well documented, virtually every social pathology in industrialized countries—including violent crime, substance abuse, and truancy, plus unwed childbearing itself in the next generation—proceed foremost from single-mother homes and fatherless children. Fatherlessness far eclipses poverty and race as the leading predictor of criminality and other anti-social behavior.[188] With fatherlessness stubbornly but falsely attributed to paternal abandonment, the only acceptable response becomes ever-more draconian but pointless "crackdowns" on allegedly dissolute fathers. Because fathers were never the main cause of the problem in the first place, these measures simply perpetuate and exacerbate the problem.

If instead we see single motherhood realistically, as the intentional and avowed choice of the Sexual Revolution, then the explosion of crime, addiction, and truancy, and with them the massive increase in the size and power of the penal system and state apparatus generally, takes on increased significance. It is then far from fanciful to suggest that sexual liberation lies behind the larger trends in violent crime and incarceration, as well as other major social ills.

188. *Father Facts* 6 (Germantown, Maryland: National Fatherhood Initiative, 2011). Attempts to attribute these behaviors to poverty or racial discrimination have been refuted by studies that control for these variables. See Urie Bronfenbrenner, "Discovering What Families Do," in David Blankenhorn et al. (eds.), *Rebuilding the Nest* (Milwaukee: Family Service America, 1990), 34; Ronald Angel and Jacqueline Angel, *Painful Inheritance: Health and the New Generation of Fatherless Children* (Madison: University of Wisconsin Press, 1993), 188; Norman Dennis and George Erdos, *Families Without Fatherhood* (London: Civitas, 2000).

Drawing upon a large body of research, some by leftist scholars, Bryce Christensen has demonstrated how feminist policies that undermine families contribute directly to the rise in criminality and incarceration. "Solid research links the nightmarish 'increases in crime and violence' among young people between 1960 to 1990 to 'the entry of large numbers of mothers into the work force [and] the rise in single-parent households.'"[189] Christensen also connects runaway incarceration rates to feminist-driven family breakdown and cites evidence that "Divorce rates are consistent predictors of the use of lethal force by police."[190] In fact, there is no dispute about the direct connection between single-parent homes and criminality.

From this perspective, the battle against crime, incarceration, and the growth of state power generally will continue to be a losing one without appreciating the central role played by sexual ideology in family breakdown and the social anomie that ensues.

The financial consequences are likewise unambiguous. The social ills bred by single-parent homes are the very problems that account for most domestic government spending, including budgets for law-enforcement and incarceration, education, health, and ever more "social services."

It is often observed that, financially, the welfare state is a "two-edged sword," as Phyllis Schlafly puts it. "At the same time that it forces government to become the financial provider for millions of children and their caregivers, it reduces the government's tax receipts to pay for the handouts."[191] In fact, the financial effects are much more devastating even than that: welfare is government's self-expanding engine for creating social pathologies for itself to solve. The effects are more than wasteful, for it is money spent to turn children into criminals, addicts, drop-outs, and rioters—precisely the problems that then rationalize more government programs, government spending, and government power.

The implications are staggering. Budgets to address the social ills proceeding from single-motherhood have mushroomed out of control. Even now, as it is bankrupting governments and bringing down prime ministers, social spending remains the largest and fastest-growing category in the budgets of Western democracies, with no end in sight. Any

189. Christensen, "Hearth or Hangman?" 6–7.

190. Ibid., 6, citing David Jacobs and Robert M. O'Brien, "The Determinants of Deadly Force: A Structural Analysis of Police Violence," *The American Journal of Sociology*, vol. 103, no. 4 (January 1998), 851.

191. "The Cost to Taxpayers of Missing Fathers," *Townhall.com*, 14 June 2011, http://townhall.com/columnists/phyllisschlafly/2011/06/14/the_cost_to_taxpayers_of_missing_fathers/page/full.

mention of cutbacks or restraint sends mobs of angry feminists, students, and civil servants marching through the streets of Athens and London, striking fear into any politician who might dare to reduce social spending. "Social services spending is the largest growing line item in Missouri's budget," writes David Usher of the Center for Marriage Policy, describing a relatively solvent and conservative American state. "The welfare state is eating Missouri alive."[192] It already devoured the democratically elected prime ministers of Greece and Italy and replaced them with functionaries appointed by the European Union.

The Western democracies are not poor. They are bankrupting themselves by bureaucratizing the family functions that are the foundation of private life and economic prosperity. Insolvency and debt inescapably result from the voracious appetite of the resulting leviathan, creating endless spirals of problems. From mortgage bubbles (caused by programs devised to further subsidize single-parent "families") to abused children, each government measure brings problems that demand more government measures.

This is why the *Wall Street Journal* and others have located the West's debt crisis entirely in the welfare state and therefore in the Sexual Revolution. "The decline of marriage is not just a moral, a social, or a cultural issue," writes Phyllis Schlafly. "It is America's biggest fiscal issue ... and marriage absence has become a major cause of national deficits." The "poor" of the Western world are not starving children with distended bellies. They are the offspring of single mothers. They are the victims not of a stingy society but of a sexually indulgent one. "Poverty is chiefly predicted by family structure," Schlafly observes. "Marriage drops the probability of child poverty by 82%.... If single moms were to marry the fathers of their children, the children would be lifted out of poverty."[193] History's most affluent societies are voluntarily bankrupting themselves financially as well as morally by underwriting sexual decadence.

The word "economy" derives from the Greek word for household management, indicating why the family must always be society's fundamental economic unit. What we call economic policy is the transference of this management from the household to the state and the attendant

192. David Usher and Cynthia Davis, "Marriage: America's Greatest Fiscal Issue," 1 October 2010, Center for Marriage Policy website: http://marriagepolicy.org/2011/09/marriage-americas-greatest-fiscal-issue/.

193. "Europe's Entitlement Reckoning," *Wall Street Journal*, 10 November 2011 (http://online.wsj.com/article/SB10001424052970204190704577026194205495230.html); Schlafly, *Who Killed*, 121, 128. See also Tom G. Palmer (ed.), *After the Welfare State* (Ottawa, Illinois: Jameson Books, 2012).

illusion that society itself—including private life—can be directed from the top down by civil servants rather than developing spontaneously from a foundation of family households upward. It cannot be sustained and neither can a civilization that attempts it.

Yet the welfare state is but one mechanism the sexual revolutionaries have devised for transforming the male population into an underclass of criminals. As we will see in the next chapter, they have many, many more.

III

Criminalizing Sex:
The New Gender Crimes

"Hysteria is not the privilege of the uneducated."
—T. S. Eliot

"Citizens, I seek among you judges, and yet I see only accusers."
—Raymond de Sèze at the trial of Louis XVI[1]

"We're going to re-educate you, boy."
—feminist university dean to a faculty member[2]

LIBERALS ARE NOT ALONE today in expressing concern about America's high and increasing rate of incarceration and the growing reach and severity of the penal apparatus. A nation that claims to be the freest on earth—that originated in constitutional principles stretching back beyond Magna Carta—is today, in terms of its criminal justice system, among the least free. The United States incarcerates a greater proportion of its population than Islamist Iran and is exceeded only by Communist North Korea. "Over the past three decades, the United States has built a carceral state that is unprecedented among Western countries and in US history," writes Marie Gottschalk. "Nearly one in fifty people, excluding children and the elderly, is incarcerated today, a rate unsurpassed anywhere else in the world."[3] These scrupulously gender-neutral "people" are overwhelmingly men.

The American prison population is exploding, with over two million

---

1. Quoted in John Laughland, *A History of Political Trials* (Oxford: Peter Lang, 2008), 48.
2. Daphne Patai, *Heterophobia: Sexual Harassment and the Future of Feminism* (Lanham, Maryland: Rowman and Littlefield, 1998), Kindle location 1258.
3. Marie Gottschalk, *The Prison and the Gallows: The Politics of Mass Incarceration in America* (Cambridge: Cambridge University Press, 2006), i.

inmates. "Today a higher proportion of the adult population in the United States is behind bars than anywhere else in the world." Even this only scratches the surface, since for every citizen actually behind bars there are many more whose lives are controlled by the penal system. "The reach of the US penal state extends far beyond the 2.2 million men and women who are now serving time in prison or jail in America," writes Gottschalk. "On any given day, nearly seven million people are under the supervision of the correction system, including jail, prison, parole, probation, and other community supervision sanctions. This constitutes 3.2% of the US adult population, or one in every thirty-two adults, a rate of state supervision that is unprecedented in US history."[4] And again, since these "people" are mostly men, this constitutes a far higher percentage of the adult male population.[5]

Even these figures seriously understate the trend. If we consider the similar "people" whose movements and finances are directly supervised by the child support enforcement machinery, then tens of millions of American "people" actually live their lives under the supervision of the penal apparatus. The trend is growing in Britain and other Anglophone countries, in Europe, and elsewhere.

Most of this growth has occurred in the last four decades, since "from the mid-1920s to the early 1970s, the US incarceration rate was remarkably stable."[6] Gottschalk asks a critical question: "Why didn't the construction of the carceral state face more political opposition?"

This rush to imprison has come at the expense of basic freedoms and constitutional protections, and it is far from self-evident that all these inmates are guilty. In America, basic civil liberties and procedural safeguards are now routinely ignored, grand juries are neutered, frivolous prosecutions abound, and the innocent are railroaded into prison through plea bargains and other high-pressure devices that border on extortion.[7] Some conservatives do not like to accept these facts, but they are indisputable. There is little doubt today that the incarceration and even execution of the innocent is a serious problem in America and is growing elsewhere. Prosecutorial misconduct, police lying, falsified evidence, judicial incompetence or corruption, attorney malpractice, and

---

4. Ibid., 1.

5. Though some 90% of these inmates are male, Gottschalk writes of the "disproportionate impact" on "the growing number of incarcerated women."

6. Gottschalk, *Prison*, 2.

7. Paul Craig Roberts and Lawrence M. Stratton, *The Tyranny of Good Intentions: How Prosecutors and Bureaucrats Are Trampling the Constitution in the Name of Justice* (Roseville, California: Prima, 2000); Bennett L. Gershman, *Prosecutorial Misconduct* (Eagon, MN: West, 1999).

more mean that huge numbers of incarcerated Americans are certainly innocent. The Innocence Project attests by its results that many are wrongfully convicted. Many never receive a trial, and many more are not even eligible for one.

These trends are usually attributed to the "law-and-order" demands of conservatives, who themselves seldom deny their own role (or indifference) but stubbornly insist that more punishment is necessary to deter crime and vigorously advocate it against the leniency of liberals. In fact, few of these conservatives understand what they are advocating. The left has developed a far more refined and effective mentality of punishment.

Much of this new criminalization comes not from the prosecution of existing crimes but from the proliferation of new ones and from the politicization of the criminal justice system. Harvey Silverglate writes that "Congress is criminalizing everyday conduct at a reckless pace," and what Congress legislates is only the tip of the iceberg: state legislatures, judges, and even civil servants also create crimes. Many new crimes are vague, defined not by a clear response to a clear danger, but by political and partisan negotiations. Many others are legislated not by elected representatives as statutes but by civil servants as regulations. Still others are effectively legislated by judges and, effectively, by prosecutors, and some even by plainclothes enforcement agents. The politicization of prosecution and weakening of legal safeguards, such as blurring the distinction between civil and criminal offenses and eliminating the principle that a crime requires criminal intent (*mens rea*), have also undermined constitutional protections.[8] "The urge to criminalize and restrict has constituted a serious and unwarranted assault on our civil liberties," writes Simon Heffer. "It reflects one of the most poisonous attitudes of the modern state, that it is considerably easier to prosecute and punish harmless people than it is to pursue serious criminals."[9]

---

8. Harvey Silverglate, *Three Felonies a Day: How the Feds Target the Innocent* (New York: Encounter, 2009), x, xxv, xxx–xxxi. The elimination of *mens rea*, requiring criminal intent, has been especially helpful in criminalizing sex. Brian W. Walsh and Tiffany M. Joslyn, *Without Intent: How Congress Is Eroding the Criminal Intent Requirement in Federal Law* (Washington: Heritage Foundation and National Association of Criminal Defense Lawyers, 2010, http://s3.amazonaws.com/thf_media/2010/pdf/WithoutIntent_1 0-res.pdf#page=10), vi. This is precisely what feminist criminology does. See Edward Greer, "The Truth Behind Legal Dominance Feminism's 'Two Percent False Claim' Figure," *Loyola of Los Angeles Law Review*, vol. 33 (2000), 963.

9. "On the Rise of Pernicious Laws that Criminalise the Law-Abiding," *Daily Mail*, 26 December 2011, http://www.dailymail.co.uk/debate/article-2078863/Hunting-speed-traps-rise-pernicious-laws-criminalise-law-abiding.html.

In fact, these trends are not the result of traditionalists' demands for law and order, which were not particularly new in the 1970s. A more innovative and far more militant force had arrived on the scene.

Gottschalk—an avowedly feminist scholar—points out that traditional conservatives were not, in fact, the prime instigators and cites "interest groups and social movements not usually associated with penal conservatism." Yet she names only one: "the women's movement."[10]

The massive criminalization of the population—almost entirely the male population—coincides precisely with the rise of organized feminism. "Women's groups and the women's movement became a vanguard of conservative law-and-order politics," Gottschalk writes, employing politically correct language. "Women's organizations played a central role in the consolidation of this conservative victims' rights movement that emerged in the 1970s."[11] As the epicenter of radical feminism, the United States also leads the worldwide expansion of incarceration.[12] In addition to promoting single motherhood and ancillary policies that, by breaking down the family, create more crime in the usual sense,[13] feminists also created a plethora of new crimes. Sexual radicalism has increased both criminality and criminalization.

From the beginning, the most authoritarian pressure group in American politics has consistently been women's rights activists. "If one looks back at the history of penal policy and reform, it is striking what an uncritical stance earlier women reformers took toward the state," writes Gottschalk. "Periodically, they have played central roles in defining violence as a threat to the social order and uncritically pushing for more enhanced policing powers."[14] No social movement or interest group has done more to politicize criminal justice or expand the penal apparatus. "Feminist groups . . . became champions of state intervention to address problems like rape and domestic violence."[15] During the 1970s—precisely the time they were spreading "no-fault" divorce throughout the civil judiciary—they were also politicizing criminal justice and commandeering the penal machinery. "Nearly every state enacted legislation designed to make it easier to convict and punish people [sic] accused of sexual assault or domestic violence."[16]

10. Gottschalk, *Prison*, 228–29.
11. Ibid., 115.
12. Ibid.
13. See chapter II, under "The Family and Criminality."
14. Ibid.
15. Ibid., 11.
16. Marie Gottschalk, "Ghosts of the Past, Present, and Future of Penal Reform in the

Despite her admirable candor, Gottschalk's language itself reveals the distorting power of ideology. To absolve her sisters of responsibility for the incarceration explosion she deplores, she invokes terms like "conservative" to describe feminist militants. Though the feminists were the "vanguard," she repeatedly blames "conservatives" for "co-opting" the women's movement. Rather than responsible adults who can be held accountable for their actions, feminists were "vulnerable to being captured and co-opted by the law-and-order agenda of politicians, state officials, and conservative groups." Much as self-professed rape victims no longer need demonstrate that they offered any objection to the alleged assault, Gottschalk provides no indication that the sisterhood offered the slightest resistance to this mass political abduction.[17]

Conservatives certainly played a role, though if anyone was unwittingly co-opted it was more likely they. This is evident from their campaigns to provide more effective recourse to crime victims, largely in response to liberal measures weakening punishments. President Ronald Reagan's 1982 Task Force on Victims of Crime led to the creation of US Justice Department's Office for Victims of Crime. A glance at that agency's website today reveals that the campaign has been taken over by feminists and homosexuals adopting a presumption of guilt: the "victims" (not "alleged victims") are women or homosexuals, the "perpetrators" (not "defendants") are heterosexual men, and the "crimes" (not "alleged crimes") are mostly sexual and political.

Gottschalk's own account makes clear that feminism, not conservatism, was the innovative and militant force. "A commitment to greater gender equality by reducing rape and domestic violence got funneled through a specific political and institutional context and got transformed in the process," she insists. "The result was a more punitive environment that contributed to the construction of the carceral state." What Gottschalk calls "the victims' movement" did include naïve conservatives, but the cutting edge was clearly the sexual left:

> Being for victims and against offenders became a simple equation that helped knit together politically disparate groups ranging from the more traditional conservative, law-and-order constituencies mobilized around punitive policies like "three-strikes-and-you're-out," to women's groups organized against rape and domestic violence, to gay

United States," in *Why Prison?* ed. David Scott (Cambridge: Cambridge University Press, 2013), 258.

17. Gottschalk, *Prison*, 116.

and lesbian groups advocating for hate crimes legislation, to the Million Moms pushing for gun control.[18]

This collusion of left and right leaves no room for dissent or opposition (which is why we never hear about it), including any defense of the innocent, which is then easily intimidated and ignored, in both the media and the courtroom. But further, it also creates a vicious cycle. Justifiable public outrage about genuine crime is claimed as a mandate to legislate ever-more draconian measures against law-abiding but defenseless citizens, whom leftist lawyers refuse to defend (*"pro bono"*) and who are not always entitled to a public defender. Such measures, increasing child support for example and with it single motherhood, exacerbate the rise of real criminality. Meanwhile, by averting our eyes from the central role of sexual radicalism in the incarceration explosion, we can only address its more obvious miscarriages of justice by further weakening the measures available to adjudicate and punish real crimes. Thus we rotate the guilty out of the prisons as we rotate the innocent in.

Here the young, low-income black male is the pivotal figure who both disguises and reveals this trend, because he tends to be a member of both groups. As the likely child of a single mother, he is most liable to commit crime in the traditional sense. This makes him a political client of the left and a villain of the right. He is also the most defenseless and therefore likely target for the state's anti-father machinery, an evicted father looted and then incarcerated by the child support gestapo. This makes him a malefactor to both the left and right. This leaves him about a 75% chance of incarceration, depending on how he is played as a pawn in others' games of political power.

Here too, Gottschalk exemplifies how ideology creates optical illusions that exacerbate the problem. She accepts the standard leftist line that crime and incarceration are driven by "racial disparities, racial discrimination, and institutional racism" but finds that "the USA would still have an incarceration crisis even if black people were sent to prison and jails at 'only' the rate at which white people are currently locked up." So instead of race, "class" becomes the substitute culprit, and the solution is more generous welfare. Yet her own account makes clear that it was neither racism nor poverty but welfare that created an African-American criminal class and prison population in the first place: "In the 1920s [after decades of segregation laws], fewer than one in three prisoners were black. By the late 1980s [after decades of welfare], for the first time in US history the majority of prisoners were black."[19]

18. Ibid., 11, 228.
19. "Ghosts of the Past," 243, 255, 257.

Gottschalk also does not question the veracity of the accusations. She assumes that all the accused are guilty and does not address what we will see to be the massive problem of knowingly false accusations, which are now out of control with both rape and domestic violence. Nor does she question or address how both rape and domestic violence have been redefined so broadly as to make almost anyone guilty, nor how they became the pattern for expanding other gender crimes. Instead, she assumes that all claims are valid and that all accusers are certifiable "rape victims" and "battered women." Still, she is troubled.

What Gottschalk has stumbled upon is the feminist version of Stalinism: the familiar process by which radical movements first challenge and then commandeer both traditional values and the instruments of state repression for their own purposes as they trade ideological purity for power. She is especially perplexed at how comfortably leftist mob justice thrives alongside the liberal impulse to excuse actual criminality: "American feminists prosecuting the war on rape and domestic violence were remarkably unaware of or untouched by developments in the field of critical criminology, which . . . understands crime primarily in terms of power relations."[20]

In fact, feminists have a very keen understanding of criminology as a weapon in "power relations"; they pioneered it, and it is their own quest for power that created the new sex crimes. Feminists and more recently homosexual radicals have marshaled the criminal law as the principal instrument of their politics, not hesitating to invoke criminal and quasi-

---

20. Gottschalk, *Prison*, 160. Ideology leads Gottschalk into further perplexity as she describes the process by which federal funding absorbed what had been local law enforcement issues into the bureaucratic federal enforcement and social work machinery (127–29). "Funding pressures eventually prompted the centers to . . . embrace more of the goals of state agencies, notably social services, mental health, and law enforcement." Here again, Gottschalk portrays this as an insidious takeover of radical feminism by "conservative" federal officials with money. Despite the candor of her report, her own ideology prevents her from seeing the Stalinization of the sisterhood, whose loss of ideological purity she laments. "Women's groups entered into some unsavory coalitions and compromises that bolstered the law-and-order agenda and reduced their own capacity to serve as ideological bulwarks against the rising tide of conservatism" (131). Obviously the federal government was bankrolling its own expansion over what should have been matters for local police by "funneling" money to the feminist lobbies: "The main vehicle for greater state involvement in the cause of violence against women was the US Department of Justice, which funneled money, expertise, and philosophy into the emerging movement." Rather than protecting all citizens' constitutional rights, as its mandate requires, "the US Department of Justice became the champion of abused women." "Ghosts of the Past," 240. Of course nothing suggests the feminist lobbies resisted the government's largesse; on the contrary, it is clear that they used it to build powerful pressure groups and lucrative careers.

criminal accusations to silence their political opponents and ordinary people with the penal apparatus. "In the last two decades, feminists have built a real political resistance to male sexual dominance," wrote the disturbed but influential Andrea Dworkin, "and we prosecute the pigs to prove it."[21]

Feminist lawyers and legal scholars have led the politicization of prosecution over four decades. "By 1990, there were at least eight law reviews devoted exclusively to feminist issues, with more appearing every year," two researchers noted two decades ago. "Hundreds of articles of the same persuasion have appeared in mainstream law journals, especially the most prestigious ones. A 1990 bibliography of books and articles on women and the law occupied 70 pages."[22] More than a quarter century later the trend has exploded far beyond this, to the point where the appearance of a journal entitled *Feminist Criminology* raises no eyebrows at the very notion that criminal justice should be openly politicized with ideology.

Sexualized legal theory, far from its liberal appearance, is today's most illiberal influence on the law and seeks to eradicate basic protections dating back centuries. "Such liberal principles as neutrality of the law, equality, and individual autonomy must be discarded because of their 'patriarchal' roots," write Cathy Young and Michael Weiss. "The new feminism attempts to replace those notions with a new breed of philosophy and jurisprudence.... Law is seen as an instrument to 'change the distribution of power,'" rather than to punish crime.

In cases where due process still protects defendants, feminist prosecutors create parallel civil cases, in which conviction is much easier (and much more lucrative) because of more relaxed rules of evidence and standards of conviction. To circumvent the double jeopardy prohibition, even when a defendant has had his day in court and been acquitted by a jury of his peers, he can still be effectively convicted and looted by the courts. The financial windfall accruing to the purported "victim" (and lawyers, and everyone else involved in this innovative jurisprudence) makes this practice all the more attractive and almost impossible to defend against.

Conservatives see left-wing bias dominating the civil and constitutional judiciary and manifesting itself as "judicial activism" in rulings on abortion, affirmative action, and school prayer. Yet the severest conservative critics have trouble accepting the equally serious corruption of

21. Quoted in Patai, *Heterophobia*, Kindle locations 885–87.
22. Michael Weiss and Cathy Young, *Feminist Jurisprudence: Equal Rights or Neo-Paternalism?* (Washington: Cato Institute, 1996).

criminal justice. Understandably attached to principles of law and order, many fail to realize how completely that principle has been politicized and inverted by ideology and continue to presume the guilt of those who fall afoul of it. "Law-and-order conservatives typically believe in increasing police and prosecutorial powers and show little concern for the plight of defendants," Stuart Taylor and K.C. Johnson write, as an explanation for the widespread refusal to recognize false rape accusations.[23] Conservatives are correct that criminals often go free but fail to understand that this happens because of a politicized judiciary that also criminalizes the innocent. They also fail to understand that when they place themselves in the service of left-wing ideologues no one remains to challenge state power.

Of course, the feminist drive to lock up men extends the existing tendency of the criminal justice system to do so regardless—not simply because men indisputably do commit most violent crime, but also because they are more harshly punished than women for the same crimes. Sonja Starr of the University of Michigan Law School found "large gender gaps favoring women throughout" the sentencing process, "averaging over 60%." "Female arrestees are also significantly likelier to avoid charges and convictions entirely, and twice as likely to avoid incarceration if convicted."[24]

The abuses in the criminal justice system cited at the start are only the beginning; at least those defendants are generally charged with a crime and can request a trial, however perfunctory these procedures may have become.

The new sex and gender crimes take the injustice to a new level. Though hazardous for journalists or academics to discuss, it is increasingly obvious that sexual radicalism has thoroughly perverted the criminal justice system and eroded centuries-old protections on which the United States and other constitutional democracies were founded.

While the incarceration of innocent people is now spreading throughout the justice system, the most flagrant and numerous instances—indeed, injustice no one denies—are attributable to the sexualization of the justice system, with crimes that are sexually specific or sexually interpreted: "rape," "sexual assault," "sexual harassment," "domestic vio-

---

23. Stuart Taylor and K.C. Johnson, *Until Proven Innocent: Political Correctness and the Shameful Injustices of the Duke Lacrosse Rape Case* (New York: Thomas Dunne, 2007), 361.

24. "Estimating Gender Disparities in Federal Criminal Cases," University of Michigan Law School, *Law and Economics Research Paper Series*, Paper No. 12–018, August 2012.

lence," "stalking," "child abuse," "bullying," "sex trafficking," "aggressive driving," and more. Most people today have little understanding of what these terms really mean. Indeed, it is not possible to understand what they mean, because their meanings change constantly or they have no fixed definition at all. It is very clear that they have been devised decidedly for the purpose of circumventing the precision of standard criminal definitions and—an intention radicals explicitly avow—increasing the number of incarcerations.

These witch hunts bear almost no relation to what is suggested by the inflammatory language. In many cases, the new gender crimes are simply the old sex crimes politicized with radical ideology. This is precisely what makes them so potent. Feminists have discovered that conservative moralists are a soft touch if they clamor for ever-harsher penalties against "sex offenders," "violence against women," and "child abuse"— all highly misleading terms for matters against which no public outcry had been heard before feminists began generating it. The penalties and punishments attract little scrutiny because they are invariably bipartisan. And they are enthusiastically supported by prosecutors and other penal officials, who recognize an easy formula for expanding their own power and earnings. Yet the expanded police powers rationalized by these alleged crimes are not likely to be used against true sex offenders (for which existing law has always provided); they are far more likely to be used against the innocent for political reasons. There is no other reason for them to have been created.

Some of these offenses have been redefined so loosely as to make them the opposite of what plain English suggests, while others have been simply concocted altogether, entailing crimes no one ever heard of before: "rape" that includes consensual sex; domestic "violence" that involves no violence or physical contact or any threat of it; "child abuse" that is routine parental discipline or homeschooling or fabricated altogether to win advantage in divorce court; "bullying" that is so vague as to be meaningless or involves criticism of the homosexual political agenda or other differences of belief and opinion; "stalking" that is involuntarily divorced fathers trying to see their own children; and much more.

It is not surprising that the public—including politically sophisticated people and even those who claim to be experts in the field—have trouble understanding the new gender crimes. Contrary to long-established principles of justice, there is usually no clear definition of the offense. Like the new statutes in other areas, they are vague, but they are vague to the point of being meaningless, where it is not clear what "crime" has been proven or can possibly be proven. The distinction between criminal acts and non-criminal human conflict or even simple disagreement is blurred; clear acts of criminal violence like rape and assault (for which, again, existing criminal law has always provided) are jumbled together with open-ended terms like "abuse" and "exploitation" to suggest that anything that might fall under these expansive terms is also a crime for which someone should be arrested. The crime is usually defined politically as resulting from a "power imbalance," or, with "the glorification of feeling,"[25] subjectively, according to the opinion or "feelings" of the one claiming to be a "victim." Guilt is determined not by the objective act of the accused but by the subjective state-of-mind of the accuser—not simply whether she gave "consent" but whether she felt "fear" or simply "offense." "To be universally acceptable and therefore effective, law must be based on objective criteria. Something is either legal or illegal. It either did or did not take place," write two leading authorities. "But this standard no longer applies to laws that affect women."[26]

But this is only the beginning: the presumption of innocence for gender crimes has been inverted into a presumption of guilt; knowingly false accusations are unpunished and even encouraged; patently innocent men (and some women) are taken away in handcuffs and put behind bars without being convicted, tried, or even charged; clear miscarriages of justice are rationalized and excused by government officials and politicians with legal jargon and weasel words about "progress" and "changing attitudes."

Seldom are these quasi-crimes adjudicated by trials or juries in standard courts. Instead, guilt (but seldom innocence) is summarily pronounced by "special" courts and various quasi-judicial, extra-judicial, pseudo-judicial bodies that are highly bureaucratic: "family" courts, "domestic violence courts," "judges surrogate," lawyers, social workers, campus tribunals, public school administrators, welfare officials, and other petty functionaries and political operatives, usually with a vested interest.[27] Traditionally, crimes are defined and quantified as they are adjudicated: if a jury convicts a defendant then a crime has been committed. But the new offenses are officially verified because "reports" have been "confirmed" not by juries but by the decree of judges and sometimes simply by civil servants such as social workers. Accusers' claims to be "victims" are officially "certified" by civil servants without

---

25. Paul Nathanson and Katherine K. Young, *Legalizing Misandry: From Public Shame to Systemic Discrimination against Men* (Montreal: McGill-Queen's University Press, 2006), 202–03.

26. Ibid., 202.

27. The rule of law requires criminal adjudication "in the ordinary legal manner *before the ordinary courts of the land.*" A.V. Dicey, quoted in John Laughland, *A History of Political Trials* (Oxford: Peter Lang, 2008), 7 (emphasis added).

any judicial proceeding, implicitly entitling the officially certified victim to have her official victimizer punished. Some accused are punished without any conviction or even formal charge. Outcomes are rigged with paid professional accusers ("victim-advocates") hired to testify against defendants they do not know and about whose alleged guilt they have no first-hand knowledge in order to secure conviction and maximum punishment, whereas no advocates are hired to testify or ensure due process protections for the accused; in fact, they often have no opportunity even to speak on their own behalf. In government documents (and media reports) accusers are labeled as "victims," while the accused are termed "perpetrators," even before any conviction or trial or formal charge (if there is any) or introduction of evidence. Convictions and punishments are promoted in official documents as goods in themselves, and increasing their number as desirable goals of government policy, to be pursued for their own sake regardless of the evidence against specific defendants in particular cases. Government statistics purporting to document and quantify the existence of these crimes are based not on convictions but likewise on "reports" and on definitions so vague that it is not clear what if anything is being reported (or by whom). By contrast, government statistics and documentation on the resulting incarcerations, which are required by law, are not published.

All this creates a culture of accusation and punishment. Though the process is openly designed to favor accusers, we hear "repeated reminders of how difficult it is for victims to come forward with accusations": "They expect not to be believed; they suffer from great emotional stress; they fear retaliation (which would be a violation of federal civil rights law)."[28] Convictions must therefore be ever-easier to obtain, or made unnecessary altogether, and punishments must always be ever-easier to inflict, preferably without trial. Activists thus demand the removal of all barriers to punishment: mandatory arrest laws, no-drop provisions, new specialized courts created with the express purpose of obtaining more convictions, "victim advocates," vocal pressure groups (funded by government prosecutors) publicly demanding more convictions regardless of evidence and threatening politicians if they do not get them.

The outcome is usually a foregone conclusion because (like the show trials of the 1930s and 1950s), the procedure is effectively scripted. Typically, the accuser will be "training herself in correct victim behavior by reading" government literature "made available for the purpose," as Daphne Patai explains. "A script is being played out. All the characters

---

28. Patai, *Heterophobia*, Kindle locations 593–95.

have roles to perform."[29] But acquittal is not part of the script, and everyone accused receives some punishment.[30]

Until recently, the new crimes have all had one common feature and one primary purpose: to criminalize males, masculine behavior, and masculinity itself. They have no other reason to exist. The alleged victims are invariably understood to be exclusively women and girls; the alleged perpetrators are almost entirely heterosexual men and boys, and the behavior for which they are punished is masculine behavior. When the equal protection of the law prevails enough to ensnare feminists in their own traps, excuses are quickly found to explain why women (or at least feminist women), by definition, cannot be guilty. As similar methods are adopted by homosexualist militants, women, religious believers, and other categories of people may also be targeted.

This perversion of criminal justice, criminalization of masculinity, and power of sexuality as a political weapon can be grasped only by understanding how central is the sex act itself to the power dynamic. The most potent but least understood feature of the new gender crimes is how smoothly they use expanded sexual freedom to diminish civil freedom.

Many have observed the paradox of feminism's promotion of licentious sex coupled with its "puritanical" intolerance, without understanding the dynamic that connects the two. "Feminists used to urge women to explore their own sexuality freely," write Patai and Koertge, "but now there is a figurative policing of the bedroom."[31] But this is not really a chronological change, and there is nothing figurative about the police. "While women's studies professors bang pots and blow whistles at anti-rape rallies," observes Heather MacDonald, "in the dorm next door, freshman counselors and deans pass out tips for better orgasms and the use of sex toys."[32] It is no coincidence but a dynamic and powerful dialectic connecting the two sides of the anomaly that makes sex a weapon.

The crime usually begins as some new sexual freedom demanded to liberate women from some "oppression"—though crucially, the new freedom is also enticing to men, especially young men with strong libidos and few responsibilities. This then degenerates into a corollary

---

29. Ibid., Kindle locations 748–49.

30. See below, under "Domestic Violence."

31. Daphne Patai and Noretta Koertge, *Professing Feminism: Cautionary Tales from the Strange World of Women's Studies* (New York: Basic Books, 1994), 3.

32. Heather MacDonald, "The Campus Rape Myth," *City Journal*, vol. 18, no. 1 (Winter 2008, http://www.city-journal.org/2008/18_1_campus_rape.html).

criminal accusation against (almost invariably) the man who indulges in the new pleasure. This often follows the woman's combined emotional disappointment that the sex is not accompanied by any commitment and realization that she suddenly wields enormous legal power to punish the man:

- Recreational sex in the evening turns into accusations of "rape" in the morning, even when it was entirely consensual. (This is especially rampant on university campuses and in the military.)

- Demands for equal access to workplaces, universities, the military, and other previously male venues invite accusations of "sexual harassment" against the men when sexual relations inevitably develop (and often turn sour), regardless of who initiates them.

- Cohabitation and easy ("no-fault") divorce are demanded to liberate women from "patriarchal" marriage but quickly generate accusations of male abandonment (even when the woman severs the relationship without grounds), as well as domestic "violence" and "child abuse," in order to procure custody of children and the financial awards and assets that accompany them.

- Defiant declarations that women do not need men's financial support quickly give way to demands to arrest and incarcerate without trial men who do not provide women with adequate income in the form of spousal or child support.

- Assertions that women do not need men for protection soon produce hysterical outcries for intrusive police powers, innovative punishments, and expanded penal institutions to punish ever-proliferating and loosely-defined forms of "violence against women," even when no physical contact or threat of it is involved.

- The proclaimed right to raise children out of wedlock and without fathers to protect and discipline them turns into demands to prosecute adolescents and even children for "bullying" one another and eventually for real crime.

- Demands to legalize prostitution are followed by efforts to find and prosecute unnamed "sex traffickers."

- More recently, demands to give "transgender" persons access to the public washrooms of their choice are said to create the need for criminal penalties against heterosexual males who might wander into the wrong facility.

In each of these cases, demands for more freedom soon become demands for less. In each case, no clear definition of the crime and no regular criminal procedures prove guilt. Instead, special courts using novel and irregular procedures can redefine the crime to fit the defendant.

But more, each of these cases involves not only a claim that women's freedom (sexual and otherwise) is restricted, but also opportunities for easier sexual contact and for men to enjoy easy sex without the responsibility that normally comes with the conventional regulation of sex through marriage: the need to establish an economically viable home; protect and provide for a wife and children; remain faithful to one woman. Indeed, men who will accept these commitments often find that they are no longer available. Here again, progressive political doctrines have not eliminated a "gender stereotype," as we were promised; they have merely politicized it. Whether by accident or design, feminists themselves have created a political version of the temptress, the seductress who lures men into a "honey trap" by offers of sexual pleasure before springing a trap that today can mean decades in prison.

Homosexual militants are now adopting similar techniques. The demanded right to engage in homosexual acts and public sexual displays is extended almost unnoticed into the power to arrest or otherwise stop the mouths of preachers, "bullies," and anyone else who objects or ridicules or impinges on homosexuals' "feelings" or "pride."

This dialectic of freedom and punishment appropriates the terms of sex and places them in the control of sexual operatives and penal officials. "It matters little whether sex is prohibited or promiscuity encouraged," observes Patai. "Either way, the management of sexuality is a key element ... which through such manipulation attempt[s] to erase the private sphere."[33]

Here too, we see the familiar pattern of how radical political ideologies create the very problems they then re-package as grievances, which then serve to rationalize increased "empowerment" and repression.[34] The distinction between "negative" rights to be free from state interference and "positive" rights to demand government intervention is elided with hardly a notice.

What is presented as the individual's "right" to exercise a new sexual freedom without restriction by the state quickly translates, by a sleight-of-hand that few perceive, into a government power to punish both those who partake of the new freedom and those who stand in the way of it. This is the logic that transforms the Rights of Man into the Reign of Terror. The fanatical Antoine de St. Just could have been speaking for

33. Patai, *Heterophobia*, Kindle locations 2651–2.
34. Milovan Djilas, *The New Class* (New York: Praeger, 1958), 37.

the Sexual rather than the French Revolution when he declared, "No freedom for the enemies of freedom!"

The shift from freedom to punishment is reinforced by the subjective nature of the transgressions, whereby guilt is determined not by the objective act of the accused but by the subjective state of mind of the accuser. Consensual sex in the evening becomes rape the next morning. Domestic "violence" is defined not as physical assault but subjective "fear." Harassment is a woman feeling harassed, and discrimination is a homosexual perceiving discrimination. Speech is punished in a litigious free-for-all allowing people to sue (some say loot) one another for giving "offense." "The danger of the experience-based standard pursued by feminists is that . . . feelings trump facts," write two scholars, who quote a feminist authority: "Just because an act may not meet the traditional common law definition of force," writes law professor Toni Lester, "does not mean that the target of the harassment does not justifiably experience the act, *in her own mind*, as force."[35] This power to dictate and alter the meaning of words renders the accused guilty by virtue of being accused. "If a woman's interpretation sets the legal standard, then it is virtually up to every woman . . . to define the guilt of the man she accuses," says one lawyer.[36] "This sets the stage," writes Patai, "for the elevation of women's word to the level of law—which was precisely the goal of feminist activists."[37]

The innocent are railroaded because the validity of both the new crimes themselves and accusations against specific persons encounter almost no challenge. Few are willing to appear to defend "sex crimes" or accused "sex offenders." The result is a spiral of silence by journalists, scholars, and other presumed watchdogs (and even friends and family), as the accused are left to dangle.

As with past revolutionary movements, guilt is attributed not to specific individuals based on evidence of specific deeds. Instead, guilt is apportioned to categories of people and individuals become liable to punishment because of their inclusion in groups: "abusers," "rapists," "batterers," "harassers," "stalkers," "deadbeats," "bullies," "pedophiles," "traffickers," "haters," "homophobes," and more. Like the old "capitalists," "bourgeoisie," and "counterrevolutionaries," criminality is defined

---

35. Furchtgott-Roth and Stolba, *Feminist Dilemma*, 96, emphasis added. The authors reproduce a feminist diagram in which "harassment" is distinguished from "flirting" by the response of the "victim."

36. Quoted in Nathanson and Young, *Legalizing Misandry*, 202.

37. Patai, *Heterophobia*, 165, quoted in Nathanson and Young, *Legalizing Misandry*, 202.

collectively as membership in a class—even a class into which one is designated by government policy beyond one's control. Compare the similar instructions of Bolsheviks and feminists describing their own criminology. First, Martin Latsis, a Cheka leader and "true Bolshevik," explains how to exterminate a category of people:

> We are not waging war on individual persons. We are exterminating the bourgeoisie as a class. During the investigation, we do not look for evidence that the accused acted in deed or word against the Soviet power. The first questions you ought to put are: To what class does he belong? What is his origin? What is his education and profession? And it is these questions that ought to determine the fate of the accused.

Next are the instructions of influential feminist Catherine MacKinnon, who advises legislatures throughout the world on how to punish men who fit a certain profile:

> Instead of asking did this individual commit a crime of battery against that individual, the court would ask did this member of a group sexually trained to woman-hating aggression commit this particular act of woman-hating sexual aggression? . . . The testimony of other women . . . would be central: How does this man treat women sexually? . . . We might have learned whether pornography . . . was part of the defendant's training.[38]

This shifts the prosecution from the legal culpability of an individual for a specific deed to the component in a political campaign against a targeted group. We are told that we "must stop the scourge of domestic violence"[39] or rape or stalking or human trafficking, but no one launches political campaigns to stop the scourge of premeditated murder or armed robbery. Here the aim is not to control crime; it is to eliminate a group that powerful interests and officials have identified as a political enemy. Specific individuals are not named and evidence not presented of precisely what deeds they have committed; let alone is there an indictment by a grand jury that has weighed evidence. Instead, we are told about new epidemics of new crimes with new names of which no one had previously heard. These crimes arise not because of increased criminality but because of changes in our collective political consciousness whereby what we previously saw as imperfections (or "power imbalances") in the human condition, become crimes of which only some can be guilty. Thus the constant demand for government

---

38. Vladimir Tismaneanu, *The Devil in History* (Berkeley: University of California Press, 2013), 5; Weiss and Young, *Feminist Jurisprudence*.

39. The phrase yielded 832 results on a Google search.

campaigns to "raise awareness" of unnamed nonviolent malefactors said to be guilty of nebulous, newfangled crimes, which no one really understands because no precise definition exists. Often the alleged "crime" is said to result from incorrect "attitudes," including political opinions or religious convictions. This necessitates official campaigns to "re-educate" law enforcement officials, defendants, and everyone else with acceptable opinions so they will see crimes of political oppression to be punished and criminal oppressors to be arrested where previously they saw only a family quarrel or hurt feelings. These propaganda campaigns transform police officers from the keepers of public order into armed political activists charged with rescuing the "oppressed," and they generate public hysteria that renders fair trials impossible for those actually accused of these catch-all offenses. "I can think of no other areas in life in which putative sufferers require so much help in order to recognize the damage supposedly inflicted on them and have come to depend on such careful instruction in how to script the accounts of their victimhood."[40] The villains are then rounded up en masse in well-publicized "raids" that visually declare their guilt to the media, the public, and any prospective jurors.

Crimes most of us never witness (and some that we had previously never heard of) are happening all around us, we are told by the "awareness" campaigns, the criminals lurking in our very midst, perhaps in our own family. The person we thought was our neighbor is a "survivor" of domestic "violence." A college student is in fact a rape "victim." The *au pair* has been "trafficked." Well, if not them, then others "just like them." Perhaps we ourselves are victims. A lawyer can tell us.

New jargon enters our daily discourse and penetrates our consciousness and the private corners of our lives. You are not just being disagreeable; you are "abusive." Perhaps it is "domestic" abuse, closely akin to "domestic violence." And by adopting the quasi-criminal buzzwords we become acculturated into the mentality of accusation and punishment.

And with acceptance comes use. The power to have one's critics incarcerated is highly intoxicating, as any dictator can attest. It is a pleasure to which today's feminist and homosexualist ideologues have succumbed. But more than that, it is a pleasure they are allowing the rest of us to taste. For one need not be an ideologue to enjoy either the new sexual freedom or the power it confers. Accusations quickly become available as weapons to be used in personal as well as political vendettas. At least one British Labour politician has discovered that criminal accu-

40. Patai, *Heterophobia*, Kindle Locations 1069–70.

sations of rape and child abuse provide an effective method of destroying political opponents.[41] (And the ultimate use of the law as a weapon against men who cannot defend themselves comes with the prosecution of dead men by feminist prosecutrixes.)[42] But more seriously, the power to have one's spouse or parent incarcerated can be similarly exhilarating and "liberating"—especially if he is "controlling" and fits the description in the "awareness" campaigns. But no society can remain free that allows criminal accusations to become weapons in political competitions, let alone in private disputes and family disagreements.

All this feeds conveniently into the increasing bureaucratization and feminization of the police. Along with government "awareness" campaigns, flimsy accusations are treated seriously because they rationalize police budgets, especially feminized and sexualized police, by turning law-abiding citizens into safe, nonviolent criminals for female and homosexual policepersons to arrest[43] (or worse).[44]

The issue here is not particular miscarriages of justice, which it is not our task here to prove. The point is that the politicized crime industry condemns itself as a systematic miscarriage of justice by its own campaigns to "redefine" crime and render guilt and innocence indistinguishable.

Perhaps the most revealing indictment against us all is that none of these draconian measures is noticed or debated. Instead of examining and scrutinizing the demagoguery, journalists and scholars—those we normally expect to investigate and analyze public policy (and who are keenly aware how easily accusations of abetting sex crimes can be turned on them)[45]—themselves fan the flames of mass hysteria, as zealots and

---

41. Fraser Nelson, "Tom Watson Had the Police in His Political Thrall," *Daily Telegraph*, 15 October 2015 (http://www.telegraph.co.uk/news/uknews/law-and-order/11934689/Tom-Watson-had-the-police-in-his-thrall-that-is-the-real-scandal.html).

42. Dan Hodges, "Even Death Will Not Spare Lord Janner from 'Justice,'" *Daily Telegraph*, 21 December 2015, http://www.telegraph.co.uk/news/uknews/law-and-order/12063128/Even-death-will-not-spare-Lord-Janner-from-justice.html.

43. Wrong Arm of the Law," leading column, *Daily Telegraph*, 31 July 2012 (http://www.telegraph.co.uk/comment/telegraph-view/9432252/Wrong-arm-of-the-law.html); "Christian Preacher Vows to Fight...," *Daily Mail*, 2 May 2010 (http://www.dailymail.co.uk/news/article-1270650/Christian-preacher-trial-public-order-offences-saying-homosexuality-sin.html#ixzz0n9nOnTGZ).

44. "A Tragedy Plays out in Little Rock...," *Washington Post*, 6 May (2016?), https://www.washingtonpost.com/investigations/a-tragedy-plays-out-in-little-rock-when-a-police-officer-kills-a-colleagues-father/2016/05/06/df77595c-ef6c-11e5-85a6-2132cf446d0a_story.html.

45. See the Introduction.

ideologues, invoking "violence" that never took place, and running wild in search of unnamed "abusers," "rapists," "batterers," "pedophiles," "deadbeats," "bullies," and "traffickers," most of whom are never shown to exist.

Yet so acculturated have we all become by the new "awareness," that accused fathers, soldiers, students, religious believers, and others themselves believe the propaganda and are convinced that they alone are being falsely accused amid epidemics of "real" perpetrators. "It is typical for a man to believe . . . the media myth of the Evil Male," writes Robert Seidenberg. "While he knows that he is a great father himself, he thinks everyone else is a deadbeat dad."[46] "According to a recent . . . survey of college and university presidents, nearly one-third agree that sexual assault is prevalent on college campuses nationwide," writes Michael Kimmel. "But only 6% believe it's prevalent at their own institutions."[47] The complaint invariably begins, "When [sexual harassment, child abuse, nonpayment of child support, domestic violence, campus rape, etc.] is such a serious epidemic, why are they targeting *me* for prosecution, when I am innocent and they have no evidence against me?" It is almost impossible to convince such people (let alone anyone else) that no such epidemic exists and that the other targets of accusations are as innocent as they are. "I do want to recognize sexual assault is real and horrible. I'm happy to know there are procedures and things put in place to bring justice to those who are sexually assaulted," says one accused student. "But in cases like mine..."[48] The reality gradually dawns on them when they find that everyone assumes (or finds it safer to assume) that they are as guilty as they assume the rest to be.

As the sexual left advances its agenda through the penal system, we must reassess, if not our values, at least their application. "Law and order" is an imperative in every society, but in ideological tyrannies where criminal law has been commandeered to serve a political agenda and punish the innocent, how far should we champion law and order uncritically as a virtue in itself? It is time to accept that this is an appropriate question to be applying in the Western democracies. We must consider the discomforting possibility that, largely under influence of

---

46. Robert Seidenberg, *The Father's Emergency Guide to Divorce-Custody Battle* (Takoma Park, Maryland: JES, 1997), 38.

47. "A Recipe for Sexual Assault," *Atlantic*, 24 August 2014, http://www.theatlantic.com/education/archive/2015/08/what-makes-a-campus-rape-prone/402065/.

48. Emily Shire, "Sexual Assault: The Accused Speak Out," *Daily Caller*, 28 January 2016, http://www.thedailybeast.com/articles/2016/01/28/sexual-assault-the-accused-speak-out.html.

sexual ideologues who feel perfectly safe in launching completely baseless accusations of the most hideous crimes, we have long since passed the point where the real lawbreakers sit as judges, prosecutors, and jailors, and the innocent are being marched off in handcuffs.

Rape and Sexual Assault

There is no crime like rape. Not only is it morally repugnant, to the point of once being considered "worse than death," but with no other traditional crime is the guilt of the accused so completely dependent on the state-of-mind of the accuser. For this reason rape is the easiest crime to politicize. One sex alone can accuse, and one sex alone can be accused. In Susan Brownmiller's famous and influential dictum, rape is "a conscious process of intimidation by which *all* men keep *all* women in a state of fear."[49] Innocence therefore is no excuse, because there is no such thing. All men are part of the conspiracy.

With rape a political crime, new crimes followed logically. Rape sets the standard for other gender crimes. As we will see again and again, it is the subjective mindset of the accuser, not the objective act of the accused, that determines guilt. Thus the definition of crime is subject to almost infinite elasticity and expansion to include almost anything and anyone, and the accused becomes guilty by definition. (In April 2014, on what authority it is unclear, the White House boasted that it has "modernized the definition of 'rape'" to mean something very different from what plain English suggests and most people understand, and it is not the first.) As the meaning of the word expands by government fiat, so does the criminal population. The debasement of the language thus contributes directly to the expanding power of the state's criminal machinery over the citizenry.

This is spreading and politicizing other areas of the law. Rape-as-political-oppression is poisoning our entire criminal justice system and turning it into an instrument of political ideology.

In recent years, a number of prominent figures have been subject to questionable rape charges: Julian Assange, Dominique Strauss-Kahn, Silvio Berlusconi, Bill Cosby. British Justice Minister Kenneth Clark was pilloried not for committing rape but for making politically incorrect statements about it. And false rape charges have dominated the headlines from time to time: Tawana Brawley, Koby Bryant, the Duke University lacrosse players. Yet when the charges invariably prove false,

---

49. Susan Brownmiller, *Against Our Will: Men, Women, and Rape* (New York: Simon and Schuster, 1975), original emphasis.

silence ensues. Commentators of both left and right conjure up excuses and blame scapegoats: right-wing political conspiracies, left-wing reverse racism or class warfare, corrupt prosecutors. No one dares to point the finger at the common perpetrator behind all these miscarriages of justice: the feminist rape industry.

It is not surprising then that the earliest crime used by feminist ideologues to politicize criminal justice was rape. Early suffragettes and female temperance campaigners advocated castration for rapists, notwithstanding the Eighth Amendment prohibition on "cruel and unusual punishment." Both Elizabeth Cady Stanton and Susan B. Anthony, who opposed the death penalty for everyone else, wanted accused rapists killed.[50]

Others may agree, until they learn that, under feminist influence, rape has been redefined to mean virtually anything, eliminating the distinction between forced and consensual sex. Legal theorist Catherine MacKinnon asks "whether consent is a meaningful concept" and has repeatedly suggested that virtually all heterosexual intercourse amounts to rape. McKinnon is highly influential at law schools throughout the United States and Canada and advises the governments of individual states and provinces. "Clearly, there is much to fear from an approach to rape law based on a theory with that sort of dogma at its core," write Michael Weiss and Cathy Young. "It means that the government can enter American bedrooms to force men to receive explicit consent to sexual activity . . . or risk a jail sentence."[51] In fact, it means that explicit consent is no defense when meting out jail sentences.

Men accused of rape today receive virtually no due process protection from either prosecutors or grand juries, which once existed specifically to protect the public from overzealous prosecutors. "Now people can be charged with virtually no evidence," says Boston defense attorney and former sex crimes prosecutor Rikki Klieman. "If a female comes in and says she was sexually assaulted, then on her word alone, with nothing else—and I mean nothing else, no investigation—the police will go out and arrest someone."[52]

Not surprisingly, false rape accusations have exploded. Almost daily we see men released after decades in prison because DNA tests prove

50. Gottschalk, *Prison*, 119.

51. Weiss and Young, *Feminist Jurisprudence*.

52. Quoted in Weiss and Young, *Feminist Jurisprudence*, and in Jack Kammer, *Good Will Toward Men: Women Talk Candidly About the Balance of Power Between the Sexes* (New York: St. Martin's Press, 1994), 153.

they were wrongly convicted.[53] And they are the fortunate ones. While DNA testing has righted some wrongs, the corruption of the rape industry is so systemic that, as the Duke University lacrosse case demonstrated, hard evidence of innocence is no barrier to prosecution and conviction. "A defendant who can absolutely prove his innocence—most obviously Reade Seligmann in the lacrosse case—can nonetheless *still* be convicted, based solely on the word of the accuser" write two principal authorities on that case. Indeed, the North Carolina statute states that an accusation is tantamount to a conviction: "naming the person accused" along with the time and place "will support a verdict of guilty of rape" of one kind or another. Stuart Taylor and K.C. Johnson write that "Such provisions are unique to rape law,"[54] meaning they are not found in standard criminal statutes, but it would be more precise to say that they are unique to feminist gender crimes, for equivalents now exist with domestic violence and child abuse, as we will see.

The feminist principle that "women never lie about rape" is unchallengeable not only in the media and academia, but in the courtroom itself.[55] "Although it may not be 'politically correct' to question the veracity of a women's complaint of rape, failing to consider the accuser may be intentionally lying effectively eradicates the presumption of innocence," writes a forensic examiner, timidly. "This constitutional right is especially significant when dealing with allegations of rape, as in most jurisdictions *sex offenses are the only crimes that do not require corroborating evidence for conviction.*"[56] This presumption of guilt highlights the danger of politicizing violent crime and encounters almost no

---

53. "Jurors in Tears as they Clear Student of Rape—Then Discover Another Man Falsely Accused by Same 'Victim' Had Killed Himself," *Daily Mail*, 25 May 2010; "Innocent Man Freed after 27 Years," *Express*, 31 July 2010. For more documented cases, see the Innocence Project site: www.innocenceproject.org.

54. Stuart Taylor and K.C. Johnson, *Until Proven Innocent: Political Correctness and the Shameful Injustices of the Duke Lacrosse Rape Case* (New York: Thomas Dunne, 2007), 379 (emphasis original).

55. Feminists have popularized an arbitrary figure of 2% of rape charges are false, but this figure is "an ideological fabrication." Edward Greer, "The Truth Behind Legal Dominance Feminism's 'Two Percent False Claim' Figure," *Loyola of Los Angeles Law Review*, vol. 33 (2000), 949 (http://ncfm.org/libraryfiles/Children/rape/greer.pdf). "Because the precise rate of false or mistaken reporting is unknowable," writes Stephen Henrick, "the argument has no empirical support." "A Hostile Environment for Student Defendants: Title IX and Sexual Assault on College Campuses," *Northern Kentucky Law Review*, vol. 40, no. 1, 88.

56. Bruce Gross, "False Rape Allegations: An Assault on Justice," *The Forensic Examiner* (2011, accessed 15 May), http://www.theforensicexaminer.com/archive/spring09/15/ (emphasis added).

opposition. "The certainty that all men accused of rape are guilty drove government policy during virtually the whole 13 years of Labour rule," writes Melanie Phillips.[57]

Likewise the feminist claim, parroted by the Obama White House, that rape and sexual assault are hugely "under-reported."[58] How can anyone say that a crime is "under-reported"? This likewise presupposes that the claimant knows that multiple people are guilty of crimes which no one has reported, for which no evidence has been presented, and for which no defendant has been accused, charged, tried, or convicted.

The reality is very different. "Any honest veteran sex assault investigator will tell you that rape is one of the most falsely reported crimes," says prosecutor Craig Silverman,

> I am unaware of any Colorado prosecutor who put as many rapists away for as much prison time as I did during my prosecutorial career.... However, during my time as a prosecutor who made case filing decisions, I was amazed to see all the false rape allegations that were made to the Denver Police Department. It was remarkable and surprising to me. You would have to see it to believe it.[59]

Purdue University sociologist Eugene J. Kanin found that "41% of the total disposed rape cases were officially declared false" during a nine-year period, "that is, by the complainant's admission that no rape had occurred and the charge, therefore, was false." A follow-up study at a university found 50% of accusations were false, again purely by the recantation of the accuser. Unrecanted accusations certainly put the actual percentage of false allegations much higher. Kanin concluded that "these false allegations appear to serve three major functions for the complainants: providing an alibi, seeking revenge, and obtaining sympathy and attention."[60] The Center for Military Readiness has encountered additional motivations: "False rape accusations also have been filed to extort money from celebrities, to gain sole custody of children in

57. "How to Restore Justice to Rape Trials," *Daily Mail*, 24 May 2010, http://www.melaniephillips.com/articles/.

58. Mark Perry, "Using White House Claim of Under-Reporting, Only 1 in 36 Women at Ohio State are Sexually Assaulted, Not 1 in 5," American Enterprise Institute website: http://www.aei-ideas.org/2014/05/using-white-house-claim-of-under-reporting-only-1-in-36-women-at-ohio-state-are-sexually-assaulted-not-1-in-5/, 9 May 2014.

59. Craig Silverman, "Craig's Court: I Call Them as I See Them," 2 February 2004, http://web.archive.org/web/20050404230831/http://www.thedenverchannel.com/kobebryanttrial/2812198/detail.html.

60. Eugene J. Kanin, "False Rape Allegations," *Archives of Sexual Behavior*, vol. 23, no. 1 (1994), 1–2.

divorce cases, and even to escape military deployments to war zones." According to a report of the Defense Department Inspector General released in 2005, approximately 73% of women and 72% of men at the military service academies believe that false accusations of sexual assault are a problem.[61]

These are not cases of mistaken identity, as media attempts to disguise the epidemic of false convictions invariably imply. They involve the politicization of the justice system for the purpose of knowingly punishing the innocent. Perhaps the clearest admission that false accusations are a political weapon is that feminists themselves vigorously oppose any prosecution of accusers for making them.[62]

In the infamous Duke University lacrosse case, Durham, North Carolina, prosecutor Michael Nifong suppressed solid evidence of the innocence of the three rape defendants for months and proceeded to prosecute men he knew to be innocent in an effort to send them to prison for as much as thirty years each.

Nothing suggests the Duke case was unusual. Nifong had willing accomplices throughout the state and local governments: assistant prosecutors, police departments, crime lab technicians, judges, and the state bar, plus the media. And again, no grand jury exercised its function to restrain Nifong. Though Nifong was eventually challenged and disbarred (but only after the evidence became overwhelming), he was never criminally prosecuted for framing innocent people. Moreover, his downfall occurred only after highly unusual media coverage; his fellow prosecutors' first response was to circle the wagons around their obviously crooked colleague and defend his prosecution of innocent men, an open admission that he did nothing out of the ordinary and that they all use similar techniques to railroad the innocent.

Tellingly, no official inquiry or investigation sought to determine how widespread such attempts by prosecutors to frame law-abiding citizens are. Neither has any systematic investigation by the media, civil liberties groups, or academic scholars determined why so many innocent men are being incarcerated on fabricated allegations and evidence of rape.[63]

Indeed, the central point to be made about the Duke case is precisely the one even few critics raised: it is far from unique. If such intentional

---

61. "Sex, Lies, and Rapes," internet site of the Center for Military Readiness (http://www.cmrlink.org/social.asp?docID=276, accessed 5 August 2008).

62. See the petition at http://womenagainstrape.net/content/sign-support-rape-survivors.

63. One exception being Taylor and Johnson, *Until Proven Innocent*, ch. 23.

injustice can be perpetrated against men whose case attracted vast media attention—the supposed "disinfectant of sunlight"—what befalls those who languish in obscurity, victims of rigged justice that is less palpable? "If police officers and a district attorney can systematically railroad us with absolutely no evidence whatsoever," said one defendant, "I can't imagine what they'd do to people who do not have the resources to defend themselves."[64] Not what they "would" do: what they now do, all the time.[65] "Innocent men are arrested and even imprisoned as a result of bogus claims," writes Linda Fairstein, former head of the sex-crimes unit of the Manhattan District Attorney's Office, who estimates that half of all rape reports are unfounded.[66]

The Duke case also demonstrates that no penalties are imposed on those who fabricate rape accusations. (The accuser was subsequently charged with other crimes, including felony arson, child abuse, vandalism, and eventually murder, but never for making false rape accusations.)[67] "Essentially, there are no formal negative consequences for the person who files a false report of rape," writes one forensic expert. "Although there are grounds for bringing legal action against the accuser, it is virtually never done. Even should a charge be filed, in most jurisdictions filing a false report is only a misdemeanor." "Rape shield" laws prevent defense attorneys not only from introducing an accuser's sexual history; "they have been used to exclude prior false accusations of rape filed by the alleged victim."[68] In Britain, women who have confessed to repeated fabricated rape charges have been exempted from jail.[69] (Also in Britain, incidentally, "A man wrongly jailed when a woman cried rape has failed to prevent being charged £12,500 for his 'board and lodging' while in prison.")[70] In one of the harshest punishments yet recorded, a woman in Washington State was sentenced to

64. Ibid., 357.

65. Taylor and Johnson, *Until Proven Innocent*, 358.

66. Ibid., 374.

67. Jesse Deconto, "Crystal Mangum Indicted in Boyfriend's Death," *Raleigh News and Observer*, 19 April 2011 (http://www.newsobserver.com/2011/04/18/1138586/crystal-mangum-indicted-for-boyfriends.html).

68. Gross, "False Rape Allegations."

69. "Woman Admits SECOND Cry Rape Offence . . . but is Spared Jail," *Daily Mail*, 1 August 2010 (http://www.dailymail.co.uk/news/article-1299310/Woman-admits-SECOND-rape-offence-spared-jail-heavily-pregnant.html).

70. Sam Greenhill, "Victim of False Rape Claim Must Pay £12,500 for Bed and Board in Jail," *Daily Mail*, 1 January 2008 (http://www.dailymail.co.uk/pages/live/articles/news/news.html?in_article_id=505428&in_page_id=1770&ito=newsnow, accessed 28 November 2008).

eight days in jail and fined $250 for filing a knowingly false accusation of rape that could have resulted in a life sentence for the accused.[71]

The title of Taylor and Johnson's book, *Until Proven Innocent*, indicates how rape law exhibits a feature we see repeatedly with feminism's new gender crimes: a presumption of guilt that forces the accused to prove his innocence, often against an accusation that is ill-defined. "The State of Washington has openly shifted the burden of proving consent to the defendant," write Weiss and Young. The state supreme court simply cited and approved "legislative intent to shift the burden of proof on the issue to the defense." As with most such changes, the effect (and the only possible intention) is not to punish more actual rapists but to criminalize more men. "The result of this unconstitutional burden-shifting will be not to jail more violent rapists—lack of consent is easy enough for the state to prove in those cases," write Weiss and Young, "but to make it easier to send someone to jail for failing to get an explicit nod of consent from an apparently willing partner before engaging in sex."[72] In fact, it does more than that: as the Common Law has long recognized, it makes conviction virtually certain.

It is not necessary therefore to marshal particular cases to show that rape adjudications are unjust. The constant innovations advocated by the rape adjudicators themselves make it very clear, as they seek every opportunity and means to expand the definition of rape to include ever-more behavior and make it easier to convict ever-more men. "Feminists themselves . . . write openly of 'redefining rape,'" notes one observer. "For those of us who still speak traditional English, this amounts to an admission that they are falsely accusing men."[73]

The *reductio ad absurdum* came with a California law requiring that, to avoid a rape conviction, male university students must "demonstrate they obtained verbal 'affirmative consent' before engaging in sexual activity." What constitutes such "consent" is unclear. Cathy Young points out that "verbal consent could always be retroactively revoked," again making all sex rape if the woman decides (at any time) that it is. A Canadian campus campaign warns that "if it's not loud and clear, it's not consent—it's sexual assault." Young remarks, "Perhaps eventually, someone

71. Peyton Whitely, "Woman Pleads Guilty to False Rape Report," *Seattle Times*, 19 March 2008 (http://seattletimes.nwsource.com/html/localnews/2004291649_false19e. html, accessed 28 November 2008).

72. Weiss and Young, *Feminist Jurisprudence*.

73. F. Roger Devlin, *Sexual Utopia in Power* (San Francisco: Counter-Currents, 2015), 16.

will calculate the appropriate decibel level at which 'Yes' becomes valid," for purposes of avoiding prison.[74] When asked how innocent people are supposed to prove that they received verbal consent, the California assemblywoman who authored the law replied, "Your guess is as good as mine."[75]

The effect is to criminalize more of the population. "Since most couples have engaged in sex without 'verbal' consent," writes attorney Hans Bader, "supporters ... are effectively redefining most people, and most happily-married couples, as rapists." Bader describes the absurdity of obtaining explicit verbal agreement to each stage (what constitutes a new "stage"?) of sex. Because verbal consent is impossible to prove, the measure effectively requires written consent—"or, better yet, a notarized signature"[76]—at each stage. How many notarized signatures must a man obtain in a given encounter in order to avoid prison? Everyone knows this will not happen, and so the effect (and clearly the purpose) is to create another tool to criminalize male sexuality and men. "The law has no bearing on the vast majority of sexual encounters," one proponent revealingly argues. "It only applies when a student files a sexual assault complaint."[77] In other words, virtually all sex is officially redefined as rape, but no one will notice unless a woman decides to exercise the ever-available option to prosecute her husband or partner for what, on her say-so, is suddenly criminal rape. "The 'yes means yes' law effectively defines every sexual encounter as rape," writes Ashe Schow, "unless neither party turns the other in to police."[78]

74. "Want to Have Sex? Sign this Contract," *Minding the Campus*, 20 February 2014, http://www.mindingthecampus.com/originals/2014/02/want_to_have_sex_sign_this_con.

75. Jason Garshfield, "The Underlying Problems of SB 967 and Affirmative Consent," *Daily Nexus*, 16 February 2016 (http://dailynexus.com/2016-02-12/the-underlying-problems-of-sb-967-and-affirmative-consent/).

76. Hans Bader, "California Activists Seek to Redefine Quiet, Consensual Sex as Rape...," *Liberty Unyielding*, 14 March 2014, http://libertyunyielding.com/2014/03/09/california-activists-seek-redefine-quiet-consensual-sex-rape/#QWsXwoqRFsRqcOzF.99; Cathy Young, "Campus Rape: The Problem with 'Yes Means Yes,'" *Time*, 29 August 2014 (http://time.com/3222176/campus-rape-the-problem-with-yes-means-yes).

77. Amanda Marcotte, "Do Not Fear California's New Affirmative Consent Law," *Slate*, 29 September 2014, http://www.slate.com/blogs/xx_factor/2014/09/29/affirmative_consent_in_california_gov_jerry_brown_signs_the_yes_means_yes.html.

78. "California's Sexual Re-Education Camps are Coming Soon," *Washington Examiner*, 2 June 2015 (http://www.washingtonexaminer.com/californias-sexual-re-education-camps-are-coming-soon/article/2565477?utm_campaign=Conservative%20Inbox:%20Top%205&utm_source=Conservative%20Inbox:%20Top%205%20-%2006/04/15&utm_medium=email).

Following predictably, the American Law Institute (ALI) began campaigning to adopt this standard federally, effectively criminalizing the entire sexually active population of the United States. "Any act of sex in which permission is not repeatedly requested and granted would put at least one of the parties, usually men, in legal jeopardy," writes Schow. "Absent the repeated 'May I…?' and affirmative responses, any woman could later have her partner locked up over unexpressed mental reservations. Men could make the same accusations." Opponents illustrate the potential: "Person A and Person B are on a date and walking down the street. Person A, feeling romantically and sexually attracted, timidly reaches out to hold B's hand. . . . Person B does nothing, but six months later files a criminal complaint." Schow summarizes the opponents' arguments: Under ALI's new rules, "Person A is guilty of 'criminal sexual contact.'" The proposed measure:

> defines "sexual contact" expansively, to include any touching of any body part of another person. . . . Any kind of contact may qualify; there are no limits on either the body part touched or the manner in which it is touched.
>
> Person A would be guilty of the act only if Person B filed a complaint, but therein lies a profound problem. . . . Everything is potentially a sexual assault unless done strictly according to their rules about obtaining prior consent to every action, no matter how innocuous, of every sexual encounter. There is no need to say "no." Without the presence of a prior "yes," the act is already an assault.
>
> By this definition, millions of Americans—perhaps almost all sexually active people—become offenders.

The ALI proposal "shifts the burden of proof from the accuser to the accused, who would now have to show he—it is usually he—obtained consent in order to prove there was no assault." Rape law is already moving in this direction, as we have seen, but this makes the lack of documented "consent" more plausible, since it sets an impossible hurdle that common sense tells any jury could not possibly have been met. Opposition groups point out that this "would make prosecutors' jobs incredibly easy."

> They could merely tell juries that they must find someone guilty because no evidence could be produced that consent was obtained. The prosecutor would need no evidence beyond the accusation, and could tell the accused: "Prove me wrong."

Criminal conviction could be avoided only by having a notary present to legitimate each physical movement: Unsurprisingly, as Schow comments in her report, presenting evidence "is not an issue that this draft really addresses."[79]

Apparently hyperbolic libertarian warnings that the government is making us "all criminals" appear to be validated, but the cutting edge of the trend is (once again) the radical sexuality that those same libertarian Cassandras ignore.

Incidentally, this legal trend is also being invoked to indoctrinate and sexualize children with "consent education," a ploy that carries other potential benefits from the standpoint of sexual radicalism. "They are trying to plant a notion that a kindergartner could consent to sexual relations," says David Usher of the Center for Marriage Policy. "A kindergartner could consent, or can consent, to a sexual relationship and needs to be taught about how to do that as a kindergartner." As we will see elsewhere, the ideologues replace traditional morality with a government-approved definition of sin. "We already do teach young children about this. It's called right and wrong, and that's what us parents teach our kids," said Dianna Thompson of the American Coalition for Fathers and Children. "Why are we going to be teaching our children about issues they are not even supposed to be concerned about at that age?" Thompson suggests a young boy could be held culpable of "unwanted touching" and be stigmatized as someone to be watched as a potential rapist.[80]

Feminists openly advocate that convicting men of rape is a goal to be pursued for its own sake, regardless of the evidence in particular cases, and they agitate for using whatever political means are available to increase convictions as a virtue in itself. "The real scandal, when it comes to rape, is that only 6% of rapes reported to the police end in a conviction," writes Christina Patterson in the *Independent*.[81] Why do we have trials and juries and due process of law, when Ms. Patterson knows that defendants of whose cases she is ignorant are guilty? (Low conviction rates for rape reflect the fact that, under feminist pressure, they are calculated differently: "'Conviction rate' usually describes the percentage of all the cases that are brought to court that end in a conviction.

79. Ashe Schow, "Has the Federal Government Ever Had Sex?" *Washington Examiner*, 15 June 2015 (http://www.washingtonexaminer.com/has-the-federal-govt-ever-had-sex/article/2565963). ALI also devised radical changes in divorce law permitting highly intrusive government intervention into private homes for non-criminal matters. See chapter II, under "Divorce."

80. "Activists: Schools Must Teach Sex Consent to Kindergartners," *WorldNetDaily*, 30 December 2014, http://www.wnd.com/2014/12/activists-schools-must-teach-sex-consent-to-kindergartners/.

81. "It's Miliband, Not Clarke, Who Should Be Ashamed," 19 May 2011.

However, when dealing with rape, the term has come to describe the percentage of all cases recorded by the police as rape that end up with someone being convicted of rape. The use of a much larger denominator has the inevitable consequence of producing a much lower figure for the conviction rate.")[82]

It is hardly surprising therefore that the process for adjudicating rape is openly rigged in favor of conviction. Rape accusers remain anonymous, but the accused do not, even after the accusation is demonstrated to be false. The past sexual history of the accuser is not admissible as evidence, but that of the accused is. Accusers are exempt from polygraph tests, but not the accused. Even a history of false accusations is not admissible.[83] Apparently police are now being instructed hide evidence that exculpates the accused.[84]

As with other new gender crimes, the rape industry has generated a corps of paid professional accusers known as "victim advocates" whose function is to secure convictions of men of whose actions they have no first-hand knowledge. While applauding this development, Taylor and Johnson note with understatement that "many of the women who choose such careers see themselves as advocates for rape accusers."[85] Indeed, they have chosen careers as rape accusers.

"Because DNA evidence has subjected rape convictions to especially exacting scrutiny, it seems probable that the error rates are higher in other cases," write Taylor and Johnson.[86] This ignores how DNA results themselves can be rigged. The *Washington Post*, among others, has documented how feminist crime laboratory technicians doctor and fabricate evidence to frame men they know to be innocent.[87]

Crime laboratories are notorious for not only backlogs and mistakes, but also for such falsified results. The Innocence Project has identified and publicized numerous such cases, though they have been less than

---

82. Guy Norfolk, "Leda and the Swan—and Other Myths about Rape," David Jenkins Professorial Lecture, Royal College of Physicians, 7 May 2010, http://falseallegations.wordpress.com/2010/12/22/8/.

83. Gross, "False Rape Allegations."

84. "University of Texas Tells Its Police to Hide Evidence that Favors Students Accused of Rape," *College Fix*, 14 March 2016, http://www.thecollegefix.com/post/26614.

85. Taylor and Johnson, *Until Proven Innocent*, 377.

86. Ibid., 360.

87. "FBI Admits Flaws in Hair Analysis over Decades," 18 April 2015, https://www.washingtonpost.com/local/crime/fbi-overstated-forensic-hair-matches-in-nearly-all-criminal-trials-for-decades/2015/04/18/39c8d8c6-e515-11e4-b510-962fcfabc310_story.html. The *Post* and every other media outlet go to great length to disguise the fact that the cases overwhelming involve rape.

candid about how many of the "wrongfully convicted" are charged with rape and how many of the falsified crime lab results involve rape. It is clear from their own accounts that the proportion is overwhelming. According to their website, 272 of 349 cases involve "sex crimes." The following is a random sampling of all their cases on a single date, before they stopped providing the daily listing.[88]

- Cases in Maryland and Florida in which crucial evidence in rape trials has gone missing. When labs are overworked and underfunded.

- North Carolina completed construction this month on an expanded crime lab. This expansion effort aims to reduce the severe backlog in North Carolina labs, which included thousands of rape cases.

- Read about the case of Ronnie Taylor, who was released Oct. 9 after DNA evidence proved his innocence of a rape for which he had served 12 years in prison. An error at the Houston crime lab contributed to Taylor's wrongful conviction.

- "It's fear," Anderson, of Hanover, VA, said of the bureaucratic resistance to clearing the way for such analyses. DNA evidence exonerated Anderson in 2001 of a rape conviction, after he was sentenced to 210 years in prison and served 15. "No one wants to admit a mistake has been made."

- Commercial Dispatch: Brewer goes free on 1992 child murder, rape charges.

- "We need to establish additional safeguards to make sure this stuff doesn't happen here," said former Attorney General Jim Petro, a Republican who while in office pushed for DNA testing that freed a man wrongfully convicted of rape and murder.

"It is time we stop kidding ourselves in believing that what happened in Dallas is somehow unique," said Jeff Blackburn of the Innocence Project of Texas about an innocent man who had just been released after 27 years in prison. "What happened in Dallas is common."[89] The district attorney attributed the miscarriages of justice to "a past culture of overly aggressive prosecutors seeking convictions at any cost," yet nothing indicates that this "culture" has changed. The Innocence Project said it

88. Innocence Project website: https://www.innocenceproject.org/all-cases/#involved-yes (accessed 15 March 2017). The daily listing was at http://www.innocenceproject.org/news/Blog-Search.php?check=true&tag=59.

89. Innocence Project website: https://www.innocenceproject.org/charles-chatman-released-15th-person-to-be-cleared-by-dna-evidence-in-dallas/.

planned to investigate 450 similar cases in Dallas alone, but it too refuses to challenge the feminist orthodoxy that women never lie.

Notwithstanding grandstanding politicians promising "to make sure this stuff doesn't happen," it will continue to happen so long as officials owe their jobs to ensuring that it does happen. Self-serving clichés about how government functionaries are "overworked and under-funded" indicate a thriving bureaucratic enterprise that can create busi-ness for itself by encouraging hysteria and accusations. After all, if they simply stop accusing innocent men they would no longer be "over-worked and underfunded"; indeed, they would no longer be necessary, and their positions could be eliminated, which is why the problem con-tinues.

Government funding in fact drives much of the injustice. It was "crit-ical to the development of the anti-rape movement," writes Marie Gottschalk, who describes how feminist groups politicized rape and positioned themselves to receive lucrative government funding. Politi-cizing rape dramatically increased federal police power where no consti-tutional justification exists for federal involvement at all. "With the help of LEAA [Law Enforcement Assistance Administration] money and other public financing, the government successfully absorbed many of the independent rape crisis centers and services . . . into its professional, hierarchical bureaucracy. Federal policy encouraged the creation of pro-grams for [alleged?] rape victims in established community agencies through incentives like grants." Gottschalk does not inquire how many rape accusations are recanted or patently false, though she does back-handedly reveal that federal funding incentivizes conviction: "The LEAA heralded those rape crisis centers that contributed to the report-ing and conviction rates for sexual assault." She also argues that feminist groups are "profoundly co-opted" by government agencies providing the funding, seemingly only to lament that their ideological purity and fervor were blunted by the money and power. "If the rape issue is viewed narrowly, these groups were a success," she concedes. But lamen-tably, "They abdicated the earlier commitment to functioning as inde-pendent sites for an oppositional ideology."[90]

If all else fails, acquitted defendants can simply be accused again. If they cannot be convicted through rape laws, they can be charged under federal "civil rights" statutes. Then they can be punished not for actually committing any rape but merely because their politically heterodox opinions and the conduct of their personal lives violates someone's

---

90. Gottschalk, *Prison*, 125–26, 132–33.

"civil rights." Catherine MacKinnon has explained the totalitarian justice.[91]

The media watchdog is more of a lapdog that never barks. "Nobody dependent on the mainstream media for information about rape would have any idea how frequent false claims are," writes Stuart Taylor of the *National Journal*, who was nominated for the Pulitzer Prize for his coverage of the case. "Most journalists simply ignore evidence contradicting the feminist line." Taylor and Johnson observe a feature of rape reporting that we will find with reporting on domestic violence and child abuse: "calling a rape complainant 'the victim'—with no 'alleged.'"[92] "Unnamed complainants are labeled 'victims' even before legal proceedings determine that a crime has been committed," according to the Center for Military Readiness. "Publicly named men accused of misconduct are treated as 'innocent until accused.'"[93] The media also give rape accusers anonymity, even when their accusations turn out to be fabrications. As rape hysteria became a frenzy in 2015, Christina Hoff Sommers writes: "Our detour into madness might never have happened had those investigative journalists . . . resisted their 'nightmare' narrative and just reported the truth."[94]

It is ironic that so much hysteria, false accusations, and distorted scholarship occur on university campuses, which supposedly exist to pursue truth. "On campus after campus," writes columnist Barbara Kay, "with virtually no statistical evidence to support their claims, feminists have promoted the idea that a woman runs a far higher risk of being sexually assaulted on a North American university campus (one in four or five, depending on the source) than a lifelong smoker has of getting cancer."[95]

It is no accident in this setting, where sexual freedom is indulged to the point of becoming not only an orgy but an "ideology,"[96] that its

91. See the introduction to this section, above.

92. Taylor & Johnson, *Until Proven Innocent*, 376. See K.C. Johnson, "The *Time's* Shoddy Reporting on Campus Rape," *Minding the Campus*, 11 May 2014, http://www.mindingthecampus.com/forum/2014/05/the_headlinetimess_shoddy_repo.html.

93. "Sex, Lies, and Rapes," internet site of the Center for Military Readiness (http://www.cmrlink.org/social.asp?docID=276, accessed 5 August 2008).

94. "The Media Is Making College Rape Culture Worse," *The Daily Beast*, 23 January 2015, http://www.thedailybeast.com/articles/2015/01/23/the-media-is-making-college-rape-culture-worse.html#.

95. Barbara Kay, "Rape Culture and the Delusions of the Feminist Mind," *National Post*, 28 February 2014 (http://fullcomment.nationalpost.com/2014/02/28/barbara-kay-rape-culture-and-the-delusions-of-the-feminist-mind/).

96. Mary Hasson, "Your Tuition Dollars at Work: How Colleges Promote a Perverse Sexual Ideology," *The Family in America*, vol. 28, no. 1 (Winter 2014).

authoritarian corollary is also most fully developed, as the sexual indulgence encouraged by today's campus culture goes hand-in-glove with politicized and perverted justice. "The baby boomers who dismantled the university's intellectual architecture in favor of unbridled sex and protest have now bureaucratized both," observes Heather MacDonald. "The academic bureaucracy is roomy enough to sponsor both the dour anti-male feminism of the college rape movement and the promiscuous hookup culture of student life."[97] In fact, the two are intimately connected, as Thomas Sowell perceives:

> Those who are whipping up the lynch-mob mentality have shown far less interest in stopping rape than in politicizing it. Many of the politically correct crusaders are the same people who have pushed for unisex living arrangements on campus, including unisex bathrooms, and who have put condom machines in dormitories and turned freshman orientation programs into a venue for sexual "liberation" propaganda.... The politically correct still want their sexual Utopia, and want scapegoats when they don't get it.[98]

Far from exercising their own calling of disinterestedly pursuing truth (which supposedly justifies their lives of taxpayer-subsidized leisure) when it involves their own institutions, the professors stand at the vanguard of the lynch mob. Before any trial commenced, Duke University faculty members created their own Maoist-style cultural revolution when they publicly demanded that the lacrosse players confess—as if professors are prosecutors, judges, and jurors: "Protesters gathered outside the lacrosse house carrying a banner with the word CASTRATE, banging pots and pans, and chanting 'Confess, confess!' Student vigilantes plastered the campus with 'Wanted' posters bearing the players' photographs. Eighty-eight Duke professors took out an ad in a local newspaper in support of the pot bangers and poster wielders."[99]

Such demands have long characterized "women's studies" programs, where trumped-up accusations have poisoned the curricula of thousands of universities and colleges with political ideology masquerading as scholarship. They have also turned students and faculty into inform-

---

97. Heather MacDonald, "The Campus Rape Myth," *City Journal*, Winter 2008 (http://www.city-journal.org/2008/18_1_campus_rape.html).

98. "Sexual Assault on Campus," *National Review Online*, 13 May 2014, http://www.nationalreview.com/article/377804/sexual-assault-campus-thomas-sowell.

99. Christina Hoff Sommers, "In Making Campuses Safe for Women, a Travesty of Justice for Men," *Chronicle of Higher Education*, 5 June 2011 (http://chronicle.com/article/In-Making-Campuses-Safe-for/127766/). See also K.C. Johnson's blog: http://durhamwonderland.blogspot.com/2014/01/a-duke-professor-on-group-of-88.html.

ers and pseudo-police against their colleagues and incited young women into believing that every personal hurt is a crime of "violence." Here the politicized scholarship of MacKinnon and Dworkin is treated as a manifesto. "If a woman did falsely accuse a man of rape," opines one graduate of such programs, "she may have had reasons to. Maybe she wasn't raped, but he clearly violated her in some way." We will find this repeatedly with gender "crimes": eliminating the very concept of innocence by eliding the distinction between physically violating a woman and hurting her feelings. A Vassar College assistant dean thinks false criminal accusations contribute positively to a man's education: "I think it ideally initiates a process of self-exploration. 'How do I see women?' 'If I didn't violate her, could I have?' 'Do I have the potential to do to her what they say I did?'"[100]

This is mob justice at its most incendiary, because it is perpetrated by the educated—starkly vindicating James Madison's observation that "Had every Athenian citizen been a Socrates, every Athenian assembly would still have been a mob."

Needless to say, none of the Duke University faculty who used their academic positions to incite a lynch mob against defenseless students were dismissed or reprimanded. The president of Duke retained his job, whereas it is standard procedure for university presidents in high-profile sexual assault and harassment accusations to be summarily dismissed after unproven accusations. "The Duke lacrosse case did not have lasting consequences for anyone involved," writes one legal authority. "Duke amended its sexual assault procedures just two years later to erode due process rights for the accused."[101]

Using criminal charges to serve a political agenda, is especially visible in this context, waging a war against a class by criminally prosecuting the most vulnerable members. "*Regardless of the 'truth' established in whatever period of time about the incident at the house on North Buchanan Boulevard*," writes Duke literature professor Wahneema Lubiano, the Duke players "are almost perfect offenders" in the sense that critical race theorist Kimberlé Crenshaw writes about: they are "the exemplars of the upper end of the class hierarchy, the politically dominant race and ethnicity, the dominant gender, the dominant sexuality, and the dominant social group on campus."[102] An academic political theory apparently

---

100. Nancy Gibbs, "When Is It Rape?" *Time*, 24 June 2001, (http://www.time.com/ti me/magazine/article/0,9171,157165,00.html#ixzz1QyYlxYPD).

101. Henrick, "Hostile Environment," 81, 83.

102. Wahneema Lubiano, "Perfect Offenders, Perfect Victim," online: http://dukeaa as.blogspot.com/2006/04/social-disaster-voices-from-durham.html (emphasis added).

makes any private citizen fair game for knowingly false criminal accusations ("regardless of the truth").

Patently false accusations continue to rage in North American and more recently British universities years after the Duke fiasco.[103] With the latest sensational campus "rape" accusation exposed as yet another hoax, the alternative subtext once again emerges that the truth and facts do not matter and that innocence is no excuse when righteous political causes offer professional journalistic accusers the intoxication of power. As a sensationalized University of Virginia "rape" case unraveled in late 2014,[104] Cathy Young collected a sampling of the weasel words from the ideological weasels whose careers depend on rationalizing fabrications:

> Amanda Marcotte blasted "rape apologists" attempting to "derail" the conversation with their talk of a hoax at UVA and asserted that Erdely's story would have been attacked no matter how thorough a job she had done. (She even not-so-subtly insinuated that the "rape denialist movement" is driven by men who are themselves rapists.) The same themes were echoed in a rant by Katie McDonough in *Salon*, who grudgingly acknowledged that Erdely's article was flawed but still denounced the criticism as "rape denial." . . . *New Yorker*'s Kate Stoeffel fretted that all the questioning feels like "presumed innocence is a privilege reserved for purported rapists and not their purported victims" and asked, "To what end are we scrutinizing?"...
>
> Some other feminists are quite openly suggesting that we shouldn't let facts get in the way. "So what if this instance was more fictional than fact and didn't actually happen to Jackie? Do we actually want anyone to have gone through this? This story was a shock and awe campaign that forced even the most ardent of rape culture deniers to stand up in horror and demand action," writes Katie Racine . . . in *The Huffington Post*. (A mostly fictional story is beneficial because it proved to "rape culture deniers" that rape culture exists? . . .) And in *Politico*, UVA student journalist Julia Horowitz opines that "to let fact checking define the narrative would be a huge mistake," since Jackie's likely fabrication points to a bigger truth. That is not journalism; it's agitprop.[105]

103. See the ongoing bibliography on the SAVE website: www.accusingu.org.

104. See the retraction by *Rolling Stone* magazine at https://www.rollingstone.com/ culture/news/a-note-to-our-readers-20141205 and the bibliography at www.accusingu .org. Yet, "The discredited Rolling Stone story about a University of Virginia fraternity rape has done little to slow the push for tougher disciplinary measures to combat what activists call the 'rape culture on campus.'" Valerie Richardson, "After UVA Fiasco...," *Washington Times*, 16 April 2015 (http://www.washingtontimes.com/news/2015/apr/16/ college-sexual-assault-crackdown-sparks-effort-to-/).

105. Cathy Young, "The UVA Story Unravels: Feminist Agitprop and Rape-Hoax Denialism," *Real Clear Politics*, 8 December 2014 (http://www.realclearpolitics.com/arti

In 2015, a sitting US Senator, Kirsten Gillibrand, publicly branded a Columbia University student who was neither charged nor convicted of any crime and against whom no evidence of any crime was ever presented—a private citizen with no comparable platform to defend himself—as a "rapist."[106]

These responses demonstrate very clearly that such cases are not matters of mistaken identity, honest mistakes, sloppy reporting, or "inefficient" adjudication by functionaries with "inadequate resources." They comprise a political agenda of radical ideologues using criminal accusations as a political weapon against innocent people.

Accordingly, ideologues have sought to by-pass the standard criminal courts, where remnants of due process are thought to prevail, to the politically charged environment of universities, where they have now devised their own archipelago of ideological pseudo-courts staffed by students and faculty who take it upon themselves to adjudicate rape accusations. "Across the country, students accused of sexual assault are regularly tried before inadequate and unjust campus judiciaries," writes Caroline Kitchens, "Cases of sexual misconduct are decided by a committee of as few as three students, faculty members, or administrators."[107]

Similar to what we have seen with family courts, these kangaroo courts bear no relation to true courts, and nothing requires that they observe due process of law or protect the constitutional rights of the accused. On the contrary, it is clear that they are created for the express purpose of circumventing such protections and meting out punishment. One attorney describes

> a disciplinary procedure where students nearly always lack lawyers, no legally trained judge oversees the process, testimony is not under oath, hearsay is freely considered, relevant evidence or even proper notice of the charges may not be given to both parties, students may be forced to incriminate themselves, and whatever "jury" is empaneled may not be of one's peers.[108]

---

cles/2014/12/08/the_uva_story_unravels_feminist_agitprop_and_rape-hoax_denialism_124891.html#ixzz3LOvBWgP4).

106. K.C. Johnson, "Shame on Gillibrand," *Minding the Campus*, 22 January 2015, http://www.mindingthecampus.com/2015/01/shame-on-gillibrand/#more-12684.

107. Caroline Kitchens, "The Rape 'Epidemic' Doesn't Actually Exist," *US News and World Report*, 13 October 2013 (http://www.usnews.com/opinion/blogs/economic-intelligence/2013/10/24/statistics-dont-back-up-claims-about-rape-culture?src=usn_tw).

108. Robert Shibley, "Due Process, Clarity Suffer As Feds Tackle Campus Sexual Assault," WGBH Radio internet site: http://wgbhnews.org/post/due-process-clarity-suffer-feds-tackle-campus-sexual-assault, 1 May 2014.

In many cases, the accused is not even told the accusation against him. At Yale, "specific accusations are not disclosed to the accused, no fact-finding takes place, and no record is taken of the alleged misconduct."[109]

Campus rape accusations thus present another pattern we have seen with family law and will see further with other gender crimes: replacing accepted due process procedures of standard courts with psychotherapeutic pseudo-judicial procedures created by special ad hoc pseudo-courts. University of Virginia students who want to politicize their sex lives have an assortment of therapeutic, quasi-judicial procedures available to "communicate their feelings and perceptions regarding the incident" and level quasi-criminal accusations in the process. One "allows both you and the accused to discuss your respective understandings of the [alleged?] assault with the guidance of a trained professional." A trained professional what? Accuser? MacDonald notes that "out in the real world . . . no counterpart exists outside academia for this super-structure of hearings, mediations, and negotiated settlements." This amounts to students playing Perry Mason, or perhaps a more apt parallel is Robespierre. "If you've actually been raped, you go to criminal court—but the overwhelming majority of campus 'rape' cases that take up administration time and resources would get thrown out of court in a twinkling, which is why they're almost never prosecuted." As we will see, domestic violence and child abuse accusations are also processed by government functionaries and specialized courts, without due process protections, rather than standard criminal courts. "Indeed, if the campus rape industry really believes that these hookup encounters are rape, it is unconscionable to leave them to flimsy academic procedures."[110]

But of course taking these cases to criminal courts would expose them for the fabrications they are. "If a college wouldn't conduct a murder trial, it shouldn't be conducting rape trials either," writes Megan McArdle. "We certainly shouldn't press them to punish these crimes because we can't get a conviction in a court of law, as it sometimes seems is happening."[111] At least this is true until the justice of the crimi-

109. Patrick Witt, "A Sexual Harassment Policy that Nearly Ruined My Life," *Boston Globe*, 3 November 2014, http://www.bostonglobe.com/opinion/2014/11/03/sexual-haras sment-policy-that-nearly-ruined-life/hY3XrZrOdXjvX2SSvuciPN/story.html.

110. MacDonald, "Campus Rape Myth." See also Christine Kitchens, "The Rape 'Epidemic' Doesn't Actually Exist," *US News and World Report*, 24 October 2013, (http:// www.usnews.com/opinion/blogs/economic-intelligence/2013/10/24/statistics-dont-back -up-claims-about-rape-culture?src=usn_tw).

111. "Rape on Campus Belongs in the Courts," Bloomburg.com, 5 May 2014, http:// www.bloombergview.com/articles/2014-05-05/rape-on-campus-belongs-in-the-courts.

nal courts themselves is further debased, a process being accelerated by the "flimsy academic procedures."

The federal government rationalizes this denial of due process protections on campuses by saying that "a Title IX investigation will never result in incarceration of an individual . . . the same procedural protections and legal standards are not required." Yet federal officials also urge institutions to share their maliciously obtained information with police. "This recommendation essentially presents the due process-free college inquiry as an assistant to police investigations—undermining the OCR's [Office of Civil Rights of the Department of Education] claim that denying accused students meaningful due process protections because the college action can't impose criminal liability." According to Joe Cohn of the Foundation for Individual Rights in Education, "statements made during these hearings will likely be admissible against them in subsequent criminal proceedings."[112] The Duke fiasco displayed the cross-fertilization between the parallel systems of "justice."[113]

Reputable scholars who investigate claims of a "rape epidemic" readily conclude that it is not simply exaggerated but a hoax. "The rape 'epidemic' doesn't actually exist," writes Kitchens, who shows how the White House statistics claiming that "one in five women has been sexually assaulted while she's in college" are completely concocted. Heather MacDonald calls the claim "preposterous." "There is no such epidemic," she states flatly. "There is, however, a squalid hook-up scene, the result of jettisoning all normative checks on promiscuous behavior. . . . There is simply no reason to concede any factual legitimacy to the rape hysterics."[114]

---

112. K. C. Johnson, "The White House Joins the War on Men," *Minding the Campus*, 29 April 2014, http://www.mindingthecampus.com/originals/2014/04/the_white_house_joins_the_war_.html; Ashe Schow, "Kirsten Gillibrand Claims Her Bill Gives Equal Rights to Accusers and Accused," *Washington Examiner*, 17 June 2015.

113. Colgate University demonstrates the intoxication with quasi-police power gripping campus officials, who seem to feel empowered as not only judge and jury but jailor. Abrar Faiaz was accused contrary to the wishes of the alleged victim. "Campus security officers then escorted him to a cramped and dirty basement room without Wi-Fi or cellular access and stood guard over the entrance. . . . After Faiaz had endured 36 hours of imprisonment, Professor Melissa Kagle…managed, despite Colgate's efforts to obstruct and dissuade her, to secure Faiaz's release." Peter Berkowitz, "Lawsuit Casts Harsh Light on Due Process at Colgate," *Real Clear Politics*, 4 October 2014, http://www.realclearpolitics.com/articles/2014/10/03/lawsuit_casts_harsh_light_on_due_process_at_colgate__1 24167.html#.VC7rlnXw4Ck.twitter#ixzz3FNvB4uXG.

114. Kitchens, "The Rape 'Epidemic'"; Heather MacDonald, "Neo-Victorianism on Campus," *Weekly Standard*, 20 October 2014, http://www.weeklystandard.com/articles/neo-victorianism-campus_810871.html?page=3; see also "An Assault on Common

But ideologues persist with tortured logic. "Activists like to claim that a constantly changing story from an accuser is just evidence of trauma," writes Ashe Schow. "When presented with evidence that the accuser did not believe the incident was sexual assault until months or years after it took place, the accuser is allowed to claim that she made such statements under duress."[115]

Because the campus accusers seldom have any real evidence of any actual crime, the latest ploy is to claim the existence of a "rape culture." This obviates the need for evidence of a specific deed in favor of a vague problem for which there is no proof but which rationalizes open-ended draconian measures against individual students. Fortunately, some scholars have begun refuting this accusation directly. "Twenty-first century America does not have a rape culture," Kitchens writes in *Time*; "what we have is an out-of-control lobby leading the public and our educational and political leaders down the wrong path. Rape culture theory is doing little to help victims, but its power to poison the minds of young women and lead to hostile environments for innocent males is immense." Barbara Kay in Canada's *National Post* has a similar assessment. "We are gripped by a baseless, but pandemic, moral panic," she writes. "Moral panic fueled by ideology and righteous indignation quickly corrodes the critical faculties and blinds even otherwise intelligent people to objective facts." Likewise, K. C. Johnson of Brooklyn College:

> That little, if any, evidence exists to sustain either of these beliefs has not deterred the "rape culture" believers; if anything, the lack of evidence for their claims appears to have emboldened them. Nor have they been deterred by the revelation of high-profile false rape claims on . . . ; if anything, the increasing build-up of sympathy for clearly railroaded males has intensified the rage of those who discern a "rape culture" on campus.[116]

Sense," *Weekly Standard*, 2 November 2015, http://www.weeklystandard.com/articles/assa ult-common-sense_1051200.html?page=1. This assertion is documented fully in Wendy McElroy, *Rape Culture Hysteria* (Vulgus, n.p., 2016), and in K. C. Johnson and Stuart Taylor, *The Campus Rape Frenzy: The Attack on Due Process at America's Universities* (New York: Encounter, 2017). Though both books appeared too late for full inclusion here, their argument is fully consistent with my own and proves it beyond a doubt.

115. Schow, "Kirsten Gillibrand."

116. Caroline Kitchens, "It's Time to End 'Rape Culture' Hysteria," *Time*, 20 March 2014 (http://time.com/#30545/its-time-to-end-rape-culture-hysteria/); Barbara Kay, "'Rape Culture' Fanatics Don't Know What a Culture Is," *National Post*, 8, March 2014 (http://fullcomment.nationalpost.com/2014/03/08/barbara-kay-rape-culture-fanatics-d ont-know-what-a-culture-is/); K. C. Johnson, "'Rape Culture' Fraud—Unmasking a Delusion," *Minding the Campus*, 18 March 2014 (http://www.mindingthecampus.com/orig-inals/2014/03/rapeculture.html#sthash.yZZqoKSk.dpuf).

The campus Jacobins were given additional power in April 2011, when the OCR decided that federal civil rights statutes could be used as a kind of criminal code. Acting without any authorization or mandate from Congress, Assistant Education Secretary for civil rights Russlynn Ali issued a directive to university officials demanding that campus tribunals adopt a lower standard of proof when convicting students and faculty of quasi-crimes. The letter did not follow standard procedures for federal regulations and "suffers from . . . a failure to conform to the laws governing administrative rulemaking," because it was not subject to public notice and comment, required of all federal regulations.[117] It was simply an arbitrary order issued from the pen of a functionary.

"Her letter provides detailed guidelines on the steps colleges should take to 'minimize the burden on the complainant,'" Hoff Sommers points out. "Not a word about the burden on the accused or his rights." This new standard had previously been considered and rejected by most institutions. "This . . . sends the message that results—not facts—matter most," writes Harvey Silverglate. "Such a standard would never hold up in a criminal trial." (Again, perhaps not yet.) The letter (from a federal office for "civil rights") cautions that constitutional rights should not be allowed to impede the freedom to accuse. Schools should ensure that steps taken to accord due process rights to the alleged perpetrator do not restrict or unnecessarily delay the Title IX protections for the complainant. "This suggests, oddly and ominously, that the statutory rights of the accuser trump the constitutional due-process rights of the accused," writes Wendy Kaminer. "The Obama administration, like the administrations of so many colleges and universities, implicitly approaches sexual harassment and sexual violence cases with a presumption of guilt."[118]

The move is a huge power grab by federal officials using campus radicals as proxies. "The letter by its own admission does not seek equal rights for both the accused and the complainant, but rather superior rights for complainants," writes Stephen Henrick. "It also effectuates a presumption that all accused students are guilty and it institutes four

117. Henrick, "Hostile Environment," 59.
118. Christina Hoff Sommers, "In Making Campuses Safe for Women, a Travesty of Justice for Men," *Chronicle of Higher Education*, 5 June 2011 (http://chronicle.com/article/In-Making-Campuses-Safe-for/127766/); Harvey Silverglate, "Yes Means Yes—Except on Campus," *Wall Street Journal*, 15 July 2011, http://online.wsj.com/article/SB10001424052702303678704576440014119968294.html?mod=googlenews_wsj; Wendy Kaminer, "Sexual Harassment and the Loneliness of the Civil Libertarian Feminist," *Atlantic*, 6 April 2011, http://www.theatlantic.com/national/archive/2011/04/sexual-harassment-and-the-loneliness-of-the-civil-libertarian-feminist/236887/.

reforms that will increase convictions without regard to guilt or inno-cence." These include:

- lowering the burden of proof in campus sexual assault trials to "pre-ponderance of the evidence";[119]

- establishing suspect evidentiary rules;

- requiring schools to inform only complainants (but not accused students) their legal rights;

- giving the Title IX coordinator unbridled discretion to revise any sanction issued in a sexual assault proceeding.[120]

Another standard right routinely violated is the prohibition on dou-ble jeopardy: "In total violation of basic principles of double jeopardy, OCR has also enticed schools to re-examine an acquitted student with-out notice to him or her until the second investigation begins." Needless to say, "a conviction upon subsequent investigation is all but assured," since "No risk-averse institution would dare defy OCR's unstated com-mand to convict on the second try."[121]

But "the letter's most problematic aspect is its formalization of a pre-sumption of guilt in campus adjudications." Henrick finds that "just two sentences out of its nineteen pages discuss due process protections," and then only to imply that "accused students at private universities ... do not have any rights at all." OCR guidelines recommend suspending accused students from their classes and evicting them from their resi-dences "because they are likely guilty." Here again, increasing the rate of convictions is advocated as a virtue for its own sake, regardless of evi-dence in specific cases, and the letter institutes procedural changes "that will lead to increased convictions irrespective of an accused student's guilt or innocence." One professional self-described "sexual assault activist," who advises some 800 universities, "publically stated he looks forward to seeing more accused students expelled." (His firm's goal is to criminalize voluntary sex resulting from "unreasonable pressure.")[122]

---

119. Phyllis Schlafly comments succinctly: "The new rule means that the feminist academics sitting in judgment on male college students need to be only 50.01 percent confident a woman is telling the truth whether or not she has any credible evidence." *Who Killed the American Family* (Washington: WND Books, 2014), 70.

120. Henrick, "Hostile Environment," 65, 59–60.

121. Ibid., 53, 71.

122. Ibid., 61–62, 13, 64. For the word games by which he accomplishes this, see Claire Gordon, "How Colleges Rebranded Rape," *Al-Jazeera*, 17 April 2014, http://americ a.aljazeera.com/watch/shows/america-tonight/articles/2014/4/17/nonconsensual-sexw henrapeisreworded.html.

Henrick's analysis highlights the power wielded over even "private" universities from the federal government's financial largesse and pressure. In sexual cases, universities are already permeated by "incentives to falsely convict accused students." "Schools have an incentive to convict anyone who is charged with sexual assault or rape as a matter of risk aversion for the institution," according to Henrick. The massive federal funding that almost all universities depend upon for their extensive building programs serves as leverage that ensures that feminist doctrine is imposed through campus pseudo-courts. "Failure to conform to Title IX can lead to financially disastrous consequences for an educational institution," Henrick writes. "Given the amount of federal money most universities receive, the mere threat of losing it is enough to secure 'voluntary' compliance with OCR's requests." Colleges and universities therefore "have a very strong incentive to convict accused students in all circumstances."[123]

Today, the federal government's "primary concern is now decidedly the rights of complainants," writes Henrick. "The agency has devoted little if any time to ensuring that sexual assault hearings are 'equitable' and 'impartial' for both the defendant and the complainant," despite the fact that they are required to do so by law. Whereas "a school's deliberate indifference to a complainant's claim that he or she was raped or sexually assaulted is automatically an actionable violation for money damages," even in the absence of a criminal standard of guilt, "deliberate indifference to an accused student's innocence, by contrast, is not actionable." Henrick describes it as "a system of adjudication in which innocent people are prone to conviction for offenses they did not commit." The published guidelines are "at best dense, vague, and self-contradictory, and all focus primarily on the rights of complainants." By contrast, "OCR has never defined a university's obligation to provide due process protections for student defendants except to say that doing so should not unduly restrict or delay complainant's Title IX rights." In fact, "no OCR publication or federal regulation mandate[s] any punish-

---

123. Henrick, "Hostile Environment," 50–51, 53, 75, 54, 81. Demonstrating the affinity between different radical sexual grievances, the Obama administration used the same financial leverage and the same civil rights statute to order schools to allow children to choose their washrooms, regardless of their biological sex. The executive *fiat* undermines not only the separation of powers but the authority of school officials. "If a . . . man wants to go shower with the girls on the soccer team," according to a congressman, "he's allowed to do that because of his will or his gender fluidity for the week [he] can tell the teacher 'this [is] what I'm feeling . . .' and she has no recourse to step in." "73 House Republicans Sign Letter," *Daily Signal*, 18 May 2016, https://goo.gl/4gvSVf.

ment for false accusations." The 2008 version of OCR's guidelines "did not mention the accused at all except to say, 'it also may be appropriate to counsel the [alleged?] harasser to ensure that he or she understands that retaliation is prohibited.'" So great is the presumption of guilt that protesting one's innocence by invoking standard constitutional rights or expecting knowingly false accusations to be punished is now branded as "retaliation" against an accuser.[124]

Having aggrandized its power by its unauthorized expansion of its own mission, OCR then predictably requested a 37.7% budget increase for one year.[125]

In April 2014, the White House itself became directly involved, releasing a report that further tightened the noose on accused men. "Missing is virtually any recognition of the need for fairness to the accused."[126] To avoid "hurtful questioning," a standard due process protection must be eliminated: the right to face and cross-examine one's accuser. "The parties should not be allowed to cross-examine each other."[127] The White House also urged campuses to dispense with what little peer review existed in favor of a "single investigator" to pronounce guilt. "In other words, one person—presumably paid by the university, whose federal funding may be at stake . . . will effectively decide innocence or guilt."[128] The term "due process" does not appear in the report.

Why are ostensibly criminal acts now treated as "civil rights" violations at all (aside from the now evidently irrelevant matter of the civil rights of the accused)? Because the courts have ruled that rape and sexual assault are forms of "discrimination." This bizarre formulation for what is supposed to be violent crime (which we will see replicated with other gender crimes) is only comprehensible when it is understood that it is devised precisely to be invoked when no violence or crime has taken

124. Ibid., 52–54, 56, 59.

125. Ashe Schow, "Senators Want More Money for Campus Sex Police," *Washington Examiner*, 31 March 2016, http://www.washingtonexaminer.com/senators-want-more-money-for-campus-sex-police/article/2587338.

126. Cathy Young, "Guilty Until Proven Innocent," *Time*, 6 May 2014 (http://time.com/88407/the-white-houses-report-on-campus-sexual-assault-relies-on-the-lowest-common-denominator/).

127. Hans Bader, "Obama Administration Attacks Cross-Examination and Due Process Rights in Campus Guidance," Competitive Enterprise Institute blog, 30 April 2014, http://www.openmarket.org/2014/04/30/obama-administration-attacks-cross-examination-and-due-process-rights-in-campus-guidance/.

128. Will Creeley, "Concern Grows over White House Task Force's Recommendations," Foundation for Individual Rights in Education: http://www.thefire.org/concern-grows-over-white-house-task-forces-recommendations/, 6 May 2014.

place, and when the police and criminal courts therefore choose not to pursue criminal charges. (It is worth asking how many victims of mugging or housebreaking or armed robbery would see themselves foremost as victims of "discrimination.") With criminal violence re-classified as discrimination, it follows that behavior deemed to constitute discrimination can be classed as criminal violence, even when it is not, in fact, violent. This rationalizes lowering the burden of proof for criminal accusations.

The latest twist is that male students are now responding with suits of their own, likewise claiming "discrimination." "There is a countertrend of civil rights suits from young men accusing colleges of wrongful, gender-biased expulsion on charges of sexual misconduct."[129] So rather than simply not pressuring the universities to violate the male students' civil rights in the first place, one group of federal government lawyers gets to pressure the universities into acts of "discrimination" for which another group of federal government lawyers then gets to sue them.[130] "The same Title IX law that federal officials and universities are citing in doubling down on what critics describe as a 'rape culture' on campus is increasingly being cited by male students who contend they have been unjustly punished, even railroaded, based on their sex."[131] Like the accused men, the universities can be presumed to be guilty of *something*, because the civil rights lawyers have erected a legal regime whereby the universities cannot avoid "discriminating" against *someone*; all that remains is for the judicial oligarchy to decide between them which set of victims has the most political clout to have their complaints punished.

Of course this regime of suits and counter-suits is fantastically expensive, with millions drained from the universities and students and tax-

129. Young, "Guilty"; also, "Another Side to the Campus Sexual-Assault Mess," *Newsday*, 26 May 2014, http://www.newsday.com/opinion/columnists/cathy-young/another-side-to-the-campus-sexual-assault-mess-cathy-young-1.8163697.

130. Once again, this pattern seems to have been set by divorce courts, who first grant mothers absolute power to prevent children from seeing their fathers and then, when they inevitably abuse the power that the courts gave them in the first place, the courts purport to remedy the problem by threatening to jail the mothers for using it (though they seldom do). The less invasive solution for everyone (but less lucrative for the legal practitioners) would be to not give them the monopoly power in the first place. Stephen Baskerville, *Taken Into Custody: The War Against Fathers, Marriage, and the Family* (Nashville: Cumberland House, 2007), 69–70.

131. Valerie Richardson, "Men Invoking Anti-Discrimination Title IX to Fight Sex Assault Charges," *Washington Times*, 1 December 2014 (http://www.washingtontimes.com/news/2014/dec/1/title-ix-invoked-by-male-university-of-colorado-st/).

payers into the pockets of lawyers.[132] This is hardly accidental. Sexual ideology allows lawyers to plunder universities with rape accusations much as it allows them to plunder fathers in divorce courts and taxpayers through welfare.

This tyranny of the "civil rights" lawyers becomes an open-ended formula for their unlimited "empowerment," since some claims of "discrimination" are more equal than others. "These lawsuits are an incredible display of entitlement," ironically declares Professor Caroline Heldman of Occidental College, "the same entitlement that drove them to rape." Here too the claim of "discrimination" is clearly a disingenuous ruse to criminalize men, since—despite perfunctory pretenses of "gender neutrality" and definitions so vague that women could indeed be found culpable—only one sex can effectively be accused. Asked for an official legal ruling about legal culpability in a case where two intoxicated students had sex ("They have raped each other and are subject to expulsion?" it was suggested), Duke University dean of students Sue Wasiolek replied: "Assuming it is a male and female, it is the responsibility in the case of the male to gain consent before proceeding with sex."[133]

Because rape accusations will inevitably be gender-specific, charges of "discrimination" and "gender bias" are a formula for unlimited litigation, since what is being re-adjudicated in each case is not the guilt or innocence of a particular man but the differences between men and women, which become subject to endless re-delineation by quasi-judicial decree.

All this is much easier to introduce in the university "kangaroo courts," in Silverglate's words, than with the real judiciary (at least for now). "While real-world courts have invalidated many of these codes," he writes, "the federal government has now put its thumb decisively on the scale against fairness on issues of sexual harassment and assault." Receiving federal funds has had the effect of turning universities into ideological police administrations—debasing the standards of both criminal justice and education and, indeed, blurring the distinction between the two. Seeking weasel words to justify ignoring evidence exonerating an accused student, the attorney for one university wrote

---

132. Bob Unruh, "Campus-Assault Crackdown Provoking Expensive Backlash," *WorldNetDaily*, 5 July 2014, http://www.wnd.com/2014/07/campus-assault-crackdown-provoking-expensive-backlash/#TyoC5rTvr977Ymsm.99.

133. *Ms.* magazine blog, 18 June 2014, http://msmagazine.com/blog/2014/06/18/men-sue-in-campus-sexual-assault-cases/; "A Duke Senior Sues the University…" *Indy Week*, 28 May 2014, http://www.indyweek.com/indyweek/a-duke-senior-sues-the-university-after-being-expelled-over-allegations-of-sexual-misconduct/Content?oid=4171302.

that the campus proceeding "was not a legal process but an educational one."[134]

The aim of these pseudo-courts is clearly neither justice nor education but political power—openly the target and ironically the aim of campus sex militants. "The campus rape industry claims that what it calls campus rape is not about sex but rather politics—the male desire to subordinate women," writes MacDonald. The University of Virginia Women's Center intones that "rape or sexual assault is not an act of sex or lust—it's about aggression, power, and humiliation, using sex as the weapon. The rapist's goal is domination." In another example of how radical ideology replicates the very problem about which it complains, this provides an apt description of precisely what feminist activists are now doing: using sex as a political weapon to gain power and domination and humiliate men.

All this amounts to little less than a reign of terror against accused men by feminists in the federal government. If an institution follows its own rules, "the accused student has no recourse no matter how unjustified his or her sentence." A letter published in the campus newspaper of an Ivy League university clearly articulates the mentality of the campus Robespierres and the logical conclusion of the hookup culture: "The university is to be applauded for . . . [its] message to all males," the student wrote:

> "You need to check your behavior carefully before you enter into a relationship with a woman. There will be no due process if you are accused of rape. The woman's version of what happened will always be accepted over the man's account." If a male student knew that was the policy hopefully this would serve as a check on sexually aggressive behavior.[135]

Revealingly, radical ideologues beyond the universities, including writers and editors of professional journals, have defended the system of knowingly false accusations as a positive good in itself in order to terrify male students. Ezra Klein argues that trumped-up accusations are a legitimate weapon precisely because they strike fear into the innocent:

> It tries to change, through brute legislative force, the most private and intimate of adult acts. It is sweeping in its redefinition of acceptable consent. . . . If the Yes Means Yes law is taken even remotely seriously it will settle like a cold winter on college campuses, throwing everyday

---

134. Silverglate, "Yes Means Yes."
135. Quoted in Henrick, "Hostile Environment," 78, 82 note 155.

sexual practice into doubt and creating a haze of fear and confusion over what counts as consent.[136]

This fear of the justice system by the citizenry is desirable: "This is the case against it, and also the case for it. . . . Men need to feel a cold spike of fear when they begin a sexual encounter. . . . To work, 'Yes Means Yes' needs to create a world where men are afraid."[137]

As we will see again and again with the new gender crimes, "ideology plays a role in sexual assault trials to the increasing detriment of the accused as some universities institutionalize the anti-due process biases of their administrators."[138] Now campus Bolsheviks (borrowing from the methods their counterparts implemented in divorce courts) are calling for secret trials of rape—"Closed Criminal Trials"—in not only universities but also regular criminal courts.[139]

US Congressman Jared Polis advocates expelling from the universities all men accused of sexual assault—even the innocent ones. What he terms a "reasonable likelihood standard" appears to suggest a certain statistical likelihood (his scenario is 20%, with no indication why) that everyone is guilty. "Even if there's a 20–30% chance that it happened, I would want to remove this individual," Polis told a committee hearing. "If there's 10 people who have been accused, and under a reasonable likelihood standard maybe one or two did it, it seems better to get rid of all 10 people."[140]

This "witch hunt" has occasioned one of the few instances of scholars starting to perceive the larger pattern of feminist-generated hysterias. "Today's college rape panic is an eerie recapitulation of the daycare abuse panic," observes Christina Hoff Sommers. "Just as the mythical '50,000 abducted children' fueled paranoia about child safety in the 1980s, so today's hysteria is incited by the constantly repeated, equally

---

136. Ezra Klein, "'Yes Means Yes' Is a Terrible Law, and I Completely Support It," *Vox*, 13 October 2014, http://www.vox.com/2014/10/13/6966847/yes-means-yes-is-a-terrible-bill-and-i-completely-support-it.

137. Intentionally spreading fear among a target population of unconvicted people also characterizes campaigns to collect "child support." See Baskerville, *Taken Into Custody*, ch. 3.

138. Henrick, "Hostile Environment," 83.

139. See the list of student demands at the University of Virginia *following* the fabricated story in *Rolling Stone*: http://media.cav.s3.amazonaws.com/10072_studentssexuala ssaultsolutionso.pdf.

140. Chuck Ross, "Dem Congressman: Expel All Students Accused Of Sexual Assault, Even The Innocent Ones," *Daily Caller*, 10 September 2015, http://dailycaller. com/2015/09/10/polis-expel-all-students-accused-of-sexual-assault-video/#ixzz3lNJJE-jHd.

fictitious 'one-in-five women on campus is a victim of rape'—which even President Obama has embraced." Even the few scholars who investigate one hysteria have been remarkably slow (or afraid) to notice parallels with others, but here Hoff Sommers sees very clearly the similar role of ideology:

> Once again, conspiracy feminists are at the forefront of this movement. Just as feminist psychologists persuaded children that they had been abused, so women's activists have persuaded many young women that what they might have dismissed as a foolish drunken hookup was actually a felony rape. "Believe the children," said the ritual abuse experts during the day care scare. "Believe the survivors," say today's rape culturalists. To not believe an alleged victim is to risk being called a rape apologist.[141]

Yet even conservative critics avert their eyes from the feminist juggernaut. In the Duke fiasco they studiously avoided any acknowledgement of feminism's role but instead emphasized the racial dimension—a minor feature of the case but a much safer one to criticize. The single-minded hype of the racial dimension made this case (like the earlier Tawana Brawley hoax) appear exceptional. But overemphasizing the racial factor avoided the most serious implications of the Duke case. Race demagogues like Jesse Jackson and Al Sharpton are soft targets for conservatives, precisely because they do not command the institutional clout to politicize criminal justice proceedings on a large scale. There is little evidence that white people are being systematically railroaded into prison on fabricated accusations of non-existent crimes against blacks. This is precisely what is happening to men, both white and black, accused of the kind of gender crimes that feminists have turned into a political agenda.

The 2003 accusation of basketball star Kobe Bryant demonstrates that a black man accused by a white woman is hardly more likely to obtain justice. Historically, of course, this was the far more traditional pattern. Our race-conscious society is frequently regaled with the shameful history of lynching and instructed by historical spin doctors to remember it as a racial atrocity. Those who politicize history neglect to mention that almost all those lynched were black men accused of rape by white women. White feminists have spun this as "the dominant white male ideology behind lynching—the thought that white womanhood was in

---

141. "Rape Culture is a 'Panic Where Paranoia, Censorship, and False Accusations Flourish,'" *Time*, 15 May 2014 (http://time.com/100091/campus-sexual-assault-christina-hoff-sommers/). For child abuse hysteria, see chapter III, under "Child Abuse."

need of protection against black men." Some include the fantastical suggestion that this was the conscious method used by the white "patriarchy" to suppress the yearning of black men and white women to join hands in a kind of political romance of progressive liberation.[142] Yet clearly this is ideology speaking rather than facts. White women accused black men of rape, just as feminists themselves are now doing with other vulnerable men, and no evidence suggests they were coerced into doing so by white men or anyone else. Where fabricated rape accusations are concerned, the races have changed, but the genders have remained constant.

As elsewhere, the criminalization of men is now extending to the criminalization of boys. In 2010, two boys aged 10 and 11 were found guilty of "attempted rape" for what was obviously a case of children playing doctor. Initially the boys were charged with rape, until the girl changed her story and said it never happened. (Learning the game young, "The girl told the court she had lied to her mother about what had happened because she had been 'naughty' and was worried she would not get any sweets.") The boys were then ordered to register as sex offenders.[143] Widespread public indignation that such a case even went to trial in the first place was not enough to deter Britain's Child Protective Services from insisting that the boys are criminals.

Political manipulation of rape accusations was highlighted when Julian Assange of WikiLeaks was charged with a vague assortment of crimes by the Swedish government. Angry with Assange for leaking classified material, the US government found the charges useful.

The set-up was obvious, and the feminist *New York Times* made it plain in invoking "wide-ranging definitions of sexual assault and rape." Translation: Legal definitions of "rape" are now so far removed from plain English that they have nothing to do with actual rapes. "Separate sexual encounters he had with each of the women *became nonconsensual after* he was no longer using a condom." Translation: The women consented, but prosecutrixes charged him anyway. As if to emphasize the politics of rape prosecutions, the *Times* added that "female empowerment—economic, social, and also legal—has a different quality in Swe-

---

142. Fairly typical are "Lynching and Violence in American Culture," online: http://amath.colorado.edu/carnegie/lit/lynch/women.htm, and Jeremy Boggs, "A New Look at the Southern Rape Myth," H-Net: http://www.h-net.org/reviews/showrev.cgi?path=1355 71160166162.

143. Philip Johnston, "Was This Really Attempted Rape—or Children Playing?" *Daily Telegraph*, 24 May 2010, http://blogs.telegraph.co.uk/news/philipjohnston/100040 818/was-this-really-attempted-rape-or-children-playing/. The comments garnered by this and almost every news account of the verdict were almost uniformly appalled.

den than in other countries." In other words, rape law is a feminist political tool and a standing miscarriage of justice. The *Times* admitted that "Sweden's current criminal code is not much stricter on sexual offenses than those of other European countries" or the US. Not content with this, "the definition of rape should be expanded to include situations in which a woman does not explicitly say no to sex."

Accounts of the Assange case confirm the manipulation of the law to debase the language and create political criminals: one accuser was a professional feminist: "the protégée of a militant feminist-academic" and a "campus sexual equity officer," according to the *Daily Mail*. "Fighting male discrimination in all forms...was her forte." Both accusers enlisted a prominent "gender lawyer" and "leading supporter of a campaign to extend the legal definition of rape to help bring more [alleged?] rapists to justice." In other words, ignore plain English and change the meaning of words to criminalize the innocent. The website of one apparently offered "7 Steps to Legal Revenge," advising women how to use trumped-up accusations to punish men for emotional hurts. After the "rape," one "raped" woman had sex with her "rapist" again and threw a party for him, while the other cooked him breakfast after being "raped."

Everyone knows there was no rape. Yet everyone involved from the left to the right had political reasons for implying there might have been, for pretending to see the emperor's clothes, for blurring the distinction between innocence and guilt, between truth and falsehood, and for pursuing criminal charges known to be fabricated. Thus we all become part of the brave new post-modernist world where words can be "deconstructed" to mean whatever we want them to mean, where there is no objective truth and—prompted by political motives—we all follow the truth that is "right for us." It is hardly surprising if governments follow our lead and legislate the meanings of words and "findings of fact" to create *their* own reality by making us all criminals. As usual, one deconstructed reality (what used to be called a "lie") necessitates another, until our political agendas require that we remain silent as we watch knowingly innocent men being led away in handcuffs. But this is a society of lackeys and tyrants, where we all find it handy to have a criminal charge available to pin on anyone who hurts our feelings or threatens our power.

Of course, men like Assange, Bryant, and students who indulge in casual sex arguably are asking for trouble and deserve what they get. In theological terms, though they receive an unjust punishment from human authorities, they are being justly punished by God. This is a valid argument theologically and one that would be very healthy for young men to absorb—though significantly, no such argument has been put forth for discussion by the churches, which simply avert their eyes and hold their tongues from matters that would seem to be in their direct purview: rampant sexual "misbehavior" (of some kind) by both sexes. Yet aside from the churches' abdication of leadership, this standard can hardly justify quasi-criminal punishments. For one thing, any secular government must distinguish sin from crime and legally punish only the latter—unless we are going to make a decision to punish fornication as a crime, in which case it must be legislated and punished equally in all and by both sexes. Ironically, the decidedly hyper-secularized radicals are the ones substituting for traditional religion a new political theology and a new definition of sin; traditional religion recognized legitimate spheres for Caesar and for God. Ironically too, it gains support from conservatives (both secular and religious) who express disapproval of the sexual license but lack the stomach to confront the perversion of criminal justice. Perhaps the biggest danger in allowing the state to define sin is to create, in Hobbes's phrase, a "mortal god."

The most graphic demonstration of how radicalism produces precisely the problems it claims to be eradicating may have occurred in 2011, when young feminists, dressed in sexually provocative clothing with signs proclaiming "Slut Pride," and "Proud Slut," took to the streets of Toronto and other cities in a series of "Slut Walks." Marchers aimed—peculiarly but revealingly (as it were)—to "take back the word 'slut.'" "Sluts and Allies, Unite!" declared a speaker. One woman wore a sexy outfit and wrote "rape me" on herself.

Perplexed, older feminists asked if these displays were a "step backwards," as the young women seemed not only willing but eager to make themselves precisely the "sex objects" their foremothers deplored. In fact, these assertions of female sexual power were the logical conclusion of unleashing sexual energy as a political weapon. The thrill these women derived from displaying their bodies in public—all in a good cause, of course—was palpable.

The international protests were ostensibly set off by a policeman's incautious but hardly inflammatory remarks, to a handful of women, that wearing enticing clothing in some circumstances is unwise. He was predictably accused of "blaming the victim." "While we are proud of our sexuality," declared one speaker (*proud* of it?), "it is by no means an invitation to violence."

But of course no one ever said that it is. The policeman's words (at a safety forum) were no more than what a father might advise his daughter. Would he be "blaming the victim" and deserving of feminist invective, or would he be concerned about his daughter's safety? (Do feminists even recognize this distinction?) Indeed, any father of a daughter will instantly recognize the adolescent sartorial rebellion on display in Toronto and elsewhere, however dressed up (so to speak) as a political statement.

The harmless advice became the occasion for a huge tantrum of undress on at least four continents. Far from suggesting that all this alleged rape might warrant some sexual restraint, we saw women marching in their underwear, defiantly proclaiming their right to "be sexual," and celebrating sex as a virtue to be indulged for its own sake with no consequences.

As with "Gay Pride" demonstrations and the Femen protests, this public exhibitionism was obviously far out of proportion to any political point about protecting women, who in industrial countries are the safest people in history. What we saw was the unleashing of deeper passions coupled with the familiar and uniquely feminine power (though one now adopted by homosexuals) to use sex for manipulation, including in this case political manipulation.

Here once again people who instinctively understood that this saturation of the public discourse with sex cannot possibly be healthy had trouble articulating precisely why. In fact, the reasons are very concrete. What is going on here is the blending of sexual and political radicalism in an authoritarian mix. The result is a vicious spiral of sexual indulgence driving political repression. In Toronto speakers repeatedly called, in Maoist fashion, for compulsory government "education" of those who disagree with them.

Such displays are not a defensive measure to prevent "violence against women"; they are an aggressive grab for, as the feminists say, "power and control." Conspicuously absent was any presumption of innocence or recognition that in a free society crime is adjudicated case-by-case according to due process of law, with protections for the rights of the accused and weighing of evidence by an impartial jury. Instead, we saw another instance of mob justice at its most incendiary, fueled by sexual energy and driven by political ideologues demanding arrests and incarcerations regardless of evidence. What chance will a man accused of rape have for a fair trial in Toronto or any other city that has witnessed an angry mob of screaming, half-naked women—especially with penal officials subject to politically doctrinaire "sensitivity training" that the Toronto Police Department say they have now implemented? That training includes the feminist insistence that rape is "political" and therefore the accused is always guilty.

Is it an exaggeration to suggest that our refusal to face the truth about rape accusations has led us to the point where we permit innocent men to be railroaded into prison so that adolescent women can experience the release of displaying their bodies in public?

Sexual Harassment

Sexual harassment is another new crime that no one understands or can understand because it has no fixed definition. The term is continually revised and expanded to ensnare ever-more wrongdoers (usually after the fact) and transfer power into the hands of feminists, lawyers, government officials, and assorted hangers-on. As generally understood, it refers to men in positions of superior authority abusing their leverage to extort sexual favors from female underlings. Such misbehavior was already prohibited by both standard rules of professional conduct and by law long before feminists used the accusations to leverage political power. "The fact that the behaviors in question were already covered by existing criminal and civil prohibitions, including assault, battery, blackmail, lewdness, breach of contract, and intentional infliction of emotional distress, was insufficient."[144] The new terminology was not only politically incendiary but intentionally vague, so that what began as unethical professional conduct could be expanded to include any male behavior. "Sexual harassment has become so loosely defined as to be incapable of serving any constructive purpose," wrote Daphne Patai, the leading academic expert on the topic and one of the few to approach it with critical detachment, more than a decade ago. "'Sexual harassment' seems often to be little more than a label for excoriating men."[145] Like other radical political campaigns, it also created a lucrative litigation enterprise hardly distinguishable from an extortion racket.

According to the US federal government, sexual harassment occurs not only "when submission [to] or cooperation [with it is] an implicit or explicit condition of employment" but also when it has the "purpose or effect of unreasonably interfering with a person's work performance or creating an intimidating, hostile, or offensive work environment."[146] In fact, it is much more expansive than even this loose definition suggests. Under feminist pressure (and much like rape), sexual harassment has now been expanded to punish any sexual or romantic interaction between men and women under any circumstances, if the woman complains to the authorities. It therefore turns ordinary personal relationships into legal offenses for which only men can be punished.

---

144. Diana Furchtgott-Roth and Christine Stolba, *The Feminist Dilemma: When Success is Not Enough* (Washington: AEI, 2001), 94.

145. Patai, *Heterophobia*, Kindle locations 218, 221.

146. Ibid., Kindle locations 353–54.

One educational resource lists "sexually harassing behaviors" (meaning legally actionable ones) as "name-calling (from 'honey' to 'bitch')," "spreading sexual rumors," "leers and stares," "sexual or 'dirty' jokes," "conversations that are too personal," "repeatedly asking someone out when he or she isn't interested," and "facial expressions (winking, kissing, etc.)."[147] In an influential article in the *Harvard Law Review*, Cynthia Bowman includes "the harassment of women in public places by men who are strangers to them," such as construction workers, because of wolf whistles, leers, winks, and remarks such as "Hello, baby." She advocates "statutes specifically targeting street harassment, and litigation aimed at redefining the torts of assault, intentional infliction of emotional distress, and invasion of privacy." So leers, stares, and winks would become crimes equivalent to "assault" or, in feminist parlance, "violence against women."[148] Patai comments that "the statute proposed by Bowman would punish a man for starting a conversation with a female stranger with any sort of implicitly sexual language—including, perhaps, an 'unwelcome' pickup line in a singles bar." In other words, for initiating any conversation at all. Weiss and Young hope, perhaps naively, that "Unconstitutional vagueness and overbreadth would appear to stand in the way of such legislation." Feminists also agitate to bring the full force of the law to make construction crews "cease engaging in 'visual harassment' of women passing their building sites."[149]

Here again, the criteria for establishing guilt are highly subjective, based entirely on a woman's feelings. Words mean what the accuser decides they mean; therefore, the offense is what the accuser decides it is, based on her own feelings. "Thus, a woman's subjective judgment of men's actions, regardless of their intent, became the standard by which complaints could be judged," writes Patai. "Subjective factors thus operate at every level of the sexual harassment scene."[150] This constitutes nothing less than "the elevation of women's word to the level of law."[151] And it can include sexual feelings and hurt feelings. One study found that "As the attractiveness and availability of the man decreased, the women's experience of feeling harassed increased."[152]

Even more than rape, therefore, sexual harassment is both subjective

147. Weiss and Young, "Feminist Jurisprudence."

148. Louise Fitzgerald, "Sexual Harassment: Violence Against Women in the Workplace," *American Psychologist* 48 (1993), 1070–6.

149. Patai, *Heterophobia*, Kindle location 2571.

150. Ibid., Kindle locations 391–92, 398–99.

151. Ibid., Kindle location 2180.

152. Furchtgott-Roth and Stolba, *Feminist Dilemma*, 97.

and vague: "an offense that even the Supreme Court cannot define."[153] Are we talking here about a breach of ethics or a crime? Once again, the effect is to blur the distinction between unpleasantness and criminality. "Sexual harassment . . . lies on the border between a crime and a mistake," one feminist reveals.[154] So one man's mistake is another man's prison term. Does this semi-crime necessarily include physical "force," as Lester indicates (if only "in the woman's own mind")? If so, why is it "harassment" and not rape or sexual assault? It is never clear. Moreover, it seems to be intentionally unclear, so that no criteria separate ethical (civil) peccadilloes from violent (criminal) assault. "What's the difference between an unwelcome request for a date and rape?" asks Wendy Kaminer. "Pursuant to the Obama administration's definition of sexual harassment, this is not an easy question to answer."[155] This ambiguity is created by feminists to "link harassment to more serious acts of violence." Deborah Rhode insists that "the dynamics of male entitlement, dominance, and control that foster harassment also contribute to more serious forms of abuse, such as domestic violence and rape." This explicit equation of political power with crime is invoked by mainstream feminist groups who describe "harassment" as "a form of violence against women, used to keep women in their place."[156] Throughout feminist literature, we meet repeated "suggestions that sexual harassment is the precursor of rape (both acts being defined as essentially about 'power,' not sex)" and "the frequent use of the honorific 'survivor' to refer to those who have experienced 'sexual harassment' . . . invites the reader to elide distinctions, to treat all instances of sexual harassment as 'equally damaging as' brutal sexual assault. Such claims violate empirical and conceptual boundaries, *and they are intended to do so.*"[157]

Equally nebulous is the adjudication. Sexual harassment is not generally prosecuted or tried in a court. Instead the employer is held legally liable, usually through civil suits. The employer must therefore police its employees, acting as a kind of proxy sexual constabulary. The entire matter is thus handled civilly, not criminally—though it ostensibly involves "violence" (of some kind). Here too the distinction is blurred, and the reality for the accused is that

---

153. Patai, *Heterophobia*, Kindle location 1683.
154. Ibid., Kindle location 1398.
155. "No Sex Talk Allowed," *The Atlantic* internet site: http://www.theatlantic.com/sexes/archive/2013/05/no-sex-talk-allowed/275782/, 15 May 2013.
156. Furchtgott-Roth and Stolba, *Feminist Dilemma*, 98.
157. Patai, *Heterophobia*, Kindle locations 611–14 (emphasis added).

being found guilty of sexual harassment is, in its consequences, far closer to being found guilty of a crime than to losing a civil suit. Admittedly, sexual harassers do not go to jail, but in all other respects, one's life can be just as ruined by being found guilty of sexual harassment as by a criminal conviction. Those found guilty of sexual harassment are typically treated as outcasts, just as criminals are. If one is accused of sexual harassment, one stands to lose one's job... and one's respectability in one's community.[158]

Here too, constitutional protections are quietly discarded. "Despite these severe consequences, those accused of sexual harassment do not enjoy anything close to the procedural protection given in our legal system to defendants in criminal trials," Patai points out. "Guilt need not be proven beyond a reasonable doubt; and culpable actions need not be demonstrated as either intentional or reckless." In fact the system is marked "with a complete absence of due process." As we will see with the other feminist somewhat-crimes, harassment law blurs the distinction between private behavior and crime: "The law about sexual harassment in employment thus affects people's lives in a manner that is normally reserved for criminal law without giving them the rights that criminal defendants normally have."[159] In what Patai describes as a "vigilante mentality," the accuser is routinely even given "the right to declare... what is to be a satisfactory punishment for the accused."[160]

At one time, of course, it was men, especially family members, who protected women from such unpleasantness. But the feminist insistence that women do not need men for protection necessitates the substitution of gendarmes and the penal apparatus for the same purpose.

So what was once a matter of enforcing manners is now a matter of enforcing the law, giving penal officials a vested interest in adjudication and punishment. "The risk of occasionally being offended is the price we pay for living in a free society," write Weiss and Young. "The Supreme Court cautions us against 'the facile assumption that one can forbid particular words without also running a substantial risk of suppressing ideas in the process. Indeed, governments might soon seize upon the censorship of particular words as a convenient guise for banning the expression of unpopular views.'" Feminists seem to have no hesitation about this. "Most feminist legal theorists do not even deny that their intent is to censor particular words because they serve as conduits for evil ideas," Weiss and Young found. "Even if one agrees with

---

158. Mane Hajdin, quoted in ibid., Kindle locations 374–77.
159. Ibid., Kindle locations 377–80, 451–52.
160. Ibid., Kindle locations, 895, 701.

their view that such 'sexual objectification' is detrimental to women's status, that hardly warrants eviscerating First Amendment freedoms."[161] Philosopher Ferrel Christensen has warned that the concept of "sexual harassment" has become "the greatest violation of freedom of speech to emerge in decades."[162]

Political opinions already qualify as "harassment" on university campuses when contrary to feminist orthodoxy. When a University of Michigan student suggested that date rape accusations could possibly be false he was informed by his dean that his opinion constituted "discriminatory harassment."[163] A statistics professor was accused of "racial and sexual harassment" for "using statistical analysis to challenge some claims of race and sex discrimination—such as the assertion that blacks were disproportionately denied mortgage approval because of race, or that women earned 59 cents to a man's dollar because of discrimination."[164] At California State University, a student can be found guilty of sexual harassment for "reinforcement of sexist stereotypes through subtle, often unintentional means" and "stereotypic generalizations," and Marshall University punishes words that cause "embarrassment" or are "demeaning" or "stigmatizing."[165] Thus men are punished not for harassing women themselves, but for questioning harassment policies and punishments and the goodness of the gendarmes who administer them. An eminent University of California biologist was suspended for refusing harassment training. He called the mandatory training a "sham": "The requirement was a naked political act by the state that offended my sensibilities, violated my rights as a tenured professor, impugned my character, and cast a shadow of suspicion on my reputation and career."[166] Alan Dershowitz recounts how—again, reminiscent of Mao's Cultural Revolution—"a group of feminists in his criminal-law class at Harvard, objecting to his discussion of false allegations of rape, threatened to file hostile-environment charges against him." "Despite the fact that the vast majority of students wanted to hear all sides of the important issues surrounding the law of rape," Dershowitz states, "a

161. Weiss and Young, "Feminist Jurisprudence."

162. Patai, *Heterophobia*, Kindle location 1178.

163. Weiss and Young, "Feminist Jurisprudence."

164. Ibid.

165. Harvey Silverglate, "What Characterizes the Modern Totalitarian, Corporatized University?" FIRE website: http://www.mindingthecampus.com/originals/2011/03/_by_harvey_a_silverglate.html, 17 March 2011.

166. "Prominent Professor May Lose Salary for Refusing 'Sham' Sexual Harassment Training," *Fox News*, 6 November 2008, http://www.foxnews.com/printer_friendly_story/0,3566,447824,00.html.

small minority tried to use the law of sexual harassment as a tool of censorship." The significance of this does not escape him: "[T]he fact that it is even thinkable at a major university that controversial teaching techniques might constitute hostile-environment sexual harassment demonstrates the dangers of this expandable concept."[167]

The ideological and authoritarian logic reaches its starkest in "anti-feminist intellectual harassment." Under this concept, dissent from or criticism of feminist doctrine constitutes an actionable offense and proceedings used to silence the "harasser": "Anti-feminist intellectual harassment ... occurs ... when any policy, action, statement, and/or behavior creates an environment in which the appropriate application of feminist theories or methodologies to research, scholarship, and teaching is devalued, discouraged, or altogether thwarted." Patai calls this "perilously close to an open declaration to the effect that no criticism of feminism and feminists shall be tolerated."[168] But it is difficult to see how it is anything less than precisely such a declaration. According to attorney Hans Bader, "Perfectly civil, non-vulgar students have been subjected to disciplinary proceedings for sexual and racial harassment, in violation of the First Amendment, merely for expressing commonplace opinions about sexual and racial issues, like criticizing feminism."[169]

The accused are then indeed treated like a disgraced party member in Maoist China, subject to ordeals of self-denunciation and re-education:

> ... the offending party is brought to the point where he agrees to spend time learning about, and even leading, activities related to women at the college. He also undertakes ... to write a letter of apology to the student, expressing his esteem for her abilities and detailing what he has learned from his training. The trainer suggests that this letter (to be submitted first to the trainer for "review") also be approved by the department chair and the university's EEO [Equal Employment Opportunity, a federally funded entity] office.[170]

Similar indoctrination is used to punish domestic "violence."

Even children are now punished for sexual harassment, as the US saw

---

167. Patai, *Heterophobia*, Kindle locations 1113–7. For a more recent case, see Robin Wilson, "For Northwestern, the Kipnis Case Is Painful and Personal," 4 June 2015, http://www.chronicle.com/article/For-Northwestern-the-Kipnis/230665?cid=db&elqTrackId=0ae58fff3f7d48058e4f33476884e86f&elq=35ee85c343ad408eb2cdd13c2ce96aab&elqaid=128 19&elqat=1&elqCampaignId=5271.

168. Ibid., Kindle locations 2484, 2486–69, 2501–02.

169. Bader, "Obama Administration."

170. Ibid., Kindle location 2195–98.

when six-year-old Johnathan Prevette was suspended from school for kissing a girl on the cheek. Such sensational cases are, again, only the tip of the iceberg, and many have followed since. Minnesota's harassment law includes kindergartners, and in one school year alone, over 1,000 children "were suspended or expelled on charges related to sexual harassment." In 1993, Cheltzie Hentz, 7, became the youngest complainant at that point to win a federal sexual-harassment suit for "abusive" language by boys on a school bus.[171] "This particularly absurd case also provided a telling example of the anti-heterosexual bias" that pervades the sexual harassment industry. "A six-year-old girl kissing another little girl would not have been the target of such vigilance."[172]

These programs invariably include the requirement to "educate" the offending child in ideology. This includes informing girls who might enjoy the attention that they should instead be scolding the boys for their criminal culpability in transgressing federal law. "Many girls consider this behavior acceptable, and they laugh and joke about it," laments one social worker. But they are instructed instead to respond to such flirtations by issuing a scripted government warning to the offender and threatening him with police: "Stop it! That's sexual harassment, and sexual harassment is against the law."[173]

Like other political crimes, sexual harassment is also subject to manipulation for those with private grievances against the targeted male. In another sensational case, a Maryland track coach was fired when accused by two girls "unhappy about failing to make the all-county cross-country team." His crimes included Marine-style yelling and derision to motivate the runners—"methods that, one plaintiff [apparently not adequately schooled ideologically] told a reporter, were fine for boys but not for girls, because 'they'll cry.'"[174]

Such manipulation became overtly politicized in such high-profile cases as Anita Hill's accusations against US Supreme Court nominee Clarence Thomas and the allegations against President Bill Clinton by Paula Jones, leading to charges from both political parties that the other was practicing "sexual McCarthyism."[175] Though such public cases are the tip of the iceberg and not typical of what ordinary men and boys endure, they do illustrate how sexual harassment charges are used

171. Weiss and Young, "Feminist Jurisprudence."

172. Patai, *Heterophobia*, Kindle locations 642–44.

173. Quoted in Young, *Ceasefire*, 182.

174. Ibid., 182. Note that the man can be punished either for treating girls differently from boys or, as opportunity allows, for treating them the same.

175. Ibid., 165.

opportunistically. "Accusations of sexual harassment are unusually well
suited to serve as a weapon," writes Patai. "A law that rests so comfortably on the victim's say-so and others' reactions to that say-so, a law that
deals so cavalierly with evidence, is ideally situated for abuse."[176] Clinton "provides a good illustration, as people condemn him or defend
him not because of his alleged actions but because of *a priori* positions
they hold in relation to his administration." Conservative politicos seem
perplexingly eager to adopt and thus legitimize feminist ideology when
it offers a weapon against their own political opponents. As Young
remarks, "Many conservatives were suddenly converted to the cause of
sexual harassment in their zeal to get Clinton."[177] Such opportunism
comes at a cost, as doctrinaire sexual militancy not only wheedles its
way deeper into mainstream politics but—more seriously—politicizes
our ethics and morality and turns it into ideology. In pursuing Clinton,
right-wing zealots credulously adopted ready-made feminist jargon,
whose full implications they could not possibly understand, rather than
simply pointing out that he was pursuing a married woman and betray-
ing his own wife. Thanks to feminist political theology, the political sin
of "sexual harassment" replaces quaint, old-fashioned transgressions
like fornication and adultery.

Feminists likewise demonstrate how selectively their principles can
be applied, depending on politics, since unlike traditional religion and
morality, sexual ideology mandates not fixed principles that apply
equally to all but political maneuvering for the "empowerment" of
some. What purports to be an ethical principle in fact eliminates ethical
principles and substitutes political ideology, whose purpose is the
advancement and power of one group over others. As Patai explains:

> The initial feminist silence in response to Paula Jones's allegations
> against the president . . . is usually attributed to unwillingness on the
> part of feminists to denounce their best political hope in Washington.
> Legal scholars such as Susan Estrich . . . rather unabashedly admits it's
> all politics. More recently, Gloria Steinem wrote an op-ed piece in the
> *New York Times* arguing that men are entitled to one grope and
> defending the president because he recognizes that "no" means "no."
> Steinem thereby confirmed the views of those denouncing the hypoc-
> risy of feminists for abdicating their usual vigilance toward men's
> behavior when, opportunistically, it suited them to do so. Where was
> she until now, critics have asked, when charges of sexual harassment
> were running out of control? Presumably in the same support group as

176. Patai, *Heterophobia*, Kindle Locations 776–78.
177. Young, *Ceasefire*, 194.

most feminists who were happy to see such charges play havoc with men's lives in the workplace and in schools—as long as their own allies weren't targeted.[178]

What is ostensibly a criminal or quasi-criminal accusation (again, it is vague) requiring the equal protection of the law is revealed as a political weapon for feminist operatives to wield against politically selected, vulnerable targets in order to maximize their own power.

While militants claim to champion "equality," and while men have brought complaints against women, sexual harassment has become one more tool to punish male behavior and men. "Rarely is there any mention of cases of women students pursuing professors, harassing male students, or making the lives of other women unpleasant."[179] Though the presumption of most people—and the feminist orthodoxy—is that it proceeds from "power," the real target is men and masculinity.

This is revealed by the dictum of influential legal theorist Catherine MacKinnon that "it is done by men to women regardless of relative position on the formal hierarchy."[180] So men in inferior positions can be accused by more powerful women for what is known as "contrapower harassment": underlings "harassing" their supervisors, students their professors, patients their doctors, but only when the accuser is female. What "power" leverage they exercise is unclear, since the term itself reveals that they have none. But in each case the "harasser" is the male (and their "crimes," one study found, consisted of suggestive looks and requests for dates). "An individual woman's 'professional power' is always trumped by a male's . . . 'social power,'"[181] so the male is always the offender. In a fairly candid admission of what is going on, one study let slip the ideologically incorrect possibility that "the vulnerability inherent in their sex appears to override their [professional] power."[182]

The political ideology governing harassment accusations is also revealed when the accusations are directed against female superiors. This usually comes from not male but female underlings, and it occurs mostly on university campuses when lesbian professors are accused by their students. It goes without saying that the accused feminists are treated much more leniently than men; indeed, they themselves usually

---

178. Patai, *Heterophobia*, Kindle locations 765–71.

179. Ibid., Kindle Location 658.

180. Quoted in Paul Nathanson and Katherine K. Young, *Legalizing Misandry: From Public Shame to Systemic Discrimination against Men* (Montreal: McGill-Queen's University Press), 197.

181. Patai, *Heterophobia*, Kindle location 655.

182. Young, *Ceasefire*, 183.

insist there is nothing wrong with what they did and even celebrate it, because they did it in the name of feminist ideology—yet another example of how ideology creates the very problems about which it complains and delivers the opposite of what it promises. For invariably the feminist professors are not only politicizing but sexualizing their classrooms far more deliberately and overtly than the male colleagues they excoriate. One sees "feminism as a simultaneous discovery of both sexual and intellectual desire" and declares, "It is because of the sort of feminist I am that I do not respect the line between the intellectual and the sexual." Thus while one ideologue complains that lecherous male professors "often" create "highly sexualized classroom climates" (an accusation for which Patai finds no evidence), her sisters in the professoriate itself are busily sexualizing their own classrooms quite openly and deliberately, engaging in more programmatic lechery under the guise of ideological liberation.

That feminists are occasionally caught in their own trap might be a source of comfort to those who hope that some vestige of "equal protection" still governs the law. Feminists are not among them. "Most people take an accusation for a finding of guilt," complains Jane Gallop, a feminist professor on the receiving end of an accusation. "Simply to be accused of a sexual crime is to be forever stigmatized." The irony is not lost on Patai, who notes the professor's "failure ever to connect her experiences with those of the dozens of men who have faced similar accusations from women in colleges and universities. That some of these men may be as innocent as Gallop feels herself to be seems never to have crossed her mind."[183]

In other words, the objection to the witch hunt is not that it persecutes the innocent but that it might diminish the power of the sisterhood. This illustrates not merely a double standard but a double standard designed decidedly to criminalize innocent men. "Female sexual harasser seems like a contradiction in terms," writes one feminist, since "feminism invented sexual harassment." Sexual harassment is not a universally recognized crime that feminists simply brought to light so that it could be applied equally to all; it is a new political crime literally "invented" by ideologues to criminalize those whose positions and power they crave for themselves and to whom they appear to be imputing their own sexual-political fantasies. Feminists by definition cannot be guilty because the criminal law has been redesigned to shift power to feminists. "For a feminist to be accused of sexual harassment is, to

---

183. Patai, *Heterophobia*, Kindle locations 1438–40.

Gallop, the mark of 'an issue drifting from its feminist frame.'"[184] In other words, it is to de-politicize the criminal justice system and disarm the law as a political weapon by applying the equal protection of the laws. Like feminism generally, it is not based on universal principles that apply equally to all; it is another power grab achieved by criminalizing others. Applying the "equal protection of the law" would bring the entire enterprise crashing down.

As always, the most effective weapon for destroying men is sex, and the battle reduces to who controls the terms of sexuality. "Sexualizing is not necessarily to women's disadvantage," one feminist confesses, with understatement. She then goes on to declare that feminists alone may decide when "sexualizing" is permitted and when it is not—and that, in Patai's words, "men are to be held legally liable if they make a wrong guess about this." As a student, one eventual feminist professor said she wanted to get her professors into bed "in order to make them more human, more vulnerable." She "wanted to see them naked, to see them as like other men." "Screwing these guys," she explains, "definitely did not keep me from taking myself seriously as a student." Sex, in other words, is a weapon to degrade and humble. "She wants sexual harassment law and regulations to exist only within a framework that provides her and other feminists with license," writes Patai, "while restraining the behavior of men."[185] License yes, but following from that, political power. Here is the true use of sex as power, the political honey trap: having used the muscle of the law to neuter their natural tendency to take the sexual initiative, feminists can then lure men into sexual encounters on feminist terms, before the police and lawyers step out of the closet.

All this manipulates sex to criminalize masculinity itself, and the feminist formulation that sexual assault and sexual harassment are about not sex but "power" plays a critical and revealing role. Cathy Young points out that "to the ideologues, sex is not about sex but about power," and MacKinnon, who "treats sexuality as a social construct of male power," makes this explicit.[186] Patai likewise shows that "Male sexual interest is not simply being construed, or interpreted, as 'power.' It has actually been redefined as such."[187]

The full force of the feminist logic equating masculinity with power, with the aim of neutering (or acquiring) it, can only be fully understood by realizing that it contains an important element of truth. As is well

184. Ibid., Kindle locations 1459, 1478–79.
185. Ibid., Kindle locations 1505–7, 1520–2, 1545–46.
186. Young, *Ceasefire*, 183.
187. Patai, *Heterophobia*, 170.

known, women (but not men) find power sexually attractive. As Henry Kissinger is reported to have remarked, "Power is the ultimate aphrodisiac," but only for women. Masculinity itself is power, and the terms we use to describe it ("potency," "impotence") indicate as much. "Women are attracted to wealthy and high-status men," observes Professor Daniel Amneus, "but men are not attracted to wealthy and high-status women." This differential is central to the attraction and harmony between the sexes:

> The powerful and high-achieving woman might suppose that her own achievements entitle her to be admired and pursued by men, as high achieving men are admired and pursued by women. It doesn't work that way. President Kennedy and President Clinton found themselves surrounded by willing females; Madeleine Albright and Janet Reno would get nowhere with their male underlings by making passes at them. Hypergamy prevents such gender-switches. If Betty Friedan, Adrienne Rich, and Marcia Clark imagined that being successful movers and shakers would make them attractive to men and allow them to become sexual predators like Kennedy and Clinton, they found out otherwise. Powerful women are not attractive to men. This is why women are lesser achievers than men.

Given other controversies provoked by sexual radicals, it may be worth pointing out here that civilized society channels this power differential into social harmony, economic prosperity, and political stability through marriage, in which context Amneus explains it very succinctly:

> Women want to marry men who are older, taller, more muscular, richer, better educated, and have higher status than themselves. When they do, their friends tell them they have made a good match. A woman who chooses to marry a man younger, shorter, less muscular, poorer, less educated, and with a lower status—or even one or two of these things—will be judged to have married beneath herself. A low-status man who pursues a wealthy, high-status woman will be deemed a gigolo.[188]

This is inequality at its most voluntary and functional. By demanding "gender equality" (not to mention marriage between members of the same sex) and depicting gender differentials as "oppression," sexual radicals are not only upsetting and sabotaging the relations between the

---

188. Daniel Amneus, *The Case for Father Custody* (Alhambra, California: Primrose Press, 1999), 321. See also Marianne Bertrand, Emir Kamenica, and Jessica Pan, "Gender Identity and Relative Income within Households," National Bureau of Economic Research, Working Paper 19023, October 2013.

sexes and the dynamic that makes for mutual attraction; they are inject-
ing government power into the most intimate human relationships at
precisely the point where the attraction is socially most constructive and
tasking it with a mission at which it can succeed only by unending
authoritarianism. They are turning sex from a force for private attraction to an instrument for permanent legal warfare between the sexes.

The very power differential that drives the sexual and marital relationship is now being perverted to "empower" the feminine by criminalizing the masculine. The feminine component is not similarly
vulnerable, because, while it is also characterized by a kind of power,
women's power is sexual whereas men's is economic and civil. "Never
discussed . . . is women's own allure created by gesture, dress, and so
forth," write Paul Nathanson and Katherine Young. "This, too, is a kind
of power."[189] By commandeering the state and criminalizing sexual
attraction, feminists seek to acquire both kinds of power. "Women are
never at fault," writes Patai. "They need not examine their own ways. . . .
They need only to learn when and how to file complaints, although,
interestingly, even this recourse is never construed as a 'power' in their
possession. Only men have power, and it is men, not women, who need
to change."[190] But the critical difference is that the male power exists
separate from the state and serves as a check on it. This new female (and
homosexual) power is always in alliance with the state, whose own
power it in turn augments.

Moreover, it is a form of power that leads to others, since only the
incurably correct politically could argue that such "harassment" is not
often a two-way street. "For every gross male harasser, there are ten
female sycophants who shamelessly use their sexual attractions to get
ahead," writes Camille Paglia.[191] Once again, it would appear that it is
the feminists who are using the state to exercise "power and control."
"Showing your cleavage is the embodiment of empowerment," says a
female spokesperson for Wonderbra, which commissioned a survey
finding that two-thirds of British women admitted using their cleavage
to advance their careers, and 14% admit they "wear plunging necklines
in the workplace to boost their career."[192] "Sexual harassment" codes do

189. Nathanson and Young, *Legalizing Misandry*, 197.

190. Patai, *Heterophobia*, 41.

191. "A Call for Lustiness," *Time*, 23 March 1998, 54, quoted in Nathanson and
Young, *Legalizing Misandry*, 222.

192. Sadie Whitelocks, "Our Secret Weapon! Two Thirds of British Women Use Their
Cleavage to Get Ahead in Life Finds Wonderbra Poll," *Daily Mail*, 30 March 2012, online:
http://www.dailymail.co.uk/femail/article-2122645/Our-secret-weapon-Two-thirds-Briti
sh-women-use-cleavage-ahead-life-finds-Wonderbra-poll.html#ixzz1qmsqoOFH.

not discourage this form of power-seeking; they render it far more effective.

Women's natural sexual attraction thus constitute what feminists characterize as their "oppression," and this is the inescapably political logic by which, "Taken to its logical conclusion, ideological feminism really does lead to lesbianism." It also shows why the kind of lesbianism thus driven is not simply a personal sexual preference but a subtle political ideology whose logical conclusion can only be the criminalization of male heterosexuality, if not all heterosexuality. "Do we really want to declare that straight men are sexist for feeling physically attracted to female bodies?" ask Nathanson and Young.[193] Indeed, criminally sexist. Patai calls this "heterophobia."

The logical conclusion is of course emasculation, which is expressed in various demands that men denounce themselves and one another for being men. In one of the latest stunts, men are expected to parade about in high-heel shoes as a form of empathy with oppressed women—a peculiar form of political protest that has the virtue of permitting women to exercise sexual allure while simultaneously claiming to be victimized by their own indulgence and power, and then blaming and emasculating men. The "Walk a Mile in Her Shoes" campaign claims to make "men better understand and appreciate women's experiences." "But women choose to wear high heels because they want their legs and feet to look sexy," Heather MacDonald observes. "Nothing forces them to be sex objects; they assume the role voluntarily."[194] In April 2015, Temple University ROTC cadets were both politicized and publicly humiliated by being ordered to wear high heels during a political march.[195]

Logically the only way to end sexual inequality and "harassment" is to end sexual difference—toward that end, now re-baptized as "gender." "Women couldn't be oppressed if there was no such thing as 'women,'" comments one feminist, apparently the product of a "sex-change" procedure. "Doing away with gender is key to doing away with patriarchy."[196]

193. Nathanson and Young, *Legalizing Misandry*, 211.

194. Heather MacDonald, "Another College Gets the Times Treatment on Sexual Assault," *National Review Online*, 14 July 2014, http://www.nationalreview.com/corner/382725/another-college-gets-times-treatment-sexual-assault-heather-mac-donald.

195. See http://www.ijreview.com/2015/04/301448-controversy-after-rotc-cadets-allegedly-forced-to-march-in-event-wearing-questionable-footwear/?utm_source=Iterable&utm_medium=email&utm_campaign=morningnewsletter.

196. Kate Bornestein, *Gender Outlaw: On Men, Women, and the Rest of US* (New York: Routledge, 1994), 115, quoted in Dale O'Leary, *The Gender Agenda* (Lafayette, LA: Vital Issues Press, 1997), 90.

In short, nothing indicates that the hysteria over "harassment" is a necessary but excessive response to a real problem; from the start it was another ideological power grab, using sexual dynamics and government power to emasculate and feminize. "Now I believe that obvious cases of true harassment are relatively rare," says one professor who volunteered to participate in his university's program, "and that most of the movement feeds off minor incidents and consensual relationships that have somehow gone sour."[197]

The result is a campaign to root out heterodox opinions that most people regard as common sense and label them as criminal. "Dissent . . . was not regarded as a difference of political opinion, but as the un-welcome persistence of pernicious 'attitudes' assumed to inspire crimi-nal behavior," writes Brian Mitchell. He cites a US Congressional com-mittee, which compares commonsense beliefs about men and women to racist bigotry: "At the root of sexual harassment is a series of cultural beliefs, attitudes, and perceptions about women. Unless we can change stereotypical thinking, sexual harassment training programs will likely prove ineffective."[198]

Like other new gender crimes, sexual harassment "has spawned an industry" that thrives by accusing. Aside from the usual proliferation of lawyers and civil servants, private companies now offer "awareness pro-grams" and "training services" that teach people how to accuse.[199]

As with rape, the vanguard of all this is in our ideological incubator: higher education. "The modern college or university is, in most instances, run primarily by the lawyers," observes Harvey Silverglate. This substitution of lawyers for educators "grows . . . out of the increas-ing role of federal and state legislation in the daily life of our colleges" and from a consequent fear of being sued. "Today no . . . decision is made without consultation with, if not outright dictation by, the [in-house law firm known as the] general counsel"—stand-in administra-tors "to whom 'No trouble on my watch' is the guiding principle." This fosters a culture not of inquiry and criticism but of obedience and con-formity. Thus, "many issues are decided not on the basis of what is con-ducive to instruction and learning, but rather in response to the ever-hovering question: How can the college reduce its legal liability and avoid being sued?" And the first example that comes to mind is sexual:

---

197. Patai, *Heterophobia*, Kindle locations 1021–22.

198. Mitchell, *Women in the Military*, 278. Mitchell is discussing the military, but the same points are applicable elsewhere, especially wherever federal funding is involved.

199. Nathanson and Young, *Legalizing Misandry*, 218.

So when ... a student accuses another student of a sexual assault, the disciplinary tribunal on many campuses tends to give excessive deference to the accuser, at the expense of the accused, for fear of being charged with some form of gender discrimination or a laissez-faire attitude toward harassment. The same attention to liability-reduction may be found in numerous decisions made by campus tribunals or administrators.[200]

Behind a front of distinguished educators who have been reduced to ciphers, feminist federal officials manipulate the nation's universities through marionette lawyers.

Here as elsewhere, the system readily degenerates into legal extortion. "Universities tend to prefer the least expensive path to resolution of sexual harassment cases, and this often means settling out of court, usually by paying off the complainant, regardless of the merits of the charges," writes Patai. "Such settlements are frequently shrouded in secrecy; all the outside world knows about them is that charges were withdrawn in exchange for undisclosed sums of money. The alleged 'harasser's' name is never explicitly cleared."[201] Such methods operate on the cutting edge of criminal law, where the plea bargain has similarly become a legalized shakedown racket, and parallel "civil" cases provide a lucrative profit motive for accusers, lawyers, and anyone else who can get their noses in the trough.

In May 2013, the US federal government continued pushing the envelope with yet more directives dictating how universities must police and micromanage the private lives of their students, to the point of stopping the ideas that come out of their mouths. The Foundation for Individual Rights in Education (FIRE) describes the initiative as "a shocking affront to the United States Constitution" that mandates "that virtually every college and university in the United States establish unconstitutional speech codes that violate the First Amendment and decades of legal precedent." According to FIRE president Greg Lukianoff, the government is demanding "campus speech codes so broad that virtually every student will regularly violate them. The DOE and DOJ are ignoring decades of legal decisions, the Constitution, and common sense."[202] Silverglate and Juliana DeVries say that by dictating the permissible

---

200. Silverglate, "What Characterizes." Note how he too conflates "assault" and "harassment," as if they are the same.

201. Patai, *Heterophobia*, Kindle locations 1081–83.

202. "Federal Government Mandates Unconstitutional Speech Codes at Colleges and Universities Nationwide," Foundation for Individual Rights in Education internet site, http://thefire.org/article/15767.html, 17 May 2013.

extent of sexual discussion, the federal agencies "have mandated the effective abolition of free speech on college campuses." As they describe the measures:

> Henceforth, "sexual harassment," for which a student must be investigated according to federal regulations, will be defined on campuses throughout the nation as engaging in "any unwelcome conduct of a sexual nature." Moreover, the "unwelcome conduct" need not be gauged by the perceptions and reactions of a "reasonable person." Instead, a student . . . must . . . be brought up on harassment charges if his conduct is, quite simply, "any unwelcome conduct of a sexual nature," including "verbal conduct" (more commonly known as "speech"), from the vantage point of the "victim."[203]

Another legal authority writes that, "The breadth of this new mandate, plucked from the mists occupied only by the most radical ideologues, is staggering."

> Under DOJ/DOE's definition of sexual harassment, a student asking another out on a date could conceivably violate the law if the person being asked out found the question "unwelcome". . . . Or if a student was taking a health class where biological reproduction was discussed, the teacher might be found guilty of sexual harassment if one student found the discussion "unwelcome," even if no one else in the class and no reasonable person found it unwelcome or offensive.[204]

Here again, the subjective perceptions of the accuser ("victim"), not the objective deeds of the accused ("harasser") determine guilt. Lukianoff says, "If the listener takes offense to sexually related speech for *any reason*, no matter how irrationally or unreasonably, the speaker may be punished." In other words, because the crime is "offending" someone, the accused is guilty by virtue of being accused.

The critics who led the outrage against the directive treat it as something unusual, isolated, and innovative and so they have trouble accounting for where it came from. But as we have seen and will see again, it is a common feature of gender crimes—already well established in, for example, divorce court and rape cases, where it is certainly very familiar to the feminist officials who devised these directives.

Here too one can see very starkly how the "hook-up" culture of easy

---

203. "The Feds Mandate Abolition of Free Speech on Campus," Minding the Campus internet site, 13 May 2013, http://www.mindingthecampus.com/originals/2013/05/the_feds_mandate_abolition_of_.html.

204. Hans A. von Spakovsky, "Making a Request for a Date Could be a Federal Crime," *PJ Media*, 15 May 2013, http://pjmedia.com/blog/making-a-request-for-a-date-could-be-a-federal-crime/.

sex that is now rife throughout the universities of the Western world—and that was started in the name of sexual liberation—has now become a massive, federally administered honey trap that lures and then criminalizes heterosexual male university students. "Libertarians are rightly outraged by the Obama administration's new puritanical speech code," Peter Lawler observes: "But others have either praised or blamed that same administration for its 'aggressive libertarianism' when it comes to sexual behavior—its promotion of the right to contraception, its opposition any limitation on abortion as religious extremism, and its firm embrace of the cause of gay rights. Some might say this is the most and least puritanical administration in history."[205] But what is critical is not the paradoxical contradiction; it is the dynamic behind it. Ken Masugi notes "the contradictory place the university has become." "Having embraced the sexual revolution and encouraged an atmosphere of promiscuity," he writes, "much of higher education has now created a legalistic, centralized crackdown on talk about sex.... We have become what Tocqueville implied our condition would be without the influence of mores: a bureaucratic nightmare. If we can't rule ourselves, we will have rules, myriad of them, made for us."[206]

But this is not really contradictory at all, and the bureaucratic nightmare is no accident. It is yet another grab for power by sexual revolutionaries, and it places them firmly in control. Indeed, consistent with our recurring theme, what escapes even critics is how smoothly the ever-expanding definition of "harassment" criminalizes, simultaneously, both personal behavior and heterodox political opinions. "This [directive] leaves a wide range of expressive activity ... subject to discipline," FIRE points out, diplomatically suggesting examples of what might be prohibited: "a campus performance of 'The Vagina Monologues,' a presentation on safe sex practices, a debate about sexual morality, a discussion of gay marriage." But of course we all know that these are not the activities that will be banned. They are precisely what are being encouraged, funded, and given official sanction because they flush out heterodoxy so it can be punished. "Inclusive enforcement of this mindlessly broad policy is impossible," Wendy Kaminer notes, adding that it is not intended to be enforced evenhandedly. "I doubt federal officials want or expect it to be used against sex educators, advocates of reproductive

---

205. "The Obama Administration's Neo-Puritanical Repression," Rightly Understood blog, 16 May 2013, http://bigthink.com/rightly-understood/the-obama-administrations-neo-puritanical-repression.

206. "The De-Eroticized University," Library of Law and Liberty internet site, 16 May 2013, http://www.libertylawsite.org/2013/05/16/the-de-eroticized-university/.

choice, anti-porn feminists, or gay rights advocates, if their speech of a sexual nature is 'unwelcome' by religious conservatives."[207] On the contrary, it will be used against religious conservatives and anyone else who challenges the federal government's consolidation of sexual power.

If any doubt can remain about the federal government's commitment to due process, officials suggest "taking disciplinary action against the harasser" *before* any investigation is even complete, and they complain that one appeal resulted in exculpation. "A Justice Department offended that a defendant might be able to go through several levels of appeal is something that should scare all of us," comments Hans von Spakovsky. "They appear to want the university to apply the Queen of Heart's admonition in *Alice in Wonderland* and lop off the heads of anyone accused of sexual harassment *before* there has even been an investigation or hearing to determine whether the accusations are true."[208] One student leader at a major university complained that by demanding rules of evidence and due process protections for the accused, "You're automatically assuming the information from the [alleged?] victim is false."[209]

"The Departments of Education and Justice are out of control," declares FIRE's Lukianoff. "Banning everyday speech on campus? Eliminating fundamental due process protections?" But the most damning indictment of all of us may be that this level of outrage can be generated on university campuses (where the most severe penalties are expulsion), whereas no remotely comparable clamor arises against innocent men jailed for decades by trumped-up accusations in criminal courts or summary incarcerations by divorce courts without any criminal conviction or even charge at all.[210]

Domestic Violence

Feminist hysteria over domestic violence is even more dishonest than that generated over rape and sexual harassment. "The battered-women's movement turned out to be even more vulnerable to being co-opted by the state and conservative penal forces than the anti-rape movement

---

207. "No Sex Talk Allowed," *Atlantic* internet site, 15 May 2013, http://www.theatlantic.com/sexes/archive/2013/05/no-sex-talk-allowed/275782/.

208. "Making a Request."

209. "College Student Lear: Requiring Substantial Evidence of a Sex Offense before a Student May be Expelled 'Automatically Assum[es] the Information from the Victim is False,'" Community of the Wrongly Accused blog, 20 May 2013, http://www.cotwa.info/2013/05/college-student-leader-requiring.html.

210. A bibliography is at http://www.saveservices.org/sexual-assault/editorials/2016-2/.

that emerged before it," writes Marie Gottschalk.[211] This is from a feminist scholar who does not question the claims of the domestic violence industry. Yet the most cursory scrutiny quickly reveals that this alleged epidemic too is fabricated. "There is not an epidemic of domestic violence," Massachusetts Judge Milton Raphaelson has stated (after his retirement). "There is an epidemic of *hysteria* about domestic violence."[212] None of the statistics purporting to quantify a problem of family violence are based on convictions through jury trials or even formal charges; they are based on "reports" that are not even necessarily "substantiated" (itself a meaningless term that has no connection with any judicial procedure), and substantial incentives exist not only for women but also for federally funded interest groups and government agencies to manufacture false accusations and exaggerate incidents.[213] Domestic violence has become "a backwater of tautological pseudo-theory and failed intervention programs," write scholars Donald Dutton and Kenneth Corvo. "No other area of established social welfare, criminal justice, public health, or behavioral intervention has such weak evidence in support of mandated practice."[214]

Even more than rape and sexual harassment, and like the divorce industry with which it is closely connected, domestic violence has become a multi-billion dollar industry and "an area of law mired in intellectual dishonesty and injustice."[215]

Feminists portray domestic violence as a political crime perpetrated exclusively by men to, again, perpetuate male power. Yet the fact that men and women commit violent acts in the home in roughly equal

211. Gottschalk, *Prison*, 139. For a more detailed treatment of domestic violence, see Baskerville, *Taken Into Custody*, ch. 4.

212. Speech at Becker College, February 2000, quoted at http://www.massoutrage.com/how-restraining-orders-work-in-real-life.html.

213. See for example from the *Washington Post*, generally a cheerleader for the domestic violence industry: Glenn Kessler, "Holder's Claim...," 18 December 2013, http://www.washingtonpost.com/blogs/fact-checker/wp/2013/12/18/holders-2009-claim-that-intimate-partner-homicide-is-the-leading-cause-of-death-for-african-american-women/.

214. "Transforming A Flawed Policy: A Call To Revive Psychology and Science in Domestic Violence Research and Practice," *Aggression and Violent Behavior* 11 (2006), 478. "In examining research on battery, one sees that respected medical periodicals uncritically indulge the feminists in their inflammatory tendencies. ... Medical journals have dropped their usual standards when reporting findings of the battery studies." Christina Hoff Sommers, *Who Stole Feminism?* (New York: Simon and Schuster, 1995), 202–03.

215. David Heleniak, "The New Star Chamber," *Rutgers Law Review*, vol. 57, no. 3 (Spring 2005), 1009.

numbers has been clearly established in so many studies that it requires no reiteration here.[216] Some feminists themselves admit and even celebrate this fact. "Women are doing the battering," wrote the iconic Betty Friedan, "as much or more than men."[217] Yet this fact is studiously ignored by today's domestic violence lobby and by law enforcement officials who derive power and earnings from concocting preposterous accusations. The US Department of Justice states that "Strategies for preventing intimate partner violence should focus on risks posed by men."[218] "In 95% of domestic assaults," officials claim, "the man is the perpetrator of the violence."[219] Even were such blatant and undocumented falsehoods true, what precisely is the point of stating them, what constructive purpose does it serve, and what are the implications that can be drawn? That being male establishes guilt? That men who have not committed domestic violence should be punished as if they did? As Phyllis Schlafly concludes, "Feminist ideology about the goal of gender-neutrality and the absence of innate differences between males and females goes out the window when it comes to the subject of domestic violence."[220]

Of course it does not matter what percentage of which category of people commits the preponderance of a particular crime (which has never been demonstrated in this case), since the important public issue is due process of law for every individual. Even if one sex were shown

216. Philip W. Cook, *Abused Men: The Hidden Side of Domestic Violence* (Westport, Connecticut: Praeger, 1997); John Archer, "Sex Differences in Aggression Between Heterosexual Partners: A Meta-Analytic Review," *Psychological Bulletin*, vol. 26, no. 5 (September 2000), 651–80; Murray A. Straus, "The Controversy over Domestic Violence by Women: A Methodological, Theoretical, and Sociology of Science Analysis," in X.B. Arriaga, and S. Oskamp, *Violence in Intimate Relationships* (Thousand Oaks, CA: Sage, forthcoming), accessed 24 October 2004 at http://www.vix.com/menmag/straus21.htm. An extensive bibliography is Martin Fiebert, "References Examining Assaults by Women on Their Spouses or Male Partners: An Annotated Bibliography," *Sexuality and Culture*, vol. 14, no. 1 (2010).

217. Betty Friedan, *It Changed My Life: Writings on the Women's Movement* (Cambridge, MA: Harvard, 1998), 126.

218. Patricia Tjaden and Nancy Thoennes, *Extent, Nature, and Consequences of Intimate Partner Violence* (Washington, DC: National Institute of Justice and the Centers for Disease Control and Prevention, July 2000, NCJ 181867).

219. Internet site of Eric Smith, Macomb County, Michigan, prosecuting attorney: http://prosecutorsmith.com/domestic-violence-information-from-the-prosecuting-att orneys-office/. Why a public prosecutor keeps a personal internet page to disseminate political opinions on prosecutions is not clear.

220. "Feminists Abuse Domestic Violence Laws," Townhall.com, 26 November 2007 (http://townhall.com/columnists/phyllisschlafly/2007/11/26/feminists_abuse_domestic_violence_laws/page/full/).

statistically to commit the preponderance of violent acts, this obviously does not justify punishing the innocent members of that sex. Yet even official government documents now use phrases like "violence against women" and "male violence," as if responsibility for crimes is assigned to categories of people rather than the individuals who commit them. The very fact that such presumptions of criminality are propagated by politicians, journalists, and scholars indicates how unhealthy and politicized the debate has become, how many vested interests have developed a stake in obfuscating rather than illuminating the truth, and how far we have accepted doctrines of collective guilt once associated with totalitarian regimes.

More important than achieving gender balance, however, is to understand how the explosion in domestic violence accusations is directly connected with divorce and child custody.[221] "All of this domestic violence industry is about trying to take children away from their fathers," writes columnist John Waters. "When they've taken away the fathers, they'll take away the mothers."[222] The panoply of punishments ostensibly directed at domestic violence was created almost entirely to win advantage in divorce and child custody cases and answered the problem of how to physically remove the father from the home. "It's an easy way to kick somebody out," says one family law specialist, who claims to see at least one case a month where patently false charges are used to remove a spouse.[223]

Among legal practitioners it is now common knowledge that patently trumped-up accusations are routinely used, and never punished, in divorce and custody proceedings. Attorney Thomas Kasper has described how abuse accusations readily "become part of the gamesmanship of divorce."[224] Elaine Epstein long ago noticed that "allegations of abuse are now used for tactical advantage" in custody cases.[225] "Whenever a woman claims to be a victim, she is automatically be-

221. Anne McMurray, "Violence Against Ex-Wives: Anger and Advocacy," *Health Care for Women International*, vol. 18, no. 6 (November–December 1997); Callie Marie Rennison and Sarah Welchans, *Intimate Partner Violence* (Washington, DC: US Department of Justice, Bureau of Justice Statistics, May 2000, NCJ 178247), 5.

222. "When Violence Becomes Something to Fight Over," *Sunday Tribune*, 2 April 2000.

223. Quoted in Donna Laframboise, "Oh Dad, Poor Dad," *Toronto Globe and Mail*, 12 April 1997, D1–2.

224. Thomas J. Kasper, "Obtaining and Defending Against an Order of Protection," *Illinois Bar Journal*, vol. 93, no. 6 (June 2005).

225. Elaine M. Epstein, "Speaking the Unspeakable," *Massachusetts Bar Association Newsletter*, vol. 33, no. 7 (June–July 1993), 1.

lieved," says Washington state attorney Lisa Scott. "No proof of abuse is required."[226]

Bar associations and even courts themselves regularly sponsor public seminars counseling mothers on how to fabricate abuse accusations. "With child abuse and spouse abuse you don't have to prove anything," the leader of one seminar quoted in the *Chicago Tribune* tells divorcing women. "You just have to accuse."[227] "The number of women attending the seminars who smugly—indeed boastfully—announced that they had already sworn out false or grossly exaggerated domestic violence complaints against their hapless husbands, and that the device worked!" writes an astonished Thomas Kiernan in the *New Jersey Law Journal*. "To add amazement to my astonishment, the lawyer-lecturers invariably congratulated the self-confessed miscreants."[228]

Open perjury is readily acknowledged. "Women lie every day," says Ottawa Judge Dianne Nicholas. "Every day women in court say, 'I made it up. I'm lying. It didn't happen'—and they're not charged."[229]

Feminists themselves point out that most domestic violence occurs during "custody battles," and the vast preponderance of cases arise among divorced and separated couples with children.[230] The dishonesty is evident from the words of feminist groups themselves, who are the most vociferous opponents of divorce and custody reform.[231] Their literature is saturated with complaints not that convicted violent assailants are avoiding prison and walking the streets—an open admission that physical violence is seldom the issue—but that fathers are retaining access to their children after becoming the target of fabricated accusations whose principal purpose is to keep them separated. So pointed is this complaint that custody, rather than safety, is the principal grievance concerning men who are portrayed, without evidence or trial, as violent

226. Lisa Scott, "Scream Queens Fuel Nightmarish VAWA System," *The Price of Liberty* website (http://www.thepriceofliberty.org/05/07/05/guest_scott.htm), 5 July 2005. See also Donald Dutton and Kenneth Corvo, "Transforming A Flawed Policy: A Call To Revive Psychology and Science in Domestic Violence Research and Practice," *Aggression and Violent Behavior*, vol. 11 (2006).

227. Eric Zorn, "A Seminar in Divorce, Down-And-Dirty Style," *Chicago Tribune* 4 November 1988, 1.

228. *New Jersey Law Journal*, 21 April 1988, letters to the editor section, p. 6, quoted in Warren Farrell, *Women Can't Hear What Men Don't Say* (New York: Tarcher/Putnam, 1999), 153.

229. Dave Brown, "Gender-Bias Issue Raises 'Optics' Problem in Domestic Court," *Ottawa Citizen*, 21 February 2002.

230. Callie Marie Rennison and Sarah Welchans, *Intimate Partner Violence* (Washington: U.S. Department of Justice, Bureau of Justice Statistics, May 2000, NCJ 178247), 5.

231. "Leave No-Fault Divorce Alone," *Daily Herald*, 26 December 2004.

criminals.[232] A PBS film on domestic violence and its promotional literature asserted:[233]

- "All over America, battered mothers are losing custody of their children."

- "One third of mothers lose custody to abusive husbands."

- "Batterers are twice as likely to contest [custody] as non-batterers. And they often win sole or joint custody."

- "75% of cases in which fathers contest custody, fathers have history of being batterers."

These undocumented statements are demonstrably false.[234] (The social science data is clear and unambiguous: an intact family is the safest environment for women and children, and most violence occurs after family dissolution.)[235] But the claims themselves are self-refuting. Were they true, one would expect the principal concern to be that men are beating their wives and not being prosecuted or imprisoned, with custody as secondary. If duly convicted criminals are incarcerated as expected, after all, questions of child custody should not arise. Instead, custody is the only grievance, confirming that the purported "batterers" have not been convicted of battering or any other infraction, because everyone knows they have not battered anyone.

So-called "battered women's shelters" have been called "one-stop divorce shops" because they are "extreme militant feminist" operations that exist mostly to separate children from their fathers, even without any demonstration of violence.[236] Erin Pizzey, who founded the first shelter in London in 1971, claims that her movement has been "hijacked" by feminists.[237] Extended investigations by Canada's *National Post* and others revealed a violently anti-male agenda, corruption, drug and alcohol use, child abuse, and even, ironically, violence against women.[238] Yet

232. Sara Catania, "Taking Away Battered Women's Kids," *Mother Jones*, 1 July 2005.

233. Michael Getler, "A Little About Me, A Lot About 'Breaking the Silence'" 2 December 2005; Carey Roberts, "PBS' 'Breaking the Silence' Not Ready for Prime Time," *ifeminists.com*, 19 October 2005 (http://www.ifeminists.net/introduction/editorials/2005/1019roberts.html).

234. See chapter II, under "Divorce."

235. The research is analyzed in Baskerville, *Taken Into Custody*, ch. 4.

236. Donna Laframboise, "One-Stop Divorce Shops," *National Post*, 21 November 1998.

237. Erin Pizzey, "How Feminists Tried to Destroy the Family," *Daily Mail*, 22 January 2007.

238. Donna Laframboise, "Battered Shelters," *National Post*, 14 November 1998.

they continue to receive government funding. One woman whose husband "didn't beat me up or nothing, we just had an argument," says shelter workers ignored her pleas and pressured her to leave her marriage. "They asked me if I was abused, and I said, 'No.' They wanted me to get a lawyer, and I said, 'For what?'" She maintains shelter employees tried to "trick" her into making incriminating statements about her husband. "Everything negative about him, they wrote it down. If I said something nice about him, they wouldn't write it down. I kept telling them, 'No, he didn't hit me.'" She was offered financial incentives to leave her husband. "They said, 'If you leave him, we can help you find a place right away.' But I said, 'I don't want to leave him.' . . . They wanted that so bad. They were trying to break up a family, and I didn't want that."[239] Journalistic investigations revealed "prison camp-like working conditions, misappropriated shelter assets, falsified documents, sex discrimination, illicit drug activities, horrific child abuse, illegal cover-ups, complacent oversight agencies, and more."[240]

Like other new gender crimes, the critical feature of "domestic violence" is that it has no definition. The fact that violent assault is already illegal in every jurisdiction on earth is ignored amid the hysteria and rush to punishment. Legally, domestic violence is adjudicated not as violent assault but as a conflict within an "intimate relationship." Like rape and sexual harassment therefore, it blurs the distinction between disagreement and crime. Indeed—and this is difficult for the uninitiated to fully comprehend—it need not be, in fact, *violent*. In fact it need not be even physical and almost never is, since true battery can be formally charged as criminal assault. "You don't have to be beaten to be abused," is now a standard slogan propagated even by ostensibly objective journalists: "Abuse also means name-calling, put-downs, control and isolation. Abuse means an intimate partner constantly refusing to let you have money, intimidating you by shouting, giving you negative looks or gestures, forcing you into sex acts, or ignoring your opinions."[241] Accusations of "abuse" against citizens guilty of no legal infraction are thus reported uncritically by news media as if "negative looks" and "name-calling" constitute "violence" mandating arrest. A poster on

239. Ibid.

240. Carey Roberts, "Abuse Shelter Head Turns to Violence and Abuse," *MensNewsDaily*, 8 July 2008, http://ejfi.org/DV/dv-76.htm, also http://www.thepriceofliberty.org/arc_roberts.htm.

241. Valerie Schremp, "Domestic Violence Is Society's Menace," *St. Louis Post-Dispatch*, 4 February 4 2001.

the New York subway urges women to call the police if they have suffered "emotional abuse," such as being called "fat" or "stupid."[242]

These definitions are now employed by law enforcement agencies. The British Supreme Court has ruled that "criticizing" and "denying money" constitutes domestic violence. The Home Office explicitly states that domestic "violence" is not violent. "Domestic violence is not restricted to physical violence," it says; "it may include psychological, emotional, sexual, and economic abuse."[243] Funded by almost $1 billion annually from the Violence Against Women Act, the US Justice Department, declares that "undermining an individual's sense of self-worth and/or self-esteem" is "violence." "Domestic violence can be physical, sexual, emotional, economic, or psychological actions . . . that influence another person," says the DOJ. Among the "crimes" that are now included in the DOJ's definition of "violence" are "constant criticism, diminishing one's abilities, [and] name-calling."[244] For such "violence" men (usually fathers) are jailed without trial. Such definitions do not merely circumvent due process protections and punish the innocent; *they are intended to do so*, since they have no other reason to exist than to target those who have committed no violent assault. Obviously it is impossible to build a defense against such vagaries. "Acts that are not criminal between strangers become crimes between members of a household," observes Phyllis Schlafly, "and such actions can be punished by depriving a man of his fatherly rights, putting him under a restraining order, and even jailing him."[245]

The New Jersey family court invokes political rationalizations for openly denying due process protections to those accused and betrays its own presumption of guilt in the process, saying such protection "perpetuates the cycle of power and control whereby the [alleged?] perpetrator remains the one with the power and the [alleged?] victim remains powerless." Attorney David Heleniak, calling domestic violence law "a due process fiasco," identifies numerous violations of standard due process protections in US statutes: no presumption of innocence; hearsay evidence is admissible; and defendants have no right to confront their accusers.[246] Omitting the word "alleged" is standard in federal and state

---

242. Young, *Ceasefire*, 97.

243. Ann Tacket, "Tackling Domestic Violence: The Role of Health Professionals" (London: Home Office, 2004), 1.

244. Department of Justice website: http://www.usdoj.gov/ovw/domviolence.htm.

245. Phyllis Schlafly, *Who Killed the American Family?* (Washington: WND Books, 2014), 65–66.

246. Heleniak, "New Star Chamber," 1036–37, 1042.

statutes (and media reports), and (as with nonpayment of child support) "the mere allegation of domestic abuse . . . may shift the burden of proof to the defendant."[247]

"Restraining orders" separating fathers and children (often for life) are routinely issued during divorce proceedings without any evidence of legal wrongdoing, often without notifying the father to be present to defend himself or without any hearing at all. These orders do not punish criminals for illegal acts they are proven to have committed but prohibit law-abiding citizens from otherwise legal acts—like being in their own homes or with their own children. With the stroke of a pen, judges can simply legislate new crimes around each individual, who will then be arrested for doing what no statute prohibits and what the rest of us may do without penalty. "Once the restraining order is in place, a vast range of ordinarily legal behavior"—most often contact with one's own children—is "criminalized."[248] Because violent assault and other statutory crimes are already punishable, the only people punished are peaceful, law-abiding citizens.

The orders are issued virtually for the asking. Elaine Epstein, past president of the Massachusetts Women's Bar Association, accuses her peers of caving into the "media frenzy surrounding domestic violence" and of doling out restraining orders "like candy." "Restraining orders and orders to vacate are granted to virtually all who apply," and "the facts have become irrelevant," she writes. "In virtually all cases, no notice, meaningful hearing, or impartial weighing of evidence is to be had."[249] Attorney Paul Patten of Fall River, Massachusetts, also says they are "issued like candy," adding, "It's a rare case that they won't be issued as long as somebody says the magic word, 'I've been hit' or 'I've been threatened.'"[250] State representative Barbara Gray told journalist Cathy Young that "judges grant the restraining orders without asking too many questions"—and apparently saw nothing wrong with that.[251] "As a judge for 10 years, I issued hundreds of restraining orders after hearing

247. Miriam Altman, "Litigating Domestic Abuse Cases under Ch. 209A," *Massachusetts Lawyers Weekly*, 23 October 1995, B6.

248. Cathy Young, *Domestic Violence: An In-Depth Analysis* (Washington, DC: Independent Women's Forum, September 2005), 22 (http://www.iwf.org/pdf/young_dom violi.pdf).

249. Epstein, "Speaking the Unspeakable," 1.

250. "Retiring Judge Reveals that Restraining Orders Are Huge Problem," *Massachusetts News*, May 2001.

251. Cathy Young, "The Abuse of Restraining Orders," *Boston Globe*, 30 August 1999, A19.

only one side," Judge Raphaelson confesses.[252] Connecticut attorney Arnold Rutkin charges that many judges view restraining orders as a "rubber-stamping exercise" and that subsequent hearings "are usually a sham."[253] "No objective proof is required," writes Minnesota attorney Daniel Butler. "If the petitioner simply says she is afraid, the order for protection will commonly be issued giving her the home, the children, child support, maintenance, etc."[254] In Missouri, a survey of judges and attorneys unearthed complaints of disregard for due process and noted that restraining orders were widely used as a "litigation strategy."[255] Massachusetts attorney Sheara Friend, says, "I don't think there's a lawyer in domestic relations in this state who doesn't feel there has been abuse of restraining orders. It's not politically correct—lawyers don't want to be pegged as being anti-abused women—but privately they agree."[256]

"Stories of violations for minor infractions are legion," the *Boston Globe* reports. "In one case, a father was arrested for violating an order when he put a note in his son's suitcase telling the mother the boy had been sick over a weekend visit. In another, a father was arrested for sending his son a birthday card."[257] Even accidental contact is punished with arrest. Cathy Young found that "Fathers hit with restraining orders based on trivial or uncorroborated allegations have been jailed for sending their kids a Christmas card, asking a telephone operator to convey the message that a gravely ill grandmother would like to see her grandchildren, or returning a child's phone call."[258]

"The restraining order law is one of the most unconstitutional acts ever passed," says attorney Gregory Hession. "A court can issue an order that boots you out of your house, never lets you see your children again, confiscates your guns, and takes your money, all without you even knowing that a hearing took place." A defendant charged with the most heinous violent crime "has all his or her rights preserved and carefully guarded when before a court.... The court is careful to explain and

252. Milton H. Raphaelson, "Time to Revisit Abuse Statute," *Western Massachusetts Law Tribune*, vol. 2, no. 16 (18–24 April 2001), 4.

253. Arnold Rutkin, "From the Editor," *Family Advocate*, vol. 18 (Winter 1996), 1020.

254. "Fathers Get the Shaft in Family Law Proceedings," *Law and Politics*, December 1995.

255. David Dunlap, "The Adult Abuse Act: Theory vs. Practice," *UMKC Law Review*, vol. 64 (1996), 686, quoted in Young, *Domestic Violence*, 23.

256. Ibid.

257. Kate Zernike, "Divorced Dads Emerge as a Political Force," *Boston Globe*, 19 May 1998.

258. Young, *Ceasefire*, 127.

watch over every constitutional right of that defendant," says Hession. "Not so with restraining order hearings, where a defendant may lose all those things, with no due process at all." Hession describes the process as a "political lynching":

> In a criminal trial, defendants . . . are presumed innocent. They have a right to a trial by jury. They have the right to face their accusers and have evidence presented and cross examine any witnesses. They may not be deprived of property or liberty without due process of law. The Commonwealth must prove guilt beyond a reasonable doubt. The law has to be clearly defined. They have a right to a lawyer, and to be provided one if they cannot afford one.

The abuse law throws out all of those protections.[259]

The violation of due process procedures is so routine that one judge directly instructed his colleagues to violate the constitutional rights of law-abiding citizens: "Your job is not to become concerned about the constitutional rights of the man that you're violating as you grant a restraining order. Throw him out on the street, give him the clothes on his back, and tell him, see ya around. . . . We don't have to worry about the rights."[260]

The next logical step is that fathers and their children are permitted to see one another only under the gaze of government supervisors. This is precisely what is taking place in the rapidly growing system of "supervised visitation centers" for which fathers must pay an hourly fee to see their children. "These centers not only get state funding, they also charge fathers for the privilege of seeing their own offspring." "People yell at you in front of the children. They try to degrade the father in the child's eyes," says Jim O'Brien. "No matter what you do, you're doing it wrong. I wish I'd never come here. . . . They belittle you." When O'Brien asked his daughter if she'd made her first communion in the six years since he had seen her the social worker jumped in and said, "You're not allowed to ask that!" Rick Brita is another father who was never convicted of any offense, and what was supposed to be a three-week arrangement was turned into a three-year ordeal. The center is described by Joseph Rizoli: "It's like being in jail. Everything the father does on the visitation has to be permissioned. Even hugging your own children could end your visit. In Rick's case three years has given him permission to pass this hoop and he can hug his kids now. But he can't

---

259. Hession press release, 30 July 2001.
260. Russ Bleemer, "N.J. Judges Told to Ignore Rights in Abuse TROs," *New Jersey Law Journal* 140, 24 April 1995.

take the children out to a park or anything else outside the center. . . . He can't even take pictures of his own children."[261] Are fathers and their children subject to this humiliation because the father is dangerous or because the centers get federal money for each case? "Are these contract centers concerned with the children or the funding?" asks Stan Rains of Victoria, Texas:

> Children are acutely aware of the ever-present, note-taking caseworkers and of the cameras located every 10 feet along the walls. I have seen a parent and child cling to one another and stare back at the narroweyed, stern visages of several caseworkers studying this parent and child clinging to one another in terror and desperation. They reminded me of two neurotic and traumatized research monkeys reacting to the observations of white- frocked researchers, conditioned to the fact that these white-coated observers had the power to inflict pain, anguish, and even death. With this parent-child pair, their desperate, mutual clinging to one another, seemed to be viewed negatively by the caseworkers. . . . The demeaning of the "visiting" parent is readily visible from the minute that a person enters the "secured facility" with armed guards, officious caseworkers with their clipboards, and with arrogant, domineering managers. . . . The child's impression is that all of these authority figures see Daddy as a serious and dangerous threat. . . . It leaves a child with an impression that their love for Daddy is dangerous and bad, and so is Daddy. . . . Caseworkers . . . correct parents and children alike, openly, for all to hear. [262]

Equally totalitarian are specialized "integrated domestic violence courts," whose mandate is less to dispense impartial justice than, in the words of New York's feminist chief judge, to "make [alleged?] batterers and abusers take responsibility for their actions."[263] These courts bear little relation to most people's understanding of due process. There is no presumption of innocence, hearsay evidence is admissible, and defendants have no right to confront their accusers. One study found there was no possibility that a defendant can be acquitted, since every man arrested for non-felony domestic violence received some punishment:

261. John Maguire, "Twenty Dollars an Hour to Visit Your Child," *Massachusetts News*, 2 August 1999, and correspondence with Joseph Rizoli (25 June 1999).

262. Stan Rains, "Visitation Center Dracula," *Fathering Magazine* (http://www.father mag.com/007/visitation-center/; accessed 8 December 2001). Rains was placed under a gag order following the publication of this article, according to his attorney, David A. Sibley of Corpus Christi, Texas.

263. Quoted in Frank Donnelly, "Domestic Violence Court to Debut," *Staten Island Advance*, 14 December 2003.

fine, jail, and/or treatment.[264] Treatment usually means "Soviet-style psychological reeducation." "The accused men are . . . assigned to classes where feminists teach shame and guilt because of an alleged vast male conspiracy to subjugate women," writes Schlafly. "His attendance at these Soviet-style reeducation sessions continues until he conforms."[265]

A Toronto lawyer describes these courts as "pre-fascist": "Domestic violence courts . . . are designed to get around the protections of the Criminal Code. The burden of proof is reduced or removed, and there's no presumption of innocence."[266] All this reinforces the illusion of a problem because "it coerces defendants into pleading guilty by depriving them of essential constitutional rights, including the right to post bond and the right to be represented by an attorney." "It's just butchering the Bill of Rights," according to attorney Kevin Donovan.[267] *Mother Jones* magazine notes that "conviction rates have risen" and "guilty pleas are way up, suggesting that prosecutors were able to build more substantial cases, leading to more plea bargaining." In other words, the certainty of conviction pressures the innocent into pleading guilty.[268]

As with rape accusations, domestic violence zealots regard sending people to prison as a virtue in itself. In San Diego, two lawyers report with glee that by suspending due process protections a court "obtains convictions in about 88% of its cases,"[269] likewise reminiscent of Soviet criminology. Convictions are supposed to be based on an impartial weighing of evidence in each individual case. Nowhere else in the law do we regard convicting people of crimes—thousands of people of whose guilt or innocence we can have no first-hand knowledge—as a goal to be achieved for its own sake.

In Britain, centuries-old protections for the accused are set aside in the zeal to punish those routinely labeled not as "defendants" but as

264. Angela Gover, John MacDonald, and Geoffrey Alpert, "Combating Domestic Violence: Findings from an Evaluation of a Local Domestic Violence Court," *Criminology and Public Policy*, vol. 3, no. 1 (2003), table 11.

265. Schlafly, *Who Killed*, 65–66, 67.

266. Quoted in Dave Brown, "Skirmish Fails to Scratch the Formidable Feminist War Machine," *Ottawa Citizen*, 9 April 2002.

267. Terje Langeland, "Railroaded for Domestic-Violence Defendants, El Paso County's 'Fast Track' May Not Always Lead to Justice," *Colorado Springs Independent*, 15–21 August 2002 (http://www.csindy.com/csindy/2002-08-15/cover.html).

268. Elizabeth Gettelman, "A New Order in the Court," *Mother Jones*, 1 July 2005 (http://www.motherjones.com/news/featurex/2005/07/court.html, accessed 3 July 2005). Six years earlier, the same magazine published a relatively truthful report on domestic violence.

269. Michael Rips and Amy Lester, "When Words Bear Witness," *New York Times*, 20 March 2006.

"abusers." "Special domestic violence courts" allow third parties such as civil servants and feminist groups to use "relaxed rules of evidence and the lower burden of proof" by bringing "civil actions" against those they label as batterers, even if their alleged "victim" brings no charges—or does not exist. "Victim support groups," with no first-hand knowledge of the alleged deed, can now act in the name of anonymous alleged victims—with no proof that such alleged victims even exist—to loot men who have been convicted of no crime.[270]

Constitutional scholar A.V. Dicey stipulated that due process of law requires adjudication "in the ordinary legal manner before the ordinary courts of the land." By contrast, special courts to try newly invented crimes that can only be committed by certain people are familiar from totalitarian regimes. New courts created during the Reign of Terror in the French Revolution were consciously imitated in the Soviet Union. In Hitler's *Volksgericht* or people's court, "only expediency in terms of National Socialist standards served as a basis for judgment." Rosemary O'Kane emphasizes that the essence of the Terror "lies in summary justice," typically executed by "newly appointed law courts" or "extraordinary courts and revolutionary tribunals."[271]

Continuing the Bolshevik logic, forced confessions, familiar from the Stalinist show trials, are extracted in family courts and domestic violence courts on pain of losing access to one's children or of incarceration. Pre-printed confessions state, "I have physically and emotionally battered my partner." The father must then describe the violence, even if he insists he committed none. The documents require him to confess, "I am responsible for the violence I used. My behavior was not provoked."[272] Scholars of totalitarianism furnish an apposite description: "Confessions are the key to this psychic coercion. The inmate is subjected to a constant barrage of propaganda and ever-repeated demands that he 'confess his sins,' that he 'admit his shame.'"[273]

With most crimes, police generally do not arrest suspects without a warrant unless they personally witness it. Yet the mob justice surrounding domestic violence has brought the innovation of mandatory arrest, even when it is not clear who has committed the deed or even that any

270. Robert Verkaik, "Crackdown Unveiled on Domestic Violence," *The Independent*, 19 November 2001 (http://news.independent.co.uk/uk/legal/story.jsp?story=105619).

271. Carl J. Friedrich and Zbigniew K. Brezezinski, *Totalitarian Dictatorship and Autocracy* (Cambridge, Mass.: Harvard, 1965), 216; Rosemary H.T. O'Kane, *The Revolutionary Reign of Terror: The Role of Violence in Political Change* (Aldershot, Hants., UK: Edward Elgar, 1991), 22, 39, 253.

272. Documents from Warren County, Pennsylvania, in the author's possession.

273. Friedrich and Brzezinski, *Totalitarian Dictatorship*, 216, 195.

deed has been committed at all.[274] One prosecutor in Hamilton County, Ohio, notes that this is "turning law-abiding citizens into criminals." Judith Mueller of the Women's Center in Vienna, Virginia, who had lobbied for the mandatory arrest law, says, "I am stunned, quite frankly, because that was not the intention of the law. It was to protect people from predictable violent assaults, where a history occurred, and the victim was unable for whatever reason to press charges. . . . It's disheartening to think that it could be used punitively and frivolously."[275]

Because mandatory arrest laws resulted in an unexpected rise of arrests of women, feminists began devising procedures effectively requiring, as clearly as possible without stating it categorically, that only men be arrested. Though about half of all incidents are mutual, with no clear instigator or victim, feminists began demanding that police arrest the "primary aggressor." "Police manuals often instruct officers to determine who is the primary aggressor based on 'who appears to be in control,'" though with no guidance on how to determine which person appears to be in "control." In many police departments, "the unofficial policy is to simply arrest the larger person. So in practice the primary aggressor standard becomes the flimsy rationale to arrest the man."[276] In Massachusetts, a training manual tells officers to ignore men's "excuses" such as, "She hit me first." The manual encourages officers to downplay the significance of a man's injuries, warning that "injury alone doesn't determine who is the abuser."[277]

"No drop" prosecution is another legal innovation requiring prosecutors to prosecute cases they would otherwise abandon for lack of evidence or because they judge that no crime has occurred at all. Advocates claim that these measures increase guilty pleas, an open admission that the innocent are being extorted into pleading guilty with threats of prosecution.[278]

The corollary of new crimes that only some people can commit is to exempt others from punishment for standard crimes—indeed, to pro-

---

274. *VAWA: Threat, to Families, Children, Men, and Women* (Rockville, Maryland: Respecting Accuracy in Domestic Abuse Reporting, March 2006), 8.

275. Young, *Domestic Violence*, 15–16.

276. *Justice Denied: Arrest Policies for Domestic Violence Cases* (Rockville, Maryland: Respecting Accuracy in Domestic Abuse Reporting, April 2006).

277. Young, *Domestic Violence*, 17.

278. Robert Davis, Barbara Smith, and Heather Davies, "Effects of No-Drop Prosecution of Domestic Violence Upon Conviction Rates," *Justice Research and Policy*, vol. 3, issue 2 (Fall 2001), 1–13. This official publication of the US Department of Justice, the principal federal agency charged with defending Americans' constitutional rights, does not mention the rights of the accused.

vide a license to kill. Harriet Harman, deputy leader of the British Labour Party and Minister for Women, proposes allowing women to kill their "intimate partners" with impunity if they kill while "claiming past, or fear of future, abuse from male partners."[279] Murder would thus be condoned if a woman claimed to have suffered "conduct which caused the defendant to have a justifiable sense of being seriously wronged."

How the dead (and unproven) "abusers" could establish their innocence is not discussed in the proposal. "Effectively, what Harman and the ultra-feminist lobby want is a licence for women to kill," writes Erin Pizzey, a long-time advocate for domestic violence victims, who has reacted in horror at the hijacking of the movement by ideological extremists. "Women can murder as long as their sense of victimhood is sufficiently powerful. . . . Rather than reducing violence, Harriet Harman's proposals could become a charter for domestic chaos, as vengeful women believe they can butcher partners they come to loathe, inventing incidents of abuse or exaggerating fears of assault."[280] Robert Whelan of the Civitas think-tank accused the government of introducing "gang law" into the legal system. Lyn Costello of Mothers Against Murder and Aggression described the changes as "utter madness." "We need clear laws, not more grey areas. . . . Unless there are really exceptional circumstances, such as self-defence or protecting yourself or family, then there is no excuse for killing someone, and it should be murder."[281]

Stalking

"Stalking" is another politicized crime that thrives on emotion and fear—and misinformation. It conjures up images of perverts hiding in bushes ready to pounce on unsuspecting women. The reality is that stalking accusations are now another political tool in the hands of sexual ideologues.

Like domestic violence, stalking is not perpetrated exclusively by men against women, yet that is how feminists portray it. Despite feminist-

279. Barbara Kay, "The New Justice," *National Post*, 13 August 2008 (http://www. nationalpost.com/story.html?id=719007&p=1). Ottawa law professor Elizabeth Sheehy proposes a similar measure in her 2013 book, *Defending Battered Women on Trial*.

280. Erin Pizzey, "Erin Pizzey, Champion of Women's Rights, Says Radical Feminist Plans to Let Victims of Domestic Abuse Get Away With Murder Are an Affront to Morality," *Mail Online*, 29 July 2008: http://www.dailymail.co.uk/news/article-1039445/Erin-Pizzey-champion-womens-rights-says-radical-feminist-plans-let-victims-domestic-abuse-away-murder-affront-morality.html.

281. James Slack, "Go Soft on Killer Wives: Women Who Kill in Cold Blood Could Escape Murder Charge," *Daily Mail*, 29 July 2008 (http://www.nationalpost.com/story.html?id=719007&p=1).

generated hysteria, no evidence suggests that any more women are being "stalked" now than in the past. Yet here too, feminist legislation criminalizing non-violent private behavior swept through the legislatures unnoticed and unopposed during the 1990s. As with all the new gender offenses, what was new was not the problem but the ideology. The result is another nebulous offence with no clear definition which allows anyone to be arrested virtually at whim. Weiss and Young write that "exaggerated claims . . . uncritically picked up by the media, have created a climate of hysteria in which the rights of mostly male defendants are easily trampled."[282]

By criminalizing "stalking" rather than assault, officials can arrest a man not for acts he has committed but for what someone says he may at some future time possibly intend to commit. According to former US Attorney Jay B. Stephens, "We should not have to wait until an overt act of violence occurs to take action."[283] This approach to law enforcement means that everyone could be presumed guilty of hypothetical crimes they have not committed, and we could just arrest the entire population. It directly violates the fundamental Common Law principle that a man can only be punished for a crime that he has actually committed. (But then, so do restraining orders, divorce procedures, and many other measures.)

Stalking laws are absurdly vague, and standards of proof almost non-existent. The District of Columbia criminalizes "conduct with the intent to cause emotional distress to another person." In Pennsylvania, prison is the penalty for "intent to cause substantial emotional distress." Florida permits warrantless arrests.[284] The US Justice Department defines stalking as "nonconsensual communication."[285]

"All kinds of people are labeled 'stalkers,' even if they haven't put people in fear of violence," writes Tessa Mayes, who cannot seem to bring herself to use the word "men." "Today, 'stalker' is used when somebody is doing something that appears uncommon or irritating even if it is not menacing or threatening. This means that when people tell researchers they are the victim of stalking, they may mean something even more

282. Weiss and Young, *Feminist Jurisprudence.*
283. Quoted in ibid.
284. Ibid.
285. Patricia Tjaden and Nancy Thoennes, *Stalking in America: Findings From the National Violence Against Women Survey* (U.S. Department of Justice, Office of Justice Programs, National Institute of Justice, Centers for Disease Control and Prevention, Research in Brief series), April 1998, 1–2, https://www.ncjrs.gov/pdffiles/169592.pdf (accessed 5 November 2016).

trivial than the kind of behaviour currently outlawed."[286] Mayes cites a Chicago man convicted of stalking his ex-girlfriend, despite evidence that during the time when he was alleged to have terrorized her, they spent time together in a motel and she listed him on a hospital form as the person to contact in case of emergency.[287]

The British Crime Survey likewise makes it apparent that official figures are heavily based on "minor acts of annoyance." Mayes found that most stalking convictions were for letter-writing or telephone calls rather than acting out the stereotypical, menacing view of a stalker who repeatedly follows or watches the victim or hangs around their home or workplace. Consistent with what we see with other feminist "crimes," Mayes notes that "definitions of 'stalking' are problematic" and hopelessly subjective and describes "the redefinition of stalking, and the constant search for it by the authorities." Again, Mayes could be describing rape or domestic violence or human trafficking. "As with offences of intimate violence generally, the definition of stalking partly relies on the victim's *emotions* (in this case, 'distress, fear or alarm'), and sometimes does not even involve physical acts against them." In fact, it almost never involves physical acts.

Mayes has discovered here what others discover independently about hysteria over rape, domestic violence, child abuse, trafficking, or any of the other "crimes" we are examining (invariably without realizing the similarity): it is a hoax. "'Stalking' is lumped in to the category of 'intimate violence' as if an emotional reaction by somebody is the same as suffering from a physical act of violence." Also like rape and domestic violence, "behaviour that wasn't considered worthy of legal intervention in the past is now being criminalised." Noting that most people "didn't report 'partner abuse' (including stalking) to the police because it was considered 'too trivial or not worth reporting,'" Mayes observes that "Clearly, many acts the Home Office regard as criminal are simply not seen as such by the 'victims.'"[288]

Something even more deceptive is probably taking place here, since another feminist-driven abuse is probably responsible for this male-only "crime." Both the US and British governments' literature makes apparent that most cases involve divorced fathers trying to see their children and that hysteria and measures claimed to prevent "stalking" provide one more tool to keep them away. The fact that the British

286. Tessa Mayes, "Stalked by an Overblown Fear of Crime," *Spiked*, 4 February 2008 (http://www.spiked-online.com/index.php?/site/earticle/4469/).

287. Weiss and Young, *Feminist Jurisprudence*.

288. Mayes, "Stalked."

Crime Survey includes stalking by family members as an intimate crime lends plausibility to this interpretation. Of course, no figures on this are made available, but it would merit further investigation.

Feminists invariably respond by invoking some grisly crime against a woman by a man. This is precisely how the stalking laws were passed in the first place, usually in response to some shocking and sensationalized crime that is already criminally punishable. Illinois enacted a new law after a woman was gunned down by her estranged husband, "who repeatedly violated a protection order."[289] Aside from confirming that most such cases are connected with divorce and child custody, such crimes can and are of course punished under existing criminal murder and assault statutes without criminalizing harmless people such as fathers who simply want to see their children. But here again, the aim is not to protect women; it is to attack the patriarchy. "Today's tendency to blur the trivial with the criminal tends to label too many of us as victims or criminals on the basis of statistical interpretation, and it suggests we are all in need of greater intervention by the authorities," Mayes concludes. "Sometimes, it would be better if the 'intimate' stayed intimate."

Child Abuse

Child abuse—both real and imaginary—may be sexual radicalism's most vicious legacy, a phenomenon subtly and cynically exploited for political purposes to the point of, even more than elsewhere, actually creating the problem in the first place as a vehicle for aggrandizing power.[290]

Here too we find the fingerprints of the radicals, institutionalized in the social work profession, fomenting hysteria to semi-criminalize more of the population, this time parents (mothers as well as fathers). As with other gender crimes (including what are still called "sex crimes"), the hideousness of the accusation easily lends itself to mob justice, a tendency the radicals have exploited to the full. "The child abuse issue . . . has been one which in recent decades has whipped the country into a frenzy, that has caused people to throw reasonableness, good judgment, and basic fairness to the wind," writes Stephen Krason. "Children are being harmed, so the response has been that we must *do something*. What has been done has occurred without careful reflection and without a judicious concern for the likely consequences."[291]

---

289. Weiss and Young, *Feminist Jurisprudence*.

290. Addressed at length in Baskerville, *Taken Into Custody*, 193–214.

291. Stephen Krason, "The Mondale Act and Its Aftermath: An Overview of Forty Years of American Law, Public Policy, and Governmental Response to Child Abuse and

In this case though the radicals have gone a step further, from exaggerating and redefining a traditional crime (rape) to coining new jargon to fabricate a new crime (domestic violence) to—in the case of child abuse—actually creating the problem they claim to be combating. This is a very serious charge, but it can easily be demonstrated.

Beginning in the nineteenth century, a new sensitivity about childrearing methods led to the founding of hundreds of societies for the prevention of cruelty to children in Britain and the United States. Though these were ostensibly private organizations at first, "New laws and court decisions gave these societies extraordinary police powers" to prosecute allegedly abusive and neglectful parents, remove children from their families, and terminate parents' rights. All this coincided with the appearance of feminists, who understood the subtle but extraordinary power they could acquire by controlling and politicizing children—to the point of effectively becoming family police. "Women's groups were integral to these child-welfare campaigns."[292]

The professionalization of social work in the early twentieth century—at the instigation of feminists like Jane Addams—quickly created a plainclothes gendarmerie with a vested political interest in other people's children. As governments wrested charitable work from churches and other private foundations, social workers became government officials with "extraordinary police powers," though without the restraints we normally impose on police to protect the rights of the accused.

The Sexual Revolution created a bonanza of opportunities for these female gendarmes to divide and rule the nation's families and a nightmare for the nation's children and parents, millions of whom found themselves separated from one another and, in various ways, turned into semi-criminals. Here again, "contemporary feminism . . . emerged at roughly the same time as the movement for the current child abuse laws."[293]

In the United States, this led to the Mondale Act of 1974, which provided federal financial incentives to find child abuse, or to concoct it, and hence to the dreaded "Child Protective Services," another plainclothes feminist constabulary, which investigates families for child abuse on highly questionable pretexts.

Neglect," in *Child Abuse, Family Rights, and the Child Protective System: A Critical Analysis from Law, Ethics, and Catholic Social Teaching* (Lanham, Maryland: Scarecrow Press, 2013), 41. (I am quoting from the online version at http://www.faithandreason.com/wp-content/uploads/2012/08/Mondale-Act-After-Forty-Years_-True.pdf?97be1a.)

292. Gottschalk, *Prison*, 118.

293. Krason, "Mondale Act," 42.

Perhaps predictably, this legislation was soon followed by waves of child abuse hysteria that swept America and (following similar legislation elsewhere) Britain and other countries during the 1980s and 1990s, resulting in torn-apart families, hideous injustices, psychologically damaged children, incarcerated parents, and ruined lives. The "witch hunt," as the American Civil Liberties Union termed one episode, shows how parents of both genders (though far more often fathers) were unjustly deprived of their children and incarcerated by setting aside constitutional safeguards while the media and civil liberties advocates (including the ACLU, which has again learned to hold its tongue) looked the other way.[294] Each case "was part of a line of what only can be called witch hunts in which state social workers badgered very young children until they came up with lurid tales—after having denied that those things occurred."[295] All turned out to be fabrications.

In each case, the pattern is similar. In fact, Stephen Krason's outline of the *modus operandi*—with its presumption of guilt and other due process violations, use of children as political instruments and weapons, and determination to punish at all costs—strikingly parallels rape, domestic violence, child support, and the other gender crimes we have examined:

1. Authorities seem to work from the premise that the parents are guilty and have to prove themselves innocent.

2. When it becomes apparent that authorities realize that no abuse or neglect has occurred, they still persist to try to find something.

3. In spite of legal strictures, they keep cases and investigations open, and efforts are made by authorities to coerce false confessions of guilt or (if a criminal investigation) to plea-bargain with the threat that children will not be returned otherwise.

4. Parents have long struggles getting their children back even after they are exonerated.

5. After their sometimes nightmarish battles with the agencies are over they find they have no legal recourse because of the state's immunity.[296]

---

294. *When Child Protection Investigations Harm Children: The Wenatchee Sexual Abuse Cases*, American Civil Liberties Union of Washington (October 1997). See also Dorothy Rabinowitz, *No Crueler Tyrannies: Accusation, False Witness, and other Terrors of our Times* (New York: Wall Street Journal Books, 2003).

295. William Anderson, "The Earl of Dook, or the Continuing State of State Justice in North Carolina," *LewRockwell.com*, 1 June 2006.

296. Krason, "Mondale Act," 12.

Here too, none of the prosecutors, judges, or social workers who ignored due process protections to frame parents they knew to be innocent on spurious charges were ever prosecuted or punished for obstructing justice or for the lives they destroyed. (One of them, Janet Reno, was made Attorney General of the United States.)[297] On the contrary, they have complete immunity from criminal prosecution or civil liability, even when their allegations are demonstrated to be fabricated and malicious.

Even more seriously—and this also parallels other gender crimes—repeated exposés of obvious and widespread injustices trigger no systematic investigation or official inquiry into the workings of the child protection system to determine why they occur. Not surprisingly they continue unabated, as the media and other supposed watchdogs lose interest. The abuse and exploitation of children by the very people and programs that claim to be protecting them is now so common and has been repeatedly and ruthlessly exposed in so many scholarly studies and popular accounts that one wonders why it is permitted to continue.

Yet continue it does.[298] Since the 1980s, scholars have warned that a "flood of unfounded reports" endangered truly abused children.[299] Critics from both the left and right charge that innocent parents are losing their children because of false or exaggerated accusations of abuse. "An antifamily bias ... pervades the policies and practices of the child welfare system," according to Jane Knitzer of the Children's Defense Fund. "Children are inappropriately removed from their families."[300] Some have alleged that children are removed unjustly and unnecessarily from parents in "staggering proportions." A California commission concluded that "the state's foster care system runs contrary to the preservation of families by unnecessarily removing an increasing number of children from their homes each year."[301] "Children everywhere are often removed from their parents without a warrant when one should be

---

297. Nat Hentoff, "Where Were the Law Guardians?" *Village Voice*, 21 April 1998.

298. Christopher Booker, "The Shameful Stories that Can't Be Told," *Daily Telegraph*, 31 July 2010, http://www.telegraph.co.uk/comment/columnists/christopherbooker/7920221/The-shameful-stories-that-cant-be-told.html.

299. Douglas Besharov, "Unfounded Allegations—A New Child Abuse Problem," *Public Interest* (Spring 1986), 22.

300. "Testimony of Jane Knitzer, Children's Defense Fund, Amendments to Social Services, Foster Care, and Child Welfare Programs, Hearing, Subcommittee on Public Assistance and Unemployment Compensation of the Committee on Ways and Means, U.S. House of Representatives," 22 and 27 March 1979.

301. Little Hoover Commission, *For the Sake of the Children: Restructuring Foster Care in California*, Report #115, 9 April 1992, conclusion.

obtained," says California attorney David Beauvais. "Parents are often tricked or intimidated. . . . Courts too often rubber-stamp CPS recommendations, and hearings are confidentially held. There is no public access and little media scrutiny. Once in the system, parents are well on their way to losing their parental rights."[302]

A San Diego Grand Jury investigation revealed "a system out of control, with few checks and little balance." This system, where justice is blocked by "confidential files, closed courts, gag orders, and total statutory immunity [for judges and social workers], has isolated itself to a degree unprecedented in our system of jurisprudence and ordered liberties."[303]

Even today, "The experience of facing false charges . . . can happen to any parent merely by a stranger picking up the telephone and anonymously calling a well-publicized hotline number . . . to say, without any evidence, that a parent maltreated his or her child," concludes a recent authority, who sites statistics showing that "this involves a massive number of children and families each year." With striking similarity to what other parents discover through involuntary divorce, "it is almost impossible to fully insulate one's family from the threat of a system that on very little pretense can simply reach into the home and take away one's offspring."[304]

While the due process and constitutional rights violations of taking away people's children might seem obvious, Mary Pride looked at the observance of basic due process protections by child abuse statutes in the United States: the right to know the accusation against one, to a jury trial, and to examine the evidence and challenge it. She found that parents had none of these rights in thirty-one US states and all of these rights in none. Only one state even permitted a jury trial.[305] Parents have no right to appeal; indeed, an appeal may be useless if they have no access to the evidence presented against them, and the very concept of an appeal may be meaningless if no solid evidence against them existed in the first place. Parents have no right to confront their accusers (who are often anonymous) or cross-examine witnesses. Like men accused of rape, they have no protection against double-jeopardy, because of parallel "civil" prosecutions. Likewise, there is no presumption of innocence, and parents must prove their innocence against an accusation of some-

302. Riya Bhattacharjee, "David Beauvais: Defender of the First Amendment," *Berkeley Daily Planet*, 28 April 2006.

303. *Families in Crisis*, report by the 1991–92 San Diego County Grand Jury (http://www.co.san-diego.ca.us/cnty/cntydepts/safety/grand/reports/report2.html).

304. Krason, "Mondale Act," 10.

305. Cited in ibid., 36.

thing that (strikingly similar to child support, domestic violence, and the rest) has no definition and whose specifics they may not be informed, and the Fourth Amendment protection of privacy and probation on "unreasonable searches and seizures" (similar to divorce proceedings) may as well not exist.[306] Attempts to challenge these statutes on constitutional grounds invariably proved pointless.[307]

Here again, feminist officials devised a new term to create a new crime with no precise definition and therefore no possibility of defense. "Nowhere [in the law] are there clear-cut definitions of what is encompassed by the terms" *child abuse* and *child neglect*.[308] In a line that could apply to any of the new gender crimes in this book, one scholar concludes that "the problem of definition has been a major reason for an ongoing explosion of false abuse/neglect reports."[309]

As with "domestic violence" between adults therefore, one must be very cautious about any statistics and assertions that claim to quantify child abuse, however "scientific" they purport to be. Here too the designation of a category of "abuse," somehow separate from violent crime but unclear precisely how, renders determinations highly subjective at best and subject to political manipulation. Like domestic violence, child abuse is seldom adjudicated as violent assault, so no objective measure of its frequency exists. Consequently, vague definitions and subjective methods of verification create uncertainties even about what precisely is the subject under discussion.

None of the government statistics purporting to quantify child abuse are based on convictions in jury trials or even court actions, even when cases are classified as "confirmed" or "substantiated" (terms which, for this reason, are largely meaningless). Here again, such figures are based on "reports" by social workers, and some represent nothing more than interviews conducted with non-specialists about alleged abuse they chose not to report. The literature on child abuse provided from official sources and from government-funded scholars and advocacy groups is carefully selected, and most is highly questionable.

The decision of when to intervene against parents thus becomes the subjective determination of social workers. "Existing standards set no limits on intervention and provide no guidelines for decision-making," observes Krason. "It is up to the social workers to decide what is meant

---

306. Ibid., 36–37, 38.

307. Ibid., 24.

308. Jeanne Giovannoni and Rosina Becerra, *Defining Child Abuse* (New York: Free Press, 1979), 2.

309. Krason, "Mondale Act," 2.

by 'abuse' and 'neglect.'"[310] Free societies do not normally permit civil servants to adjudicate crime *ad hoc* and decide who is a criminal.

In their relentless determination to punish, the family police have little regard for the rights of children (that elsewhere they claim to champion). Long and intrusive interrogations of children, with relentless suggestions of the alleged brutality and lust of their parents against them, poison their relationships with their parents, sometimes permanently. "Long, repeated interrogations by social workers—and the outright intimidation that sometimes accompanies them—forced physical and sexual examinations in some cases to determine if they have been sexually abused, and (essentially) forced therapy by psychologists, counselors," is described by Krason (and others), who suggests they could be "considered torture under international human rights law."[311] The foster care into which children are placed after being taken from their parents is a far more likely setting for serious abuse than the children's natural family, with more than 10 times the rate of physical abuse and more than 28 times the rate of sexual abuse of children in group homes than in the general population.[312]

Like child support enforcement agents and other feminist gendarmes, child protective services blur the distinction between social work and law enforcement. In effect, they constitute another form of plainclothes family police. "Although spoken of in terms of social services," writes Susan Orr, "the child-protection function of child welfare is essentially a police action." Yet because they are not called police and do not wear uniforms, these social workers are not required to follow due process procedures; nor are the courts before which parents accused by them are summoned. Orr calls child protective services "the most intrusive arm of social services," because of their power to remove children from their parents. Yet because the parents are seldom charged criminally, they are not afforded due process protections and are unable to defend themselves in proceedings that (like divorces) are usually secret and without public record. Like Orr, Krason argues that "child abuse and neglect should be treated as criminal matters to be dealt with in regular courts, where accused persons have the full range of due process and other constitutional rights."[313]

310. Krason, "Mondale Act," 28.

311. Ibid., 48. See also Baskerville, *Taken Into Custody*, ch. 4.

312. Cited in Krason, "Mondale Act," 48.

313. Susan Orr, *Child Protection at the Crossroads: Child Abuse, Child Protection, and Recommendations for Reform* (Los Angeles: Reason Public Policy Institute, October 1999), 10–12; Krason, "Mondale Act," 58.

Also like divorce proceedings, child protection blurs the distinction between civil and criminal law. It is "civil of a special type,"[314] where officials can punish parents by taking away their children or incarcerating them without trial. For the few parents who do receive jury trials, "A verdict of not guilty in a criminal court will not effect [*sic*] the 'true [substantiated] finding' in Juvenile Court because that finding is based on a different and lower evidentiary standard." So parents who have received their day in court and been found innocent are still guilty in the eyes of social workers and family court judges, who base their determination of guilt on . . . apparently whatever they feel like.[315] "Even if parents are exonerated by a criminal court, agency actions and proceedings against them in juvenile and civil courts often may still go ahead," notes Krason. "Criminal exoneration is no guarantee they will get their children back."[316]

Much like secret police operations in totalitarian states, the child abuse gestapo turns citizens into informers by providing for anonymous reporting, requiring mandatory reporting by doctors and other professionals of even suspected child abuse (whatever that might be), complete immunity from criminal prosecution or civil liability for knowingly false reports, and confidentiality of records and proceedings. "Much as we see in totalitarian regimes," writes Krason, "The laws . . . have created a system driven to a certain extent by fear . . . Physicians, teachers, day care center workers, and other mandated reporters make reports—often on the slightest pretext—because they figure that it is better to speak up than not speak up for the sake of self-protection."

Some US states mandate that *every citizen* must report even *suspected abuse*, and federal legislation has been introduced to require all states to do so. "This almost certainly would mean that, as with the mandated professional reporters currently, any person could face civil or criminal liability if he failed to report" something that has no definition.[317] "Forcing the states to make every single adult a mandatory reporter with no exceptions will lead to a police-state environment, where every adult is forced to act as an informer against friends, family, and neighbors, or face possible charges."[318]

---

314. Krason, "Mondale Act," 40.

315. *Child Sexual Abuse, Assault, and Molest Issues*, Report No. 8, A Report by the 1991–92 San Diego County Grand Jury, 29 June 1992 (http://www.co.san-diego.ca.us/cnty/cntydepts/safety/grand/reports/report8.html).

316. Krason, "Mondale Act," 38.

317. Krason, "Mondale Act," 33, 3.

318. Internet site of the Homeschool Legal Defense Association, 12 December 2011, http://www.hslda.org/Legislation/National/2011/S1877/default.asp.

As with divorce and other government measures to forcibly break up families, cases are shrouded in secrecy. Ostensibly, this is to protect family "privacy," though in reality it provides a cloak to violate privacy with impunity. "Confidentiality laws are supposed to protect kids; instead they shield bureaucrats," notes one commentator. "They were supposed to protect families; instead, they provide a basis for assaulting them."[319]

Also like child support agents, child protection officials are recruited largely from the ranks of divorced women and from graduates of social work and "women's studies" programs, where they are trained in feminist ideology that is hostile to parents and especially fathers. It appears that homosexuals are also entering the social work profession in large numbers.[320]

Child abuse hysteria was carried into adulthood through "recovered memory therapy," another fabrication by feminist theories in the psychotherapy industry. One eminent Johns Hopkins University psychiatrist describes "a craze reminiscent of the Salem witch hunts," where wild, preposterous tales of lurid childhood sex crimes were manufactured from a psychological theory and used to demonize and arrest mostly fathers (who, as we shall see, commit very little sexual or physical child abuse). As a result, "many men (and a few women) were being found guilty of crimes they never committed and receiving punishing prison terms."[321] In *Victims of Memory*, Mark Pendergrast shows how the recovered memory hoax destroyed families, ruined lives, and sent innocent parents to prison with no evidence that they had committed any crime or abuse. Yet it is embarrassingly clear that, as the price for getting published, Pendergrast must issue repeated, seemingly gratuitous protests, unconvincing and contrary to his own evidence, that this hysteria was not incited by feminist ideology.[322]

319. Krason, "Mondale Act," 34, partly quoting Trevor Armbrister, "When Parents Become Victims," *Reader's Digest* (April 1993), 106.

320. See Mary Pride, *The Child Abuse Industry: Outrageous Facts About Child Abuse and Everyday Rebellions Against a System that Threatens Every North American Family* (Westchester, IL: Crossway, 1986), 241, and Brenda Scott, *Out of Control: Who's Watching Our Child Protection Agencies?* (Lafayette, LA: Huntington House, 1994), 58.

321. Paul R. McHugh, *Try to Remember: Psychiatry's Clash Over Meaning, Memory, and Mind* (New York: Dana Press, 2008), introduction, Kindle locations 820–21, 1302–03. McHugh acknowledges that "feminists attacked it [efforts to refute the accusations] because they believed 'recovered memories' confirmed their views about patriarchal oppression in family life." Yet "90% of accusers are women," and the main targets are "parents" (almost always fathers). Otherwise, like Pendergrast (see next note), he conspicuously avoids ideology. Kindle locations 815, 818, 820.

322. Hinesburg, Vermont: Upper Access Books, 1995. A writer who doth seem to protest too much on this point, Pendergrast never tells us who suggests that it *is* the creation of feminist ideology.

Yet no one should doubt the ideological subtext. "The abuse therapists were joined by an influential group of conspiracy-minded feminists," writes dissident feminist Christina Hoff Sommers. "When a few civil libertarian feminists . . . tried to blow the whistle on the witchhunt, they were vilified by the conspiracy caucus as backlashers, child abuse apologists, and 'obedient daddies' girls of male editors.'"[323]

Feminist-dominated administrations in the United States have elevated child protection to a paramilitary operation. In 1993, US Attorney General Janet Reno used unsubstantiated child abuse rumors to launch military operations against American citizens in Waco, Texas, resulting in the deaths of 24 children that she was ostensibly protecting. The militarization of child protection was seen again in the largest seizure of children in American history, when almost five hundred children were seized from their polygamous parents in the Fundamentalist Church of Jesus Christ of Latter Day Saints without any evidence of abuse. "A night-time raid with tanks, riot police, SWAT teams, snipers, and cars full of Texas Rangers and sheriff's deputies—that is the new face of state child protection," writes attorney Gregory Hession, "social workers backed up with automatic weapons."

The media obfuscated the central role of feminist ideology in the action, which was nevertheless revealed when a spokeswoman for the state's child protection agency described the "abuse": "There is a mindset [among the sect] that even the young girls report that they will marry at whatever age, and that it's the highest blessing they can have to have children." As Hession comments, expressing respect for motherhood is "abuse," and legally innocent American citizens can now be attacked militarily on their own soil by their own government for rejecting feminist ideology and practicing traditional values within their own homes.[324]

As with other new gender crimes, the feminist gestapo's "attempt to monitor and control vast numbers of people in the minutest of details about how they conduct their lives and raise their children is more than a touch of totalitarianism."[325]

So does this mean that the entire child abuse epidemic is just another hoax? Stephen Krason and others do argue plausibly that, despite the

---

323. "Rape Culture is a 'Panic Where Paranoia, Censorship, and False Accusations Flourish,'" *Time*, 15 May 2014 (http://time.com/100091/campus-sexual-assault-christina-hoff-sommers/). As we have seen (above, under "Rape and Sexual Assault"), Hoff Sommers sees a parallel with the current hysteria surrounding "campus rape culture."

324. Gregory A. Hession, "Whose Children Are They Anyway?" *New American,* 23 June 2008 (http://thenewamerican.com/node/8344#SlideFrame_1,).

325. Ibid., 61.

explosion of "reports" generated by the child abuse lobby, "the 'epidemic' of child abuse—*real* child abuse—that the American public heard so much about in the 1960s, 1970s, and 1980s is just not there, and probably never was."[326]

Yet it may be more serious even than that. The plausibility of the accusations stems from the possibility that, ironically, there may indeed be a child abuse epidemic, and it is being created by the "protectors." Britain's notorious Baby Peter case demonstrated that child protection is virtually useless against real abuse, though the extensive media attention given to that case refused to confront the corollary victimization of innocent parents. Popular exposés by journalists like Christopher Booker have likewise highlighted the bizarre combination of abusing innocent children and victimizing innocent parents.[327]

The explanation once again appears to be that the radicals have not eliminated child abuse so much as they have politicized and bureaucratized it. For the child abuse phenomenon is almost entirely the creation of the feminist welfare bureaucracies themselves. Here is one more textbook example—albeit an unusually horrifying one—of radicalized government creating a problem for itself to solve.

Real child abuse correlates directly and demonstrably with the rise of single-mother homes that are the setting for almost all of it. This is very clear from unambiguous figures from the US government, the British government, and numerous scholarly studies.[328] In fact, no reputable scholar even tries to deny it, though feminists confirm even as they try to excuse it ("battered women who maltreat their children").[329] Overwhelmingly, the most likely physical abuser of a child is the child's own single mother, and the most likely sexual abuser is the mother's lover. Contrary to the innuendo of divorce and child abuse advocates—who intentionally and knowingly use fabricated abuse accusations in family courts to remove fathers from the home—it is not married fathers but single mothers who account for almost all child abuse. "Contrary to public perception," write Patrick Fagan and Dorothy Hanks of the Heritage Foundation, "research shows that the most likely physical abuser of a young child will be that child's mother, not a male in the household." Mothers accounted for 55% of child murders, according to a Justice Department report (and natural fathers for a tiny percentage). Despite

---

326. Krason, "Mondale Act," 10.

327. See above, note 298.

328. Surveyed in Baskerville, *Taken Into Custody*, ch. 4.

329. Gregory Parkinson, et al., "Maternal Domestic Violence Screening in an Office-Based Pediatric Practice," *Pediatrics*, vol. 108, no. 3 (September 2001), e43.

later efforts to disguise it, the US Department of Health and Human Services shows that women aged 20 to 49 are almost twice as likely as men to be perpetrators of child maltreatment: "almost two-thirds were females." Given that "male" perpetrators are not usually fathers but much more likely to be boyfriends and stepfathers, fathers emerge as by far the least likely child abusers. A study by London's Family Education Trust found children are up to 33 times more likely to suffer serious abuse and 73 times more likely to suffer fatal abuse in the home of a mother with a live-in boyfriend or stepfather than in an intact family.[330]

In other words, the most effective protection for children is precisely the rival figure the feminist welfare and divorce bureaucracies love to hate and are most intent on removing from the home: the father. "The presence of the father ... placed the child at lesser risk for child sexual abuse," concludes one study in a typically defensive tone. "It is solidly clear that an ongoing, co-residential social and biological father decreases, by far, the dangers to that child of being abused."[331] The very concept of fathers as protectors is so politically incorrect that researchers must hedge their findings with politically acceptable weasel words: "The protective effect from the father's presence in most households was sufficiently strong to offset the risk incurred by the few paternal perpetrators."[332] In fact, the risk of "paternal perpetrators" is miniscule. While men are assumed more likely to commit sexual than physical abuse,[333] sexual abuse is much less common than severe physical abuse and is almost entirely perpetrated by boyfriends and stepfathers (who are falsely classified as "fathers" in most statistical studies).

Yet feminists would have us believe that father-daughter incest is rampant, and feminist child protection agents implement this propaganda as policy, rationalizing the forced removal of fathers and creating

---

330. Robert Whelan, *Broken Homes and Battered Children: A Study of the Relationship between Child Abuse and Family Type* (London: Family Education Trust, 1993), 29. Whelan's findings led the British government to stop publishing figures. "Whitehall no longer wants them to be collected." Melanie Phillips, "The Darkest Secret of Child Sex Abuse," *Sunday Times*, 26 November 2000.

331. Nancy Coney and Wade Mackey, "The Feminization of Domestic Violence in America," *Journal of Men's Studies*, vol. 8, no. 1 (October 1999), 45.

332. David L. Rowland, Laurie S. Zabin, and Mark Emerson, "Household Risk and Child Sexual Abuse in a Low Income, Urban Sample of Women," *Adolescent and Family Health*, vol. 1, no. 1 (Winter 2000), 29–39 (www.afhjournal.org/docs/010110.asp).

333. Despite the ubiquitous stereotype of the pedophile male, it now appears to be female teachers who are engaged in an epidemic of raping underage boys. None seem to be seriously punished. The March 2006 issue of Whistleblower magazine is devoted to this problem. See "Another Woman Gets No Jail Time," *WorldNetDaily*, 1 June 2006, http://www.wnd.com/2006/06/36416/.

the very problem they claim to be solving. "An anti-male attitude is often found in documents, statements, and in the writings of those claiming to be experts in cases of child sexual abuse." These scholars document techniques by social service agencies to systematically teach children to hate their fathers, including inculcating in the children a message that the father has sexually molested them. "The professionals use techniques that teach children a negative and critical view of men in general and fathers in particular," they write. "The child is repeatedly reinforced for fantasizing throwing Daddy in jail and is trained to hate and fear him."[334] From the father's perspective, the real child abusers have thrown him out of the family so they can abuse his children with impunity.

On the other hand, feminist groups consistently defend mothers, single and otherwise, who abuse and kill their children, such as the notorious Andrea Yates, who confessed to murdering her five children. "One of our feminist beliefs is to be there for other women," Deborah Bell, president of Texas NOW told the Associated Press. "We want to be there with her in her time of need."[335] Perhaps Andrea Dworkin's view is illuminating here: "Under patriarchy, every woman's son is her betrayer and also the inevitable rapist or exploiter of another woman."[336]

It is implausible that judges are unaware that the most dangerous environment for children is precisely the single-parent homes they themselves create when they remove fathers in custody proceedings. Yet they have no hesitation in removing them, secure in the knowledge that they will never be held accountable for any harm that comes to the children. On the contrary, if they do not they may be punished by feminist-dominated family law sections of the bar associations and social work bureaucracies whose earnings and funding depend on a constant supply of abused children. A Brooklyn judge, described as "gutsier than most" by the *New York Law Journal*, was denied reappointment when he challenged social service agencies' efforts to remove children from their parents. A lawyer close to the Legal Aid Society said that "many of that group's lawyers, who [claim to] represent the children's interests in abuse cases, and lawyers with agencies where [allegedly?] abused children are placed, have been upset by Judge Segal's attempts to spur fam-

334. Ralph Underwager and Hollida Wakefield, *The Real World of Child Interrogations* (Springfield, IL: Charles C. Thomas, 1990), 127.

335. Quoted by Phil Brennan, "NOW Throwing Lifebelt to Mom who Drowned Five Kids," *NewsMax*.com, 30 August 2001.

336. Cathy Young, "The Misdirected Passion of Andrea Dworkin," *Boston Globe*, 18 April 2005 (http://www.boston.com/news/globe/editorial_opinion/oped/articles/2005/04/18/the_misdirected_passion_of_andrea_dworkin/).

ily reunifications." Though no evidence indicated that his rulings resulted in any child being abused or neglected, "most of the opposition [to his reappointment] came from attorneys who represent children in neglect and abuse proceedings."[337] An Edmonton, Alberta, judge was forced by feminists to apologize for saying, "That parties who decide to have children together should split for any reason is abhorrent to me," in a case involving a divorcing mother whose two young sons were hospitalized for heat stroke after she left them in a hot parked car.[338]

Seldom does public policy stand in such direct defiance of undisputed facts, to the point where the cause of the problem—separating children from their fathers—is presented as the solution, and the solution—allowing children to live with their fathers—is depicted as the problem. It is unambiguous and undeniable that if you want children abused, take them away from their fathers.

The logic is marvelously self-justifying and self-perpetuating, since by eliminating the fathers, feminist officials can then present themselves as the solution to the problem they themselves have created. The more child abuse—whether by mothers or foster care providers or even by social workers themselves (which is often the case)—the only option on the table is to further and endlessly expand the child abuse bureaucracy. Even when the horrors are exposed, meaningful reform is then deftly deflected with the self-serving argument that the welfare agencies are "overworked and underfunded," thus rationalizing expansion of the very machinery creating the horrors. "State agencies ... frequently complain that they are understaffed and overworked—even while justifying more and more intervention into families."[339]

Whether it is evicting the father from the home, establishing visitation centers where he may see his children under the surveillance of social workers, protecting the children from the abusive single mother and her boyfriend, treating the emotionally devastated children with drugs or psychotherapy, or removing them altogether into the control of state-sponsored foster homes and, later, juvenile detention facilities—the solution to the problems created by each cadre of officials is to create more cadres of officials.

This appalling conclusion is simply a commonplace of political science: bureaucracies relentlessly expand, often by creating the very prob-

337. Daniel Wise, "Mayor's Panel Rejects Brooklyn Family Court Judge for Second Term," *New York Law Journal*, 14 March 2001, 1.

338. Gordon Kent, et al., "Judge Apologizes for Saying He Finds It's 'Abhorrent' When Parents Split," *Edmonton Journal*, 9 January 2003.

339. Krason, "Mondale Act," 47.

lem they exist to combat. This time we have created a massive army of functionaries with a vested interest in creating as much child abuse as possible, and they are doing precisely that.

Bullying

Criminalizing fathers and mothers is closely followed by the criminalization of children. Another recent hysteria concerns "bullying," another new quasi-crime with no clear definition. Yet it is replete with programs and spending to "raise awareness," in the words of First Lady Michelle Obama, so that what everyone thought was adolescent misbehavior is in fact a federal civil rights violation and perhaps a federal crime. The US government's "interagency bullying-resource web site" includes such infractions as "teasing," "name-calling," and "excluding someone from a group on purpose."[340]

Almost all US states now have "anti-bullying" legislation. Massachusetts has enacted "the strongest anti-bullying legislation in the country," according to Representative Martha Walz.[341] Georgia's law is also said to be "among the toughest in the nation," according to the Associated Press (AP). But whom and against what precisely does it protect? Apparently "the state doesn't collect data specifically on bullying occurrences," so we do not even know that bullying is a problem. And how can we, since no one seems to know precisely what it is?

As with other nebulous new gender crimes, we are relying yet again for our evidence of this alleged problem on "reports" that may or may not be "confirmed" (by whom, and according to what criteria?). We cannot quantify it through conviction rates, since it is not adjudicated as we usually understand that term—that is, by a jury trial or other due process protections. "Bullying experts point out that the rising numbers may reflect more reports of bullying, not necessarily more incidents," says the AP. But what is the difference between a "report" and an "incident"? Here again the definition becomes highly subjective (meaning non-existent). "Many children reported teasing, spreading rumors, and threats." Will teasing and spreading rumors be prosecuted as crimes under the new laws? "How do you quantify bullying?" a school official asks, sensibly enough. "It could even be as simple as a rolling of the eyes." For this children will be prosecuted? How precisely, for "a rolling of the eyes"?

---

340. US Government website: http://www.stopbullying.gov/topics/what_is_bullying/index.html.

341. Peter Schworm, "Anti-Bullying Law Clears Conference Committee," *Boston Globe*, 28 April 2010.

The AP writes that "Most states require school districts to adopt open-ended policies to prohibit bullying and harassment." Open-ended indeed, since nothing else is possible. "It needs to be written into the law that bullying has the same consequences as assault," insists Brenda High, who operates a web site revealingly called Bully Police. Then why not simply use the existing assault laws, if this really is violent assault, in which case standard due process protections would apply? Or is it more "open-ended"—like "a rolling of the eyes"?

The AP does not ask these questions or probe any deeper into this alleged crime wave, and neither apparently do the officials who would have us believe that we need more intrusive law enforcement machinery to deal with the children who are perpetrating yet another new "crime."[342]

Bullying laws like the one proposed in Massachusetts will dramatically expand the bureaucratic machinery in the schools. According to MassResistance:[343]

• Every school must have a comprehensive "bullying prevention and intervention plan," updated every two years.

• "Relevant" parts must be sent to all parents every year in their native languages.

• All curriculum, kindergarten through grade 12, must include "instruction on anti-bullying prevention."

• All faculty and staff must be trained annually in "bullying prevention and intervention."

• All school employees and volunteers must report "any instance of bullying or retaliation" (which has no definition). As with "child abuse" informers, the bill immunizes the "mandatory reporters" from responsibility for mistaken or false accusations.

• Mandatory psychotherapy (much like domestic violence), with guidelines requiring schools to teach children "to recognize and manage their emotions, demonstrate caring and concern for others, establish positive relationships..."

• Schools may implement programs for "remediating any discrimination or harassment" based on "a person's membership in a legally protected category," principally homosexuality.

---

342. Dionne Walker, "Anti-Bullying Laws Lack Any Regular Enforcement," *Washington Times*, 15 September 2009, B3.

343. MassResistance site: http://www.massresistance.org/docs/govt09/bully_bills/final_0503/index.html.

• "Bullying" is defined not by objective or specific acts, but by how others feel about any particular act, gesture, etc.

• The bill pertains to students "regardless of their status under the law" (i.e., illegal aliens).

Children who at one time would have been educated to understand constitutional protections extending back to Magna Carta are now being schooled in the techniques of accusing, with accusers enjoying the power to accuse anonymously while (once again) accused children have no right to face their accusers, possibly even when the accuser is an adult school official. Georgia's statute, held up as a model by the federal government, allows "a teacher or other school employee, student, parent, guardian, or other person who has control or charge of a student, either anonymously or in such person's name, at such person's option, to report or otherwise provide information on bullying activity."[344] So apparently the accused child and the rest of us must simply take the word of the adult accuser that "such person" in whose name the accusation is being made actually exists. Here again, the Massachusetts law does not qualify its identification of the accused "perpetrator" or self-described "victim" with the word "alleged."[345]

Bullying hysteria also provides occasions to re-educate children in the techniques of homosexuality. Piggy-backed on anti-bullying legislation, gay groups push mandatory programs to instruct children as young as kindergarten age on homosexual sex. The claim is that children are bullied because they are perceived to be gay, and so it is necessary to "educate" potential bullies in homosexual pleasures from a young age. The Massachusetts law is patterned after model legislation written by the Gay, Lesbian, and Straight Education Network and includes provisions for incarcerating children.

Yet granting the questionable assumption that such an ill-defined offense can be quantified, "homophobic" bullying appears to occur at about the same level as bullying generally. A study by the homosexual group Stonewall in Britain in 2007 claimed that 65% of gay students had experienced bullying, whereas a national survey of bullying of pupils generally in 2006 found that an even higher percentage, 69%, complained of being bullied.[346]

---

344. Letter from US Secretary of Education Arne Duncan, 16 December 2010, http://www2.ed.gov/policy/gen/guid/secletter/101215.html, 98.

345. Ibid., 99.

346. *Christian Concern For Our Nation and the Christian Legal Centre Response to the Government Equalities Office UK Consultation on the European Commission's Proposal for an Equal Treatment Directive* (London: CCFON, 2009), 9, https://goo.gl/Y6MWzH.

So connected is the anti-bullying campaign to homosexualist advocacy that the Massachusetts law also served as the vehicle for measures criminalizing any criticism of homosexuality that have nothing to do with school bullying. One proposed provision would stop the mouths of critics by imprisoning them:

> Whoever publishes any false material whether written, printed, electronic, televised, or broadcast with intent to maliciously promote hatred of any group of persons in the commonwealth because of race, color, religion, national origin, ancestry, sex, sexual orientation, or disability shall be guilty of libel and shall be punished by a fine of not more than one thousand dollars or by imprisonment for not more than one year, or both.

In the name of "anti-bullying," US states are now requiring that "transgender" children in public schools be permitted to use the washrooms and join the sports teams of their chosen "gender," regardless of their actual biological sex. California and others have enacted statutes requiring school officials to allow children to choose either male or female washrooms or sports teams.[347]

There is little evidence that federally funded officials are any more effective than parents in solving the alleged problem. Researchers at the University of Oregon conducted a review of studies on the effectiveness of bullying intervention programs in the United States and Europe across 25 years. They found such programs had little effectiveness, and none demonstrated a significant reduction in bullying behavior. In fact, "the average teacher actually reported more bullying after intervention than before."[348]

As elsewhere, some accept that anti-bullying measures are a legitimate endeavor against a serious problem that has simply been hijacked by homosexualist groups. Seen in the larger perspective however, it is likely that the phenomenon of "bullying" itself (whatever it is) is likely the work of sexual activists and their campaign against patriarchy. Traditionally, bullies were sorted out by fathers. Fathers protected their children against bullies, taught them how to handle themselves against bullies, and prevented them from bullying others. But with the systematic banishment of fathers by feminist-controlled divorce courts (invari-

---

347. "California Law Allows Transgender Students to Pick Bathrooms, Sports Teams They Identify With," *CBS News* website, http://www.cbsnews.com/news/california-law-allows-transgender-students-to-pick-bathrooms-sports-teams-they-identify-with/, 12 August 2013.

348. Quoted in Neil Swidey, "The Secret to Stopping a Bully," *Boston Globe Sunday Magazine*, 2 May 2010.

ably reinforced by school authorities), the single mothers—who in alliance with homosexualists appear to be the principal advocates pushing for anti-bullying measures—can only cope by criminalizing one another's children.

Here yet again we can see how government, in collusion with sexual ideologues, creates the very problems it claims to be solving. We can also see how undermining the family drives the sexual and political indoctrination of children and increases state power. The most cynical bullies may be adult officials who, having deprived them of the natural protection and guidance of their fathers, target defenseless children for criminal prosecution.

Bullying is now a cause for intervention not by fathers but federal officials. In 2010, the Department of Education hosted a Federal Bullying Prevention Summit, and in 2011 President Obama hosted a White House Conference on Bullying Prevention. We are now told that bullying is yet another form of "discrimination" that constitutes a federal "civil rights violation." In 2010, Russlynn Ali circulated another letter to the nation's educational administrators informing them (again, using the leverage that comes with federal money) that the children entrusted to their care were potential "civil rights" violators and that Big Sister is watching. "I am writing to remind you," she wrote, "that some student misconduct that falls under a school's anti-bullying policy also may trigger responsibilities under one or more of the federal antidiscrimination laws enforced by the Department's Office for Civil Rights."[349]

The tattletale culture now reaches to the highest political level of adulthood, where no less a rascal than British Prime Minister Gordon Brown was accused of "bullying" his staff. These are grown men and women complaining that verbal outbursts make their head of government a "bully."[350] Kevin Jennings, head of the US federal Safe and Drug Free Schools office, includes in his professional credentials that he was bullied as a schoolboy. President Obama, who says he too was bullied as a child, tells his White House Conference that a third of middle and high school students have "reported" being bullied, and almost 3 million students "say they were pushed, shoved, tripped, even spit on." Only 3 million? Who on the planet is not qualified to issue such a report? Are we all now certifiable "victims"? At the risk of political

349. Letter from Assistant Secretary of Education Russlynn Ali, 26 October 2010, http://www2.ed.gov/about/offices/list/ocr/letters/colleague-201010.html, 83.

350. "Gordon Brown 'Bullied Staff and Undermined Ministers,'" *Daily Telegraph*, 21 February 2010, http://www.telegraph.co.uk/news/newstopics/politics/7285584/Gordon-Brown-bullied-staff-and-undermined-ministers.html.

incorrectness, it is tempting to suggest that dealing with bullies without tattling to government agents, is part of the process of maturation. Is it even possible to suggest what at one time would have gone without saying (and what may actually be heart of the matter): with guidance from a father, is defending oneself and one's siblings and friends not part of the process of becoming a man?

More Gender Crimes

Breastfeeding

A homely but succinct example of how the new sexual liberation exploits the impoverishment of our political culture to "empower" radicals and functionaries is new laws that purport to "permit" breastfeeding in public. Realization of the value of breastfeeding, along with more women in the workplace, has led to attempts to develop more tolerant attitudes toward public nursing. What is not noticed, however, is that the new measures do not merely "permit" it (something that could be effected simply by removing prohibitions); they inflict penalties on anyone who objects. In some jurisdictions it is now a crime to "interfere" (whatever that means) with a woman breastfeeding. It is one thing to repeal laws prohibiting public nursing, so that women are not subject to legal punishments for doing it; it is another altogether to then inflict punishments on anyone who exercises their right to express their disapproval—which in a free society is the principal alternative to legal punishments. According to legislation introduced by US Senator Olympia Snow, a private employer who does not permit breastfeeding in his or her workplace is guilty of sex discrimination and may be punished under federal law.

But along with the stick comes a carrot. Businesses could receive tax credits for assisting with nursing, including supplying breast pumps (federally approved of course).[351] The state thus becomes economically involved in the process, not simply leaving everyone alone to mind their own business, but actively promoting and enforcing the new form of liberation with its financial and coercive muscle.

Another subtle sleight-of-hand—and power grab—is taking place here, between not prohibiting public nursing and prohibiting private beliefs about public nursing. No one after all is proposing that we criminalize public breastfeeding. We are being urged to criminalize anyone

---

351. Douglas Weimer, *Breastfeeding: Federal Legislation* (Washington: Congressional Research Service, 2005), http://maloney.house.gov/documents/olddocs/breastfeeding/20050505_CRS_Federal%20Legislation.pdf.

who objects to public breastfeeding, even if they do so privately. The fact that this distinction is not acknowledged in the debate indicates something unhealthy in our political culture: the inability to distinguish between legally permitting a practice and marshaling the law against beliefs expressed about that practice. Without this distinction no room is permitted for moral disapproval as an alternative to legal prohibition. Thus no middle ground is left between criminalizing one side or the other. This traps us all in a subtle but deadly revolution, in which the penal apparatus is up for grabs, a political prize that can be, and indeed must be, marshaled against someone, if only by those who do not want it marshaled against themselves. That "someone" in practice becomes whichever group is stronger or more determined politically, more able or willing to seize the government machinery and use it against the other.

This corresponds to the distinction—so often blurred by the new sexual politics and unnoticed by the rest of us—between demands to liberalize prohibitions, to allow people greater individual freedom, and an ideology that seeks power over the people. Even in something so apparently innocuous as public nursing, we can see radical ideology taking the opportunity to cross that line.

This is now writ large in the politics of society and is strikingly manifest in the politics of homosexuality. Michael Brown's progression of homosexual liberation applies throughout the sexual agenda:

1. First, gay activists came out of the closet;

2. Second, they demanded their "rights";

3. Third, they demanded that everyone recognize those "rights";

4. Fourth, they want to strip away the rights of those who oppose them;

5. Fifth, they want to put those who oppose their "rights" into the closet.

And the sixth step now appears to be arrest and incarceration. The pattern is similar throughout: liberalize the sex, then criminalize the sexists. Create a new sexual freedom, and then use it as a weapon against anyone who presents an obstacle to the power it confers. Perhaps the peculiar line, attributed to one lesbian professor who turned her classroom into a "bacchanalian frenzy" (bringing accusations of "sexual harassment") is not so preposterous after all: "Our breasts were political."[352]

---

352. Quoted in Patai, *Heterophobia*, Kindle location 1491.

Washrooms

The politicization of sex on university campuses and in schools leads logically to the latest controversy: the politicization of public washing facilities. This has appeared on the media radar screen because it involves access to facilities of the opposite sex by self-identified "transgendered persons." But this manifestation of "gender ideology"[353] also began under the radar screen with feminism and the same federal regulations and financial leverage that encourage accusations of rape, sexual harassment, and more.

For some unexplained reason, feminists began demanding and receiving unisex bathrooms in university housing. This too is said to be mandated by federal non-discrimination laws, which carry the threat of loss of federal funds for universities who fail to comply. Conservatives and others who objected (such as parents) cast the issue in terms of the privacy rights of female students, who suddenly found men in their bathing rooms.[354] Here again, the corollary danger to male students goes, if not unnoticed, at least unmentionable. But the trend constitutes such an obvious intake mechanism for the sexual harassment and prison industries that one wonders if we are wasting our money educating the average male student, whose suitability for a university education must be seriously questioned if he lays himself open for such an obvious trap. As Wendy Shalit alone seems to recognize, a new freedom leads once again to a new authoritarianism: "In the world of the co-ed bathroom, young women are 'free' to perform strip teases and parade about in wet towels secure in the knowledge that their college administration will come down like a hammer on any young man found guilty of 'objectifying' them with the 'male gaze.'"[355]

And here again, feminist demands open the door to those by homosexualists, who insist that students and others (including minor children) should be permitted to select the washing and changing facilities according to their self-selected "gender identity" rather than biological sex. In 2016, the Obama administration complied by issuing sweeping guidelines to all institutions that hope to keep their federal funds,

---

353. Mary Rice Hasson and Theresa Farnan, "Bathroom Guidelines Open Cultural Fault Line," 16 May 2016, Ethic and Public Policy Center internet site: http://eppc.org/publications/bathroom-guidelines-open-cultural-fault-line/.

354. Scott Jaschik, "A Bathroom of Her Own," 21 December 2009, Independent Women's Forum website: http://www.iwf.org/media/2435346/IWF-in-the-News:-A-Bathroom-of-Her-Own.

355. Wendy Shalit, "A Ladies' Room of One's Own," *Commentary*, 1 August 1995 (http://www.commentarymagazine.com/article/a-ladies-room-of-ones-own/).

requiring that "transgender students must be allowed to participate in such activities and access such facilities consistent with their gender identity." The selection is entirely subjective on the part of the student, since under federal law, "there is no medical diagnosis or treatment requirement that students must meet as a prerequisite to being treated consistent with their gender identity." To the objection that heterosexual men can use the option to enter female facilities (which apparently does happen), the administration responds with the familiar remedy: more criminal accusations, this time against those who "abuse" the new rule by being the wrong "gender." Thus again the pretense of gender neutrality evaporates when the time comes to criminalize those who fail to choose the correct gender: heterosexual men. Conservatives seeking the easiest path to avoid confronting the militants will probably acquiesce in this solution.

And More

Once the principle has been established only heterosexual men can be guilty of certain crimes, few limits remain against criminalizing the peculiarities specific to them. This is greatly facilitated by eliminating traditional codes of conduct and etiquette, which recognized differences between the sexes and consequently allotted both special privileges and special restrictions to both men and women. Discarding these apolitical and private moral codes and replacing them with a legally mandated and state-enforced policy of official gender neutrality left no other terms to mediate the persistent differences between men and women other than the one understood by state officials: that of criminal and victim.

Almost daily we see new crimes being legislated, usually by regulatory authorities, to criminalize what had previously been discouraged by moral disapproval. Most can only be committed by men. Two men were recently arrested on the New York subway for sitting with their legs too far apart. The male-only nature of this criminal practice is indicated by the terminology: "manspreading." Subway authority posters scolding riders for this infraction are addressed to "Dude."

When "feminists convinced [Madrid's] left-wing council that men invading the space of others with their splayed legs was a problem that needed to be tackled," with a statute "aimed specifically at 'male transport users,'" the transport chief pointed out its redundancy: "Current rules state that it is one seat per passenger."

One observer notices what we have seen elsewhere: that such measures are so unavoidably (or intentionally) vague as to invite abuse: "This 'law' gives the police more power to selectively arrest whoever they like," writes Joel Snape. "The main problem with arresting people for anti-social behaviour is that anti-social behaviour shouldn't be illegal in the first place."

> Criminal acts have clear boundaries, as in the case of murder...; sitting with your legs too wide on a subway seat does not. Every commuter instinctively knows the difference between a man who's tall enough to need a bit of extra room and someone who's just being an arse, but in order to effectively prosecute it you'd need some sort of complex formula to determine guilt, which included variables like limb-length, testicular size, the number of other commuters on the train during the time of the offence, and the always important willingness-to-be-accommodating-when-the-carriage-gets-crowded matrix.[356]

As Cathy Young points out, no arrests appear planned for women who occupy extra space with shopping bags.[357]

Feminists now agitate against "manslamming" and "mansplaining"[358] —interactions between men and women recast as criminal-victim encounters and where the terminology again makes clear which sex is guilty by definition.

Religious Belief

Gender crimes are not the only offenses in the cross-hairs of sexual radicals, though they certainly furnish the precedents that can be marshaled to justify punishing opposition, including dissenting beliefs about sexual morality. The targets of most gender crimes are heterosexual men and boys (though women and girls are not immune). But since most opposition to sexual freedom (though not to the criminalizations) comes from religious believers, sexual militants are now looking for justifications to stop their mouths by restricting their religion.

It is thus not surprising that the greatest threat to religious freedom—and therefore to freedom generally—in the West today is sexual radicalism. The most serious cases restricting religious expression in the

---

356. "'Manspreading Arrests': The Long Arm of the Law Just Invaded Our Personal Space," *Daily Telegraph*, 1 June 2015, http://www.telegraph.co.uk/men/thinking-man/11643052/Manspreading-arrests-the-long-arm-of-the-law-just-invaded-our-personal-space.html; "Madrid Bans 'Manspreading' on Buses," *Daily Telegraph*, 7 June 2017, http://www.telegraph.co.uk/news/2017/06/07/madrid-bans-manspreading-buses/.

357. "Feminists Treat Men Badly. It's Bad for Feminism," *Washington Post*, 30 June 2016, https://www.washingtonpost.com/posteverything/wp/2016/06/30/feminists-treat-men-badly-its-bad-for-feminism/.

358. See http://www.telegraph.co.uk/men/thinking-man/11335383/Man-slamming-another-reason-to-slam-men.html and http://www.washingtonexaminer.com/feminists-upset-over-statue-of-man-and-woman-talking/article/2565164.

Western democracies almost all now proceed from sexual innova-tions.[359] Even conflicts that appear to be between religions or cultures, such as religiously mandated clothing, usually involve components of sexual and family life, such as the role of women or children's educa-tion.

Even so liberal a body as the United Nations Economic and Social Council, observes that "Christianity is . . . under pressure from a form of secularism, particularly in Europe" and attests that "This form of prejudice against Christians or ideas based on religion, which exists both in Europe and in the United States, mainly concerns questions relating to sex, marriage, and the family."[360]

Sexual radicalism is now on a direct collision course with the Chris-tian faith. As predicted by a lesbian attorney in 1997, "the legal struggle for queer rights will one day be a showdown between freedom of reli-gion versus sexual orientation."[361] Today, when the two come into direct confrontation, freedom of religion almost always loses. "I'm having a hard time coming up with any case in which *religious* liberty should win," says homosexual activist Chai Feldblum, who, as federal Commis-sioner for the Equal Employment Opportunity Commission, is sworn to uphold the US Constitution's First Amendment. "There can be a con-flict between religious liberty and sexual liberty, but in almost all cases the sexual liberty should win."[362]

Sexual militants with expansive definitions of "discrimination," "ine-quality," and most recently "violence" now claim the authority to silence Christians and others whose consciences will not permit participation, endorsement, or acquiescence in government policy concerning family life: state employees, contractors, entrepreneurs, parents, and private citizens. Another UN agency makes clear its view that no middle ground is possible and that religious expression and practice is simply incompatible with sexual liberation. "In all nations, the most significant factors inhibiting women's ability to participate in public life have been

359. See cases in *Marginalising Christians* (Newcastle: Christian Institute, 2009), http://tinyurl.com/754k8qa, and *Shadow Report*, 2005–2010 (Vienna: Observatory on Intolerance and Discrimination Against Christians in Europe, 2010), http://tinyurl.com/2wvteq5;); Stephen Baskerville, "The Sexual Agenda and Religious Freedom," *International Journal for Religious Freedom*, vol. 4, no. 2 (2011).

360. Quoted in *Shadow Report*, 11.

361. Quoted in Teresa Wagner and Leslie Carbone, eds., *Fifty Years After the Declara-tion: The United Nations' Record On Human Rights* (Lanham, MD: University Press of America, 2001), 121. I owe this reference to Benjamin Snodgrass.

362. Quoted in Maggie Gallagher, "The (Gay) Public Intellectual," *CBS News* web-site: http://www.cbsnews.com/news/banned-in-boston-part-two/, 8 May 2006.

the cultural framework of values and religious beliefs," insists a UN committee. "True gender equality [does] not allow for varying interpretations of obligations under international legal norms depending on internal religious rules, traditions, and customs."[363] People whose religious traditions and customs conflict with the UN committee's view of sexual liberation must apparently find new traditions and customs.

Throughout the Western democracies, almost all major restrictions on religious freedom now come from the ever-expanding sexual agenda. Churches, religious organizations, businesses, and individuals have been punished for exercising their religious beliefs, often on grounds of "discrimination" or simply "offense":[364]

- Preachers have been arrested for expressing ideas about sexual morality, to the point where offending a homosexual is now a crime.

- Town clerks and registrars have been forced out of their jobs and even incarcerated for refusing to officiate same-sex marriages.

- Bed-and-breakfast owners have been put out of business for "discrimination" against cohabiting couples.

- Catholic adoption agencies have been closed because they will not place children with same-sex couples.

- Firemen have been ordered to participate in "gay pride" demonstrations that publicly mock their religious beliefs and police to display symbols of "gay" liberation in police stations. (Pressuring state employees to support political causes is normally considered a serious breach of administrative neutrality.)

- Churches and charities must abolish requirements that their employees accept their principles, and they have been punished for upholding their own beliefs among their employees and for not hiring people whose beliefs and practices violate their principles.

363. United Nations Division for the Advancement of Women, General Recommendations Made by the Committee on the Elimination of Discrimination Against Women. No. 19, 11th session (1992), http://tinyurl.com/sputw; *Report of the Committee on the Elimination of Discrimination Against Women*, 13th sess. (A/49/38), 39 (New York: UN Women, 1994), 39.

364. Unless indicated otherwise, specific cases are discussed and documented in the following articles: Paul Coleman, "The 'SOGI Movement' at the United Nations: From Obscurity to Primacy in Ten Years and the Implications for Religious Liberty," *International Journal for Religious Freedom*, forthcoming; Nicholas Kerton-Johnson, "Governing the Faithful," *International Journal for Religious Freedom*, vol. 4, no. 2 (2011); Baskerville, "Sexual Agenda and Religious Freedom."

• Government-funded universities have refused to recognize religious student groups because of their beliefs about sexual morality, prohibited them from expressing their moral beliefs on campus, and attempted to expel them from the university.

• Private religious schools have been forced to recognize student groups that violate their religious and moral principles and prohibited from using the groups to counsel students on their beliefs.

• Private universities have been forced to accept cohabitation in their housing.

• Private businesses have been punished for refusing to advocate sex that violates their religious beliefs.

• Businesses and professionals are sued and threatened with jail for refusing to violate their religious beliefs.

• Counselors have been dismissed for advocating reparative therapies for same-sex attraction and for not endorsing practices that affirm homosexuality.

• At least one home for elderly Christians was punished for "institutionalized homophobia" when it refused to interrogate its residents about their sexual morality and indoctrinate them in sexual political ideology.[365]

• European Union directives would allow private citizens to be punished for expressing their convictions about sexual issues.[366]

While the new homosexual militancy is the source of many new restrictions on religious expression and practice, it is not the only cause arising from sexual liberation. Homeschoolers have lost their children to school authorities pushing an increasingly sexualized curriculum.[367] In the US, the "Obamacare" system of government healthcare includes coercive measures over both the finances and religion of private citizens. It is much less about medical care than about sexual liberation. Mandates forcing private citizens and family businesses to finance policies that fund abortion and contraception mean that for the first time Americans must, as a condition for living in their own country, purchase a specific product, even when it is contrary to their consciences, or face criminal penalties. Also proceeding from demands for sexual

---

365. *Marginalising Christians*, 62.

366. Paul Coleman and Roger Kiska, "The Proposed EU 'Equal Treatment' Directive," *International Journal for Religious Freedom*, vol. 5, no. 1 (2012).

367. Mike Donnelly, "Religious Freedom in Education," *International Journal for Religious Freedom*, vol. 4, no. 2 (2011).

freedom is its role in facilitating single-motherhood, and it is no accident that single-mothers and unmarried women comprise the principal lobbying constituency in its favor.[368]

Seldom appreciated is that many new restrictions on religious freedom have arisen because of state involvement. "Today, there is growing pressure to marginalize Christian groups which receive public funding" in Britain, according to the Christian Institute. "Projects in receipt of public funds have been pressurized to lay aside aspects of their religious ethos or risk losing Government finance. Government ministers have told Christian groups that they are welcome to apply for grants as long as they don't try to promote their faith."[369]

State employees must now choose between their faith and their professional duties. Britain's Employment Appeal Tribunal held that a local authority could require all registrars to perform all services without accommodating religious objections, suggesting that employees who objected were free to "resign and take up other employment." The Tribunal also ruled that "the limitations imposed on freedom of religion are particularly strong where a person has to carry out state functions."[370] Likewise in the United States, New York Governor Andrew Cuomo, who pushed through the state's same-sex marriage law, has said that "those who cannot follow the new law should not hold the position of town clerk." He added, "When you enforce the laws of the state, you don't get to pick and choose." MP Lynne Featherstone has similarly stated in the House of Commons that "carrying out public services cannot be a matter of conscience" and that people with strong faith convictions "might ultimately make different choices about their careers." On her blog she adds, "In the delivery of public services you have to do the job, and if there are elements of the job that you cannot do in all conscience then it isn't the job for you."[371]

On the surface, this principle in itself is valid. Employees, including government functionaries, must perform the tasks to which they agree when they assume employment. Yet the argument that scrupulous consciences may resign and seek employment elsewhere ignores several considerations. The fact that there is only so much other employment

368. "Unmarried Women on Health Care: Unmarried Women Driving Change on Leading Domestic Issue," Greenberg Quinlan Rosner internet site: http://www.greenbergresearch.com/articles/2066/3853_wvwv%20_health%20care%20memo_%200807m9_FINAL_.pdf, 8 August 2007.

369. *Marginalising Christians*, 61.

370. Kerton-Johnson, "Governing the Faithful," citing R. Trigg, *Free to Believe? Religious Freedom in a Liberal Society* (London: Theos, 2010), 11.

371. *Marginalising Christians*, 46.

available to people trained in one profession is not in itself the most serious. Suffering for one's conscience is something believers must and do expect.

More serious is that the state is changing the rules after the employment agreement. Ms. Featherstone's assertion that "it isn't the job for you" disregards the fact that it was the job to which both parties agreed in the employment contract and that the state has rewritten the job description after the fact. Governments do routinely enact policy innovations that civil servants must implement. Yet to insist that they may do so without regard for ethical implications or the consciences of those who must implement them—to the point where civil servants may simply be discarded for moral scruples that had been assumed in the previous policies and in their duties before the innovations—is to exorcise ethics from public policy altogether and reduce government employees to amoral robots. Any task, especially one in the public service, must be performed as "a matter of conscience" and the conscientious objections of public servants serve as a valuable warning sign about morally questionable government measures. (At least two clerks in New York did resign rather than implement the new policies.)[372] The world's most successful and admired systems of civil administration (the Roman Empire, the ancient Chinese mandarins, the British Civil Service) have all rigorously inculcated some ethic of moral rectitude and conscientious public service (Stoicism, Confucianism, Christianity). Yet Ms. Featherstone's insistence that "carrying out public services cannot be a matter of conscience" suggests the opposite. This pushes not only believers out of public service but ethics itself.[373]

The larger problem of expecting civil servants to operate as amoral and mindless functionaries is that the steady expansion of state proprietorship into new areas of life is itself continually narrowing alternative employment opportunities and with them alternative moral voices. As

372. Efrem Graham, "Town Clerks Bullied over NY Gay Marriage Law," *CBN News*, 7 November 2011, http://tinyurl.com/7j5rtg9.

373. This confrontation reached a new level in August 2015 when a Kentucky clerk, Kim Davis, was summarily incarcerated for refusing to issue same-sex marriage licenses. Davis was elected and could not be dismissed, so she was summarily jailed for "contempt of court" (the same method used against fathers) by a federal judge. In other words, this was not a simple case of the individual conscience versus the state but a direct standoff between the judicial and executive branches and between the federal and local governments. One official jailed another, not for personal corruption following conviction but without trial over a policy disagreement—a serious matter in a democracy. Davis clearly violated a court ruling, but the ruling again greatly expanded and centralized judicial power by criminalizing a political difference. With the separation of

the state turns entire spheres of economic and personal life into state monopolies, it restricts the range of other options, both for employees and consumers. With the state claiming a near-monopoly over the availability of newly "public" services such as education, medicine, elder care, child care, foster care, adoption, and (most problematic of all) marriage, it is not clear what alternative employment is or ever can be possible.

This trend is itself attributable to the Sexual Revolution, since many of the new government functions were at one time performed privately in the home, mostly by women, or by the local community, private charities and churches, and the private market. Demand for adoption and foster care has also exploded with the increase in single motherhood encouraged by feminism. With the expansion of the welfare state (which itself further encourages family dissolution and single motherhood), these services have been taken over by the state, whose functionaries (still mostly women) can be pressured more easily to accommodate their consciences to the official morality. If ideologically inspired political innovations are driving people out of work for the sake of their consciences, this should be raising concerns about the propriety of not only the policy innovation itself but also the expansion of public power into previously private realms. Perhaps above all, it should be raising questions about the radically innovative sexual morality that rationalizes both. When this brings stipulations that the tasks of government functionaries "cannot be a matter of conscience," we can see the danger of socializing private life. As Communist governments should have taught us, when the state becomes a monopolist, alternative employment—along with the diverse moral voices that go with it—disappears.

A similar trend operates for consumers in education. Clashes with school authorities—likewise occasioned mostly by innovative "education" in sexual technique or radical sexual ideology—arise mostly in government schools. In countries like Germany and Sweden parents are prohibited from removing their children from the state system for home

---

powers, the normal constitutional procedure in such a case is not summary confinement by a judge but deliberative impeachment by the legislature. That legislators chose not to impeach should have ended the matter, not authorized one official to arrest the other. Conservatives complained that Davis was "indefinitely incarcerated without a trial despite the fact she violated no actual law anywhere on the books"—again describing precisely what routinely happens to fathers in divorce court and demonstrating where these methods originated. Steve Deace, "Why Kim Davis is the First Game-Changing 2016 Moment," *Conservative Review*, 8 September 2015, https://www.conservativereview.com/commentary/2015/09/why-kim-davis-is-the-first-game-changing-2016-moment.

education, and teachers are squeezed out of alternative employment opportunities by the taxpayer-funded near-monopoly of public education.[374]

The state's claim to be the sole arbiter of sexual morality thus squeezes out the moral voices of its citizens and confers a monopoly of moral authority on state officials: not only do policy innovations in sexual matters create ethical conflict with citizens' consciences; the state's growing financial leverage over their livelihoods and control of their family lives allows it to silence their voices.

Having acquired this leverage, which increases its scope and power with each newly acquired function, the state extends its reach to those who have nothing to do with its services and ask for no part in them. Thus even private schools receiving no state funding find the content of their instruction dictated by state officials—and here once again, most likely when it involves sexual matters.[375] This illustrates how state power extends itself over private transactions, even when no state support is involved.

It is perhaps a measure of the impoverishment of our political culture as we abdicate moral decisions to the state that this distinction is now lost on many people, who accept government orders without questioning their legitimacy. Arguably, this in turn results from the erosion of religious values, which require that we at least try to distinguish what is legitimately Caesar's and what is God's.

Openly criminal measures are the logical next step, for example against street preachers who have been arrested and fined for expressing views about sexuality.[376] In continental Europe, criminal punishments such as incarceration are also meted out to parents for educating their own children at home instead of in school.[377]

This too may proceed in part from both the Sexual Revolution and an expanding social services sector in another sense, since these together have contributed to the "gendered" and bureaucratic quality of policing, as well as the creation of new plainclothes quasi-police functionaries such as social workers and child protective services, who are largely

374. Donnelly, "Religious Freedom"; "Student Punished for Christian Beliefs About Homosexuality Pushes Back," Liberty Counsel website: http://tinyurl.com/7c82yc6.

375. Observatory on Intolerance and Discrimination Against Christians website: http://tinyurl.com/7egpjn8; http://tinyurl.com/7399v3z.

376. James Tozer, "Christian Preacher Vows to Fight after He's Arrested for 'Public Order' Offences after Saying Homosexuality is a Sin," *Daily Mail*, 3 May 2010, http://tinyurl.com/7ymxvjw.

377. Donnelly, "Religious Freedom"; "Mother Jailed Upon Taking Son Out of Sex Ed," Observatory on Intolerance website: http://tinyurl.com/7l6f9f7.

unrestrained by due process protections. These gendarmeries are increasingly staffed largely by ideologically trained and ideologically driven feminists and homosexualists, and consequent pressures to justify those functions by creating new categories of crime that can only be committed by non-violent, politically defined criminals such as heterosexual males, married heterosexual parents, and religious believers.[378] Dale McAlpine was arrested for preaching about homosexuality by a policeman who identified himself as the "liaison officer for the bisexual-lesbian-gay-transsexual community" and who admitted taking the action because of his own personal feelings. "I am a homosexual, I find that offensive," officer Sam Adams apparently told McAlpine before arresting him.[379] The power to arrest and incarcerate people with whose beliefs they disagree is not one that free societies normally leave to individual policemen. Nor do they normally create special police units with mandates to protect only certain citizens or ignore the distinction between hurt feelings and crime. Only those classing themselves in sexual categories enjoy these privileges.

This erosion of religious and other freedom freedoms results not only from politicizing sexuality but, more subtly, from entrusting increasing areas of private and family life to an expansive state sector. It proceeds from a failure or refusal to understand and delineate distinctions of church and state or public and private and the role that the new sexual politics plays in overturning our understandings of these distinctions. The most prominent example in today's politics is also the most fundamental for standing at the fault line of church-state jurisdiction and for its critical role in mediating the boundary between public and private life: marriage. For all the recent controversy, it is still the most poorly understood.

The Sexual Revolution's confrontation with religious belief did not begin with radical homosexualism. The erosion of marriage over decades (and even centuries) has significantly weakened both families and churches vis-à-vis the state and with it their leverage to protect themselves from government intrusion and domination. Significantly, this has occurred with hardly a word of opposition or protest from the

---

378. The politicization and feminization of policing and criminal justice have been explored somewhat in child protection and domestic violence, but not other areas. See Susan Orr, *Child Protection at the Crossroads: Child Abuse, Child Protection, and Recommendations for Reform* (Los Angeles: Reason Public Policy Institute, 1999); Donald Dutton, *Rethinking Domestic Violence* (Vancouver: UBC Press, 2007); Gottschalk, *Prison*.

379. James Tozer, "Christian Preacher Vows to Fight after He's Arrested for 'Public Order' Offences after Saying Homosexuality is a Sin," *Daily Mail*, 3 May 2010, http://tinyurl.com/7ymxvjw.

churches themselves. As Gabriele Kuby has recently written, "Abandonment of Christian sexual morality is the core of the Church's self-secu-
larization."[380]

Family decline—and with it the decline of the church—has probably
been continuous throughout modern history and has progressed in
inverse relation to rising power of the modern state.[381] Yet the consequences of the state's creeping control over marriage and family became
fully evident not when (centuries ago) it took from the church the role
of officiating marriages, but only when it began claiming the power to
dissolve them—and above all, since the 1970s with the advent of "no-
fault" divorce, which may yet prove to be the greatest legislative corrosive to religious freedom enacted in the Western democracies. For, as we
have seen, it allowed the state, unilaterally and without cause, to abrogate the marriage covenant and thus override and nullify the ministry in
a realm of fundamental social and ecclesiastical importance. Under no-
fault provisions, divorce is decreed automatically and physically
enforced by the state with no say whatever not only to a legally guiltless
spouse but also to the church that consecrated the supposedly sacred
bond.[382]

Especially striking is the almost complete lack of protest or opposition from pastors, priests, and churches as one of their most important
offices was simply countermanded and, for all practical purposes, eradicated.[383] A parishioner facing unilateral and involuntary divorce today
who approaches his clergy may receive an offer of prayer and advice on
finding a lawyer, but he will certainly find no intervention or resistance
or even protest from the church, which will remain silent as state officials sever his marriage covenant, evict him from his home, separate
him from his children, confiscate his property, and even incarcerate him
without trial.[384]

Presaging today's developments, forcibly divorced parents have for
years faced almost complete abrogation of their religious freedom over
their children, whose religious upbringing passes into the hands of government officials. Even when the divorce is involuntary and literally "no

---

380. Gabriele Kuby, *The Global Sexual Revolution: Destruction of Freedom in the
Name of Freedom* (Kettering, OH: Lifesite, 2015), 202.

381. Carle Zimmerman, *Family and Civilization* (repr. Wilmington: Intercollegiate
Studies Institute, 2008).

382. See above, chapter II, under "Divorce."

383. Mark H. Smith, "Religion, Divorce, and the Missing Culture War in America,"
Political Science Quarterly, vol. 125, no. 1 (Spring 2010).

384. Baskerville, *Taken Into Custody*, chapters 2–4; David Heleniak, "The New Star
Chamber," *Rutgers Law Review*, vol. 57, no. 3 (Spring 2005).

fault" of one parent (some 80% of divorces are unilateral), that parent loses all say in the religious upbringing of his children, including what religious worship they may or must attend and even how he may instruct them in private. This too has found no challenge by churches or religious advocates. An exception proving the rule was a 1997 ruling of the Massachusetts Supreme Court prohibiting a father from taking his children to Christian services. The ruling received some media attention but no opposition from either churches or civil libertarians.[385]

"This willingness of courts to disfavor a broad range of parental ideologies—... atheist or fundamentalist, racist or pro-polygamist, pro-homosexual or anti-homosexual—should lead us to take a hard look at the doctrine that allows such results," writes Eugene Volokh.[386] Volokh documents how routine practices and rulings in American divorce courts directly violate First Amendment protections and control intimate details of innocent citizens' private lives: "Courts have ... ordered parents to reveal their homosexuality to their children, or to conceal it. They have ordered parents not to swear in front of their children, and to install internet filters." One parent was ordered to "make sure that there is nothing in the religious upbringing or teaching that the minor child is exposed to that can be considered homophobic." To compound the connection with the revolution we have been addressing, most cases Volokh cites involve beliefs about gender relations and sex.[387]

Parents' attempts to educate their children in their own beliefs and instill in them religious or civic values are prohibited by family court judges. "Courts have restricted a parent's religious speech when such speech was seen as inconsistent with the religious education that the custodial parent was providing." This is based on "the theory ... that the children will be made confused and unhappy by the contradictory teachings." One court ordered that "each party will impress upon the children the need for religious tolerance and not permit any third party to attempt to teach them otherwise." It is important to realize that each step in this process of depriving citizens of their religious freedom is effected by judicial fiat, without having to demonstrate any legal fault by

385. "Custody Wars: SJC Sets Dangerous Precedent," *Boston Globe*, 15 December 1997; "In Divorce, Court Can Have Say in Child's Faith," *Boston Globe*, 10 December 1997, A1.

386. Eugene Volokh, "Parent-Child Speech and Child Custody Speech Restrictions," *New York Law Review* 81 (May 2006), 643.

387. Ibid., 640–41. As with no-fault divorce itself, Anglo-American family law practitioners, especially involving divorce and custody of children, create the major innovations that are subsequently adopted elsewhere, including in international conventions. Stephen Baskerville, "Globalizing the Family," *Touchstone* (January–February 2011).

the parent. By first forcing guiltless parents to divorce, officials thereby empower themselves to then prohibit the same legally unimpeachable parents from confusing their children with religious convictions.[388] Naturally this includes the self-serving prohibition on the religious principle that divorce is morally wrong and so is the consequent power of the state to force it upon guiltless people and then use it to rationalize setting aside rights that are guaranteed by the Constitution of which those same judges are ostensibly the foremost guardians.

While parents arguably surrender certain freedoms over their children when they agree to divorce, the point here is that a parent who has neither agreed to a divorce nor given any legal grounds for one can still be summarily stripped of these rights. "No-fault" divorce thus becomes a backdoor method of restricting the religious freedom of legally unimpeachable citizens. "Child custody speech restrictions may be imposed on a parent even when the family's unity was abrogated by the other parent," Volokh observes. "The law here doesn't distinguish the leaving parent from the one who gets left." Thus a law-abiding citizen minding his own business summarily loses not only his children but his First Amendment protections the moment his spouse files for divorce, without any grounds, and thereby transfers the children into government control.

Finally, this also provides a wedge for restricting the freedom of all parents. "The law almost never restricts parental speech in intact families," Volokh notes. "You are free to teach your child racism, communism, or the propriety of adultery or promiscuity. Judges won't decide whether your teachings confuse the child, cause him nightmares, or risk molding him into an immoral person." At least, for now. Anyone experienced in the law knows that this firebreak will not protect even married parents indefinitely. "It's not clear that ideological restrictions limited to child custody disputes will stay limited," Volokh warns. "The government sometimes wants to interfere with parents' teaching their children even when there is no dispute between parents.... Many of the arguments supporting child custody speech restrictions ... would also apply to restrictions imposed on intact families."[389]

And again, throughout all of this no church will raise its voice or become involved, and no pastor will defend the religious freedom of his parishioner or the parental prerogatives arising from the supposedly sacred bond he consecrated. Neither have any of the advocacy organizations claiming to promote "pro-family" principles and "traditional

---

388. Volokh, "Parent-Child Speech," 642–43.
389. Ibid., 673, 707–8.

Christian values," and who now vigorously oppose same-sex marriage (sometimes in the name of religious freedom), ever defended the religious freedom of legally guiltless, forcibly divorced parents.

Arguably this failure, more than any other, has weakened the churches' moral authority. More than any other ecclesiastical ordinance, marriage exerts a direct impact on people's daily lives. The failure to defend it has certainly weakened the churches in relation to the state, which has unequivocally declared its sole supremacy over marriage and reduced the churches to the role of ornament. Albert Mohler calls this failure "the scandal of the Evangelical conscience."[390] By refusing to defend not only their parishioners but their own marriage ministry from this massive aggrandizement of state power, the churches deprived themselves of any institutional defense for themselves or their flock as the state redefined marriage out of existence and then assumed as bureaucratic "public services" the tasks once performed within the married household. Compared with all this, same-sex marriage is relatively trivial, and resisting it pointless.

If the churches could not or would not defend their authority over marriage from government takeover, it is not likely that they can now defend their or their parishioners' authority over education, adoption, foster care, or the rest—services which have themselves expanded largely because of the Sexual Revolution and consequent breakdown of marriage and the family. And this is precisely why they are now helpless to defend it against same-sex marriage. In the most critical contest between church and state begun four decades ago with no-fault divorce in the United States, the churches surrendered without a fight.

Hate Crimes and Hate Speech

The preceding "crimes" are in many ways similar to the more visible "hate crimes" legislated in recent years. They may well have been the model for these more contested statutes. The original hate crimes law in the United States (though prudently, never called that) is the Violence Against Women Act, since it allowed lawmakers to circumvent the protections of standard criminal statutes and punish only heterosexual men, much as "hate crimes" laws now do. It might seem remarkable that laws on rape and "domestic violence" have not been incorporated into hate crimes laws, since they obviously proceed from similar ideology, but this is largely because they are already politicized, with much less controversy, and no need existed to endanger these achievements by

---

390. Albert Mohler's internet site: http://www.albertmohler.com/2010/09/30/divorc e-the-scandal-of-the-evangelical-conscience/.

linking them to new laws that provoked more opposition. Here as else-where, the same conservatives who accurately warned that speech would be criminalized allowed their fear of confronting feminists to blind them to the fact that their prophecy had already been fulfilled. VAWA spread federal money around local law enforcement agencies to entice them into arresting men for ever-more-loosely defined forms of "domestic violence," "rape," "stalking," and other "violence" that is not violent.

When "hate crimes" laws were first enacted, we were likewise assured that they were only to punish "violent" crime and that non-violent, law-abiding citizens would not be criminalized for expressing their convic-tions about sexual morality, even though religious beliefs could, from the start, be used as evidence to establish that a non-hate crime is actu-ally a hate crime, and therefore to increase the punishment. "Your pen-alty is being enhanced because of your religious beliefs," explained Professor Douglas Laycock of the University of Michigan Law School. "But you're being prosecuted for the crime."[391] Either way, religious beliefs constitute federally defined and proscribed "hate" and therefore criminal culpability.

As should be clear by now, sexual radicals have very fluid and expan-sive definitions of "crime" and "violence," which can include almost anything, however non-violent and non-physical. Feminists pioneered this debasement of the language to criminalize men, and homosexual-ists are now learning from them to criminalize their critics, such as reli-gious believers. Eerily reminiscent of Pastor Martin Niemoeller's famous lines about the Nazis, conservatives and Christians who averted their eyes when this ploy was used against men by feminists now find that it is being used against them by homosexualists.

Anyone experienced with sexual radicalism quickly learns that the letter of the law means almost nothing when the political climate and the articulate mob demand arrests of politically defenseless people with unpopular views. So many Christians are arrested in Britain, despite the absence of any legal authority, that Christian Concern was compelled to request that the head of London's Metropolitan Police issue guidelines to officers informing them that describing homosexuality as a sin is not a criminal offence for which they should be arresting people.[392]

Elsewhere the law is no longer so helpful to the innocent. Canada's

---

391. Dan Gilgoff, "Does the Hate Crimes Bill Threaten Religious Liberties?" 17 July 2009, website of *US News and World Report*: http://www.usnews.com/news/blogs/god-and-country/2009/07/17/does-the-hate-crimes-bill-threaten-religious-liberties.

392. Christian Concern website: http://gallery.mailchimp.com/bed173cc9adfcad1e oe 442a35/files/20130727_Letter_Met_Police_Tony_Miano.pdf, 27 July 2013.

Supreme Court has ruled that the country's hate speech ban "is a reasonable limit on freedom of religion and is demonstrably justified in a free and democratic society." Throughout the ruling, the Court is far more preoccupied with its own political opinion of the law than—the Court's proper purview—its consistency with Canada's Constitution:

> Courts have recognized a strong connection between sexual orientation and sexual conduct and where the conduct targeted by speech is a crucial aspect of the identity of a vulnerable group, attacks on this conduct stand as proxy for attacks on the group itself. If expression targeting certain sexual behaviour is framed in such a way as to expose persons of an identifiable sexual orientation to what is objectively viewed as detestation and vilification, it cannot be said that such speech only targets the behaviour. It quite clearly targets the vulnerable group.[393]

Even truth itself is no excuse for offending a sexual ideologue: "Truthful statements can be presented in a manner that would meet the definition of hate speech," the Court adds, "and not all truthful statements must be free from restriction."

But perhaps most revealing is that very little journalistic and virtually no academic scrutiny is permitted even to raise these questions of whether a "hate crime" is even a legitimate concept in the law and whether citizens can be punished for their beliefs. A search for academic articles exploring the equal protection implications of punishing people based on their religious or political beliefs turned up no articles. On the contrary, the concept of "equal protection" is used—in academic articles that make no pretense being detached or anything other than ideological advocacy—to justify unequal treatment of accused criminals based on their beliefs, and the equal protection implications for the accused are not even questioned.[394]

Though media attention focuses on alleged "hate crimes" involving race, homosexuals were a major influence from the start. Here too, no evidence exists that these measures are needed to punish violent crime; as elsewhere, existing statutes are more than adequate to punish crimes of violence. The killers of Matthew Shepard, after whom the US hate crimes law was named—even aside from the likely fact that they turned out to be his lovers rather than his haters—received two consecutive life sentences without possibility of parole under the conventional statute,

---

393. Gospel Coalition website: http://thegospelcoalition.org/blogs/tgc/2013/03/06/canadian-supreme-court-ruling-has-implications-for-christian-witness/, 6 March 2013.

394. See for example, Anthony Winer, "Hate Crimes, Homosexuals, and the Constitution," *Harvard Civil Rights-Civil Liberties Law Review*, vol. 29 (1994), 387.

not any hate crimes law, which was not on the books. There is no reason to believe that any such hate crimes law, had it existed, would have prevented the murder. "There is no reason to believe that . . . those who commit violent crimes were not or could not be punished severely enough under generic criminal laws," write two legal authorities.

> The passage of hate crimes laws . . . did not occur because of a lacuna in the criminal law, or because some horrendous criminals could not be adequately prosecuted and punished under existing laws. Insufficient or unduly lenient criminal law is not a problem that afflicts the United States. Law enforcement officials certainly have adequate tools to prosecute criminals who commit murders, rapes, assaults, or other crimes, whether they are motivate by prejudice or not.[395]

In other words, activists politicize crime to grab political power, including the power to intimidate and incarcerate people whose beliefs the sexual radicals wish to eradicate. "Soon, instead of punishing expression that accompanies a crime, we'll be penalizing pure speech," warns Don Feder. "Evangelicals, traditional Catholics, Orthodox Jews, Mormons—any group that clings to Judeo-Christian morality and isn't willing to knuckle under—will be a target."[396]

Yet far from challenging or rejecting the concept of "hate crimes" in principle, Christian organizations seem more intent to legitimize it by compiling their own list of incidents of which they themselves are allegedly victims. One list consists mostly of desecration of churches and religious scenes and disruption of religious services by left-wing radicals.[397]

"Hate speech" laws are even more totalitarian than hate crimes, because they criminalize free speech itself. These laws originated in post-war human rights documents, when (under the name of "human rights") Soviet delegates pushed for clauses criminalizing speech they termed "fascist" (defined as any speech criticizing Communism). Western democracies that strenuously opposed those provisions as promoted by Communists are now the very ones enacting them under pressure from sexual radicals. "Despite the principled defences of free

---

395. James Jacobs and Kimberly Potter, *Hate Crimes: Criminal Law and Identity Politics* (Oxford: Oxford University Press, 2000), 65, 5.

396. Quoted on the website of the American Civil Liberties Union: http://aclu.pro-con.org/view.answers.phP?questionID=000743, accessed 15 November 2013.

397. Observatory on Intolerance and Discrimination Against Christians in Europe, Data Collection and Submission to the Office for Democratic Institutions and Human Rights [Organization for Security and Cooperation in Europe], 2013 Annual Report on Hate Crimes, 9 April 2014, http://www.intoleranceagainstchristians.eu/fileadmin/user_upload/Hate_Crimes_Report_2013_Submission_OIDAC.pdf.

speech . . . during the drafting process of the international documents, 'hate speech' laws gradually spread throughout the liberal democratic nations that had once opposed them," writes Paul Coleman. "The liberal democratic nations that once opposed such laws have become some of the most enthusiastic users of them."[398]

While the initial impetus was to criminalize allegedly "racist" expression, the laws have been used far more to punish dissenting views on sexuality. "While the issue of race and ethnicity was the first 'group' to be addressed in 'hate speech' laws, further groups have inevitably been added," writes Coleman. "If race is protected, why not religion? If religion is protected, why not sexual orientation?" Coleman likens hate speech laws to blasphemy laws in Pakistan and other Islamic countries, noting such laws have been strongly condemned by the same European countries that are now criminalizing expressions of traditional sexual morality.[399]

The European Union has come close to criminalizing "homophobia," defined as "an aversion to gay, lesbian, bisexual, and transsexual people." "Thus a *feeling* is criminalized," comments Gabriele Kuby, "not a clearly defined act." Again, precisely what we encountered with domestic violence and other gender crimes. The European Parliament proposes measures whereby "homophobia-based hate speech or incitement to discrimination is avenged with extreme efficiency."[400]

Here yet again is the same *modus operandi*: hate speech also has no definition. "There is no universally accepted definition of the expression 'hate speech,'" observes Coleman. "Indeed, it is not even clear what is meant by the term 'hate speech.'" Coleman quotes a Council of Europe fact sheet: "The identification of expressions that could be qualified as 'hate speech' is sometimes difficult because this kind of speech does not necessarily manifest itself through the expression of hatred or of emotions. *It can also be concealed in statements which at a first glance may seem to be rational or normal.*" So here again, anything by which ideologues claim to be offended can be prosecuted, since obviously "labelling some speech as 'hate speech' can be an effective tool in silencing controversial views and shutting down debate." In Germany, "committing 'an insult' is a criminal offence, and an 'insult' is defined as 'an illegal attack on the honour of another person by intentionally showing disrespect or no respect at all.'" Yet only insults involving religious or

398. Paul Coleman, *Censored* (Vienna: Kairos Publications, 2012), 21, 25.

399. Ibid., 6–7, 22.

400. Gabriele Kuby, *The Global Sexual Revolution: Destruction of Freedom in the Name of Freedom* (Kettering, OH: LifeSite, 2015), 170.

political convictions disliked by political activists are criminal: "If someone is insulted because of his appearance—for example, because of his
weight or because he is a certain age, or even because he has a disability—then very often there will be no grounds for a case. However, if that
same person is insulted on the basis of his skin colour, or his religious
beliefs, or sexual orientation, it may very well give rise to criminal proceedings."[401]
All this is exacerbated by other features of hate speech laws. What
Coleman considers dangerous characteristics are already familiar to us
from other gender crimes:

• "Hate speech" laws are vaguely worded.

• "Hate speech" laws contain a large subjective element.... "Hate
speech" laws turn the attention on to the perception of the listener.

• "Hate speech" laws do not necessarily require falsehood.

• "Hate speech" laws rarely require a victim.... Most "hate speech"
laws allow prosecutions to be launched when ... there is simply an
unidentifiable group of alleged "victims."

• "Hate speech" laws often only protect certain people.

• "Hate speech" laws are arbitrarily enforced.

• "Hate speech" laws are often criminal.[402]

The only possible purpose is to criminalize political opposition. As
the European Union's Fundamental Rights Agency laments, "There is
currently no adequate EU binding instrument aimed at effectively
countering expression of negative opinions against LGBT people." Coleman notes that "The comment is all the more remarkable for appearing
under the section headed 'Protection from anti-LGBT expression and
violence *through criminal law.*'" Demonstrating the connection between
"hate speech" and "hate crime," the FRA opines that "Deep-rooted prejudices and misunderstandings in society ... can result in homophobic
and transphobic speech, discrimination, hate crime and bullying at
school." The Council of Europe Commissioner for Human Rights has
insisted that "the step from 'hate speech' to hate crime is easily made."[403]

---

401. Ibid., 7, 8, 9–10.
402. Ibid., 8–10.
403. Ibid., 44, 46, 52 (emphasis added).

IV

Globalizing Sex—and Sexual Power

"Why is the West so obsessed with sex?"
—Nigerian delegate to a UN conference[1]

*"Military missions and foreign interventions
are [now] defined as a form of social work."*
—Henry Kissinger[2]

SEXUAL POLITICS is now worldwide, and radical sexual ideology is ascendant in the politics of virtually every country on earth. Yet it is entirely a Western and largely an Anglo-American export. Though Americans, Britons, and other English speakers like to see themselves as set apart, these countries are the epicenters of the new sexual politics. For decades, Britain and especially the United States have been exporting an aggressive sexual radicalism. "In America," Czechoslovak president Thomas Masaryk observed in 1925, "abortion has become a business, and . . . the number of divorces is legion."[3]

Here too it is more than a matter of culture. As institutionalized in the foreign policies of the United States and other Western nations and in organizations like the United Nations (UN) and European Union (EU), sexual politics is in many ways in the vanguard of political globalization. Sexual liberation now rationalizes major foreign policy adventures, including acts of aggressive war. It has dominated campaigns for "human rights" with authoritarian measures that actually violate human rights as generally conceived.[4] The UN and EU are feminist

1. Quoted in Sharon Slater, *Stand for the Family* (Gilbert, AZ: Inglestone, 2009), 8.
2. "Power Shifts," *Survival*, vol. 52, no. 6 (2010), 206. See Michael Mandelbaum, "Foreign Policy as Social Work," *Foreign Affairs*, vol. 75 (January–February 1996).
3. Thomas Masaryk, *The Making of a State* (New York: Howard Fertig, 1969), 216.
4. Stephen Baskerville, "Sex and the Problem of Human Rights," *The Independent Review*, vol. 16, no. 3 (Winter 2012).

strongholds whose policies undermine families and other traditional values, foment instability and poverty, and create myriad social problems for their operatives to solve. Here too, homosexualists are following suit. These organizations proliferate the programs described throughout this book and impose them on poor countries, creating extensive transnational sexual bureaucracies. Much like Western welfare states, transnational "aid" programs generate the very poverty and social turmoil they claim to be alleviating.

Sex and the International Regime

US Foreign Policy

Government agencies in democratic countries are supposed to remain ideologically neutral and not advocate religious, political, or other doctrines as if they are official policy. All our controversies over "separation of church and state" proceed, ostensibly, from this principle that career officials are functionaries, not advocates, who implement policies in the name of all the people but who may not in the process lobby for any particular policy on behalf of a special interest.

This principle is less rigorously enforced abroad than at home. In principle, we do not allow government propaganda machinery to disseminate political or other ideas, however apparently unexceptionable, within our own borders, whereas they may do so overseas.

This loophole has been exploited by feminists and homosexualists, who alone are exempt from the principle. Throughout the foreign (and increasingly domestic) policy apparatus of the United States and other Western governments, feminist ideology (or "gender perspective") is treated as official government policy, with no dissenting opinions even acknowledged, let alone aired, and no objections permitted. Homosexualist ideology has recently achieved similar status.[5] US embassies host "gay pride" events, ambassadors march in "gay pride" parades and regularly take positions on internal controversies within their host countries when they involve sexuality, and the US government actively interferes in the internal politics of other countries by funding feminist and homosexualist pressure groups.[6]

---

5. Presidential Memorandum—International Initiatives to Advance the Human Rights of Lesbian, Gay, Bisexual, and Transgender Persons, White House press release, 6 December 2011, http://www.whitehouse.gov/the-press-office/2011/12/06/presidential-me morandum-international-initiatives-advance-human-rights-l.

6. White House Fact Sheet, "Promoting and Protecting the Human Rights of LGBT Persons," 29 June 2016, https://www.whitehouse.gov/the-press-office/2016/06/29/fact-sh eet-promoting-and-protecting-human-rights-lgbt-persons.

Strangely, the Obama administration seemed to make "LGBT" issues the very cornerstone of its foreign policy. "Throughout the Obama Administration, the promotion and protection of the human rights of lesbian, gay, bisexual, and transgender (LGBT) persons has been a specific focus of our engagement around the world," the administration itself notes. While often criticized for incoherence and reticence in foreign affairs, on one issue it has demonstrated resolution and consistency. "The Obama Administration defends the rights of LGBT people as part of our comprehensive human rights policy and as a foreign policy priority," states then Secretary of State Hillary Clinton.[7] While invoking "human rights," the Administration has been virtually silent at the mass slaughter of religious groups by the Islamic State and other extremist movements that seriously threaten the broader international order. "Internationally, this Administration has bent over backwards to promote LGBT rights globally but stays silent as Christian minorities abroad suffer persecution and in the Middle East genocide," a former senior State Department official has said.[8]

Likewise, "USAID has a special interest in the advancement of women worldwide and is working to improve women's equality and empowerment," says the website of the US Agency for International Development. "Not only because it is just, but because it is necessary for successful development." As we will see, this reflects a conception of "human rights" that "empowers" some humans by disempowering others. This statement could have been written by any number of feminist pressure groups that enunciate this claim (with no proof). This opinion proceeds from an ideology with which not all Americans agree, and their government is not authorized to be representing the opinions of such special interests. Most impoverished countries likewise do not share these ideological stances on sexual morality, but money from wealthy democracies is used to twist their arms into accepting radical agendas in their domestic politics, a clear interference in their internal affairs. "USAID supported development of legislation against domestic violence in Albania; landmark legislation to address sexual harassment in Benin; draft legislation on trafficking in persons in Mozambique; and proposed amendments to the existing family code in Madagascar."[9] Similarly, "the State Department's Global Equality Fund . . . has allo-

---

7. Ibid.

8. Quoted in Wendy Wright, "Obama's Foreign Policy Legacy: Chaos and LGBT," 5 May 2016, website of Center for Family and Human Rights, https://c-fam.org/friday_fax/obamas-foreign-policy-legacy-chaos-lgbt/.

9. USAID website: http://www.usaid.gov/our_work/cross-cutting_programs/wid/.

cated more than $30 million to frontline advocates in 80 countries. In 2015, the Global Equality Fund provided nearly $11 million ... to support civil society organizations and activists around the globe."[10] In other words, US agencies operate as feminist and homosexualist pressure groups in the internal politics of other nations, an activity they may not legally pursue within the US (though other federal agencies are reimporting similar practices).

US foreign policy thus operates a global patronage machine, using financial leverage to control the internal politics of recipient states by creating client pressure groups and taking sides in their internal politics to "empower" one part of their population over others.[11] This is reminiscent of Soviet "salami tactics" that engineered Communist coups in post-war Eastern Europe.

American sexual imperialism is also seen in the International Violence Against Women Act, perennially pending in the US Congress. I-VAWA represents a campaign to export American feminism to poor countries, keeping them dependent on international welfare from the US and UN and therefore very likely in a state of permanent underdevelopment, and to make feminism the official ideology of US foreign policy.

As we saw earlier and will see further, the entire concept of "domestic violence" is an artificial political category created specifically to circumvent due process protections of standard criminal assault statutes and punish people who cannot be convicted in standard trials on the basis of evidence.[12] Like its domestic counterpart, I-VAWA contains provisions to shield and encourage accusers but none to protect the accused. It funds legal services for women but not men and programs on sexual abuse of girls but not boys.

The measure has little to do with "violence." It declares feminism ("gender analysis") to be the official US ideology, and officials must "actively promote and advance the full integration of gender analysis into the programs, structures, processes, and capacities of all bureaus and offices of the Department of State and in the international programs of other Federal agencies." The bill funds propaganda to indoctrinate foreign populations in feminist ideology, empowering US diplomats to "change social norms and attitudes" in other countries.

---

10. White House Fact Sheet.

11. This memo has been removed from the USAID internet site, but it is quoted in "Women in Development," 11 June 2009 (accessed November 5, 2016), here: http://am ksbd.blogspot.com/.

12. See above, chapter III, under "Domestic Violence."

Here too, the US government would finance pressure groups in other sovereign countries, taking sides in their internal politics and funding ("foreign aid") feminist groups or "nongovernmental organizations led by women." Of course such organizations would no longer be "nongovernmental" at all; they would be paid US agents operating in other countries' domestic affairs.

I-VAWA also includes provisions to politicize the US military and international peacekeeping forces to make them instruments for "the empowerment of women."

I-VAWA would create an Office of Global Women's Issues headed by an Ambassador-at-Large for Global Women's Issues, with sweeping powers beyond any other "ambassador": to direct the "activities, policies, programs, and funding" to advance women and girls in both the State Department and the "international programs of all other federal agencies." She will also ensure that feminism is central to US foreign policy and "coordinate efforts . . . regarding gender integration and advancing the status of women and girls in United States foreign policy." She will "represent the United States in diplomatic and multilateral fora on matters relevant to the status of women and girls." This official is required to coordinate her duties with feminists ("organizations with demonstrated experience in . . . promoting gender equality internationally") but not others. A similar czarina (Senior Coordinator for Gender Equality and Women's Empowerment) is also created within USAID.[13]

The European Union

The European Union, like the United Nations, has become a bureaucracy in search of a purpose. As its original mission is increasingly challenged and untenable, it seeks a renewed mission in sexual matters. As one observes notes, "The EU has exhibited a lopsided focus on egalitarian and anti-discriminatory policies in the areas of human life and sexuality."[14]

The EU is mandated to address only issues within its "competence." It was founded on the principle of "subsidiarity," meaning that governing authority rests at the most local level of competence whenever possible,

13. See "Analysis of the 2013 International Violence Against Women Act," website of Stop Abusive and Violent Environments, http://www.saveservices.org/dvlp/policy-briefings/ivawa-2013-analysis/, 5 December 2013.

14. Maciej Golubiewski, *Europe's Social Agenda* (New York: Catholic Family and Human Rights Institute, 2008, http://www.c-fam.org/publications/id.278/pub_detail.asp), 36.

and that the default authority remains with member governments. Yet subsidiarity is often ill-defined and "practically ineffectual on social policy matters."[15]

The European Union has no competence to legislate family policy, which falls within the authority of member countries. Yet like all governments and quasi-governments, it is constantly pushing back the boundaries of its own jurisdiction and is now moving into family and private life. A major driver of this "competence creep" is politicized sexuality. "Gender policy has a dominant role in the moral regulation of Europe," Maciej Golubiewski writes, "and gender equality principles are increasingly embedded in its founding documents."[16]

The EU usually rationalizes its forays into family and sexual issues as promoting "human rights," specifically efforts to eradicate "discrimination" against women and homosexuals[17] and to promote the expansive field of "children's rights."[18] In 2010, the EU funded a conference in Dublin on adoption, clearly outside its competence, because the aim was to promote same-sex adoption. Ironically, the conference was billed as an advance in children's rights. An earlier conference to promote same-sex marriage was rationalized in terms of "non-discrimination." "The funding of this conference highlights an issue that caused many Irish voters to reject the Lisbon Treaty—the problem of 'competence creep' in the European Union," says Irish Senator Ronan Mullen. "This happens when European institutions . . . extend their policy and decision-making into areas that are supposed to be matters for individual member states."[19] Here yet again, sexual radicalism is the cutting edge of expanding government power.

The EU is far from ideologically neutral, as true governments in free societies are required to be, but actively promotes and funds organizations that advance feminist and homosexualist ideology. The Network for European Women's Rights (NEWR) is an EU-funded project advocating return to Soviet abortion laws in East-Central Europe. "The opening of the EU to the East has brought in strong, religion-based

15. Ibid., 52.

16. Ibid., 36.

17. See the website of the European Union's Fundamental Rights Agency: http://fra.europa.eu/en.

18. EU Guidelines for the Promotion and Protection of the Rights of the Child, Council of the European Union website: http://www.consilium.europa.eu/uedocs/cms Upload/16031.07.pdf (n.d., accessed 16 October 2010).

19. Iona Institute website: http://www.ionainstitute.ie/index.php?id=994 (10 August 2010).

views on abortion," NEWR laments, "and the relatively liberal abortion legislation from the Soviet era is gradually being overturned."[20]

The EU experience demonstrates once again how the sexual agenda threatens freedom and democracy. Already strongly criticized for its "democratic deficit"—the practice of governing by anonymous and unelected civil servants and diplomats rather than elected and account-able representatives—the EU has pursued a largely hidden social agenda that pushes this realm of unaccountable government to new depths. A study of the EU's social agenda warns about "the profoundness of the EU's 'democratic deficit'" in the area of social policy especially:

> Its consultative operation is selective in the choice of privileged part-ners, biased in its ideological coloring, and largely removed from the democratic oversight process by EU member states. Indeed, one of the most dangerous trends in EU governance is the technocratic view that representation of social views on the EU level is done better by uncriti-cally involving "civil society organizations" [i.e., favored pressure groups], rather than democratically elected bodies of the member states.

This privileged status of "non-governmental organizations" is indeed deceptive. As indicated, they now call themselves "civil society," suggest-ing a Tocquevillian role akin to churches, charities, civic groups, unions, and other truly private organizations. Yet unlike true civil society insti-tutions, these groups are funded by the EU itself, raising the question of precisely how "non-governmental" they really are. "These self-styled representatives of civil society are the main recipient of EU funds often with their own budget lines, such as the European Youth Forum, itself a member of the Social Platform, European Women's Forum, and the International Lesbian and Gay Association [ILGA]," writes Golu-biewski. ILGA receives 70% of its funding from EU taxes.[21]

Again, democratic governments are supposed to be ideologically neutral, listening to various interests as they implement policy but not funding and favoring some ideological interests to tell themselves what to implement. "That they enjoy EU funding . . . in no way legitimizes their rise and their claim to represent truly European interests."[22] Indeed, the great irony is that these semi-governmental entities actively undermine their competitors, precisely the institutions that truly do constitute autonomous, non-governmental "civil society" such as fami-

20. Golubiewski, *Europe's Social Agenda*, 45.
21. Gabriele Kuby, *The Global Sexual Revolution: Destruction of Freedom in the Name of Freedom* (Kettering, OH: Lifesite, 2015), 83.
22. Ibid., 48.

lies, churches, and local community groups—all reminiscent of their predecessors in the Soviet bloc, which established sham institutions specifically to prevent the formation of real ones. "Through a biased political sponsorship and funding of civil society groups mostly inimical to traditional values, the European Commission has sponsored community programs that directly question the reserved competence and rights of the intermediary institutions of family, education, and the church," Golubiewski concludes. "Unaccountable 'expert networks' attached to the EC and EU agencies act with no democratic surveillance and their 'independent' reports have been used by the EC to bully countries such as Slovakia into compliance with the 'expert' interpretation of EU law."[23]

By posing as a supranational government over half of Europe, while not actually being a real government that answers to the people it claims to govern, the EU blurs the distinction between a government that is supposed to represent all the people within its territory, and an ideological pressure group that represents a limited private interest, which it promotes at the expense of others. And again, this is especially pronounced with social and sexual issues.

As we will see, the UN is similar on a less intensive but much grander scale. Importantly, neither the UN nor the EU contains a clear separation of policy making from policy implementation, a bedrock principle of free societies and the main protection against the politicization, intimidation, and corruption of civil servants. Policymaking is an inherently political process subject to partisan competition, whereas its implementation must, in free societies, be conducted by nonpolitical functionaries. (Legislators are chosen based on their party affiliation; policemen should not be.) In both the EU and UN however, functionaries are highly politicized. They are free to advocate for specific programs and then implement and administer the very program for which they advocated, increasing their own power by marginalizing or punishing any who question it. In other words, they can use their positions as the implementers of policy to lobby for more of the policies they are implementing, a fundamental conflict of interest.

The boldest measure yet may be the proposed Directive on Equal Treatment, pending since 2008 behind closed doors at the EU's Council of Ministers. This is a blanket order prohibiting "discrimination" virtually by anyone against anyone, including private individuals. It adopts precisely the methods of criminalization explored in the previous chapter. Nothing requires that accusers prove their accusations against their

23. Ibid., 49–50.

alleged discriminators; instead, the burden falls on the accused—who may be private citizens minding their own business—to prove their innocence. But it is formulated so that an accusation in itself constitutes a finding of guilt. It also offers rich financial rewards to accusers and inflicts crushing financial penalties on the accused.

Though the Directive includes a number of grounds for alleged victimization, sexual ideology is again the driving force. Anyone claiming discrimination based on "sexual orientation" can sue and collect from the alleged discriminator. "Discrimination" includes simply expressing religious or political beliefs.

Further expanding methods pioneered with "domestic violence" and "sexual harassment," victim status is entirely a subjective determination. An accuser automatically becomes a "victim" merely by being "offended" by someone else's beliefs, essentially by accusing. Discrimination is defined as being treated by someone "less favorably" than someone else, and the determination of whether the accuser has been treated less favorably is left to the accuser. Sophia Kuby of European Dignity Watch explains:

> Discrimination is defined as treating a person "less favourably" compared to another, because he or she belongs to one or more of the mentioned groups: disability, age, religion or belief, sexual orientation. Throughout the ... directive, "less favorable treatment" refers to a subjective perception of offense or the violation of one's dignity. There are no objective criteria given in order to define which behavior is deemed to be discriminatory and which is not. Anybody can claim to having been treated in a "less favorable" or "offensive" way, in large part subjective states, which could be automatically conceded as being true.[24]

Because the legal transgression is offending someone, all accusations are automatically true. It is impossible to defend against an accusation of offending someone; one is guilty by virtue of being accused.

Moreover, an even more vague standard than this "direct discrimination" is possible: "Indirect discrimination shall be taken to occur where a rule or a practice which seems neutral, has a disadvantageous impact upon a person or group of persons having a specific characteristic. The intention to discriminate is explicitly not relevant."[25]

24. Sophia Kuby, "'Principle of Equality' to Overrule Fundamental Freedoms," European Dignity Watch (EDW) website, 16 October 2010: http://www.europeandignitywatch.org/reports/detail/article/principle-of-equality-to-overrule-fundamental-freedoms.html.

25. Ibid.

As with all the new gender crimes (but perhaps especially drawing from the model of divorce proceedings), emotions rather than objective facts constitute the "evidence" against the accused. "The Directive, in assuming the equality of all sorts of couples, arbitrarily refers to 'emotion' as the sole criterion for equality," writes Kuby. "Such a distorted concept of 'equality' leads to injustice, not to justice."[26]

The "harassment" provision is taken directly from the novelty of sexual harassment, which it broadens to make even more vague and subjective. Harassment is defined as anything having "the purpose or effect of violating the dignity of a person and of creating an intimidating, hostile, degrading, humiliating, or offensive environment." This allows an individual to accuse another individual merely for expressing something the individual perceives as creating an "offensive environment." According to Christian Concern:

> "Harassment," as vaguely defined in the Directive ... allows an individual to accuse someone of harassment merely for expressing something the individual allegedly perceives as offensive. Thus, even if a Christian or Christian organisation possesses no intent to offend or harass, once someone decides to perceive the Christian's expression as offensive, that person can commence legal action. Once legal action commences against the Christian (or a Christian organisation), the burden of proof shifts to the Christian to prove that the accuser was not "harassed."[27]

The Directive is thus highly subjective and vague in what it prohibits, making it impossible to know if one has transgressed. "These concepts, which at times refer even to completely subjective sentiments, perceptions, and states of mind, lead to dangerous legal uncertainties," writes Kuby. "The question of whether something constitutes harassment therefore largely depends on the subjective perception of the 'victim,' not on any verifiable and objective criteria." Here too, the expansive language expands the population of the culpable: "The Directive is thus drafted in a way that everybody could be found guilty of 'discrimination' at any time. But it must be expected that it will not be applied uniformly, but in a selective manner. The creation of general legal uncertainty that puts everybody under threat of legal persecution."[28]

26. Ibid.

27. *Information and Action Pack on the European Union "Equal Treatment" Directive* (London: Christian Concern, 2009), 4 (http://www.ccfon.org/docs/CCFON_&_CLC_Information_&_Action_Pack_on_the_EU_Equal_Treatment_Directive_FINAL.pdf).

28. S. Kuby, "Principle of Equality."

The vagary turns the law into a weapon for whoever is able or willing to be the first to take advantage of it. According to Christian Concern, "The ambiguous language of the harassment provision fails to provide the public with adequate notice of the kind of conduct that is prohibited by the law."[29] If citizens cannot determine what is prohibited, not only can they not know if they have transgressed; they also cannot know if anyone else has either. Everyone is guilty from the moment they are accused. The distinction between justice and injustice is erased from the law, leaving it simply a weapon in the power competition, a bludgeon with no moral or ethical grounding available to whoever has better access to the legal machinery for use against whomever they choose.

As we have seen with similar gender offenses, the presumption of innocence is inverted and the burden of proof placed on the accused to prove his innocence, not on the accuser to prove his guilt: "It shall be for the respondent [the accused] to prove that there has been no breach of the prohibition of discrimination." Christian Concern comments: "The burden of proof shifts to the accused, who must then prove a negative (...that the alleged expression did not create an offensive environment as perceived by his or her accuser)."[30] This is patently impossible and, again, amounts to guilt by accusation. The accuser determines the guilt of the accused simply by his or her state of mind. "Under the Directive, 'discrimination' occurs even when an accused individual's expression is not accompanied by any intent to harass or offend . . . a violation nonetheless exists if the accuser perceives the requisite offense."[31] Kuby writes similarly:

> whoever is accused of 'discrimination' must prove his innocence, whereas any person claiming to have been a victim of discrimination is automatically presumed to be one. The reversal of proof puts the defendant into a trap from which there is no escape: it is impossible for him to disprove that something has had the effect of 'intimidating' or 'offending' the victim (because that solely depends on the victim's subjective perception). At the same time, it is also hardly possible for the defendant to disprove the Directive's legal assumption that he acted the way he did solely out of a prejudice against the plaintiff's religion, belief, disability or sexual orientation.[32]

The law becomes a shakedown, because the accuser may then demand to be paid virtually any sum from the accused. Being offended

---

29. *Information and Action Pack*, 5.
30. Ibid., 6.
31. Ibid.
32. S. Kuby, "Principle of Equality."

brings lucrative payoffs, and being offensive means ruin. Since failure or inability to pay can mean incarceration, criminalization is the next step in this ostensibly "civil" process. With striking resemblance to the Anglo-American divorce system on whose principles it is clearly (and perhaps consciously) modeled, the law becomes an extortion racket, in which hurt feelings can be avenged with plunder and prison.

This obviously creates yet more financial incentives to bring as many accusations as possible, creating another windfall for lawyers, who can then pressure courts to reward accusers with generous payoffs. One amendment proposes paying the legal fees of accusers while leaving the accused to pay for their own defense.

The Directive also creates new armies of civil servants who can justify and finance their own existence by generating complaints and lawsuits ("promotion of equal treatment"). Governments must create new functionaries to provide "independent assistance to [alleged?] victims of discrimination in pursuing their complaints." As Kuby observes, these officials will mount legal cases in the names of the alleged victims and assume (and then recoup) the legal costs. No officials are created to assist or protect the accused. Private groups may even launch legal complaints in the name of alleged victims and share in the spoil. "Any NGO, who has the necessary financial power, could henceforth accuse alleged offenders and appear in court as complainant although the presumed discriminatory behavior is not directly related to them," says Kuby. Such groups may then figure their own "costs" into the inevitable award, creating a risk-free invitation to loot anyone whose views "offend." "This possibility of litigating at no cost and no risk will, in conjunction with the reversal of the burden of proof, further encourage frivolous [but lucrative] litigation."[33] This is not equality; it is thievery.

The Directive also penalizes discrimination based on "age," without specifying what this means. Because it can include children, it can probably be used against parents. Though children are not bound by contracts, they could potentially sue their parents for "discrimination."

The Directive contains no exemption for freedom of speech, religion, or conscience, and "no balancing mechanisms to arbitrate between competing sets of rights."[34] The measure purports to protect "religious belief," but with breathtaking irony this is inverted to mean not the freedom to express one's beliefs but the power to *sue* others for expressing their beliefs. As Kuby explains, "explanation of one's religious tenets to a

---

33. Ibid. See also Paul Coleman and Roger Kiska, "The Proposed EU 'Equal Treatment' Directive," *International Journal for Religious Freedom*, vol. 5, issue 1 (2012).

34. *Information and Action Pack*, 5.

person of another faith could also be interpreted as harassment." Religious faith is not a belief to be exercised, expressed, and defended from state interference but a badge of victim status and a claim to wield government coercion to silence other religions. Ironically, this intertwines religion and government rather than separating them.

Notable here is the convergence of the radical sexual with the radical Islamist agenda: both are protected against being "offended" by Christians. Despite their theoretical antithesis, both sexual radicals and religious radicals aim to use government power to stop the mouths of their critics. They share a common antipathy to Christianity and a fear of free expression.[35]

As so often with radical ideology, this Directive creates precisely the problem it claims to combat. A measure advertised to protect religious freedom will instead curtail it. If anyone is creating an intimidating and hostile environment it is the EU, and if anyone is being harassed, it is those expressing unpopular views. As noted by Andrea Williams of Christian Concern, "Rather than protecting people against harassment, the harassment provisions become nothing less than a licence to harass those who disagree with one's views."[36] Some suggest the first action under the Directive should be a suit against the EU (which of course claims immunity for itself).

It is difficult to imagine a more draconian prescription for suppressing freedom of expression and enriching those intent on doing so. In what amounts to a *coup d'état*, comparable in scale to the Nazi Enabling Law, the proposed Article 13 provides that all existing law deemed contrary to the vague "principle of equal treatment" are summarily repealed: "any laws, regulations, and administrative provisions contrary to the principle of equal treatment are immediately abolished."

Any unguarded comment will become grounds for a crippling suit by anyone who chooses to take offense—or to make a quick profit. "When a law vaguely regulates free expression, as does the Directive, an ominous chill on the exercise of fundamental freedoms accompanies its implementation. The chill is especially bitter when an accused faces unlimited monetary sanctions, as one does under the Directive," argues Christian Concern. "Compelled by the piercing chill of an unpredictable

35. See chapter IV, under "Islamism as a Sexual Ideology."
36. *Christian Concern For Our Nation and the Christian Legal Centre Response to the Government Equalities Office UK Consultation on the European Commission's Proposal for an Equal Treatment Directive* (London: Christian Concern, 2009), 5 (http://www.ccfon. org/docs/CCFON_and_CLC_Response_to_GEO_Consultation_on_the_EU_Equal_Tre atment_Directive_24_July_2009.pdf).

financial penalty, members of the public cease to exercise their basic liberties. They fear to assemble, pray, preach, worship, or even speak."[37]

The very method by which this measure is being enacted reflects a culture of censorship. It is being negotiated in secret at the EU, and requests for documents by citizen groups have been denied. Christian Concern's apocalyptic scenario is not far-fetched: "Those with an anti-Christian agenda will wield a weapon capable of extinguishing Christian expression in Europe."[38] If not all dissenting expression.

Finally—and this cannot be emphasized enough, especially for Christians who now claim persecution—it is striking how much of this *modus operandi* originated in Anglo-American divorce law: the vagary and nebulousness of the transgression, the central role of the accuser's subjective "feelings," the presumption of guilt against the accused, the power of the accuser to loot the accused through civil procedures that require no concrete proof, the ease with which a "civil" matter turns into incarceration without trial—all this was put in place by feminists for use against fathers and men, while Christians (who once claimed authority over marriage and in whose churches the marriages often took place) steadfastly look the other way. As Pastor Martin Niemoeller famously warned, those who hold their tongues as others are led away in handcuffs will have no one to speak out when the persecutors come for them.

The United Nations

Critics of the UN often dismiss it as an ineffectual, and therefore innocuous, international debating forum with little tangible impact on international affairs. Yet beneath the media radar screen, UN operatives are active in ways most people are completely unaware. Feminists in particular, write Paul Nathanson and Katherine Young, "have turned the United Nations, which began with the limited goal of preventing wars, into the global headquarters of feminist missionaries." In UN documents, "'peace', 'justice', and 'development' are linked over and over again with women," they point out. "The unavoidable implication is that only women want these good things or that only women have the innate skills to produce and sustain them."[39]

Some 1,300 "gender focal points" exist to address "women" or "gen-

37. *Information and Action Pack*, 5.
38. Ibid., 4.
39. Paul Nathanson and Katherine K. Young, *Legalizing Misandry: From Public Shame to Systemic Discrimination against Men* (Montreal: McGill-Queen's University Press), 401, 398.

der" in the UN system, according to feminists who insist it is not enough.[40] Whereas governments of free societies do not adopt official ideologies for officials to impose on citizens, feminism ("gender perspective") is unquestionably the official political doctrine of the UN, whose agencies are required to incorporate it "in all policies and programs."[41] One UN administrative office—the equivalent of a civil service agency that is normally required to be a politically neutral implementer of policy and refrain from political advocacy—promises that it "will advocate for legal reforms and adoption of policies and programmes that will raise the status of girls and women both in the family and in society."[42] Hundreds of offices and officials, "including the United Nations Secretariat, regional commissions, funds, programmes, specialized agencies, and academic and research institutions" are all devoted to (in the ubiquitous if oxymoronic phrase) the "promotion of gender equality and the empowerment of women," according to Womenwatch, which describes itself as "the central gateway to information and resources on the promotion of gender equality and the empowerment of women throughout the United Nations system." This agency is itself the creation of an "interagency network" of agencies devoted to gender and women: "It was founded by the Division for the Advancement of Women (DAW), United Nations Development Fund for Women (UNIFEM), and United Nations International Research and Training Institute for the Advancement of Women (INSTRAW)." It is administered "by a taskforce of the Inter-Agency Network, led by the Division for the Advancement of Women. A Policy Advisory Group (currently comprised of the Gender Focal Points in DPI, FAO, ILO, INSTRAW, ITU, Regional Commissions (ECA, ECE, ECLAC, ESCAP, ESCWA, and Regional Commissions New York Office), UNDP, UNESCO, UNFPA, UN-HABITAT, UNICEF, UNIFEM, WHO, and DAW) . . . [sic]."[43]

Virtually every UN agency has its own internal office dealing specifically with women's "empowerment." Not a single such agency exists for men (or for families that include men), despite the fact that men are the overwhelming majority of war casualties, AIDS victims, victims of occupational injuries and deaths, victims of incarceration, and more.

40. Jacqui True, "Mainstreaming Gender in International Institutions," in Laura Shepherd (ed.), *Gender Matters in Global Politics* (London: Routledge, 2010), 196.

41. Ibid., 190.

42. Quoted in Douglas Silva, *The United Nations Children's Fund: Women or Children First?* (New York: Catholic Family and Human Rights Institute, 2003), 85, https://c-fam.org/white_paper/united-nations-childrens-fund-women-or-children-first/.

43. *Womenwatch* website: http://www.un.org/womenwatch/ianwge/activities/womenwatch.htm (November 2010).

Not content with this, feminists have long agitated for the creation of a single mega-agency, which duly came into existence in 2010 (though without abolishing the 1,300 "focal points," which continue to exist) and is known as UN Women. It is not entirely clear what this means, but like any government agency, UN Women is already spawning its own clientele of pressure groups clamoring for their share of funding. Though ostensibly "non-governmental"—and, like the hangers-on of the EU, referring to themselves as "civil society"—these groups are in fact funded by the UN itself and Western governments, giving them a stake in the UN's own funding, and effectively making them extensions of it. GEAR advertises itself as a coalition of hundreds of women's groups, all with a stake in expanding the UN's feminist apparat. GEAR's website contains little on substantive issues; instead, every page indicates a single-minded pursuit of "power" and "empowerment," seemingly for its own sake. GEAR was a major force in creating UN Women. Having achieved that, they now claim that the mega-agency will usurp power from the 1,300 mini-agencies. So one women's agency at the UN oppresses other women's agencies at the UN, who in turn oppress the mega-agency, and more women than ever are oppressed, a lamentable situation that can only be remedied by creating more paid positions for members of GEAR. Despite these hundreds of agencies and six worldwide conferences on women, GEAR believes that the UN itself is engaged in the "systematic oppression of women" using "the most destructive cultural practices of all time." "Its culture . . . is harmful to women," insists GEAR (in a paper published by the UN). "It's time to remove the UN's 'aura of morality.'"[44]

As indicated, the UN has now devoted some six major international conferences to women, far more than on any other topic. "Conferences" is in fact a misleading term for gatherings whose purpose is to finalize manifestos that have already circulated in draft among feminists, while excluding others. These taxpayer-funded "conferences" are closed to the public and press.

The outcomes are largely a foregone conclusion, since they are organized, controlled, and dominated throughout by feminists who are well-practiced at marginalizing anyone who disagrees with them. Feminists receive favored treatment in almost all events and venues and are

44. Paula Donovan, "Gender Equality Now or Never: A New UN Agency for Women," Office of the UN Special Envoy for AIDS in Africa (2006), 3. This paper, advocating an expansion of UN power, is published by an office of the UN itself. Ethical democratic governments prohibit their functionaries from engaging in advocacy that increases their own authority.

invited to official meetings from which their opponents are excluded. The discrimination is so blatant that two feminist scholars observe, albeit with some understatement, that feminists' opponents "have to counter UN bureaucracy and unfair treatment used to keep them out of important UN meetings." Many governments, foremost the United States, "have occasionally included feminists on state delegations sent to UN conferences and meetings, thus giving some feminists access to negotiation sessions from which NGOs are otherwise unrepresented." Non-feminists expecting to be heard at the women's conferences "found themselves not only encountering a strongly organized feminist NGO sector with some 'inside' connections, but also a draft agreement, the bulk of which had been negotiated months earlier. In effect, they arrived too late to set the negotiations agenda and . . . were left countering only the most extreme effects of feminist policies."[45] And this account is from feminist scholars.

Non-feminist groups naturally concur that the process is rigged. UN officials limit their numbers (though not feminists') at UN conferences, and committee chairs employ diversionary tactics to prevent them being heard.[46] Kathryn Balmforth claims "unfair negotiating procedures, deliberately designed to place the more socially conservative countries at a disadvantage":

> Long documents are negotiated under severe time pressure. Contentious issues are allowed to accumulate at the end of a session, when they are negotiated in non-stop meetings. Often, there are several controversial items being negotiated simultaneously in separate groups, usually without translation. Smaller delegations simply don't have the manpower to be everywhere at once, and damaging language is sneaked into documents before all delegations have time to review it, digest it, and react.

Balmforth describes "stacking of the deck," when "the Secretariat—which is supposed to be neutral—presents documents for negotiation which are heavily skewed toward the anti-family ideology" using "vague and obscure language" whose meaning is subject to manipulation and alteration.

Balmforth and others allege that feminists exert "economic and other pressure on developing countries, forcing them to drop opposition to the anti-family agenda." Here again, the distinction between a country's

---

45. Doris Buss and Didi Herman, *Globalizing Family Values* (Minneapolis: University of Minnesota Press, 2003), 41–42.

46. Ibid., 148 note 4.

official delegation, that ostensibly speaks for all its people, and a pressure group or "non-governmental" organization, that represents an ideological interest, is blurred. "Special interest groups can claim seats on national delegations, from which they negotiate documents calling for more money and power to be given to themselves," Balmforth adds. "At the ... Cairo + 5 meetings, over 40 seats on national delegations were occupied by so-called 'family planning' groups, who have a vested interest—sometimes a monetary interest—in promoting abortion and radical concepts of 'reproductive rights' for children."[47]

Sharon Slater of Family Watch International argues that wealthy nations with feminist agendas use their muscle to push aside smaller and poorer developing countries, who are much less sympathetic to radical sexual changes. At one conference, the chairperson announced that the UN delegates would be negotiating various segments of the conference document simultaneously in different rooms. This immediately put poor nations at a disadvantage as many did not have enough delegates to send to each room. It is the developing nations that usually support pro-family positions at the UN, so it seemed this was a calculated move. The lack of translators means that "people from the United States, Canada, and fluent English speakers from the European Union dominated the proceedings." Here again, feminists from ostensibly private pressure groups upstage official delegates representing entire nations. "Some UN delegates also had to remain standing even though NGO representatives, who are supposed to be observers, had prominent places at the table." "One NGO representative proceeded to present her feminist 'wish list' of proposed amendments to the document. It seemed that the feminist NGO representatives were running the show, and it was difficult to distinguish between them and the UN government delegates."[48]

Feminists respond that conservative Christian activists during the Bush administration were able to imitate such practices. "Under Bush ... CR [Christian Right] activists have been included as official representatives on the US state delegation to US conferences, such as the 2002 World Summit on Children, a position the CR heavily criticized when occupied by feminists."[49] One is tempted to ask what choice they had, if those are the rules that feminists had already established. But the

47. Kathryn Balmforth, "Hijacking Human Rights," speech delivered at the World Congress of Families, 14–17 November 1999, WCF website: http://www.worldcongress.org/wcf2_spkrs/wcf2_balmforth.htm.

48. Slater, *Stand*, 3.

49. Buss and Herman, *Globalizing Family Values*, 53.

larger criticism shows once again how feminist politics, particularly in the international sphere, is spearheading the larger degeneration of political ethics.

Over 3,000 such organizations have accredited consultative status with the Economic and Social Council of the UN, the main body dealing with social, family, and gender issues, authorizing them to lobby the UN. (The UN chooses and vets the groups it permits to lobby itself.) Of these, "only about 20 work . . . to protect the family, and, of those 20, only a small number regularly participate in UN conferences."[50]

As we just saw, the UN blurs the distinction between official delegations who represent member countries and NGOs (or interest groups). In free societies a distinction between public and private is essential to preventing improper influence. Yet, because the UN is not really a government (though it is funded by taxpayers), few rules regulate its relations with "non-governmental" organizations (since, in some undefined sense, it is one itself). Thus its agencies are free to "partner" with sympathetic pressure groups, while ignoring or excluding those its employees do not like, blurring the distinction between public and private, which is always a prescription for corruption.

UN officials and feminist groups are in constant contact with one another through backchannels and informal methods to advance the sexual agenda, largely by placing feminists from ostensibly private groups into UN positions. Feminist groups "are constantly calling upon their sister groups throughout the world to submit nominees for UN treaty monitoring committees and high-level UN positions to fill positions with their people."[51] In 1996, feminist groups, high-level UN officials, and members of treaty committees held an unofficial, closed-door meeting in Glen Cove, New York to advance feminist goals without dissenting groups permitted to attend.[52]

As in the EU, these UN-approved pressure groups refer to themselves as "civil society," but here too they are inverting the meaning of that term to the precise opposite of what plain English suggests and cashing in on the moral authority earned by true civil society institutions. The term became fashionable after the 1989 collapse of European Communism to signify pluralistic social institutions that sustain a free society

---

50. Slater, *Stand*, 2 note 4.

51. Ibid., 26.

52. Douglas Silva and Susan Yoshihara, *Rights by Stealth: The Role of Human Rights Treaty Bodies in the Campaign for an International Right to Abortion* (New York: Catholic Family and Human Rights Institute, 2009, http://www.c-fam.org/docLib/20100126_IOR G_W_Paper_Number8FINAL.pdf).

precisely because they are not controlled by the state: churches, charities, reform movements, nonprofit organizations, unions. These stood in sharp contrast to the officially approved—and therefore fraudulent—versions sponsored by the Stalinist states of East-Central Europe. By supporting and co-opting these groups with taxpayer money, the UN, EU, and national governments are creating neo-Soviet mockeries of "civil society." Balmforth describes how the UN sponsors so-called "civil society" events. These events are funded with public money, but the participants are hand-selected and the outcomes pre-determined. The outcomes of these events are then presented to UN delegates as the view of all of "civil society," in an attempt to make them feel isolated and to pressure them into submission.[53]

With the deck thus stacked, the results are profoundly hostile to families, parents, religious believers, and men. Austin Ruse describes the "agreement" reached at the "Cairo +5" conference:

> the word "father" appears twice in the document, "men" once, "boy" four times. The word "family" appears 29 times but almost always in the phrase "family planning." The word "parents" appears once and then only to tell governments that parents should be taught about the need for childhood sex-ed. On the other hand, "sex" appears 62 times, "gender" 59 times, and the term "reproductive health," always a code word for abortion, appears 103 times.[54]

One agency starkly illustrates the transformation of the UN from effectively a humanitarian organization to an ideological lobby that "consciously and consistently embrace[s] a newly dominant ideology ... of radical feminism." The UN Children's Fund (UNICEF) was so effective in its early years at raising levels of immunization that it saved the lives of some 25 million children. But changes culminating in the appointment of feminist Carol Bellamy as director in 1995 began its descent into political advocacy. Douglas Silva emphasizes (as we have elsewhere and will again) the ideological dimension of the change: "The intellectual and philosophical underpinning for this transformation was radical feminism." UNICEF's politicization began with feminist-driven programs to "protect" children not from specific health risks but from ill-defined "violence, exploitation, abuse, and discrimination"—in other words, from their own parents. Silva poses questions that might profitably be asked of others claiming to advocate for victims of "discrimination": "What exactly is meant by discrimination? Who is being

53. Balmforth, "Hijacking Human Rights."
54. Quoted in Buss and Herman, *Globalizing Family Values*, 112.

discriminated against, and how does UNICEF address this discrimination?"[55] One might also ask why their parents cannot protect them from violence, exploitation, and abuse, and whether parents themselves, rather than disease, have become the main targets of UNICEF's efforts at eradication.

Friction soon developed between an agency dedicated to children's welfare and feminists trying to liberate women *from* their children. "These pro-women activist groups" thought that UNICEF needed "to focus on a woman's own priorities . . . rather than decide for her that her children must come first," writes one participant in a program whose top priority was supposed to be children. "A woman had a right to be the person she wanted to be and not be forced into carrying out male-defined stereotypes." Indeed, as "the battle raged over whether 'children must come first' at the UN Children's Fund," feminists eventually ensured that UNICEF put women's empowerment first and children's welfare second by insisting that programs be "based on the principle of equal sharing of family responsibilities and . . . consistent with the policies for promoting women's employment." Feminist ideology was codified when its board required that "within each programme and sector, women's roles needed to be analyzed, and the inequalities stemming from gender had to be made a target of affirmative action," according to one account. "From then on, every UNICEF situation analysis and country programme must fully incorporate the gender dimension."[56]

One program targeted girls specifically for education in "gender theory and radical feminist thought." "Programming for girls would now become programming . . . based on explicitly feminist thought." Indoctrinating girls politically allowed feminists "to re-dedicate themselves to the work of aiding children, work some of them had come to ignore because of children's association with motherhood and traditional female roles." Girls would be educated in "gender-sensitive schools" that give "particular attention to the gender dimensions" of education "by removing gender bias and discrimination from textbooks, teaching methods, classroom interactions, and curricula . . . and by recruiting and training teachers, principals, supervisors, and other administrators to be sensitive to gender."[57]

The campaign had the added virtue of keeping boys in ignorance.

55. Silva, *United Nations Children's Fund*, 1, 6–7, 68, 9.
56. Ibid., 69, 88, 72.
57. Ibid., 74, 75, 80–81.

"Not a word is said about any direct intervention to increase the enroll-ment of boys, even though 73% of boys in sub-Saharan Africa do not attend school," and boys were already disadvantaged compared to girls in entire regions such as Latin America and the Caribbean. "In a world in which children, both boys and girls, suffer on a massive scale . . . the suffering of girls now seems to take precedence at UNICEF," writes Silva. "When boys are disadvantaged, for whatever reason, it simply seems that this disadvantage does not matter." To the extent that they merit any attention, boys (like men) need ideological consciousness-raising and political re-education. In UNICEF's words: "For the rights of girls and women to be fulfilled, boys and men must be educated—in schools, health clinics, youth clubs, religious institutions, businesses, the military and police—to 'unlearn' negative patterns of behaviour and learn positive new behaviours."[58]

UNICEF's re-education and behavior-modification techniques would not be limited to public institutions. UNICEF not only violates the ethical principle that administrative agencies should not endorse ideology and engage in advocacy, it likewise imposes that ideology on private households. UNICEF demands "parent and caregiver education programmes that incorporate components of behaviour change and development, in order to develop attitudes and practices that demon-strate and promote gender equality." Parents who fail to exhibit the required "behaviour change" and inculcate it in their own children will feel the presence of UNICEF officials, who promise to "Intervene early to stem the negative consequences of discrimination against girls, ste-reotyping of male and female roles and models of behaviour, and the belief that male domination and violence against women and girls are natural, all of which start very early in the family."[59]

Predictably, fathers have no role in UNICEF's understanding of chil-dren's well-being. "Fathers are mentioned as perpetrators of gender bias and discrimination, and therefore in need of re-education or re-social-ization," writes Silva. "They are not mentioned as positive role models, as integral to the upbringing of healthy and well-adjusted children." Consistent with the absence of any UN agencies to address the problems of men, "according to UNICEF, there is not one current infringement of fathers' rights or the rights of men that is worthy of being addressed."[60]

Until recently, attempts to introduce homosexual politics at the UN

58. Ibid., 81, 76, 79, 86.
59. Ibid., 83–84.
60. Ibid., 84–85.

have been frustrated by nations from the global South, with mostly traditional values. No binding UN document has ever recognized "sexual orientation" as a human right, and homosexuality has never been made a protected category in any binding UN document. "However, in just ten short years the issue has gone from relative obscurity to human rights primacy," writes a recent observer. "A radical shift has taken place at the UN, leading to the first ever resolution being adopted on 'sexual orientation' and 'gender identity' in 2011."[61] Under feminist tutelage, homosexuals are learning to use the same high-pressure methods. As of this writing, a battle rages at the UN over creating a czar to combat "discrimination and violence" against homosexuals. The 54-nation African Group was "disturbed" by the incessant focus on "sexual interests and behaviors." "The African Group is strongly concerned by the attempts to introduce and impose new notions and concepts that are not internationally agreed upon," said Botswana's ambassador.[62]

Human Rights: Still More Gender Crimes

The entrenched and growing power of sexual ideologues at the UN and other international organizations is subtly but dramatically altering the nature of diplomacy. The traditional diplomatic instruments were treaties, agreements between sovereign states on external matters such as alliances and trade. Under UN influence, treaties increasingly resemble domestic legislation, regulating the behavior not of sovereign states but of the populations and individuals within them. Here again, the vanguard of the trend is sexual radicalism.

The principal justification allowing treaties to become instruments for breaking down national sovereignty and controlling individuals' behavior is "human rights." At one time human rights entailed pressuring authoritarian regimes to end repression of their people, and it was on (and only on) this assumption that the public was brought on board the human rights campaign.[63] With little discussion or scrutiny, "human rights" has expanded into a free-for-all, a grab bag into which one can toss almost any political agenda, however distantly connected

---

61. Paul Coleman, "The 'SOGI Movement' at the United Nations: From Obscurity to Primacy in Ten Years and the Implications for Religious Liberty," *International Journal for Religious Freedom*, vol. 6, nos. 1–2 (2013).

62. "Countries Take up Positions Ahead of UN Vote on LGBT Rights," C-Fam internet site, 11 November 2016, https://c-fam.org/friday_fax/countries-take-positions-ahead -un-vote-lgbt-rights/.

63. James Nickel, *Making Sense of Human Rights* (Oxford: Blackwell, 2007), 1, 7, 12.

to the original understanding of the term. In the name of human rights, we now undertake campaigns to legislate contentious social policies and claim the authority to control other nations' spending decisions and mandate welfare programs. Recent innovations demand the prosecution of not only government officials but private citizens for "human rights" violations. Ironically, "human rights" is even used to rationalize suspension of due process protections and incarcerations without trial. We now presume to supervise how private individuals conduct their personal lives in the privacy of their own homes and prosecute them as human rights violators if we disapprove. Some campaigns conducted in the name of human rights now have aims precisely opposite to what the term suggests in plain English, to the point where "human rights are threatened in the name of human rights."[64]

Here too, the cutting edge is sexual. According to UNICEF, "if a husband and wife arrange their lives so that the husband works outside the home and the wife works within the home, caring for the children, the husband actually violates his wife's human rights," writes one observer. "The husband, therefore, must be re-educated."[65]

This shift has been driven by a view of human rights that makes it the property not of the universality of humanity (as the term itself was created to suggest) but of political groups seeking "power" over others. As one advocate writes, "Today, recourse to human rights discourse in order to make claims on behalf of individual people or specific social groups is so widespread in international politics that it might be described as 'hegemonic.'" Not substantial and specifically defined rights, but a nebulous "human rights discourse" is openly acknowledged to operate as a "useful political tool" less to protect individuals from repression than to advance political agendas. (One target is "multinational corporations.")[66] On this view, human rights are not "universal" and equally applicable to all. Instead they are a means or "instrument" to other, more political ends that benefit particular interests competing for "power" with others. "International human rights law is a peaceful but powerful instrument of change," writes Geraldine Van Bueren. "Human rights is about peacefully redistributing unequal power. The essence of economic and social . . . rights is that they involve

---

64. "On Human Rights: A Statement of the Ramsey Colloquium," *First Things* 82 (April 1998), 18–22 (http://www.leaderu.com/ftissues/ft9804/articles/ramsey.html).

65. Silva, *United Nations Children's Fund*, 83.

66. Jill Steans, "Body Politics: Human Rights in International Relations," in Laura Shepherd (ed.), *Gender Matters in Global Politics* (London: Routledge, 2010), 76.

redistribution, a task with which, despite the vision of human rights, most constitutional courts and regional and international tribunals are distinctively uncomfortable."[67]

Here human rights is no longer a constitutional limitation on government power and its abuse to preserve the freedom of all. Instead it is what Van Bueren calls an "ideology," conferring increased government power on some groups for use against others.[68]

Nowhere is this more advanced than where human rights is invoked to support innovations in social policy, specifically in the area of the family, gender relations, and sexuality (from which the last few quotations are all taken). As Paul Nathanson and Katherine Young point out, the very concept of "women's rights" is inconsistent with "human" rights. "Human Rights are universal; they apply by definition to all human beings," they write. "Women's rights, by definition, apply only to women."[69]

Today this is by far the most militant and ideologically charged area of human rights politics: "The incorporation of women's rights issues into human rights practice is a revolutionary and evolutionary process."[70] Feminists celebrate how their "revolutionary" methods have altered the very meaning of "human rights," overriding the objections of those whose aim was to control repression:

Campaigns and interventions of feminist movements all over the world have forced the human rights movement to undergo a radical change by redefining the concept of "human rights." Although committed to the notion of "universal human rights," feminist activists and scholars have nevertheless argued that human rights are not static and fixed but are determined by historical moments and struggles . . . in the process, expanding the meaning of "rights" to incorporate their own hopes and needs.[71]

67. Geraldine Van Bueren, "Combating Child Poverty—Human Rights Approaches," *Human Rights Quarterly*, vol. 21, no. 3 (August 1999), 680–1, quoted in Michael Farris, "Nannies in Blue Berets: Understanding the United Nations Convention on the Rights of the Child," *Regent Journal of Law and Public Policy*, vol. 2, no. 1 (2010), 95.

68. One enterprise advertises its services as "a human rights practitioner." Apparently human rights is now a marketable commodity where customers can expect to receive the quantity they pay for (Nathanson and Young, *Legalizing Misandry*, 218–19).

69. Nathanson and Young, *Legalizing Misandry*, 393.

70. Dorothy Thomas and Michele Beasley, "Domestic Violence as a Human Rights Issue," *Human Rights Quarterly*, vol. 15, no. 1 (February 1993), 62.

71. Saba Bahar, "Human Rights Are Women's Rights: Amnesty International and the Family," *Hypatia*, vol. 11, no. 1 (Winter 1996), 105.

This openly acknowledges that feminists have politicized human rights and appropriated it to advance the political "struggle" against men and other opponents. "Women's groups . . . are increasingly utilising the language of rights in gender struggles" one feminist scholar acknowledges.[72] Here again, human rights changes from a universal code of specific rights to be protected equally for all and becomes a "language" or "discourse," a rhetorical "tool" to be invoked when convenient to advance what is in reality the pursuit of self-interested "power" by "specific social groups": "The language of human rights and human rights convention provide a useful tool for activists seeking to 'empower' women." Rather than fixed principles, the influential Charlotte Bunch argues, "human rights are dynamic and flexible, providing a useful language in which to frame issues and a powerful political tool to advance feminist objectives" because they lend "gravitas" to that political agenda.[73] This refrain is repeated almost verbatim in dozens of articles that saturate the self-referential world of feminist scholarship: "Human rights discourse is a powerful tool for affecting political processes at the national and international level," writes Donna Sullivan. "Gender-specific abuses have yet to be fully integrated into that discourse."[74]

This shift is huge. Moral capital built up by decades of high-risk campaigning against repression, torture, mass killings, and other atrocities by regimes of left and right is appropriated to justify a grab for political power by an ideological interest. Feminists even boast that they are undermining the foundations and principles that have protected the rights of individuals for centuries:

> Feminist human rights activists are . . . doing more than merely expanding the notion of human rights. They are questioning the political and social foundations on which the notion of "rights" rests; they are undermining the distinction between public and private and challenging the social contract which is the basis of such distinctions. . . . To incorporate the demands . . . of this movement, therefore, involves more than merely focusing on woman's human rights; it demands a reconsideration of the definition of "human rights," of social contract

---

72. "The principle of struggle," wrote Polish dissident Tadeusz Mazowiecki, "sooner or later leads to elimination of one's opponent." Gale Stokes (ed.), *From Stalinism to Pluralism: A Documentary History of Eastern Europe Since 1945* (Oxford: Oxford University Press, 1996), 229.

73. Steans, "Body Politics," 75, 85, 78.

74. Donna Sullivan, "The Public/Private Distinction in International Human Rights Law," in Julie Peters and Andrea Wolper (eds.), *Women's Rights Human Rights: International Feminist Perspectives* (London: Routledge, 1995), 126.

theory, of theories of the family, and of the relationship between the state and the gendered citizen.[75]

As this passage openly celebrates, the feminists' redefinition of human rights directly inverts the traditional understanding of the term. Far from protecting the private individual from state intrusion, feminism creates an invasive ethic that denies any distinction between public and private or any private sphere of life beyond the reach of state power. The main targets are family and personal privacy.

The earliest modern human rights agreements explicitly treated private life and the family as realms to be protected. The Universal Declaration of Human Rights (1948) states (Article 16.3), "The family is the natural and fundamental group unit of society and is entitled to protection by society and the State," and it makes other provisions for the protection of family privacy and marriage. It also declares (Article 26.3) that "Parents have a prior right to choose the kind of education that shall be given to their children."

Noteworthy here is that the Western democracies were the sexual innovators. Britain and the United States joined the Soviet Union in strenuously opposing this language, and the three post-war powers resisted any recognition of the family in the Universal Declaration.[76]

The Declaration is backed by the International Covenant of Economic, Social, and Cultural Rights (1966) which states even more strongly (Article 10.1), "The widest possible protection and assistance should be accorded to the family, which is the natural and fundamental group unit of society, particularly for its establishment and while it is responsible for the care and education of dependent children." It also assumes marriage as the basis of the family and provides for the rights of parents (Article 13.3): "The States Parties to the present Covenant undertake to have respect for the liberty of parents and, when applicable, legal guardians to choose for their children schools, other than those established by the public authorities, which conform to such minimum educational standards as may be laid down or approved by the State and to ensure the religious and moral education of their children in conformity with their own convictions." The International Covenant on Civil and Political Rights (1966) protects the family (Article 23) and parental rights (Article 18.4) in language largely identical to the other measures.

---

75. Bahar, "Human Rights," 107.

76. Daniel Cere, "Human Rights and the Family," *Academic Questions*, vol. 22, no. 1 (Winter 2008–2009), 72.

Some provisions of these early treaties do appear self-contradictory. While recognizing marriage as the basis of family life, they also set it up for failure by providing for the rights of spouses at its "dissolution"— rights that as we have seen, are not remotely enforced in any country.[77]

Yet two more recent treaties go much further in undermining family integrity and private life by specifically targeting private citizens as human rights violators. Both have been the work of a small number of operatives, and it is apparent that many governments have signed them with little understanding of their full implications or commitment to enforcing their provisions. Yet their implications are nothing short of revolutionary. At a stroke, they undermine virtually every traditional authority other than the United Nations, from the national sovereignty of signatory states down to the family and parents. As such, they vividly demonstrate why the family supports all other social institutions and why its destruction undermines all social order and freedom.

Like the early treaties but more controversially, the newer treaties establish committees of unelected officials who monitor and evaluate compliance by signatory governments and their citizens. Though in theory purely advisory, these committees issue reports on the comportment of countries (and individuals within those countries) and instructions they must follow. The committees, composed of "experts" in "women's" issues, also issue gratuitous opinions or "general comments" (on what authority it is not clear) about the meaning of the treaties that often expand their reach.

Women's Human Rights

The Convention on the Elimination of All Forms of Discrimination against Women (CEDAW) has radically transformed the treaty-making process into a vehicle for social engineering. Drafted in the 1970s at the height of the Sexual Revolution, CEDAW requires countries to codify feminist ideology as official doctrine—a practice forbidden by the constitutions of most democracies, which recognize that beliefs cannot be given official status if expression is to remain free. Under CEDAW (Article 10c), signatories must "take all appropriate measures to eliminate discrimination against women ... and ... any stereotyped concept of the roles of men and women at all levels and in all forms." This is taken literally; even personal beliefs are not exempt from UN oversight. "It commits governments to intervene in virtually any setting, no matter how private or consensual, where, in the view of the CEDAW commit-

---

77. Ibid.; Stephen Baskerville, *Taken Into Custody: The War Against Fathers, Marriage, and the Family* (Nashville: Cumberland House, 2007).

tee, women are not considered equal," writes one observer. "It contains language calling for the most intrusive government imaginable—government which intrudes into the most private and sacred areas."[78] One passage (Article 5a) requires signatory governments to engineer changes not only in society but in people's minds:

> [Governments] shall take all appropriate measures . . . [t]o modify the social and cultural patterns of conduct of men and women, with a view to achieving the elimination of prejudices and customary and all other practices which are based on the idea of the inferiority or the superiority of either of the sexes or on stereotyped roles for men and women.

The CEDAW monitoring committee insists that governments disseminate propaganda to their populations. "States should introduce education and public information programmes to help eliminate prejudices that hinder women's equality" and "public information and education programmes to change attitudes concerning the roles and status of men and women."[79] The CEDAW committee has repeatedly expressed its view that governments have a duty to indoctrinate their citizens in ideology and suppress non-feminist heresies. Toward Indonesia, the committee expressed "great concern about existing social, religious, and cultural norms that recognize men as the head of the family and breadwinner and confine women to the roles of mother and wife, which are reflected in various laws, Government policies, and guidelines" and demanded to know "what steps the Government is proposing to take to modify such attitudes." Likewise, the "Committee is particularly concerned about the consistent emphasis placed on women's roles as mothers and caregivers in Croatian legislation pertaining to a variety of areas."[80]

CEDAW insists that even "private" persons are punishable for how they "discriminate" in their personal associations. "Under CEDAW, even private behavior—such as how couples divide household and child-care chores—is subject to government oversight and modification," accord-

---

78. Kathryn Balmforth, "Human Rights and the Family," paper presented at the World Family Policy Forum, 1999 (http://www.law2.byu.edu/wfpc/forum/1999/balmforth.pdf), and "Hijacking Human Rights."

79. UN Division for the Advancement of Women (UNDAW), General Recommendations Made by the Committee on the Elimination of Discrimination Against Women, No. 19, 11th Session, 1992 (http://www.un.org/womenwatch/daw/cedaw/recommendations/recomm.htm#recom19).

80. Quoted in P. Fagan, W. Saunders, and M. Fragoso, *How UN Conventions on Women's and Children's Rights Undermine Family, Religion, and Sovereignty* (Washington: Family Research Council, 2009), 10–11.

ing to Christina Hoff Sommers.[81] "The UN monitoring committee routinely censures countries like Denmark, Norway, and Iceland for failing to prevent women from taking primary care of children, a practice it deems 'discriminatory.'"[82] Anyone can thus be designated a human rights violator simply based on his most private and personal relationships. "Discrimination under the Convention is not restricted to action by or on behalf of Governments," the committee points out. Article 2(e) requires governments "to eliminate discrimination against women by any person." Article 2(f) requires governments forcibly "to abolish existing . . . customs and practices which constitute discrimination against women." The committee concludes: "States may also be responsible for private acts if they fail to act with due diligence to prevent violations of rights."[83]

CEDAW extends this government-enforced orthodoxy to education, including private schools and private families. "CEDAW prohibits making distinctions between the roles of mother and father, and teaching a traditional understanding of the family," writes one analyst. "Children are to be taught that they can get along just as well with two mothers or two fathers, and any attempt to show otherwise could be considered discrimination against women."[84] Children must be taught this in their own homes.

Having reduced public policy questions into matters of "human rights" and "discrimination," CEDAW officials may issue decrees at whim and without having to consider whether they are feasible, what the cost might be, or if they might be mutually inconsistent. Thus the CEDAW committee pushes governments to simultaneously legalize prostitution and prosecute men for engaging in it. A team of scholars observes:

> This progression, from urging countries that prohibit prostitution to move quickly to foster a national debate on legalizing the activity to chastising Germany for not elevating it to the status of a legally protected profession, is even more startling when one considers that it contradicts the reasonably clear language of the CEDAW treaty itself,

81. Christina Hoff Sommers, *The UN Women's Treaty: The Case against Ratification* (Washington: American Enterprise Institute, 2010, http://www.aei.org/docLib/20100323-CEDAW-Sommers.pdf), 5.

82. Christina Hoff Sommers, "The Case against the U.N. Women's Treaty," *National Review Online*, 16 November 2010, http://www.nationalreview.com/corner/253400/case-against-un-womens-treaty-christina-hoff-sommers#.

83. UNDAW, General Recommendation No. 19.

84. William Estrada, "CEDAW and Homeschooling Families," HSLDA internet site, 16 July 2009, http://www.hslda.org/docs/nche/Issues/U/UN_CEDAW_7162009.asp.

which says, "States Parties shall take all appropriate measures, including legislation, to suppress all forms of traffic in women and exploitation of prostitution of women." In the CEDAW committee, it seems that enabling prostitution is a form of suppressing it!

The contradiction is no accident and captures once again the authoritarian dynamic, whereby sexual liberalization is the first step in selective criminalization. Though CEDAW feminists advocate the legalization of prostitution, in practice they want laws that criminalize only men. While the CEDAW committee has pushed Mexico to legalize prostitution, in the next breath it "strongly recommends that new legislation should not discriminate against prostitutes but should punish pimps and procurers."[85]

The envisioned equality is more than equality before the law, and here too CEDAW officials can rule by decree without considering the costs. Citizens must finance "necessary supporting social services," including "a network of child-care facilities" (Article 11(2)(c)). In fact, the CEDAW committee seems particularly concerned to engineer the collectivization of childrearing. As Hoff Sommers notes, "Throughout the treaty, the drafters show a determination to eradicate gender stereotypes, especially those that associate women with care-giving and motherhood." Accordingly, governments must supervise private households to "ensure that family education includes a proper understanding of maternity as a social function."[86] The CEDAW committee admonishes New Zealand that "rates of participation [in day care] for mothers of young children and single mothers remain below the average for States members of the Organization for Economic Cooperation and Development."[87] Women's workforce participation seems to be the primary criterion directing CEDAW family policy decrees, and maximum day care is a goal in itself. The UN scolds Slovakia because the "decrease in preschool childcare is particularly detrimental to women's equal opportunity in the employment market since, owing to lack of childcare, they have to interrupt their employment career." The committee demands that Slovenia create "more formal and institutionalized childcare establishments for children under three years of age as well as for those from three to six." Having as many children as possible in institutional care is apparently a virtue for its own sake: "The committee expressed disdain that only 30% of the children under age three were placed in formal day care, while the rest were cared for by family members and other private

85. Fagan et al., *How UN Conventions*, 23.
86. Hoff Sommers, *UN Women's Treaty*, 13.
87. Quoted in Fagan et al., *How UN Conventions*, 9–10.

individuals." Collectivized child-rearing seems to be the committee's foremost panacea to combat gender inequality. In Germany, the committee was "concerned that measures aimed at the reconciliation of family and work *entrench stereotypical expectations* for women and men. In that regard the Committee is concerned with the unmet need for kindergarten places for the 0–3 age group."[88]

CEDAW operatives claim authority to curtail religious freedom and democratic rights when voters disagree with their agenda.[89] The fact that Irish voters have voted down several referenda to legalize abortion is apparently grounds to limit the freedom of Ireland's lamentably Catholic voters: "Although Ireland is a secular State, the influence of the Church is strongly felt not only in attitudes and stereotypes, but also in official State policy," the committee notes. "Women's right to health, including reproductive health [i.e., abortion], is compromised by this influence." Norway's protection for religious minorities likewise leaves them free to disagree with feminist doctrine, so Norway should think twice before allowing religious freedom:

> The Committee is especially concerned with provisions in the Norwegian legislation to exempt certain religious communities from compliance with the equal rights law. Since women often face greater discrimination in family and personal affairs in certain communities and in religion, they asked the Government to amend the Norwegian Equal Status Act to eliminate exceptions based on religion.

Indonesia should also curtail religious freedom: "Cultural and religious values cannot be allowed to undermine the universality of women's rights."[90]

CEDAW officials openly acknowledge that they are innovating new, political rights contrary to the values of most societies. The UN's Special Rapporteur on Violence Against Women acknowledges that "The most controversial [area] is the issue of sexual rights":

> The right to self-determination [of nations] is pitted against the CEDAW articles that oblige the state to correct any inconsistency between international human rights laws and the religious and customary laws operating within its territory.... While international *human rights law moves forward to meet the demands of the international women's movement*, the reality in many societies is that women's rights are under challenge from alternative cultural expressions....

88. Ibid., 11–12 (emphasis added).
89. See chapter III, under "Religious Belief."
90. Quoted in Fagan et al., *How UN Conventions*, 24–25, to which I owe these points.

The movement is not only generating new interpretations of existing human rights doctrine ... but it is also generating new rights. The most controversial is the issue of sexual rights.... One can only hope that the common values of human dignity and freedom will triumph over parochial forces attempting to confine women to the home.[91]

Complete gender equality as feminists conceive it, after all, is virtually impossible to achieve, short of truly totalitarian regulation of citizens' private lives, since many women make choices different from men's, especially once children appear. "If, for example, more women than men routinely take care of children, the CEDAW committee recommends ... government-imposed quotas and 'awareness raising' campaigns," notes Hoff Sommers. Her account of Iceland's experience shows how open-ended and insatiable the radical agenda must always be:

Iceland is a very small country, but it has one of the most extensive gender-equity bureaucracies in the world. As Hanna Gunnsteinsdottir, head of Iceland's Department of Equality and Labor, tried to explain to the CEDAW committee, her country has equity ministers, equity councils, equity advisers, and a Complaints Committee on Gender Equality whose rulings are binding. Every other year, a state-mandated "National Symposium on Gender Equity" educates citizens about sex-role stereotyping. More than 80% of Icelandic women are in the labor force, and parents enjoy paid maternity and paternity leave, including one month of pre-birth leave. Its current prime minister is the first openly lesbian head of government in the world. No wonder Iceland is ranked first in the World Economic Forum's 2009 *Global Gender Gap Report*. It would appear to be a model of egalitarianism. Yet it falls short. The committee praised the island nation for its "strides" toward gender parity, but several members found it to be remiss in its efforts to stamp out sexism. Hanna Beate Schopp-Schilling of Germany was concerned that, despite the government's multiple gender and equity committees, the parliament of Iceland itself had no committee on gender equity. The expert from Algeria wanted to know why so few women were full professors at the University of Iceland. Magalys Arocha Dominguez, from Cuba, was unhappy that many Icelandic women held part-time jobs and spent much more time than men taking care of children. She was also displeased by survey findings that Iceland's women were allowing family commitments to shape their career

91. Radhika Coomaraswamy, "Reinventing International Law: Women's Rights as Human Rights in the International Community," Harvard Law School, 1997 (http://libra ry.law.columbia.edu/urlmirror/11/ReinventingInternationalLaw.htm, emphasis added).

choices: "What government measures have been put in place to change these patterns of behavior?"

The same committee advised Spain to organize a national "awareness raising campaign against gender roles in the family." Finland was urged "to promote equal sharing of domestic and family tasks between women and men." Slovakia was instructed to "fully sensitize men to their equal participation in family tasks and responsibilities." Liechtenstein was questioned about a "Father's Day project" and reminded of the need to "dismantle gender stereotypes."

Proponents claim that the treaty is needed for countries where women are truly oppressed (most of which simply ignore it) and that it would have minimal affect in the liberal democracies, where its provisions are already observed. But this is not the view of the feminists who advocate it. Insisting that "American women need legal tools to fight patriarchy," Janet Benshoof, president of the Global Justice Center maintains that "If CEDAW were fully implemented in the United States it would revolutionize our rights."[92] CEDAW would immediately commit American officials to legislate *de facto* "equality" (however the feminists pressuring them might choose to define that). According to the authors of *Human Rights for All*, "CEDAW calls upon state parties to adopt temporary special measures aimed at accelerating *de facto* equality between men and women." Such "temporary special measures" are mandatory quotas. "CEDAW ratification would reflect the country's commitment to maintaining temporary special measures that advance the equal participation of women in civil, political, economic, social, and cultural arenas until that goal is achieved." However discriminatory against men, quotas are not "discrimination" according to CEDAW's prerogative to dictate the meanings of words. Article 54 allows that the guardians of anti-discrimination may themselves discriminate: "Temporary special measures aimed at accelerating *de facto* equality between men and women shall not be considered discrimination."[93] As Orwell predicted.

As we will see elsewhere, CEDAW would alter the structure of the US government and the authority of the Constitution to limit and define it, since treaties override internal constitutional provisions limiting the power of government. US federalism, which precludes federal intervention into areas such as family law and education, would be effectively abolished and power centralized in the national government to super-

92. Quoted in ibid., 7.
93. Ibid.

vise adherence. CEDAW mandates programs and policies that Americans have explicitly rejected, such as paid maternity leave, government-funded daycare, and equal pay for comparable (rather than equal or the same) work. Kathryn Balmforth argues that "It would be the sheerest folly to subordinate, in even the slightest degree, our right to make our own laws in this purely domestic area to any international treaty body."[94]

The effects would be, effectively, a *coup d'état*. Feminist operatives could simply sue their way into political office, appealing to their allies in the judiciary while bypassing the electorate and democratic checks and balances. "Under CEDAW," Benshoof exults forthrightly, "we could . . . sue the government to address the shameful fact that there is only one woman on the Supreme Court, no women running the Pentagon, and a Congress with only 16% women."[95] Though these ratios have increased since she stated this, the principle of filling offices by lawsuit would be further institutionalized. In short, CEDAW would give "the activists and lawyers of NCRW, NOW, and the Feminist Majority the license to sue, re-educate, and re-socialize their fellow citizens—opportunities that have eluded them under the [US] Constitution."[96]

Finally, CEDAW prohibits all sex differentiation in one area where it is essential: the military. "CEDAW would invalidate all Defense Department regulations that treat women differently, including women's exemptions from direct combat on land, sea, and in the air," according to the Center for Military Readiness. "At risk are countless laws, rules, and private practices that distinguish between the sexes or benefit women as a class. Military regulations governing personal misconduct such as adultery also would be subject to challenge by CEDAW bureaucrats."[97]

Children's Human Rights

The UN's Convention on the Rights of the Child (CRC) is even more invasive than CEDAW. Like the Anglo-American divorce law after which it is modeled, the CRC uses children as leverage to control the intimate private lives of their parents. As Phyllis Schlafly writes about "children's rights" defense:

94. Quoted in ibid., 5.
95. Quoted in Ibid., 8.
96. Ibid., 15–17, 20.
97. "CEDAW = US Military Under UN Control," Center for Military Readiness internet site: http://www.cmrlink.org/content/families-and-children/34450/cedaw_u_s_military_under_un_control, 10 October 2002.

The movement declares itself to be more interested in the welfare of children than their own parents are. It promises to give children legal sanctions against their parents, and in so doing, pits the interests of children against mom and dad. The inescapable implication is that children are not in safe hands with their own parents and that a whole movement must be called into being in order to protect them. Anti-family propaganda teaches that mothers and fathers are, at best, inadequate and, at worst, hostile to the needs of their children.[98]

The UN and other international bodies have long professed deep concern about the sufferings of children. Yet by their own account, none of their extensive assortment of programs over decades seems to have helped children in the least: "In spite of the comprehensive framework of instruments, standards, and commitments on the rights of the child ... the daily reality for millions of children worldwide is still in sharp contrast to these commitments and objectives." Or perhaps because of them:

> Children still face major threats to survival, lack opportunities for quality education, proper health and social care; they are victims of [the] worst forms of child labour, sexual exploitation and abuse, diseases, armed conflict, [and] various forms of violence; they are forced into early marriages and have to endure harmful traditional practices. Children belonging to vulnerable groups or children in particularly difficult situations face particular risks and are exposed to discrimination, marginalization, and exclusion. Girl children face specific risks and need particular attention.[99]

It is not clear how a UN treaty can possibly protect children from this hodgepodge of disparate and ill-defined horrors ("harmful traditional practices"). Most of these problems—the ones that are problems and not ideological grievances—proceed largely from the poverty and instability chronic in much of the world. Children suffer them in common with the rest of the population, including their parents. Most are not crimes in any ordinary or enforceable sense of that word, and to use them to rationalize separating out children from everyone else, including their own parents, and accusing their parents of crimes, is the most cynical posturing and simply constitutes another form of exploitation in many ways far more cruel than what the children already endure. These problems certainly cannot be solved by creating new global pow-

---

98. Schlafly, *Who Killed*, 205.

99. EU Guidelines for the Promotion and Protection of the Rights of the Child (http://www.consilium.europa.eu/uedocs/cmsUpload/16031.07.pdf, n.d., accessed August 2010), 3.

ers to confiscate children from their parents and criminalize parents. Yet that is precisely the sleight-of-hand that the CRC tries to pull off.

Like CEDAW, the CRC claims to govern the internal affairs and populations of signatory states and creates a compliance committee to scold them for inevitably falling short. But the CRC goes further: it undermines not only national sovereignty but the authority of elected representatives at the national, state, and local levels; it diminishes the authority of state and local governments vis-à-vis federal or national ones; it bypasses constitutional protections for citizens' freedom; and above all it extinguishes the authority of parents. At a stroke, the CRC undermines every authority below the UN level: parents and the family, local and state governments, and national or federal governments, each of whose authority is transferred up to the next level and ultimately to the UN. As such, one sympathetic writer comments, "the CRC provides an *ideology* for state intervention" into not only social and economic matters but even the most intimate corners of private life.[100] Like CEDAW only more so, it is not a limitation on government power but, precisely the opposite, a rationalization for expanding and centralizing it. "Ten individuals will dictate to the hundreds of millions of parents in the world how to raise their children."[101]

The CRC constitutes one of the most dramatic power shifts imaginable by a single document. Children cannot claim "rights" against anyone other than their own parents, since their parents are their defenders against everyone else. The CRC therefore has the power to set children against their parents, criminalize law-abiding citizens, centralize power away from local to national government, mandate increases in government spending without taxpayer consent, bypass elected representatives and all democratic decision-making, and abrogate virtually all constitutional limitations on government power.

Areas of jurisdiction now constitutionally forbidden to national or federal governments would become subjects of mandated government intervention. In countries like the US, where family law is still (in theory) within state jurisdiction, the CRC transfers an array of powers from states to the central government, including such vast areas of policymaking as education and health care. National and federal govern-

---

100. Van Bueren, quoted in Farris, "Nannies," 96 (my emphasis).

101. Stephen Krason, "The Mondale Act and Its Aftermath: An Overview of Forty Years of American Law, Public Policy, and Governmental Response to Child Abuse and Neglect," excerpt from his edited book, *Child Abuse, Family Rights, and the Child Protective System: A Critical Analysis from Law, Ethics, and Catholic Social Teaching* (Lanham, MD: Scarecrow Press, 2013), 44.

ments in turn themselves become the marionettes of the UN and its monitoring committee. The entire federalist principle—the original justification for the US Constitution and government—would become worthless.[102]

In the case of the United States, however, ratification would have dramatic reverberations throughout the world.

The US is effectively the only country that has not ratified the CRC. US ratification would have huge implications, not only for the US itself but globally. This is not simply because of the size and influence of the US but also because of its unique method of implementing treaties. In other countries, treaty enforcement is a political matter carried out as part of a country's foreign policy but unenforceable by domestic courts, who generally refrain from involvement in foreign relations.[103] The US makes a treaty, by constitutional stipulation, the "supreme law of the land," equal to the Constitution itself. This requires domestic courts to enforce its provisions automatically, without recourse to international tribunals.

While the monitoring committee's role is in theory only "advisory," their interpretation of compliance would be authoritative in the US and effectively bind US courts, government agencies, and parents. Not only family policy but the relations among family members in the privacy of their own homes throughout the United States would be dictated by a UN committee of feminists.

This logic is facilitated by pressure groups invoking the questionable concept of "customary international law" to incorporate treaty provisions such as the CRC into domestic legal decisions—*even where the treaty has not been ratified*. The US Supreme Court has invoked international law (when striking down a sodomy law) and the CRC itself. Federal courts have applied unratified treaties as binding in the United States. Thus an *unratified* treaty can be declared the "supreme law of the land"—equal to the Constitution itself—through nothing more than the opinions of a legal elite with a vested interested in expanding their own power.

This expansion of "customary international law" has made it nebulous to the point of nihilism. Originally the concept pertained to a very limited number of uncontroversial practices. Because no sovereign legislature from which to derive international law existed, jurists aimed to codify existing "customary," meaning universal, practice. This pertained

---

102. For details, see Farris, "Nannies."
103. Though the Vienna Convention has tried to establish otherwise; Farris, "Nannies," 90.

to such undisputed matters as diplomatic safe passage and piracy. "For customary law to emerge ... there must be uniform universal state practice ... for a long time," Austin Ruse points out. "Customary international law cannot be established from non-binding documents and neither can it be established in only 15 years. It takes decades and even centuries." Yet in recent years, sexual radicals have tried to accelerate the process of having their own highly innovative and contentious opinions ratified as "customary" law, despite the fact that they have provoked sharp disagreement and have not been practiced for any length of time. "Proponents of abortion make the case that if the phrase 'reproductive health' is repeated enough times in non-binding UN documents then a customary international law has been achieved."[104]

This turns law into a grab bag for whatever ideological fashion jurists wish to promote and a formula for pushing aside dissent: no legislature need enact it; no citizens need approve it; no public need agree to it; no election need ratify it; no mechanisms must exist to repeal it; no one can be held responsible for it. No vote is ever held, and no precise wording is ever codified. Nothing more than the momentary opinions of a judicial *clique* is necessary to declare as instant "custom" whatever fancy may take them, and without even having to state precisely what it is, it immediately becomes "law" throughout the world, even if the vast majority of humanity has never heard of it, has not approved it, or is adamantly opposed to it. This is a prescription for arbitrary government on a global scale. "Equality of women and men ... does not only constitute a crucial treaty obligation, but is also emerging as a principle of customary international law," says the CEDAW committee. "All states can be held accountable for complying with this principle which can be seen as the cornerstone of all human rights."[105] Does preventing repressive governments from killing political dissidents depend on achieving an open-ended and probably unrealizable egalitarianism, that is now "the cornerstone of all human rights" and binding on every human being in the world? At the least, this constitutes a peculiar understanding of what most of the world has traditionally understood by human rights.

But the essence of the CRC is its attack on parents. Governments must override parental decisions when social workers disagree with the parents' decisions. Children could seek government review of every homework assignment or restriction imposed by their parents. Areas of

---

104. Austin Ruse, "Rulers Without Borders," *Touchstone*, January–February 2010 (http://www.touchstonemag.com/archives/article.php?id=23-01-045-c).

105. CEDAW Committee, quoted in Fagan et al., *How the UN Conventions*, 7.

jurisdiction now constitutionally forbidden to a government become subject to mandated government intervention.

A key concept in the CRC gives governments the power to determine the "best interest of the child." This sounds unexceptionable. In fact, as Americans, Britons, and others have already discovered in domestic family law, the "best interest" standard is highly destructive of parental and family rights. It allows government officials to decide the "best interest" of other people's children, usurping that prerogative from parents, to the point of overriding parental decisions, removing children from parents who have done nothing legally wrong, and banishing the parents.[106]

Traditionally, legal authority over children has long been recognized to reside with their parents, unless they somehow forfeit it. "For centuries it has been a canon of law that parents speak for their minor children," observed Justice Potter Stewart. "So deeply embedded in our traditions is this principle of the law that the Constitution itself may compel a state to respect it." Parents, not governments, traditionally decide what is in the best interest of their own children; otherwise, they are not parents. The Supreme Court has recognized "that natural bonds of affection lead parents to act in the best interests of their children."[107]

This principle has already been all but abolished in American and British domestic law, largely because of divorce and child-protection practices, and the CRC is not the only threat to it. Contrary to these seemingly unequivocal precedents, it is now the norm in American family law to assume precisely the opposite: that "the child's best interest is perceived as being independent of the parents," as one practitioner writes, "and a court review is held to be necessary to protect the child's interests."[108]

The CRC would put added international pressure on this principle. As Professor Van Bueren forthrightly reveals:

> Best interests provides decision and policy makers with the authority to substitute their own decisions for either the child's or the parents', providing it is based on considerations of the best interests of the child. Thus, the Convention challenges the concept that family life is always in the best interests of children and that parents are always capable of deciding what is best for children.[109]

---

106. Farris, "Nannies"; Baskerville, *Taken Into Custody*, ch. 1.

107. *Parham v. J.R.*, 422 US 584, 602 (1979).

108. Robert Williams, "An Overview of Child Support Guidelines in the United States," in Margaret Campbell Haynes (ed.), *Child Support Guidelines: The Next Generation* (Washington: Office of Child Support Enforcement, 1994), 2.

109. Quoted in Farris, "Nannies," 107.

But it does not challenge the substitute presumption that government intervention in family life is always in the best interests of children and that government officials are always capable of deciding what is best for other people's children. Article 9 permits government functionaries to remove children from their parents not on the basis of proven abuse or neglect by the parents but on their simple judgement that it is in "the best interests of the child."

Noteworthy is that most cases eroding parental rights in domestic law are divorce cases. Noting that the best interest "standard also applies in divorce cases on the presumption that the family unit has been broken," Michael Farris observes, "If this treaty becomes binding, all parents would have the same legal status as abusive parents, because the government would have the right to override every parental decision if it deemed the parent's choice contrary to the child's best interest."[110] This is precisely the status divorced parents now have, abusive or not. Non-abusive parents in intact marriages who think they and their children are safe from government intervention are burying their heads.

A connected provision requires the "child's right of participation." Article 12 stipulates that signatory governments "shall assure to the child who is capable of forming his or her own views the right to express those views freely in all matters affecting the child, the views of the child being given due weight in accordance with the age and maturity of the child." Against whom must governments enforce this right of children to express whatever opinions occur to them? This essentially institutionalizes the right of children to rebel against their parents and puts the state on the side of the child, with the backing of international law. "The Children's Convention potentially protects the rights of the child who philosophically disagrees with the parents' educational goals," writes Van Bueren.[111] What is the difference from a child who (philosophically) simply does not wish to do his homework?

A striking irony is the claimed protection of children's "privacy." Article 16 provides that "No child shall be subjected to arbitrary or unlawful interference with his or her privacy, family, home, or correspondence" and "the child has the right to the protection of the law against such interference or attacks." But again, protection from whom? His or her parents? Authorizing state officials to "protect" this "privacy" justifies massive state intervention into the family's privacy.

All these provisions might sound innocuous if their purpose was to

---

110. Michael Farris, "Parental Rights: Why Now is the Time to Act," *The Home School Court Report*, vol. 22, no. 2 (March–April 2006).

111. Quoted in Farris, "Nannies," 108.

protect adults against government repression. When applied to children, they have the effect of abolishing parents and all authority between children and the state. This starkly illustrates how the family is essential to freedom, and how the state, when it claims to be protecting "rights" and "freedom" and "privacy"—without the mediating authority of the family—is the fox protecting the henhouse.

These provisions allow government officials to pose as the mouthpieces and defenders of other people's children, children they do not know and do not love. Yet the altruism of these functionaries is assumed without question, while parents are depicted as selfishly promoting their own interests, which are cast as contrary to those of their own children. This makes the child the pawn of various adult manipulators, as revealed clearly by one law school professor:

> The interests of the child should be at the center of any decision-making. If the child is capable of articulating a perspective, the child should have client-directed counsel to get that voice before the court and the court should seriously consider it. Even if the child is unable to articulate a view, the child's attorney can offer a child-focused assessment of the child's needs. Because the child's best interests may be different than one or both of the parent's interests, the child should have a voice.

What is described as "the child's" voice comes out of the mouth of a lawyer or some other official. Parents are left with no greater authority over their own children than that of another "voice" that officials may heed or ignore as they please. According to another law professor: "Giving the child a voice, however, does not necessarily 'conflict.' Listening to the child does not mean not listening to the parents or others involved in the dispute. The key is to add the child's voice to the voice of others being presented."[112]

Parents and children are equal voices—essentially they are made lobbyists for their own private lives—but it is the officials who decide.

Indeed, it is difficult to see how the CRC has any purpose other than to abolish parenthood, effectively abolishing the family. "No criticism was leveled against either Ireland or the UK for failing to consider the child's viewpoint in those cases where the parents allowed their child to attend sex education classes," writes Farris. "Nor was there any criticism for failure to consider the child's views in the decision to enroll the child in the government schools." Farris concludes that "The child's wishes

---

112. Linda Elrod, "Client-Directed Lawyers for Children: It is the 'Right' Thing to Do," *Pace Law Review* 27 (Summer 2007), 869, 882–83, quoted in Farris, "Nannies," 111.

seem to get special attention only when the parents want something different from the wishes of the government."[113]

The entire system attempts to harness and exploit the rebelliousness of children and adolescents and focus it on their parents. "Normally, when children rebel against their parents, society frowns," one team of scholars observes. "Yet the UN is attempting to put in place, in policy and law, structures that foster this type of rebellion." Another example:

> The UN committee report to Belize recommends that the government set up legal mechanisms to help children challenge their parents, including making an "independent child-friendly mechanism" accessible to children "to deal with complaints of violations of their rights and to provide remedies for such violations." In other words, the CRC committee is suggesting that the state create some entity *to supervise parents*, a structure that enables children in Belize to challenge their mother and father's parenting in court.[114]

The CRC committee has also "begun calling for the creation of 'ombudsmen,' so that children can turn in their parents when the children feel their rights have been violated. The committee has even called for national laws to make sure that parents pay adequate attention to the views of their children."[115]

The CRC also allows UN and government officials to demand expenditures on certain policies and, effectively, control budgets. One report cites Moldova (the poorest country in Europe) for "inadequate financial support out of the state budget": "The Committee strongly recommends that the State party . . . further increase budget allocations for the implementation of the rights recognized in the Convention."[116] Under the guise of "human rights," the UN is trying to control the spending decisions of a sovereign nation. The committee has also cited Austria, Australia, Denmark, the UK, and others for not spending enough on social welfare programs. According to the CRC committee's existing interpretation, it is illegal for a nation to spend more on national defense than on children's welfare.[117] In the US, the federal government would be

---

113. Ibid., 100.

114. Fagan et al., *How UN Conventions*, 13.

115. Balmforth, "Hijacking Human Rights."

116. Consideration of Reports Submitted by States Parties Under Article 44 of the Convention, Concluding Observations: Republic of Moldova, UN Committee on the Rights of the Child, 50th Session, 2009, 3–4 (http://www2.ohchr.org/english/bodies/crc/docs/co/CRC-C-MDA-CO3.pdf).

117. Quoted in Farris, "Nannies," 96.

empowered to control education, health care, family life, or any other area the UN deemed appropriate.

This is a prescription for patronage payoffs to favored clients, in this case groups professionally involved in child welfare. The UN demands that Moldovan taxpayers fund its *nomenklatura* of pressure groups—again, euphemistically termed "civil society"—and "recommends that the State party continue to provide financial and material support to NGOs working for the protection and promotion of children's rights." Despite the ostensibly altruistic pretext of children's welfare, UN officials are trying to loot Moldova's impoverished citizens and funnel their tax revenues to their cronies. This creates what some call "GONGOs" or oxymoronic *government organized* non-governmental organizations. "At what point does government funding of NGOs make them no longer NGOs?" asks ParentalRights.org, an organization opposing the CRC. "If Moldova were to accede to the UN's wishes and fund these non-government organizations, just how 'non-government' could they hope to remain?"[118]

CRC's committee also tries to criminalize spanking: "The right of the child to protection from corporal punishment and other cruel or degrading forms of punishment." The comment deals with any physical punishment, "however light," and makes no distinction between disciplinary spanking and serious physical abuse, like kicking and biting. As such, it calls for states to ban all physical punishment of children through criminal law—equating spanking with battery. Furthermore, the comment demands vast educational campaigns to "raise awareness" about the right not to be spanked. States must submit data on their progress toward eliminating "corporal punishment" during periodic reviews.[119]

While the UN lacks criminal jurisdiction to enforce such "elimination," the more advanced criminal enforcement powers of the EU may be marshaled, likely as a prelude to expanding police power to the UN. The EU has expressed its willingness to serve as an enforcement arm of the UN, to both advocate and implement UN instruments and policies.[120] The limited but growing EU law enforcement powers would be marshaled to criminalize "violations of children's rights"—principally

---

118. Considerations of Reports . . . Moldova, 4–5; "Moldova: Poverty Demands Control?" http://www.parentalrights.org/index.asp?Type=B_BASIC&SEC={11B6B020-AFAC-4C50-800D-B12C4D224D57}.

119. Fagan et al., *How UN Conventions*, 15–16. The CRC committee calls on states to ban spanking through criminal law and aims "to treat spanking as it would the battery of an adult."

120. European Union website: http://eur-lex.europa.eu/LexUriServ/LexUriServ.do?uri=CELEX:52006DC0367:EN:NOT.

by their parents: "encouraging and supporting the enhancement of capacity of law enforcement agencies for the investigation of the violation of children's rights and the development of child friendly procedures for the investigation and prosecution of violations of children's rights." The EU maintains "data bases and surveillance systems" in order "to gather, analyse, and promote dissemination of child-rights disaggregated related data" about how parents raise their children.[121]

The CRC is breathtaking in its consolidation and centralization of power. Effectively, it surrenders the authority of parents, of democratically elected governments at all levels, and of national constitutions, of the people in all the nations on earth—all to an unelected UN committee of 18 feminists. As such, it places the beginning of global government in one hand that may be the most powerful in the world: "the hand that rocks the cradle."

Homosexuals' Human Rights

The committees monitoring CEDAW and the CRC often act more as lobbies than international authorities and constantly seek to augment their power. This can take on a life of its own, beyond what is actually written in the treaties. "The fact that abortion is not mentioned in . . . [CEDAW] has not prevented the committee charged with its implementation from censuring more than 60 countries for failing to include legal abortion services in their domestic laws."[122]

This trend toward global government by committee was advanced with the "Yogyakarta Principles." Here international functionaries, on their own initiative and on no authority other than their own opinions, have devised a series of axioms about sex which they are now trying to impose on the world as "binding" law. The authors are a self-appointed group who pretentiously nominate themselves "the International Panel of Experts in International Human Rights Law and on Sexual Orientation and Gender Identity." These "experts" are feminist and homosexualist members of UN treaty committees.

No governments have agreed to these opinions promoting a homosexualist political agenda. Indeed, no UN treaty has ever recognized or even mentioned sexual orientation, "and repeated attempts to pass resolutions promoting broad homosexual rights have been repeatedly

---

121. EU Guidelines for the Promotion and Protection of the Rights of the Child (n.d.), 11–12.

122. D. Brian Scarnecchia and Terrence McKeegan, *The Millennium Development Goals in Light of Catholic Social Teaching* (New York: Catholic Family and Human Rights Institute, 2009), 47.

rejected by UN member states."[123] Nevertheless, these rules are advertised as "binding international legal standards with which all States
must comply."[124]

The "Principles" assume that young children may be classified permanently as homosexuals, and if their parents object to this categoriza-
tion then government social workers may intervene to punish the
parents. In effect, they criminalize parents for trying to ensure that their
children have a healthy and normal sexuality. Principle 5 demands "all
necessary policing" and "criminal penalties" for "harassment" of children for sexual activity by anyone "in all spheres of life, *including the
family*" (emphasis added). Parents who "harass" their children about
any matter regarding sex must be "prosecuted, tried, and duly punished." Financial rewards would entice children into bringing complaints against their parents. Schools must inculcate in children
"understanding of and respect for . . . diverse sexual orientations and
gender identities" (Principle 16).

Parents who object to this sexualization of their children can have
their mouths stopped. "The exercise of freedom of opinion and expression" may be curtailed if the words somehow "violate the rights and
freedoms of persons of diverse sexual orientations and gender identities," including their own minor children. In Orwellian Newspeak, the
Principles explain how human rights, in this case, freedom of speech
and religion, must be repressed in the name of human rights: the state
must "ensure that the expression, practice, and promotion of different
opinions, convictions, and beliefs with regard to issues of sexual orientation or gender identity is not undertaken in a manner incompatible
with human rights" (Principle 21). The document requires legal punishments for anyone who dissents from the sexual activists' opinions or
objects to anything they do. Governments must "take all appropriate
measures to combat actions or campaigns targeting human rights
defenders working on issues of sexual orientation and gender identity,
as well as those targeting human rights defenders of diverse sexual orientations and gender identities" (Principle 27).

As with the other measures transferring control of other people's
children to government "experts," this one invokes "the best interest of
the child," now defined ideologically and sexually: "The sexual orienta-

123. Piero Tozzi, "Six Problems with the 'Yogyakarta Principles,'" International
Organizations Research Group website: http://www.c-fam.org/publications/id.439/pub_
detail.asp, 3.

124. Yogyakarta Principles website: http://www.yogyakartaprinciples.org/principles
_en.htm. See also Kuby, *Global Sexual Revolution*, ch. 5.

tion or gender identity of the child or of any family member or other person may not be considered incompatible with such best interests." So by government decree "the best interest of the child" is to be homosexual—or ... whatever the child wishes or can be persuaded to do. As Piero Tozzi points out, nothing limits what may be considered acceptable "sexual orientation," including polygamy, pedophilia, bestiality, and necrophilia. It protects "the freedom to seek, receive, and impart information and ideas *of all kinds*, including with regard to human rights, sexual orientation, and gender identity, through any medium and *regardless of frontiers*" (Principle 19, emphasis added). But no corollary right to question such practices is permitted; on the contrary, criticism must be punished, and officials must "ensure that the exercise of freedom of opinion and expression does not violate the rights and freedoms of persons of diverse sexual orientations and gender identities" (Principle 19).[125] Nations' constitutional protections for their citizens' freedom of conscience and religion are abolished: "may not be invoked by the State to justify laws, policies, or practices which deny equal protection of the law, or discriminate, on the basis of sexual orientation or gender identity" (Principle 21).

Homosexualist groups, by contrast, are free not only to agitate publicly but to do so with immunity from the rules governing other groups: "must not be restricted" by regulations governing "public order, public morality, public health, and public security."[126]

Domestic Violence (again)

Carrying forward the logic of CEDAW and the CRC is the sexual agenda's clearest threat to human rights in the name of human rights: the campaign to politicize criminal law enforcement—"human rights" —for the protection, not of the accused, but of the accusers. According to this logic, alleged criminals are human rights violators—equivalent to dictators—politicizing the accusations, denying them the due process protections of formal criminal charges, and rendering their guilt or innocence subject to determination by political activists.

Here yet again, the cutting edge is sexuality and the family. The most innovative development is the campaign to classify "domestic violence" as a human rights violation. "Until recently, it has been difficult to conceive of domestic violence as a human rights issue under international law," feminist scholars acknowledge. There are logical reasons why this should be difficult. "Human rights" is supposed to be about *government*

125. Tozzi, "Six Problems," 4–5, 7.
126. Kuby, *Global Sexual Revolution*, 70.

repression, not ordinary crime. Even on its face, "domestic violence" has no connection with human rights. No one suggests that theft or mugging, when not perpetrated by government agents, are "human rights" violations. They are crimes for which the criminal justice system either provides or it does not. If not, the system is dysfunctional, but it has nothing to do with "human rights." "In traditional human rights practice states are held accountable only for what they do directly or through an agent, rendering acts of purely private individuals—such as domestic violence crimes—outside the scope of state responsibility," the feminists acknowledge. "Systematic nonenforcement of laws against armed robbery by private actors alone is not a human rights problem; it merely indicates a serious common crime problem." To maintain otherwise is to place all criminal law enforcement within the nebulous realm of "human rights" politics. "States cannot be held directly accountable for violent acts of all private individuals because all violent crime would then constitute a human rights abuse for which states could be held directly accountable under international law."[127] The other implication, not mentioned by the feminists, is that accused individuals themselves, not merely the states in which they live, would be directly subject to international law.

Yet that is precisely what these feminist scholars and others then proceed to do: replace apolitical criminal law, with its due process protections for the rights of defendants, with political campaigns of the kind mobilized against dictators. The result is predictable, if ironic: to turn "human rights" into a prescription for mob justice not against public political figures but against private individuals who have been convicted of no crime and who (unlike the dictators) have no public platform to defend themselves. "More recently, however, the concept of state responsibility has expanded to include not only actions directly committed by states, but also states' systematic failure to prosecute acts [allegedly?] committed either by low-level or para-state agents or by private actors," we are told. "In these situations, although the state does not actually commit the [alleged?] primary abuse, its failure to prosecute the [alleged?] abuse amounts to complicity in it."[128]

What justifies this innovation? Again, the alleged oppression of women, though with little definition of what precisely this means or evidence that it has even occurred. "Modern studies suggest ... that far from being a place of safety, the family can be [a] 'cradle of violence' and that much of this violence is directed at the female members of the fam-

127. Thomas and Beasley, "Domestic Violence," 37, 41–43.
128. Ibid., 41.

ily."[129] No evidence is presented for these vague assertions of unspeci-fied "violence"; they are one scholar quoting another scholar quoting "studies," of which only one, by the UN, is cited. The UN report like-wise offers no evidence but only additional vague generalizations: "Women . . . have been revealed as seriously deprived of basic human rights. Not only are women denied equality with the balance of the world's population, men, but also they are often denied liberty and dig-nity, and in many situations suffer direct violations of their physical and mental autonomy."[130] What precisely constitutes "violations of their physical and mental autonomy" is not explained, but unspecified (and unconvicted) persons apparently are guilty of these violations and must be arrested and punished.

Feminists in fact acknowledge that they have no evidence for their assertions about violent families. "Although anecdotal evidence of an overwhelming incidence of domestic violence exists, hard facts or large scale surveys of specific aspects of spousal murder, battery, or rape have often been hard to obtain, or altogether unavailable," they admit.[131] In other words, there is no evidence whatever that women suffer crime any more than anyone else, or from any serious or widespread problem of "human rights" deprivation.

As we have seen, it is clearly established that an intact family is the safest environment for women.[132] Far from having any evidence for the "cradle of violence" thesis, feminists are ignoring clear data that demon-strates precisely the opposite.

Yet even could it be provided, it is still not clear how statistical evi-dence of a crime problem justifies reclassifying it as an international human rights violation. But apparently it becomes a human rights mat-ter because it is "discrimination." "Gender-based violence is a form of discrimination that seriously inhibits women's ability to enjoy rights and freedoms on a basis of equality with men," according to the CEDAW committee.[133] Here once again, criminal violence is re-classified as dis-

---

129. Ibid., 43–44, quoting Jane Francis Connors, "Violence Against Women in the Family" (New York: United Nations, 1989). Catherine Moore, "Women and Domestic Violence: The Public/Private Dichotomy in International Law," *The International Jour-nal of Human Rights*, vol. 7, no. 4 (Winter 2003), 95, quotes the same passage, also with-out offering any specific evidence, as do other feminist scholars.

130. Connors, "Violence Against Women," 3.

131. Thomas and Beasley, "Domestic Violence," 57.

132. Baskerville, *Taken Into Custody*, ch. 4.

133. UN Division for the Advancement of Women (UNDAW), General Recommen-dations Made by the Committee on the Elimination of Discrimination Against Women, No. 19, 11th Session, A/47/38, 1992.

284 The New Politics of Sex

crimination in order to rationalize classifying acts said to constitute discrimination as criminal violence, even when no physical contact or threat of it takes place. The peculiarity of describing an allegedly violent crime as "discrimination" is said to be justified by "the widespread failure by states to prosecute such violence and to fulfill their international obligations to guarantee women equal protection of the law." Yet even granting this logic, no evidence is presented for this alleged failure because, as scholars again acknowledge, none exists. "Although information about government response to this problem is still minimal, the research suggests that investigation, prosecution, and sentencing of domestic violence crimes occurs with much less frequency than other, similar crimes."[134] But once again, no such "research" is presented, because no evidence for this assertion exists.

In fact, these assertions as well are not only unsupported but the precise opposite of the truth, as reputable scholars have already established. Even if one accepts the "discrimination" logic, it is undercut by one simple but incontrovertible fact on which the feminists are silent: no evidence suggests that "domestic violence" is even perpetrated primarily against women. On the contrary, it is well established by studies over decades (including many by feminist scholars) that men are victims of violent attacks by women at roughly the same rates as women by men.[135] This alone suggests serious problems about defining violence against women as "discrimination"—the sole justification for not leaving it to ordinary criminal law.

As for the claim of government complicity in domestic violence because it is punished "with much less frequency" than other crimes, this too is the diametrical opposite of the truth, as we have seen.[136] Even in domestic law, domestic violence is indeed adjudicated very differently from standard criminal assault: "Relaxed rules of evidence and the lower burden of proof" ("preponderance of the evidence" rather than the normal criminal standard of "beyond a reasonable doubt") enable courts to convict and punish defendants against whom no evidence exists.[137] As we have seen, domestic violence accusations seldom involve a trial, almost never a jury, and no one accused is ever acquitted. Special "domestic violence courts" exist for the express purpose of expediting

134. Thomas and Beasley, "Domestic Violence," 48, 46.
135. See chapter III, under "Domestic Violence." An extensive bibliography is Martin Fiebert, "References Examining Assaults by Women on Their Spouses or Male Partners: An Annotated Bibliography," *Sexuality and Culture*, vol. 14, no. 1 (2010).
136. See chapter III, under "Domestic Violence."
137. Robert Verkaik, "Crackdown Unveiled on Domestic Violence," *The Independent*, 19 November 2001.

pre-determined convictions and meting out more punishments, and forced confessions are extracted on pre-printed forms on pain of incarceration.[138] It is patently ludicrous to suggest that it is punished "with much less frequency"; it is punished with far more.

This strained reasoning constitutes yet another rationalization for by-passing due process protections and provides further proof that the entire category of "domestic violence" is artificially created specifically to circumvent the due process protections of criminal assault law and punish those who cannot be convicted with evidence. This is precisely why it lends itself to further politicization as a "human rights" issue, since human rights accusations likewise are inherently political, nebulously defined, loosely adjudicated, presume guilt, require a low burden of proof, and weighted toward conviction and punishment.[139]

Claims that police do not pursue domestic violence accusations are simply an admission of the most astounding feature of domestic "violence": that it need not be, in fact, *violent.* Recall that the British and US governments (the two most influential exporters of gender law) officially include "criticizing" and "denying money" as "violence," as well as "psychological, emotional, sexual, and economic abuse" and "undermining an individual's sense of self-worth and/or self-esteem." After going through a litany of purported horror stories from around the world where officials allegedly refused to prosecute domestic "violence" (all from an undocumented UN report), one feminist scholar reveals that the reason they failed to prosecute was because they adhered to "a narrow definition of domestic violence as it refers only to physical violence and so therefore excludes sexual and psychological violence."[140] In other words, officials did not prosecute anyone for committing violence because there was no violence.

This rather arresting feature of domestic violence campaigns, difficult to comprehend for the uninitiated, also accounts for the otherwise peculiar tendency of feminist and increasingly homosexualist scholars to wax eloquent and at length about why violence is bad. "Violence is an egregious affront to the core and basic notions of civility and citizenship," declares one. "Violence assaults life, dignity, and personal integrity. It transgresses fundamental norms of peaceful coexistence."[141]

---

138. See chapter III, under "Domestic Violence," and Baskerville, *Taken Into Custody*, ch. 4.

139. See John Laughland, *A History of Political Trials* (Oxford: Peter Lang, 2008), 7.

140. Catherine Moore, "Women and Domestic Violence," 97.

141. Celina Romany, "Women as Aliens: A Feminist Critique of the Public/Private Distinction in International Human Rights Law," *Harvard Human Rights Journal*, vol. 6 (Spring 1993), 87.

Such grandiloquence over matters that no one denies is only necessary to stop the mouths of those who, once they discover what is actually meant by this "violence," might be tempted to conclude that it is not really very serious after all.

As may be apparent, if anyone has been the victim of gender "discrimination" and the unequal protection of the laws concerning domestic violence, it is the accused. Indeed, the virtual persecution of men under domestic violence hysteria—including patently fabricated accusations, loose rules of adjudication, suspension of due process protections, incarcerations without trial, special politicized courts that never acquit, forced confessions, manufactured and paid witnesses—fits standard descriptions of human rights violations as practiced by some of the world's most repressive dictatorships. Yet "human rights" advocacy groups are not only silent about these practices; they support them.

Elsewhere in human rights law attention is focused on protecting the accused against criminal charges unjustly used for political purposes. Yet here "human rights" advocates become the accusers and urge more punishment, to the point of suspending due process safeguards. Armed with ill-defined open-ended domestic violations accusations, Amnesty International and other groups advocate more arrests and more punishments in the name of human rights, regardless of whether any evidence indicates that the accused are guilty. We even learn that domestic violence constitutes "private torture,"[142] and that "Amnesty International considers domestic violence a form of torture,"[143] demonstrating an Orwellian willingness to redefine words and cheapening their own campaign against real torture.[144] Here again we hear echoes of the fanatical St. Just, who might have justified the Terror with the cry, "No human rights for the violators of human rights!"

That human rights is being used to politicize law enforcement is clear from efforts not only to prosecute alleged criminals but also to change

142. Bonita Meyersfeld, "Reconceptualizing Domestic Violence in International Law," *Albany Law Review* (Winter 2003), 373.

143. This line was apparently removed from the Amnesty International website following an article in *LewRockwell.com* (http://archive.lewrockwell.com/baskerville/baskerville13.1.html), but it is still quoted on feminist websites: http://evilslutopia.com/2008/10/domestic-violence-awareness-month-2008.html and http://momma-momo.livejournal.com/ (accessed 2 November 2016).

144. Here too a pattern seems to be developing involving other items from the radical sexual agenda. A UN report has also identified laws prohibiting abortion as "torture." Stefano Gennarini, "Denial of Abortion is Torture, UN Bureaucrat Says," C-FAM internet site:https://c-fam.org/friday_fax/denial-abortion-torture-un-bureaucrat-says/. Likewise, homosexualists now insist that conversion therapy—a method of helping people

political opinions. "Domestic violence is not random—i.e., it is directed at women because they are women and is committed to impede women from exercising their rights," we are told. "As such, it is an essential factor in maintaining women's subordinate status." Feminists deride "the false conclusion that all they [governments] need to do to eliminate domestic violence is prosecute [alleged?] aggressors equally with other violent criminals"—in other words, observe the equal protection of the laws. Instead, governments must supplement the punishments by propagating to their populations the correct political opinions. The "international community" must "direct a state to adopt a particular social program to change discriminatory attitudes." Law enforcement thus becomes a tool of political ideology, which must be disseminated among (and financed by) the population to avoid becoming a nation of "human rights" violators. "As the concept of state responsibility in international law evolves further, human rights organizations may more easily hold governments accountable for failing actively to counter the social, economic, and attitudinal biases which underpin and perpetuate domestic violence."[145] Failing to control the thoughts of their people will be a human rights violation, and democratic electorates must be required to accept that new forms of crime proceed from their own ideologically incorrect opinions, or what one scholar calls "insidious forms of thought" that must be rooted out by the state machinery. Government re-education must "modify existing ideological, social, and cultural constructs that perpetuate the idea, in any way, that women are inferior to men." "Such educational programmes are imperative if one is attempting to change people's attitudes toward religious and customary practices."[146]

Along with Maoist re-education comes Stalinist Newspeak. It turns out that women are oppressed not only by gender discrimination but also by precisely what feminists themselves have been clamoring for with equal stridency: gender *neutrality*. Both sexes are equal, but one is more equal than the other:

---

overcome unwanted same-sex attraction—is torture and therefore a violation of international law that governments must criminalize. The Torture Convention is very clear that it was intended to stop "a public official" intentionally causing physical or mental pain in order to obtain information or a confession, or causing pain and suffering as a punishment. Austin Ruse, "LGBT Activists Urge UN to Designate 'Reparative Therapy' a Form of Torture," *Breitbart*, 10 November 2014, http://www.breitbart.com/Big-Peace/2014/11/07/Gays-Want-UN-to-Name-Reparative-Therapy-a-Form-of-Torture.

145. Thomas and Beasley, "Domestic Violence," 58–60.

146. Moore, "Women and Domestic Violence," 106–10.

Treating domestic violence as merely an issue of equal protection, and by inference therefore, setting up the treatment of men as the standard by which we ought to measure the treatment of women in our societies, may in fact disserve women and mask the ways in which domestic violence is not just another common crime. The norm of gender neutrality itself, embodied in the human rights treaties and international customary law, may unintentionally reinforce gender bias in the law's application and obscure the fact that human rights laws ought to deal directly with gender-specific abuse, and not just gender-specific failures to provide equal protection. The gender-neutral norm may appear to require only identical treatment of men and women, when in fact, equal treatment in many cases is not adequate.[147]

Gender neutrality is gender bias. Non-violence is violence. Due process and equal protection safeguards are human rights violations. War is peace. As Orwell predicted, words can be redefined to mean whatever a political agenda demands that they mean.

Yet further, feminists demand that the state subject all family and private life to its control in the name of human rights. "The binary concept of the public opposing the private, in law and society, negatively impacts women's enjoyment of fundamental human rights with specific reference to . . . domestic violence." In the inbred world of feminist scholarship, this too is repeated over and over like an incantation, as feminist scholars not only refuse to recognize any distinction between public and private, but argue vehemently against it: "Violence in the family can ultimately be traced back to . . . assumptions regarding gender roles and hierarchies within the family. As a result, the liberal distinction between private/family and public/state falls."[148]

Punishing true violent crime of course does not necessitate invading and controlling the private lives of innocent citizens. Acts of true physical violence perpetrated in the home or anywhere else can be punished criminally without violating the realm of personal and family privacy, let alone denying that any such realm exists. "Since domestic violence in essence perpetrates harm on others, such action should not legitimately be protected by the private element." In plain English, punishing crime does not require abolishing private life. Yet feminists want to abolish it anyway. Indeed, if there is one central theme in feminist literature on human rights, it is that no private sphere of life is legitimate if, in Catherine Moore's words, it "is not regulated by the state." "This lack of regulation of the private sphere manifests itself in an absence . . . of laws that

---

147. Thomas and Beasley, "Domestic Violence," 61.
148. Moore, "Women and Domestic Violence," 93; Bahar, "Human Rights," 106.

specifically condemn domestic violence" (which is defined to include "psychological" violence), even though there is no absence of standard laws against violent assault. Because the claimed "violence" is not violent, this has nothing to do with protecting anyone from physical harm. It is a purely political agenda, to use knowingly false criminal accusations to eradicate protections for family privacy and acquire government power over the most private corners of citizens' lives. "Void of such regulation the private sphere . . . facilitates and encourages the continuance of female suppression to male dominance in the most basic unit of society, the family." In respectable academic journals, scholars are repeating, formulaically and without any fear of challenge, that the state should not respect or recognize a private sphere of life:

> There is a critical need to place gender-based violence within the context of women's structural inequality as a means of breaking down the distinction between public and private life that operates to exclude gender-based violence from the human rights agenda. An analysis of women's structural inequality should be substituted for the current "mainstream" preoccupation with the public/private distinction.[149]

In short, domestic violence law, both domestic and international, has been formulated not to punish violent crime (which it does not punish), but to subject citizens' private lives and beliefs to penal oversight. "In this regime," writes Jeannie Suk, "the home is a space in which criminal law deliberately and coercively *reorders* and *controls* private rights and relationships . . . not as an incident of prosecution, but as its goal." Though ostensibly criminalizing violence (which is already criminal), domestic violence measures result "not only in the criminalization of violence proper," but also in the "criminal prohibition of intimate relationships in the home." Spouses and sexual partners cannot live their private lives "without risking arrest and punishment."[150]

Here is where "human rights" politics becomes its own opposite, since human rights accusations are never judicial but always political. Accusations of "crimes" by dictators are never qualified by a presumption of innocence because they are openly political, a logic that carries over to pseudo-judicial proceedings against private individuals accused of gender crimes like "domestic violence." Evidence is irrelevant, because like the dictator, the accused domestic abuser is condemned by politics.

One scholar forthrightly declares that domestic violence is a purely

---

149. Moore, "Women and Domestic Violence," 104, 93, 95, 121; Sullivan, "Public/Private Distinction," 126–34.

150. Jeannie Suk, "Criminal Law Comes Home," *Yale Law Review*, vol. 116, no. 2 (2006), 7–9 (original emphasis).

political category, artificially distinguished from violent assault only by ideology: "The clear distinction between the type of harm under examination and the many other types of violence within any society is the mooring of 'domestic violence' in its historical roots of gender subordination and feminist activism." The ideology, not the deed, creates the crime, so any accused male is simply a manifestation of universal guilt, the moment a complaint is lodged. "A binding characteristic of communities throughout the world, almost without exception," writes a scholar (again without evidence), "is the battering of women by men."[151]

The Council of Europe has recently codified this campaign in a treaty, the Istanbul Convention, which entered into force in 2014. The document explicitly politicizes law enforcement with what it terms (Article 18.3) a "gendered understanding of violence against women." The treaty asserts that violent crime results from "unequal power relations between women and men, which have led to domination over, and discrimination against, women by men and to the prevention of the full advancement of women" and that "violence against women is one of the crucial social mechanisms by which women are forced into a subordinate position compared with men" (Preamble). The "violence" is not necessarily violent and can be "psychological and economic" (Article 2). It acknowledges the novelty of using a treaty to "punish" the alleged criminality of individuals and populations ("non-State actors") within sovereign states (Article 5.2) and repeatedly makes reference to unspecified "victims" and "perpetrators" without the qualification of "alleged." It requires (Article 2.2) that "Parties shall pay particular attention to women victims of gender-based violence in implementing the provisions of this Convention" but also recognizes its own double-speak with the stipulation (Article 4.4) that "Special measures to protect women from gender-based violence shall not be considered discrimination under the Convention." Nine matters are "criminalized"—starting (Article 35) with "physical violence" (which of course is already criminal everywhere) and leading (Article 33) to "psychological violence" (which can have no definition) and (Article 40) "sexual harassment" (which as we have seen, also has no definition, though it is usually considered not "criminal"). Standard due process protections are precluded (Articles 53 and 55): the accused is denied the right to face his accuser; proceedings are demanded *ex parte* (without the accused being present to defend himself); and citizens may be charged without proof that an alleged victim even exists. Ideological indoctrination of both adult and juvenile populations, with "awareness-raising campaigns" (Article 13) and "edu-

---

151. Meyersfeld, "Reconceptualizing Domestic Violence," 379, 371.

cation" is mandatory: signatory governments must (Article 14) direct the educational system to disseminate "teaching material on issues such as equality between women and men, non-stereotyped gender roles, mutual respect, non-violent conflict resolution in interpersonal relationships, gender-based violence against women and the right to personal integrity . . . in formal curricula and at all levels of education." As domestic violence measures do elsewhere, it provides a silver bullet to circumvent immigration restrictions (chapter III).

The International Criminal Court (ICC), ostensibly created to prosecute government repression, has already shown a special zeal for prosecuting sexual matters like domestic violence. The Rome Statute creating the ICC makes "sexual and gender violence" a top priority and is littered with coded references making it clear that cases "where the [alleged?] crime involves sexual or gender violence or violence against children" (Article 68(1)) the court is expected to ensure that men are found guilty. The statute (Article 36(8)(b)) provides for hiring "judges with legal expertise on specific issues, including, but not limited to, violence against women or children,"[152] and the prosecutor likewise must "appoint advisers with legal expertise on specific issues, including, but not limited to, sexual and gender violence and violence against children" (Article 42(9)). In both provisions, these are the only specific issues singled-out for mention. The prosecutor must also (Article 54(1)(b)) "ensure the effective investigation and prosecution of crime" by respecting the "interests and personal circumstances of [alleged?] victims and witnesses," including their "gender," and to "take into account the nature of the [alleged?] crime, in particular where it [allegedly?] involves sexual violence, gender violence, or violence against children." The ICC may hold secret trials "in the case of a [alleged?] victim of sexual violence or a child who is a [alleged?] victim or a witness." In deciding whether to hold secret trials the Court must regard "particularly the views of the [alleged?] victim or witness" but not the accused. The definition of sexual crime is likewise fluid. "Hurting someone's feelings could even be a war crime," writes Dore Gold, who observes that the statutes criminalizes (Article 8(2)(b)(xxi)) "humiliating and degrading treatment."[153] The ICC's first cases were sexual.

---

152. Farooq Hassan, "International Criminal Court: Family Related Issues," synopsis of paper presented at the World Congress of Families III Mexico City, Family and the UN Mexico, 30 March 2004 (http://54.165.152.74/worldcongress.org/wcf3_spkrs/wcf3_hassan.htm).

153. Dore Gold, *Tower of Babble: How the United Nations Has Fueled Global Chaos* (New York: Three Rivers Press, 2005), 187.

Sex Education

Sexualizing and politicizing children is a top UN priority. At the 2002 Special Session on Children, children were apparently made to serve on official government delegations and to wear T-shirts declaring, "I Support Sexual Rights and Services for Everyone."[154]

A UN report issued in 2009 advocated mandatory instruction in masturbation to children as young as five. "Sexuality education is part of the duty of care of education and health authorities and institutions," says the UN document. *International Guidelines on Sexuality Education*, though withdrawn following enormous public indignation and replaced by a toned-down version, is a revealing manifesto for governments to assume control over the "sexual education" of children, instruct them in ideology about not only sex but sexual politics, and undermine and marginalize their parents.

The document professes to be concerned with HIV infection and prevention, with extensive discussions about condoms. Yet it invokes numerous and ill-defined "threats" and promotes the sexual liberation of children. "The threat to life and their well-being exists in a range of contexts, whether it is in the form of abusive relationships [i.e., parents], exposure to HIV, or stigma and discrimination because of their sexual orientation." At one point, the report complains that children "are actively discouraged from becoming sexually active."

Among the "key stakeholders" in this campaign to sexualize the world's children no mention is made of parents. Indeed, parents are dismissed for their multiple inadequacies and failures. "Sexuality education is an essential part of a good curriculum" in the schools, because "parents are often reluctant to engage in discussion of sexual matters with children because of cultural norms, their own ignorance, or discomfort." How the authors can peer into hundreds of millions of homes, let alone people's thoughts, to see what parents "often" do or their level of knowledge or discomfort is not made clear. No specific parents are named, and no documentation is provided for this claim of parental deficiency.[155] Yet parents are to be permitted only such author-

---

154. Slater, *Stand*, 108. See also Kuby, *Global Sexual Revolution*, ch. 12.

155. A paper circulated in 2013 by the World Health Organization displays similar omniscience about parents' deficiencies and feelings: "most parents do not possess all the relevant knowledge children and young people need to acquire ... parents are not always the most suitable people to discuss sexuality with their adolescent children ... many parents feel themselves unable to discuss difficult issues related to sexuality, and they are grateful if professionals do it in their stead." "Standards for Sexuality Education in Europe: Guidelines for Implementation," World Health Organization (n.p., n.d.), 24–25.

ity over their own children as state officials allow: "Teachers and school managers are called upon to balance the rights of parents and the rights of children," as if they are in conflict, and government functionaries must act as referees.

Suffused throughout with impenetrable political jargon ("rights-based, culturally sensitive, respectful of sexual and gender diversity"), the paper enunciates various peculiar and unsupported aphorisms concerning sex, which is encouraged as a virtue for its own sake:

- "'Being sexual' is an important part of many people's lives."

- "Young people want and need sexual and reproductive health information."

- "Getting the right information that is scientifically accurate, non-judgemental, age-appropriate and complete, *at an early age*, is something to which all children and young people are entitled."[156]

Entitled? By whom? By what authority is it asserted that children have a "right" to be exposed to sex "at an early age"? To be instructed, at the age of five, in government approved techniques of masturbation? Most parents strive to ensure that their children enjoy the innocence of childhood and protection from sexual predators, whether individual or bureaucratic.

For indeed, if anyone else exposed young children to sex it would be classed as pedophilia and child sex abuse (unsubstantiated accusations of which, as we have seen, radicals frequently launch against parents). Here is yet another, unusually stark example of how bureaucratic officials not only create the problem they are supposed to be solving; in this case, they are the problem—in politicized form—where none previously existed. Radicalized teachers and social workers become officially authorized to sexually molest children.

But perhaps most revealing is how "sexual education" is inseparable from political indoctrination. This is consistent with what we see elsewhere and has a long pedigree. In Sweden, where sex education has been compulsory since 1956, "sex education is not the mere abolition of technical ignorance, but a link in the mechanism of changing society." In his classic study, Roland Huntford found that "attitudes learned at home are to be discarded" and "the state has sided with youth against its

---

156. *International Guidelines on Sexuality Education* (Paris: UNESCO, June 2009; http://www.foxnews.com/projects/pdf/082509_unesco.pdf), 5–8 (emphasis added). For similar language in other official documents see, Jokin de Irala et al., "The Politics of 'Comprehensive Sexuality Education,'" Briefing Paper #12, International Organizations Research Group, 10 April 2014.

elders" in what he describes as an "attempt to win over the young through their gonads."[157]

This has expanded dramatically in today's UN. Paralleling its step-by-step program of "age appropriate" immersion in sexual technique, the UN offers a similarly systematic sequence of instruction in political ideology. From age 5, children must be taught to reject "gender roles" and "stereotypes." Beginning at age 9, they are to believe that "gender role stereotypes contribute to forced sexual activity and sexual abuse." (How precisely this is true is not explained.) At age 15, children will be required to participate in "advocacy" campaigns as part of their "education" and forced to promote political agendas, including "advocacy to promote the right to and access to safe abortion."[158]

It is no accident that children are being simultaneously sexualized and politicized. Once prised from their parents, children become vulnerable to manipulation as political tools. Their adolescent rebellion, which is inseparable from their sexual awakening and often begins as a rebellion against parental authority, is easily expanded into a political rebellion against all authority. At the same time, this sexual-political liberation from traditional authorities may find its corollary in an authoritarian identification with and loyalty to the officials, ideologies, and state machinery that facilitate their independence from their parents and in whose power they increasingly acquire a stake. Here once again, much as Plato predicted, sexual license degenerates into political liberation and then leads to authoritarianism.

This close connection between sexual and political indoctrination was developed in a subsequent UN report ostensibly treating simply "education" but drawing upon the revised guidelines. Here too, the "education" consists entirely of intermingled sexual and political doctrine. As economist Vincenzina Santoro points out, the document is saturated with sex, and in twenty-one pages "used the words 'sexual' and 'sexuality' a total of 233 times." Santoro notes "the elevation of the topic of sex by some UN bodies to the status of sacred cow or golden calf."[159]

Yet political ideology is equally pervasive in what is ostensibly a program for childhood education. Basic decorum regarding sex, and almost every society's effort to harness sexual energy for socially constructive purposes such as reproduction, is blamed on male supremacy.

157. *The New Totalitarians* (Briarcliff Manor, NY: Stein and Day, 1979), 329.

158. *International Guidelines*, 42.

159. Vincenzina Santoro, "Promoting Compulsory Sexual Education at the UN," *MercatorNet*, 29 October 2010 (http://www.mercatornet.com/articles/view/promoting_c ompulsory_sexual_education_at_the_un/#).

Sex "is usually kept hidden or is associated exclusively with reproduction for various cultural, religious, and ideological reasons, most of them related to the persistence of patriarchalism." By contrast, religious principles, which "have provided high-quality education to millions of children across the globe for centuries" in Santoro's words, "are censured for providing sexual education tarnished by 'undue ecclesiastical influence'":

> The modern State . . . must not allow religious institutions to set patterns of education or conduct that are claimed to apply not only to their followers but to all citizens, whether or not they belong to the religion in question. Consequently, the Special Rapporteur has noted with particular concern various instances in which sexual education has been obstructed in the name of religious ideas.

For no apparent reason having any obvious connection with education, the report begins with a proclamation of feminist political doctrine: "Patriarchalism is a system of social order imposing the supremacy of men over women," we are told. "Patriarchalism is therefore a system which causes and perpetuates serious and systematic human rights violations, such as violence and discrimination against women." What is the connection with educating children? Education apparently exists not to transmit learning and culture from one generation to the next but to inculcate politically approved right thinking in the young: "Education is the main fundamental tool for combating patriarchalism," the quasi-Maoist proclamation begins. "One of the main methods used by the patriarchal system and its agents ['the capitalist system and its running dogs'?] to maintain their sway is to deprive people of the possibility of receiving a human rights education with a gender and diversity perspective."

> The right to sexual education is particularly important to women's and girls' empowerment and to ensuring that they enjoy their human rights. It is therefore one of the best tools for dealing with the consequences of the system of patriarchal domination by changing social and cultural patterns of behaviour that affect men and women and tend to perpetuate discrimination and violence against women.[160]

Furthering the politicization, compulsory feminist-homosexualist sex instruction is now declared to be a human right. "The starting point of 'holistic sexuality education' is a human rights viewpoint," declares

---

160. Report of the United Nations Special Rapporteur on the Right to Education (n.p., 2010), 4, 19.

the World Health Organization.[161] So parents who teach their own children about sexuality rather than turning them over to government sex teachers become human rights violators. Moreover, exposing children to sex is the first step in further political indoctrination: "The right to comprehensive sexual education is part of the right of persons to human rights education," including "the right to information and sexual and reproductive rights." Sex education is therefore inseparable from recruitment in political advocacy. "Sexual education, to be comprehensive and to meet its goals, it must have a solid gender perspective," the standard euphemism for feminist and homosexualist ideology. "Many studies have shown that young people who believe in gender equality have better sexual lives." No such "studies" are cited, and no definition is given for "better sexual lives" or indication of how this is measured.

What is clear from this document is that sex education is no longer limited to instruction in the physical aspects of sex; it includes inculcating correct political doctrines and attitudes. "Sexual education should therefore focus on gender norms, roles, and relationships." This includes not only feminist but homosexualist orthodoxy: "Sexual education is a basic tool for ending discrimination against persons of diverse sexual orientations."

Again and again, sex education is defined in terms of political ideology, as if women's and homosexuals' rights include the right—indeed, the imperative—to control the formation of other people's children and use it to indoctrinate them politically. "Protection of the human right to comprehensive sexual education is especially important in ensuring the enjoyment of women's right to live free of violence and gender discrimination, given the historically unequal power relations between men and women." Criminalizing those who disagree with or fail to implement this program is implied in the repeated hammering of "violence against women," which runs as a mantra throughout the report. Parents who fail to inculcate sexual correctness in their children are apparently accomplices in this "violence."

Yet the report itself betrays the fact that (yet again) this ubiquitous "violence" is not really violent. "Around the world, *as many as* one in every three women has been beaten, coerced into sex, or *abused in some other way*."[162] Throughout international conventions, "violence" means not physical contact but traditional beliefs shared by most people and

---

161. Quoted in de Irala et al., "The Politics of 'Comprehensive Sexuality Education,'" 21.

162. UN Population Fund website: http://www.unfpa.org/gender/violence.htm (emphasis added).

societies about the differences between men and women. The report points out that "the Inter-American Convention on the Prevention, Punishment, and Eradication of Violence against Women . . . states that the right of women to be free from violence includes the right 'to be valued and educated free of stereotyped patterns of behaviour and social and cultural practices based on concepts of inferiority or subordination.'"[163] The much-touted "violence" is another false alarm.

The remedy for all this undefined abuse and nonviolent violence is, as always, yet more "power" for professional sexual activists and operatives: "The Special Rapporteur considers that the empowerment of women, of which sexual education forms an essential part, is a powerful defence against violation of the human rights of girls and adolescent women." In the end, sex education is not really about education at all; it is entirely about politics and "power."

Significantly, programs emphasizing abstinence until marriage are singled out for invective. "In the Special Rapporteur's view [which is the only view considered in the report], this type of programme normalizes stereotypes and promotes images that are discriminatory because they are based on heteronormativity; by denying the existence of the lesbian, gay, transsexual, transgender, and bisexual population, they expose these groups to risky and discriminatory practices." Why? Are homosexuals not capable of abstinence or restraint? Is this an admission that promiscuity is inherent to these groups? That seems to be the implication.

The only mention of parents and parental rights is to disparage them: "Although fathers and mothers are free to choose the type of education that their sons and daughters will have" (a right explicitly guaranteed in the Universal Declaration of Human Rights and several binding human rights treaties), this protection is now apparently subject to veto by government officials at their pleasure: "this authority [it is a "right" in the binding treaties] may never run counter to the rights of children and adolescents, in accordance with the primacy of the principle of the best interests of the child," though the treaties say no such thing. Once again, Anglo-American divorce law is invoked to overturn explicit human rights guarantees in binding treaties, much as it is used domestically to rationalize the direct violation of clear constitutional rights in Britain and the United States. The report draws upon propaganda disseminated by the CEDAW and CRC committees and the Yogyakarta Principles. The CRC committee likewise criticized "barriers" to political-sexual

---

163. Report of the UN Special Rapporteur, 7, 10.

education, the report emphasizes, "such as allowing parents to exempt their children from such education."[164]

The UN is constantly endeavoring to push back the boundaries of not only sexual freedom but also political radicalism. In 2011, Diane Schneider of the National Education Association (NEA) told the UN's Commission on the Status of Women, that "Oral sex, masturbation, and orgasms need to be taught in education." She claimed that sex education remains an "oxymoron" if it is abstinence-based or if students may opt-out. Again, the "education" is as much political as sexual: "the only way to combat heterosexism and gender conformity." The incorrectly educated "are stuck in a binary box that religion and family create."[165]

Homosexual technique too is increasingly pushed in the sex-ed agenda. According to Family Watch International, a Swiss school board introduced a "sex box" into the curriculum for four-year-olds. The box contains "fabric models of human genitalia in order to teach them that 'contacting body parts can be pleasurable.'" Over 3,000 parental protests failed to get it removed. California mandates gay and lesbian history in its required curriculum, and Massachusetts schools teach children as young as five about gay and lesbian relationships.[166]

Sex education is even said to encourage economic development in some peculiar way, by re-defining "development" not as economic prosperity or political stability but as a utopia of sexual release. "Comprehensive sexual education is a basic tool for achieving many of the Millennium Development Goals (MDGs), such as promoting gender equality and empowering women."[167]

Significantly, the UN education report was resoundingly denounced by numerous UN delegates and most vehemently by those representing the less developed countries, including the African Group, the Caribbean Community, the League of Arab States, and the Organization of the Islamic Conference. The delegate from the African Group "unequivocally denounced the report in some of the strongest language ever heard at the UN," and others followed.[168] The reasons are not difficult to understand. Undermining families to promote free sex will do nothing

164. Ibid., 8, 16–19.

165. Lauren Funk, "'Schools Need to Teach about Orgasms,' Says NEA to UN," C-Fam website: http://cdlmn.org/news/?p=490.

166. "OHCHR Report on Sexual Orientation and Gender Identity," Family Watch International internet site (n.d.): http://www.familywatchinternational.org/fwi/documents/fwipolicybrief_2011_UNHRC_Report_SO_GI.pdf.

167. Report of the UN Special Rapporteur, 10.

168. Santoro, "Promoting Compulsory Sexual Education."

to further development and almost certainly impede it. It has already caused enormous suffering, as we will see.

Politicizing AIDS

Africans and others in the global South may be especially skeptical about programs promoting sexual liberation because of the mind-boggling levels of death these programs have already wrought there. As a response to the AIDS epidemic, and under the influence of sexual radicals, "the best and the brightest in medicine and public health have led us to a global disaster of epic proportions," according to Edward Green, former director of the AIDS Prevention Research Project at the Harvard School of Health. Green calls it "the greatest avoidable epidemic in history."

When AIDS first appeared, African countries like Uganda responded with successful campaigns based on a multiplicity of principles, including ethical imperatives like sexual fidelity and abstinence. Green describes how Uganda, with the world's highest AIDS rate, successfully and at little cost, implemented an AIDS prevention program based on the common-sense principle of sexual restraint: delay of sex, abstinence, and fidelity, all with involvement of religious leaders.[169] The result was a dramatic reduction in the disease.

Yet despite their proven efficacy, radicals found these responses threatening to their agenda of sexual liberation and deliberately undermined them with a single alternative method: distributing condoms. "This approach was the most egregious backfire in the history of public health," writes Green, "wasting billions of tax dollars and shouldering aside low-cost, low-tech, community-based, culturally grounded strategies like Uganda's that had saved millions of lives."[170] Sexual radicals sabotaged Uganda's straightforward remedy and insisted condoms alone were the panacea. When a study commissioned by the UN's AIDS prevention agency found the condoms campaign without effect, the finding "had no impact on prevention policy. Instead, UNAIDS commissioned another study, which reached the same conclusion and went into the same drawer."[171]

Restraint campaigns advocated by Green and others included con-

169. Ibid., 37. "Leading scientific journals published several analyses concluding that decline in casual, multi-partner sex had been the major factor in Uganda's earlier success against HIV" (155).

170. Edward Green, *Broken Promises: How the AIDS Establishment Has Betrayed the Developing World* (Sausalito, CA: PoliPoint Press, 2011), x, 199.

171. Ibid., 51.

doms, but only as a last resort. ("ABC": abstain, be faithful, and use a condom.) Why should this provoke organized opposition? Green's own explanation is strikingly consistent with the larger argument of this book: "the ideology of sexual freedom." Because of what he calls the "pro-sex ideology," Green writes, "AIDS has become the most politicized disease in the annals of public health."[172]

Here again, attempts to encourage sexual restraint were eclipsed by the demand for unlimited sexual freedom: the critical message was that "you can keep enjoying all the sex you want." "Throughout the first quarter century of AIDS prevention, this value has trumped essentially all other concerns, even health and life," Green claims. "The message has been, 'Do it, and we'll help you do it safely.'" "An ideology of sexual freedom demands a technology that allows—perhaps encourages—unrestrained sex even in the era of HIV, even in ravaged Africa. Thus we see emphasis on using condoms, getting tested, and treating STDs, *along with invitations to become advocates for sexual freedom and gay rights.*" The same combination we saw with sex education and day care: blending political ideology with the promotion of sexual indulgence. "'Sex-positive' is the laurel bestowed on approaches that encourage sexual liberation," Green continues.[173] Green adds the obvious but ideologically incorrect point that is seldom heard above the strident chorus of victimization: "There is no credible evidence that gender inequality, poverty, discrimination, stigma, war and civil disturbances, racism, or homophobia actual drive HIV epidemics in Africa."[174]

Eventually the victimization view again reduces the problem to "human rights"—i.e., punishment. The Open Society Institute wants to "put legal and human rights protections at the center of HIV effort." Here again is the sexual radicals' all-purpose solution to every problem: bring in lawyers and start arresting people. "Responding to gender inequality is especially crucial for effective prevention," OSI concludes, with no logical explanation. What is the next step in implementing these "human rights protections"? Are advocates for sexual discipline denying the radicals their right, as one puts it, "to have as much sex as they want, with as many people as they want"?[175] Are advocates for traditional sexual values or simply common-sense restraint now "human rights" violators?

172. Ibid., 77, 225, 94.
173. Ibid., 23, 97–98 (emphasis added).
174. Ibid., 91–92.
175. Ibid., 93, 165.

The "gay" lobby objects vehemently to anything that limits their freedom to have sex, even if it saves the lives of homosexuals. The lives of
Africans are obviously a lower priority and can apparently can be sacrificed as pawns in a game of ideological power. (AIDS in Africa is primarily heterosexual, not homosexual.)

But feminists too have an axe to grind. As a form of contraception,
condoms are components in programs for population control, whose
rationalizations have shifted in recent decades from environmentalist to
feminist grounds. Condoms thus provide liberation from both disease
and unwanted babies. "One of many arguments used to attack Uganda's
ABC program was that 'it does not apply to women,'" Green writes, per-
plexedly. "Another argument was the greater absurdity that it is harmful
to women." Aid experts told Ugandans that abstinence and fidelity campaigns "disempowered women."[176]

Illogically but not unusually, the AIDS establishment even attacked
marriage as "the most dangerous thing an African woman can do."
Despite clear indications that "marriage is a relative haven" from AIDS,
in Green's words, UN officials try to vilify husbands for spreading AIDS
and urge women to insist on condoms by parroting this empty assertion
that "one of the riskiest propositions for a woman today in Africa is to
be married."[177]

Here yet again, the ever-present specter of "abusive men" and "violence against women" somehow invalidates the principles of sexual
restraint, and the institution that does most to encourage it: marriage.
"What kills young women is often not promiscuity but marriage,"
claims *New York Times* columnist Nicholas Kristof, also without explanation. "Just about the deadliest thing a woman in southern Africa can
do is get married." In fact, Green shows that "Married women always
have a lower HIV prevalence than unmarried women." He also points
out that "young women have much higher infection rates than young
men in Africa" and that it is far more often the wives who infect the husbands.[178]

How do "abusive" men cause AIDS? The tortured logic—whose bottom line naturally is a prescription for yet more sexual freedom—runs
something like this: "Abused women" apparently have a reduced "ability
to trust men or expose themselves emotionally to men," but—strangely
indeed—"*enhancing perceptions that a woman should get something tangible from relationships*" means that they have no choice but to become

176. Ibid., 44, 70.
177. Ibid., 115–16.
178. Ibid., 171–72.

prostitutes so they can acquire some money, further spreading the disease.[179]

How can abstinence and fidelity possibly harm women—especially when philandering husbands are said (implausibly) to be the main cause of spreading the disease? The only possible explanation is that anything that encourages sexual restraint is a threat to the sexual radicals' basic weapon, which is unrestrained sex. Feminists instinctively sense this threat to their core power: not any particular policy measure that tangibly harms any identifiable individuals in any specific way (like intentionally encouraging unrestrained sex amidst an AIDS epidemic), but any form of self-control or chastity.

Green is scathing in his indictment of the AIDS establishment, though what is uncanny is how the dishonest ploys resemble those we have found throughout the sexual agenda: the ubiquitous "gender equality" as a silver bullet to rationalize irresponsible sexual abandon, the attack on marriage and chastity, the reflexive demonization of men, and the marginalization and punishment of academics or journalists who tell the truth. "How else would governments cough up cash for 'deviant outcasts' like hookers, transvestites, junkies, and gays?" Green asks. "Here's how: use wide-eyed babies and violated wives as bait and you can bundle AIDS with women's emancipation, sexual liberation, and poverty eradication too."[180] It is hardly surprising, as Green notes, that "greater women's emancipation repeatedly correlates with higher HIV rates."[181]

Poverty and Development (and Sex)

The economic development of the global South is another field increasingly dominated by sexual ideology. To glance through the literature is to be subject to pictures of suffering women and girls and told that they "suffer most." Likewise, as a Nigerian diplomat told the UN, "Right now every issue . . . every discussion reduces the problem of Africa just to sexual orientation. It is unforgiving and unfair. . . . We do not hold for those that want sexual orientation to be a way of life in their cities and villages."[182]

This reflects fashions in the industrialized world, from whence it comes. For all the "multiculturalism" and cultural relativism being pro-

179. Ibid., 168 (emphasis added).
180. Ibid., 199.
181. Ibid., 171.
182. Quoted in "Obama's Sexual Agenda," Stand for Families Worldwide website: http://www.standforfamiliesworldwide.org/sffww/obamas-sexual-agenda (March 2014).

moted, it is Western feminism that is being imposed on the impoverished nations along with the "development" aid that does so little to
promote development that it is almost certainly retarding it. Most
nations of the global South are very conservative in their social and sexual morality.

Thirty years ago, development literature was similarly dominated by
quasi-Marxist principles, with global poverty explained by neo-Leninist
theories of imperialism, colonialism, "neo-imperialism," "neo-colonial-
ism," "dependency," and so forth, which blamed failure to develop on
exploitation by the capitalist West. These theories were themselves Western imports and left little in their wake but devastation: not only impoverishment but corruption, bureaucracy, mass displacement, political
instability, and endless wars of insurgency and counter-insurgency.

The collapse of European Communism—along with the depravity of
the regimes it sponsored in the underdeveloped world—rendered these
ideological theories largely discredited. As in the domestic policies of the
West, overt Marxism has now been largely transfigured into a subtler
neo-Marxist sexual ideology that implausibly blames underdevelopment on various but ill-defined exploiters of women, turning economic
development aid into a kind of global welfare that creates in the global
South, as it does in the West, huge populations of dependent single-parent homes. Similar to its domestic equivalent, this international welfare
claims to help impoverished "families" but in fact does precisely the
opposite.[183]

The aid business is now big business, though it has been subject to
devastating and unanswered criticism for decades, to the point where it
is now almost wholly discredited. In recent years some scathing critiques, mostly by economists who deal with undeniable facts and do not
have the luxury of indulging in fashionable ideologies, have left little
doubt that aid does far more harm than good and leaves little in its wake
but continued poverty, disease, social pathology, corruption, dictator-

---

183. Fittingly, Harriet Harman of the British Labour Party has linked the two campaigns by calling for extra welfare payments in Britain to be given to those who send
them to relatives in their home countries, making Britain's domestic welfare an instrument of foreign aid. She praised foreign-born welfare recipients, along with people
working for wages, as "hidden heroes of development through developing new policies
on remittances." "The idea that it [welfare] is to be used instead as a kind of global poor
relief fund is utterly bizarre," writes Melanie Phillips. "Ms. Harman is suggesting that
immigrants should be encouraged to come to Britain precisely so that they can act as a
conduit for British taxpayers' money to be funneled to Africa and other Third World
countries." "Harriet Harman's Bizarre Proposal," *Daily Mail*, 13 December 2010 (http://
www.melaniephillips.com/articles/).

ship, and war.[184] Some $2.3 trillion[185] has been sunk into development aid since 1945, with little to show for it but *increased* poverty in regions like Africa. To this has been added political criticism that aid money fuels corruption and is used by dictators to finance the repression of their own people. Yet the aid machine rolls on, dispensing more largesse, propping up more repressive regimes, and disrupting more families and communities.

Why is the aid business so impervious to decades of criticism by reputable scholars, criticism that has not been and cannot be refuted? Perhaps because it has less to do with the economics of development than with the politics of philanthropy. Here too, a major contributor is the feminization of international aid, which has given it a new lease on life and rendered it—like the feminization of domestic welfare—largely off-limits to criticism.

Aid For Africa (AFA) advertises extensively on the Washington Metro and hires students to hustle for money on its streets. Its head, Geralynn Batista, advertises her credentials in the US welfare system: affiliated with "one of the largest full service child care agencies in the United States, where she helped create a pioneering program for children and families with AIDS in the foster care system." "Aid for Africa members," we are told, "support children in school, provide safe havens for orphans, advocate for funding for children's issues. They . . . work to prevent rape and trafficking, and help women start small businesses." AFA's list of affiliated "charities" chants the mantra of "women and children":

- Action Africa "works with local communities to build free medical clinics for families and provide micro-loans for entrepreneurial women."

- African Children's Haven "helps African orphans and children living in extreme poverty lead healthier, more productive lives. Priority programs emphasize the education, well-being, and safety of young girls."

- Alliance for African Assistance "provides assistance in the U.S. and Uganda to refugees, immigrants, asylum seekers, and war and torture victims, particularly women and children."

184. A sampling: Simeon Djankov, Jose G. Montalvo, and Marta Reynal-Querol, "The Curse of Aid," *Journal of Economic Growth*, vol. 13, no. 5 (September 2008); Raghuram G. Rajan and Arvind Subramanian, "Aid and Growth: What Does the Cross-Country Evidence Really Show?" *The Review of Economics and Statistics*, vol. 90, no. 4 (November 2008); Peter Bauer, *Reality and Rhetoric: Studies in the Economics of Development* (Cambridge: Harvard University Press, 1984); William Easterly, *The White Man's Burden* (New York: Penguin, 2006); Robert Calderisi, *The Trouble with Africa* (New York: Palgrave Macmillan, 2006); Dambisi Moyo, *Dead Aid* (New York: Farrar, Straus, and Giroux, 2010).

185. Easterly, *White Man's Burden*, 4.

And so on down the alphabet:

- The Boma Fund is working "to break the cycle of poverty in northern Kenya by helping individuals earn an income and care for their families. Supports women's micro-enterprise projects."

- The Green Belt Movement International provides "income to millions in Kenya through tree-planting. Mobilizes communities for the environment, women's rights, good governance and civic empowerment."

- The Maasai Girls Education Fund "works to improve the literacy, health, and economic well-being of Maasai women in Kenya through scholarships for girls and community education."

- Medicine for Mali "provides medical services, including eye surgeries, supplies, health classes for women and children."

- Solar Cookers International "helps African women ... to make, use, and sell solar cookers for meal preparation and water pasteurization in order to benefit their families, communities, and environments."

- Vitamin A for Africa "works with women farmers to eliminate a major cause of blindness in African children."

Groups advertised here as "charities" are obviously political lobbies. They do not provide food and medicine; they promote political activism—closely connected to precisely the radical political activism that devastated Africa and other impoverished regions in the first place. The Southern African Legal Services Foundation is a member "charity" of Aid For Africa, but it "fights for environmental justice, children's and women's rights, land and housing rights, and the rights of those living with HIV/AIDS through support of public interest law and legal education in South Africa." Though never disclosed, the vast bulk of cases handled by such "legal services" are divorce and child custody cases, the aim being to dissolve families and remove fathers, thus increasing the hardships to children and further need for their own "services." Yet this is sold to the public and to potential donors as a "charity" that somehow promotes "development."[186]

Why this mantra, so unexceptionable to those devoted to the rescue of others, on "women and children"? Is it because men and adolescent boys do not also suffer from underdevelopment? Yes, we are assured, but women and girls "suffer more." And what precisely are the implications of this? If we are devoted to assisting these societies, should we not

---

186. Aid for African website: aidforafrica.org.

be helping "families" and "communities"—favorite terms in this literature—in their entirety?

No, this is precisely and decidedly what must not be done. First and foremost, these are feminist organizations, and the aim is to separate the women and children as objects of permanent relief, to marginalize and eliminate the males and dissolve the families that could actually build prosperous and self-sufficient societies, and make the societies permanently dependent on the foreign aid workers, advocacy organizations, lawyers, foreign governments, and international organizations. UNICEF is very explicit that its role is to subsidize women and girls economically, not to assist and strengthen their families as a whole but for the express purpose of separating them from their male family members: "Education can also provide vocational skills, potentially increasing her economic power, thus freeing her from dependence on her husband, father, or brother."[187]

Despite this massive outpouring of money and good intentions, the poverty not only continues but increases. That is because the development literature is based on the same fallacious reasoning as welfare. Throughout this public relations propaganda, "families" means single mothers and fatherless children, and "helping families" means depriving children of the fathers and family lives that would build family wealth and impart the work ethic they need to escape poverty. In all these organizations, men and fathers are marginalized, excluded, sometimes demonized, and replaced by aid organizations and government officials—in effect, global social workers. "Humanitarian responses," writes one advocate, "...can be compared to the emergence of social work in domestic politics."[188] These organizations trap children in poverty and make them permanently dependent, generation after generation, on the West's professional humanitarians whose livelihoods depend on an endless supply of impoverished clients.[189]

---

187. "Women: Commentary," *The Progress of Nations*, UNICEF, 1998, quoted in Silva, *United Nations Children's Fund*, 80.

188. Amir Pasic and Thomas Weiss, "The Politics of Rescue," in *Ethics and International Affairs*, ed. Joel Rosenthal (Washington: Georgetown University Press, 1999).

189. One historian, turning the tables on orthodoxy, argues that the US failure in Vietnam is attributable to the emergence of this mentality. "Vietnam was the first war in which the United States dispatched its military forces overseas not for the purpose of winning but just to buy time for the war to be won by civilian social programs," writes Walter McDougall. "South Vietnam's cities—like much of inner-city America—soon became corrupt and dependent welfare zones." *Promised Land, Crusader State: The American Encounter with the World Since 1776* (New York: Houghton Mifflin, 1997), 189, 193.

CARE is another high-profile group that runs high-tech advertising campaigns and hires students to solicit on the streets of Washington. CARE describes itself as "a leading humanitarian organization fighting global poverty." In fact, it is a feminist political lobby. Each page of its internet site features a woman's photograph with the caption, "I am powerful." CARE describes its vision with standard leftist buzzwords: "a world of hope, tolerance, and social justice, where poverty has been overcome." And today's buzzwords are in the feminine gender: "We place special focus on working alongside poor women because, equipped with the proper resources, women have the power to help whole families and entire communities escape poverty. Women are at the heart of CARE's community-based efforts."

Yet decade after decade, the "families" and "communities" do not and cannot "escape poverty," because the aim is not to allow economic development; it is to create a political client base of dependents. "We help families and communities create lasting solutions to poverty and discrimination," says CARE. Poverty "and discrimination"? Third World poverty results from discrimination? How? What kind of discrimination? Against whom? By whom? What measures can address this "discrimination" and how precisely can they also relieve poverty and build a prosperous economy? These questions are not even addressed, let alone answered.

"Women play a key role in the fight against poverty because as mothers, caregivers, and providers women touch so many lives every day," says CARE. "Through investments in women and girls, US international assistance helps women fulfill their potential and build a brighter future for their families and communities." How "touching so many lives" combats poverty is likewise not explained. This is not simply gushy sentimentality; insofar as it rationalizes programs that sunder families, it is perpetuating poverty.

Instead the poor and especially poor children are held as moral hostages and used as what one scholar calls "mutilated beggars"—comparable to the physical mutilation of children common in poor countries and designed to make them more pitiable and therefore more effective panhandlers.[190] Handouts to their mothers encourage the mutilation of more children. The aid business has simply politicized and bureaucratized this phenomenon, and feeding this machine with more funds has a roughly similar effect.

190. Daniel Amneus, *The Garbage Generation* (Alhamba, CA: Primrose Press, 1990), ch. 5.

CARE betrays its role as a political lobby: "We ask our elected officials to adopt policies that address the underlying causes of poverty, such as gender inequality." Yet nowhere is it explained how "gender inequality" is an "underlying cause of poverty." Peculiar but meaningless statistics seem designed to convey a vague message that heroic women and girls are suffering deprivation because ... *someone* seems to be oppressing them. As we often hear: "Women work two-thirds of the world's working hours, produce half of the world's food, yet earn only 10% of the world's income and own less than 1% of the world's property. More than 850 million people—most of them women and children—suffer from chronic hunger or malnutrition."

In fact, as the *Washington Post* has clearly demonstrated, these figures are "bogus." The UN has also explicitly confessed that "the facts quoted are indeed wrong," as has Oxfam, both of whom propagated the falsehood with no subsequent correction.[191]

But here too a little common sense makes evident that they are meaningless. If most people facing hunger or malnutrition are women and children, it may be because most people are women and children. "Women and girls suffer disproportionately from the burden of extreme poverty," CARE insists. "They make up 70% of the 1 billion people living on less than a dollar a day." That may be because women and children make up about 70% of the population of most countries in the global South.

As for the proportion of food produced by women, no source is provided for this figure or any of these figures, because here again none exists. But it is difficult to see in what sense they can possibly be true. "Quite frankly, I don't know what this statistic could mean and how we could actually assign a number to the amount of food produced by women," says one researcher. "How do we figure out who produced the food when men and women both work on the same plots, producing some crops together?" Yet here again, political necessity triumphs over scholarly integrity and truth: "When I presented the paper on how much of the world's food do women produce at FAO [Food and Agriculture Organization of the United Nations]—they were quite upset with me. They kept saying that they needed this statistic!"

191. Glenn Kessler, "The Zombie Statistic about Women's Share of Income and Property," *Washington Post*, 3 March 2015 (http://www.washingtonpost.com/blogs/fact-checker/wp/2015/03/03/the-zombie-statistic-about-womens-share-of-income-and-property/). Other researchers have reached the same conclusion: Cheryl Doss et al., "Ownership and Control of Land in Africa: Myths versus Reality," International Food Policy Research Institute, December 2013 (http://cdm15738.contentdm.oclc.org/utils/getfile/collection/p15738coll2/id/127957/filename/128168.pdf).

Further, if women and girls live in families with men and boys, why would they not all share the same living standard? But of course increasingly they do not live in families. Thanks to the Sexual Revolution (including imported Western divorce laws and domestic "violence" programs, engineered by free "legal services"), which Western feminists have been assiduously proselytizing to the global South via aid groups like CARE and Aid For Africa, women and girls do not live in families with fathers and husbands. Predictably, this traps them in the same dependent poverty as does welfare in the West.

Above all, it is never explained how targeting women and girls with financial payments promotes economic development; certainly no such theory has gained any currency in respectable academic literature. Nor is any evidence presented that this focus does in fact contribute to economic development or has any other effect than, by undermining family formation, to dig nations deeper into poverty. "Recognizing that women and children suffer disproportionately from poverty, CARE places special emphasis on working with women to create permanent social change." Yet no data is presented demonstrating that "women and children suffer disproportionately" nor that giving them money contributes to eradicating poverty or can possibly do so. "Social change" is the standard leftist code for socialism, which historically is largely responsible for Africa's impoverishment in the first place.

While CARE talks of "self-sufficiency" and "attacking poverty at its roots," it is clear that their agenda is devoted to marginalizing men and fathers and redefining "families" to mean single mothers, who must be supported by welfare disguised to look like entrepreneurship: "CARE's economic development programs assist impoverished families by supporting moneymaking activities, especially those operated by women. CARE initiates community savings-and-loan programs and provides technical training to help people begin or expand small businesses that will increase family income."

This is not business or development; it is welfare couched in terms of business. "Moneymaking" schemes are not development, especially when they depend on official aid. Families are what create wealth and pass it on to the next generation, which is the basis of economic prosperity. This is how the West developed. But the aid agenda undermines precisely this process and replaces families with international bureaucracies and patronage networks of social workers and other officials ("governments and partner organizations at many levels").

Thus the latest fad: the proliferation of "micro-lending" schemes ostensibly once again to encourage development but usually directed exclusively to "women" and serving as another form of disguised welfare. It is hardly surprising that these schemes have quickly degenerated into scams, exploited by unscrupulous lenders enticing the poor with money before trapping them in impossible debt.[192] Not wholly surprising too is that the more radical feminist ideologues scorn these projects as oppressors of women as well, which on some level perhaps they are.[193] "Small-scale income generating women-only projects ... often forced women's economic marginalization and related them to secondary roles."[194]

For CARE, every aspect of "development" presents an opportunity to advance the feminist agenda, break up families, marginalize men, and, it is worth noting, promote abortion. Among programs for disaster and "emergency relief" are "family planning and reproductive health services."

Aid funds confer political as well as economic dependence of the poor upon the rich. As noted, the poor nations are determined and sometimes defiant dissenters on liberal sexual morality. To break their opposition, Western elites use aid money to twist the arms of Southern leaders to accept radical sexual measures. By keeping impoverished countries dependent on foreign aid, the wealthy can impose their radical sexual agenda, which further exacerbates their impoverishment and creates a vicious cycle of penury and subordination. "These things are allowed to come in the debate because the developing world needs money," says Austin Ruse of the Catholic Family and Human Rights Institute. "So a developing world country will say, 'OK, we will allow this radical language and we may institute these changes in exchange for development money from the UN and the World Bank and IMF.'"[195] In 2010, the European Parliament passed a resolution reminding Africa that "the EU is responsible for more than half of development aid and remains Africa's most important trading partner," before stating that in all EU partnerships sexual orientation is a protected category of non-discrimination.[196] Likewise, at a meeting of the UN's Committee on the Status of Women:

192. Rama Lakshmi, "In India, Microloans Can Trip up the Poor," *Washington Post*, 31 October 2010, A20.

193. Penny Griffin, "Development Institutions and Neoliberal Globalisation," in Laura Shepherd (ed.), *Gender Matters in Global Politics* (London: Routledge, 2010), 227.

194. True, "Mainstreaming Gender," 190–91.

195. Quoted in Buss and Herman, *Globalizing Family Values*, 50.

196. Terrence McKeegan, "Countries Reject 'Sexual Orientation' Language in Treaty with Europe," Catholic Family and Human Rights Group website: http://www.c-fam. org/fridayfax/volume-14/countries-reject-sexual-orientation-language-in-treaty-with-europe.html, 30 December 2010.

The delegate from Nicaragua refused to accept any definition of "gender" other than male and female. The Swedish government threatened Nicaragua with the withdrawal of aid unless Nicaragua sent home its recalcitrant delegate. Nicaragua is a poor country, dependent on foreign aid, so the hapless delegate was ordered home and a new delegate was sent to New York. When the debate on "gender" resumed, the new Nicaraguan delegate innocently said: "But in my country, gender is male and female . . . ," so Sweden was back to square one. This is but one example of the way wealthy countries bully third world nations into accepting their sexual fetishes.[197]

So what will help the impoverished South? The most efficacious solution is probably the one now being sought by Africans themselves and others in the underdeveloped world, though it incites nothing but sneers and contempt from the global development elite. It is the same solution that produced unprecedented prosperity in the West and everywhere else it has been adopted: some form of effective work ethic such as Christian faith. The fact that highly evangelical Christianity is now sweeping Africa and other regions of the global South is not unconnected to the material poverty of the continent and, more importantly, provides the most effective solution. As Matthew Parris, an avowed atheist, attests:

> I used to avoid this truth by applauding . . . the practical work of mission churches in Africa. It's a pity, I would say, that salvation is part of the package, but Christians black and white, working in Africa, do heal the sick, do teach people to read and write; and only the severest kind of secularist could see a mission hospital or school and say the world would be better without it. I would allow that if faith was needed to motivate missionaries to help, then, fine: but what counted was the help, not the faith.
>
> But this doesn't fit the facts. Faith does more than support the missionary; it is also transferred to his flock. This is the effect that matters so immensely. . . . The Christians [in Africa] were always different. Far from having cowed or confined its converts, their faith appeared to have liberated and relaxed them. There was a liveliness, a curiosity, an engagement with the world—a directness in their dealings with others—that seemed to be missing in traditional African life. They stood tall. . . .
>
> Those who want Africa to walk tall amid 21st-century global compe-

---

197. Babette Francis, "Gender Bending: Let Me Count the Ways," Mercatornet.com, 21 March 2011 (http://www.mercatornet.com/articles/view/gender_bending_let_me_co unt_the_ways/).

tition must not kid themselves that providing the material means or even the knowhow that accompanies what we call development will make the change. A whole belief system must first be supplanted.

And I'm afraid it has to be supplanted by another. Removing Christian evangelism from the African equation may leave the continent at the mercy of a malign fusion of Nike, the witch doctor, the mobile phone, and the machete.[198]

This and worse is precisely what did happen in Africa and elsewhere with the demonization and expulsion of Christian evangelism by leftist ideologues: from the Marxist-inspired wars of "national liberation," to the destructive social engineering schemes in the name of "African Socialism," to the herd of white elephants bred and released by the World Bank and other aid organizations, to the true neo-imperialism of the Western aid elites—all of which has produced little besides poverty, corruption, and death.

Today, many in Africa and throughout the global South have already discovered the wisdom in Parris's advice. Christian faith is spreading like wildfire throughout Africa and other poor regions.[199] This is not the liberal Christianity of the Western elites but instead a rigorous and puritanical appeal to biblical principles.[200] And here too, the main fault line between the complacent Christianity of Western liberalism and the vigorous faith of the emerging South runs unmistakably through the politics of sex. "Most of the reasons" for differences between the Christianity of the affluent countries and the poor "involve disputes over gender and sexuality," writes Philip Jenkins. "These have proved the defining issues that separate progressives and conservatives, ecclesiastical left and right." Jenkins, who is determined to maintain scholarly detachment, is clear which side brought the novelties: "Over the last thirty years, religious attitudes in North America and Europe have shifted beyond recognition, with the advance of feminist and progressive causes, and the growth of sexual liberalism . . . symbolized by the general acceptance of women's ordination and by the free discussion of gay causes." And yet strikingly, as with the early Christian Church, as with the Protestant Reformation (and as we shall see shortly, with radi-

198. Matthew Parris, "As an Atheist, I Truly Believe Africa Needs God," *The Times*, 27 December 2008, http://www.timesonline.co.uk/tol/comment/columnists/matthew_parris/article5400568.ece.

199. Philip Jenkins, *The Next Christendom: The Coming of Global Christianity* (Oxford: Oxford University Press, 2011).

200. Philip Jenkins, *The New Faces of Christianity: Believing the Bible in the Global South* (Oxford: Oxford University Press, 2006).

cal Islam), far from being "anti-woman," women have figured very prominently in the new Christianity of the global South.[201]

Yet More Gender Crimes

Child Soldiers

Child soldiering is another new hysteria connected to the deterioration of the family and the politicization of children. The militarization of children is their politicization with a vengeance.

But as with other family crimes, the real exploiters of children may not be the ones that appear at first glance or that the media are intent on demonizing. Fortunately, David Rosen has cut through the sensationalism and critiqued this problem so effectively that we now have a fairly clear picture of what is taking place. Properly understood, we are presented with a phenomenon of not only mindboggling cruelty, but one also tragically defiant of any hope of restoring justice and order. Once again, we might begin by dismounting our high horses to consider our own responsibility for the horrors.

The dominant understanding of this problem as set forth by humanitarian and human rights groups like Child Soldiers International, is, as Rosen summarizes it, "that children should not bear arms and that the adults who recruit them should be held accountable and should be prosecuted for war crimes." Rosen questions this, pointing out that children have long served in armed conflict and that "the child soldier as an abused and exploited victim of war is a radically new concept."[202]

At one time, there was nothing remarkable about adolescent boys serving in arms. "For both working-class and upper-class boys, to be a boy soldier was to be part of a well-trained, highly skilled group to which society generally accorded honour and respect," he points out. "Children were part of virtually every partisan and resistance movement in World War II."[203]

With today's superficial humanitarianism, we see precisely the oppo-

---

201. Jenkins, *New Faces*, 246 and ch. 7.

202. David M. Rosen, *Armies of the Young: Child Soldiers in War and Terrorism* (New Brunswick: Rutgers University Press, 2005), 1, 6. What Rosen writes (159, note 1) about child soldiers is also applicable to human trafficking, though no comparably critical scholarly study exists for that problem: "Much of what we know about contemporary child soldiers comes from the accounts of journalists and the investigative reports of human rights organizations. These accounts are not only shocking but are also deliberately crafted to emblematically illustrate the concerns of humanitarian and human rights groups."

203. Ibid., 8, 22.

site, yet another attempt to discredit and criminalize masculine behavior. "They are part of a tendency in the contemporary world to criminalize war and to paint the military and its associated cultural and social links with the brush of criminality or deviancy." Consistent with our theme, Rosen sees new complaints about child soldiers as part of "a global politics of age, of which the child soldier is only one part." His emphasis on "the *ideological and political manipulation* of the concepts of childhood, youth, and adulthood" is also consistent with what we have encountered elsewhere.[204]

But to leave it at that is plainly inadequate. Rosen himself and others paint a grim picture of today's child soldiering that certainly should not be dismissed. Often both victims and perpetrators at once, armed youth both suffer and commit hideous and apparently gratuitous atrocities, far out of line with the traditional standards of just warfare. Rosen's skepticism makes his own accounts all the more credible: "Youth set people on fire, burned down their houses, shot children, paraded citizens about naked and beat them, brought opponents before youth-run kangaroo courts, and hacked men and women to death with machetes."[205]

What is new about the current generation of child soldiers—and what does make this phenomenon grotesque—is not children serving as soldiers as such, but how the warfare they are waging is driven by radical political ideologies. This is especially disturbing with the realization of how appealing such ideologies are to both boys and girls of adolescent age, especially in dismal political and social conditions that make those ideologies plausible and superficially "liberating." These ideologies are what have given to modern warfare its totalizing, unrestrained, and savage character—which is exacerbated when the warfare is waged by children.

It is evident from Rosen's account and others that most child soldiers are not abducted, passive victims of unscrupulous adults. They are far more likely to be politicized and radicalized adolescents who are recruited by others close to their own age whom we have "empowered" with the means to act out dreams of adolescent rebellion with deadly force. Every case study Rosen examined involves a radicalized and militarized youth culture.

This is fueled in part by "a background of destroyed families and failed educational systems" that cut the youth loose from familial and local bonds to serve in militias and armies. One recurring theme in Rosen's account is how children find in soldiering "surrogate forms of

204. Ibid., 9–10 (emphasis added).
205. Ibid., 78.

family and kinship." (And what would bear further investigation is how much of this problem stems from family breakdown and why so many children are cut off from their parents and thus available for recruitment as soldiers.) Potential recruits in Vilnius "were asked whether they could abandon their families and were rejected if they felt they could not."[206]

This is apparent in all Rosen's case studies: Jewish resistance fighters in Nazi-occupied Europe, rebel insurgents in Sierra Leone, and Palestinian suicide bombers. One can sympathize with these movements or condemn them, but the trend appears common to them all: modern war radicalizes youth, cutting them off from their families and encouraging them to take up radical and revolutionary politics.

Jewish resistance fighters had backgrounds in socialist Zionism and "imagined themselves as a revolutionary vanguard." They were actively rebelling against not only the Nazis but their own elders. It clearly involved an element of adolescent rebellion, which is rebellion for its own sake. "We did everything that was forbidden because it was forbidden," Rosen quotes one. "That is how the resistance began." The elders in turn saw the resistance as "childish."[207]

Likewise in Sierra Leone, students "began to dabble in revolutionary ideologies and politics" and acted out their violence as disciples of Marcus Garvey, Kwame Nkrumah, Muammar al-Qadhafi, Marx, Lenin, and Castro. "A murderous army cloaked in revolutionary ideology, the RUF [Revolutionary United Front] was drenched in the blood of the people for whom it claimed to be fighting." This army recruited "alienated and homeless children and youth," in part because they had no families to protect and shelter them.[208]

Palestinian youths were similarly politicized before being militarized, their upbringings saturated with ideology and often dominated by radicalized single mothers. "I was in a refugee camp in which everyone spoke about politics day and night," one boy recounted, "and when my mother and grandmother spoke about politics how could I not speak?" Another believed "the Palestinian youth were leading an intergenerational revolution as well as a war against Israel." Rosen quotes another as saying, "It's a real social revolution." Suicide bombers are the logical extension of ideological war and present an especially grisly side of it, from the standpoint of both the youth and their victims. "From the beginnings of the conflict, the conviction that young people have a duty

---

206. Ibid., 17, 33, 37.
207. Ibid., 22, 35, 36.
208. Ibid., 80, 81.

to sacrifice themselves for the Palestinian cause has held a central place in militant forms of Palestinian political consciousness."[209]

Here too, Rosen is clear that this is a form of political *radicalism*, and that "the radicalization of the Palestinian population developed out of the radicalization of its youth." As with the Jews and with most radicalism of the 1960s and 1970s, it is an intergenerational conflict, where the youth are going a step beyond their elders. "The peoples' committees in the villages are run by boys of fifteen, who are challenging the authority of old sheiks and imams." Contemporary descriptions were "not of a community exploiting its children, but of a community in ecstasy, enthralled by the power of youth." Reminiscent of other resistance fighters, Palestinian youth were later to look back with nostalgia on their struggle. "I miss those days a lot," Rosen quotes one. "They were the most beautiful days of my life."[210]

These "child soldiers" are being doubly politicized and thereby doubly exploited. The more obvious is provided by their circumstances and by the intoxicating thrill of bearing arms for their liberation. Beyond that however, they are made political pawns by the Western humanitarian culture that insists on casting them as victims of exploitation by yet more unnamed malefactors. Here is another instance of the open political radicalism of the 1960s and 1970s—in this case, the movements for "national liberation"—giving way to the subtler sexual ideology, as the therapeutic culture increasingly transforms the UN's mission to prevent armed aggression from a matter of diplomacy into a matter of social work: "Charges of *child abuse* have . . . been levelled against Palestinian parents for their unwillingness or inability to police the behaviour of their children" in the *intifada*.[211]

Child soldiering thus follows the other gender crimes we have examined: radical ideology first creates the problem of politicized and deracinated children and then complains about its consequences, offering yet further radical solutions that lead to more problems. The trend is embodied in the figures of Samora and Graca Machel. Samora Machel was prominent in the anti-colonial wars of "national liberation," leading the Marxist resistance to Portuguese rule in Mozambique and serving as that country's first president. His wife Graca Machel was an avid participant in those wars and then became Mozambique's education minister. These liberation movements systematically recruited huge numbers of

209. Ibid., 115, 116, 91–92.
210. Ibid., 116, 117, 118.
211. Ibid., 153 (emphasis added).

boys and youth as soldiers, and no objection was then raised by the humanitarian elites who sympathized with these movements. Two generations later, similar practices, which are the legacy of those wars, are being classed as criminal child abuse, creating employment as social workers for the wives and daughters of the freedom fighters, with leaders sought for prosecution. Especially as postcolonial regimes like the Machels' are themselves confronted by insurgencies that challenge their own authority, they (in alliance with politicized humanitarian groups and the UN) are attempting to use indignation over child soldiers to criminalize precisely the practices they themselves pioneered. Graca Machel wrote the leading UN report, *Impact of Armed Conflict on Children* (1996), arguing for the criminalization of child soldiering.[212] Marxist freedom fighters have given way to feminist social work bureaucrats, who now build thriving careers on the turmoil created by their husbands and fathers.

Perhaps not surprisingly, female soldiers also seem to find the new military life "empowering and liberating." In the older and better-educated culture of the Jewish resistance, the demands of war seem to have led to a self-imposed regimen of sexual "puritanism." Elsewhere however, sexual license appears more common. "For these women [in Mozambique], revolutionary ideologies played an important role both in organizing the meaning system in which they operated as child combatants and in helping them create new roles and identities," Rosen observes. "Many of these women interpret their war experiences as freeing them not only from colonial rule but also from male structures of dominance in 'traditional' Mozambique society." Once unleashed, radical youth can fasten on an assortment of grievances.[213]

One is tempted to ask what do these young women want liberation *for*? What do they want to be free to *do* that they could not do in traditional society? One answer is have sex and children without "male structures of dominance" such as marriage—practices that almost certainly have contributed to the child soldier phenomenon in the first place.

As Rosen observes, the means these women employ to achieve liberation are, according to current orthodoxy about child soldiering, precisely what allow the humanitarian professionals to portray them as "victims." "Virtually every activity these girls participated in [to assist the fighters] . . . would nowadays be recast as criminal forms of child abuse under the humanitarian narrative," he notes. "None of these wom-

212. Ibid., 146, 157, 12–14.
213. Ibid., 17, 39.

en regarded themselves as having been powerless or having been victimized."[214]

Sierra Leone's experience is also a warning against credulous acceptance of the "trafficking" narrative. "Not every girl who joined the rebel ranks was a sex slave," Rosen notes. "Like boys, many joined because of the excitement, power, and material gain it offered. Some of the most powerful and violent girls, the mammy queens, were expected to play a major part in fighting and acts of terrorism."[215]

It is hardly an exaggeration to say that child soldiering is largely the result of radical insurgency movements during de-colonialism and their Marxist ideology. Until this politically incorrect truth is faced, this problem too will continue, abetted by the successors to these radical movements who have ensconced themselves in today's international organizations, where they continue promoting in more subtle form the very neo-Marxist and radical feminist agendas that created the problem in the first place.

As with other instances of humanitarian indignation, little evidence suggests that the social engineering approach can have any significant impact. Child Soldiers International (CSI), along with the UN, propose a treaty: the Optional Protocol to the Convention on the Rights of the Child (CRC). As we have seen, the CRC is itself a highly problematic document that, by weakening parental authority, likely does more harm than good. Yet even being charitable, it is not at all clear how an unenforceable treaty can ameliorate this problem. CSI summarizes its own achievements as entirely a matter of exchanging words, with no clear concrete results:[216]

- Playing an instrumental role in the negotiation, adoption, and entry into force of the Optional Protocol to the Convention on the Rights of the Child.

- Actively engaging influential inter-governmental agencies, such as the UN Security Council, the Human Security Network, the European Union, the UN Committee on the Rights of the Child and the International Labour Organization.

- Publishing three Child Soldiers Global Reports.

- Publishing research on issues relevant to child soldiers, including gender and sexual exploitation.

214. Ibid., 17–18.
215. Ibid., 87.
216. These items have been removed from the CSI internet site, but they are still listed at https://prezi.com/dw1zsacq8xng/heroes/ (accessed 16 March 2017).

Sex Trafficking

On both the left and right, enormous attention is now devoted to what is variously termed "human trafficking," "sex trafficking," "trafficking in persons," "sexual slavery," "forced labor," or other terms. This began on the American sexual left during the Clinton administration, but it quickly spread to conservative groups and was taken up with some enthusiasm by the Bush administration and other Western governments. Yet it remains a gender crime, tacitly understood to be perpetrated by men (despite evidence that most of the practices comprehended under the term are in fact perpetrated mostly by women). Here again the epicenter is American feminists' search for tools to "empower" themselves by criminalizing others. "The issue was initially raised in the feminist movement in the USA and was part of a broader concern about violence against women—including rape, domestic violence, pornography, and prostitution," writes a feminist scholar. "It was argued that women of all races shared a common oppression as victims of men's violence."[217] After the term was taken up by Christian conservatives however, and used in campaigns against ordinary prostitution and illegal immigration, some feminists have recoiled from the term as politically unacceptable.[218]

In a global economy, it is predictable that the sex trade, like any other, should operate across international borders. The internationalization of prostitution, pornography, and other forms of commercialized sex involve sordid practices that are certainly worthy of attention. Throughout the world, and especially in the poor countries of the global South, people live in degraded conditions and are forced to eke out a living with practices that most of us regard as deplorable and often exploitative. When these practices involve crimes—specific practices that have been determined by a sovereign legal authority to be judiciable—they obviously should be identified and prosecuted, and, where an effectively legal machinery exists, they usually are.

Yet it is not clear that vague catch-all terms like "trafficking" are helpful in identifying and addressing these complex and varied problems, and they may be counterproductive. Inflammatory language invoking past atrocities like "slavery" may in fact refer to very different matters that call for wholly different responses. Lumping together an assortment of phenomena—of different degrees of seriousness, some illegal

---

217. Barbara Sullivan, "Trafficking in Human Beings," in *Gender Matters in Global Politics*, ed. Laura J. Shepherd (New York: Routledge, 2010), 90.

218. Laura Maria Agustin, *Sex at the Margins: Migration, Labour Markets and the Rescue Industry* (London: Zed Books, 2007).

and judiciable and some not—under one general term obfuscates more than it illuminates. Moreover, taking complex and entrenched problems of poverty and underdevelopment and trying to simply eradicate them by designating them as crimes for which someone can presumably be found to punish—even in or across societies where there may be no law to enforce, no effective law enforcement authority, and no orderly judicial procedure to guarantee due process protections for those accused—is at best naïve and may be highly dangerous.

The first striking feature of "trafficking"—that should immediately raise red flags because it connects the term so clearly with other invented new offenses we have examined—is that no one can seem to come up with a definition. Advocates themselves recognized that "historically there have been inconsistencies and disagreements regarding the definition of human trafficking among politicians, practitioners, and scholars."[219] This is no accident; it reflects the fact that, like the other new gender crimes, it arises from ideology. Thus it becomes yet another grabbag into which any political agenda can be thrown. "From girls denied schooling or coerced into under-aged marriages, to ethnic minorities without citizenship or birth registration, to migrant workers forced to work against their will by employers who abuse legal processes. . . ."— these are encompassed under the term "trafficking" by former US Secretary of State Hillary Clinton.[220] No doubt these are hardships. But are they crimes? Who precisely is the perpetrator of "ethnic minorities without citizenship," and how are they to be prosecuted? What legal action do we take against those accused of denying schooling to girls? What authority is responsible for trying them? What kind of due process protections are afforded those accused of "abusing legal processes" when by definition the legal process is open to abuse? If the "abuses" are legal, in what sense and according to what authority or whose opinion are they punishable as a crime? Secretary Clinton wants "to eliminate all forms of human trafficking." Yet her own definition of "trafficking" is so broad that it can encompass anything of which she disapproves. Without some definition, the Secretary's goal is a prescription for open-ended expansion of domestic and international police powers into areas we do not yet understand.

---

219. "Human Trafficking into and within the United States: A Review of the Literature," US Department of Health and Human Services (n.p., n.d.), http://aspe.hhs.gov/hsp/07/HumanTrafficking/LitRev/index.pdf.

220. Letter from Secretary, Office to Monitor and Combat Trafficking in Persons, *Trafficking in Persons Report 2009* (Washington: State Department, 2009; http://www.state.gov/g/tip/rls/tiprpt/2009/123147.htm).

This appears to be one more instance of blurring the distinction between crime and behavior that, while perhaps deplorable, is not necessarily criminal in order to expand government power and criminalize people who have broken no law. It has arisen not because of any new waves of crime but because ideological activists and officials have reclassified existing conditions and practices as crimes even when they do not lend themselves to judicial resolution. They are the product of an ever-expanding ideology of "legal salvationism"[221] that has become so habituated to seeing government—and in particular courts—as the solution to every problem that it demands government measures even where no government exists.

The very term "trafficking," like the other new crimes we have examined, is vague to the point of meaninglessness. "Trafficking" has become an all-encompassing term to eradicate commerce we consider wrong but which, for various reasons (perhaps because it takes place across international boundaries), is beyond the reach of conventional criminal prosecution. In some instances this may be appropriate, but the term is invoked to obfuscate rather than illuminate. We hear of "trafficking" in arms or "trafficking" in drugs, but it is not always clear whether the "traffickers" have actually broken any law, whether any law even exists and in what jurisdiction, whether any such law as they might have broken meets our standards for due process protection or is even enforceable at all.

"Trafficking" has come to suggest commerce in sex, which arguably should be outlawed (and, when it can be, usually is). But the term is also used for non-sexual labor. Is such buying and selling *ipso facto* wrong—or criminal, or "slavery"? When does it become so? What realistically can be done about it?

If Wikipedia can be taken as indicative of the informed consensus, its article on "human trafficking" defines the multitude of activities comprehended in the term as "*legal* and illegal, including both *legitimate labor activities* as well as forced labor" (added emphasis). Yet the article then goes on to refer to everything included under the term as "crimes." So "legal and legitimate" labor activities are "crimes"? Many actions included are not normally considered criminal, such as "lying," "deception," and unspecified "abuse of power."

It is evident from this article and many others like it that virtually anything can be made criminal or semi-criminal or quasi-criminal if

---

221. The phrase is Kenneth Minogue's, "The Fate of Britain's National Interest," website of the Bruges Group, 14 April 2004, http://www.brugesgroup.com/mediacentre/index.live?article=206#legallegal.

someone with enough political power disapproves of it and chooses to include it under the term "trafficking." Official definitions only illustrate the vagueness. The widely accepted *United Nations Protocol to Prevent, Suppress, and Punish Trafficking in Persons Especially Women and Children*, defines trafficking as "the recruitment, transportation, transfer, harbouring, or receipt of persons, by means of the threat or use of force or other forms, of coercion, of abduction, of fraud, of deception, of the abuse of power or of a position of vulnerability or of the giving or receiving of payments or benefits to achieve the consent of a person having control over another person, for the purpose of exploitation."[222]

This could describe the entire working populations of some societies, and they would be the fortunate ones who are working at all. It might equally describe the workforce of most multinational corporations or of governments like that of China in its operations in Africa. Are all these enterprises criminal, and is there the remotest chance of prosecuting them? Is every prostitute being passively "trafficked"? (Some do argue precisely this, but if so, why is it not punished locally, as in the past?) Is every child who works long hours in agriculture rather than attending school being "trafficked" or a "slave"? If so, who are the traffickers and slave-drivers and whom do we prosecute? His overseers—or perhaps his parents? What if he is working to provide for his family? A child working long hours in a field is at least likely to be eating, which is more than do many children in impoverished countries. Are we to criminalize his only livelihood and that of his family? Who decides where the line runs between providing low-wage jobs or requiring that children contribute to the family economy in societies where such practices are still routine, on the one hand, and "forced labor" and "slavery," on the other? One feminist scholar's evidence for sex trafficking is that in Iranian families, "Prior to marriage and especially among very young families, daughters assume their domestic role in cooking and caring for the family at a very young age."[223] This is a crime? So are we then to regulate the household labor of private families? Under what governmental authority? What agenda is being slipped in here?

Impoverished countries contain a lot of misery that is the product of poverty, underdevelopment, ignorance, superstition, and complex circumstances that have bedeviled generations of development experts. To try to eliminate these problems at a stroke by designating them as crimes and looking for scapegoats to prosecute is to invite serious trouble.

222. New York: United Nations, 2000, 2.
223. Tiantian Zheng, *Sex Trafficking, Human Rights, and Social Justice* (Oxford: Routledge, 2010), 14, quoting Sholeh Shahrokhi in the same volume.

Even assuming that "trafficking" is an identifiable offense, what are we being asked to do about it? What authority is being asked to curtail it? Is the US State Department appropriate to act as an international police agency? The Justice Department? The United Nations? The US federal trafficking law requires these agencies to monitor the enforcement practices of other countries, effectively placing them in the role of supervising other nations' police.

Many poor countries have little effective law enforcement and adjudication. Often it is impossible to distinguish the police from the criminals. "In some countries, people cross the street when they see a policeman or soldier coming their way...from a reasonable fear of being assaulted or robbed."[224] The "persistent belief by Western governments, agencies, and individuals—despite massive evidence to the contrary—that there exists in Africa a 'government' that cares about its people, represents their interests, and is responsive to their needs" is what George Ayittey calls "a delusion on a grade scale": "In many African countries, the institution of government has been corrupted and transformed into a criminal enterprise."[225] Providing such enterprises with expanded and open-ended new law enforcement powers—especially to eradicate something as vague as trafficking—is less likely to see them directed at some Western idealist's notion of a social problem than to be hijacked for personal gain or politicized to increase someone's power. Western governments themselves are far from immune from such degeneration, and crusades like this are precisely the way to encourage it.

Despite emotive terms like "modern slavery," all this stands in stark contrast with the chattel slavery of the 18th and 19th centuries. In the Anglophone world at least, slavery was a glaring anomaly and a direct threat to the free institutions of the countries that permitted it. The United States and Britain had inherited traditions of individual rights and procedures of law to defend individual freedom dating back to at least the 13th century. These principles applied at first to only a small minority of the population, and centuries passed before the rest of the population was affluent, educated, and politically articulate enough to claim inclusion. Indeed, when slavery became controversial it was only recently that even educated and politically experienced Englishmen and Americans had managed to secure these rights for themselves, and it would be decades more before they were extended to the common peo-

---

224. Robert Calderisi, *The Trouble with Africa* (New York: Palgrave Macmillan, 2006), 60.

225. George B.N. Ayittey, *Africa Unchained: The Blueprint for Africa's Future* (New York: Palgrave MacMillan, 2005), 48. I owe this reference to Colton Wilson.

ple. Constitutional protections were far from perfect, but they were integral to the identities of Englishmen and Americans, who were fiercely determined that they should be preserved. Americans had recently shed their blood in defense of those freedoms in the American Revolution, as had the English in the revolution of the 1640s, codified in 1688–89. These made the inconsistencies with slavery not simply hypocritical but threatening to the entire justification of Anglo-American freedom, including the legitimacy of the Hanoverian dynasty and the American republic itself. Abolishing slavery helped consolidate the hard-won freedoms that were still insecure for even affluent whites.

Modern Western freedom also required centuries of economic development, urbanization, aristocratic and then middle-class and later working-class agitation, legal institutions and procedures, and—not least—Christian evangelism. All this constituted training in active citizenship and was made possible by the economic achievements (inseparable from the growing political sophistication) first of the commercial and middle classes and later of the working class, which rendered slavery uneconomical and unnecessary.

All this contrasts sharply with conditions in most of the global South today. These societies have few traditions of natural rights and institutions for legal adjudication. They lack the large educated middle class that can agitate for individual rights. And many live in abject poverty that makes them liable to economic exploitation that now takes place on a global scale, where the boss may be a foreign corporation or foreign government and one against which the host government is powerless to act or with which it may be in active collusion. Trying to criminalize "exploitation" in these circumstances is like trying to criminalize poverty, which is really what is being attempted here.

If outside authorities such as the United States or United Nations are going to impose new quasi-legal requirements on impoverished countries, then outside authorities will have to enforce them. A new kind of bureaucratic imperialism will be required and is indeed developing in countries like the US and UK, working increasingly through international organizations such as the UN and the EU.

So isn't that what our foreign relations and the UN should be doing, spreading Western standards of freedom to the rest of the world?

Not necessarily. The US State Department or the British Foreign Office, by the very nature of the environment in which they operate, are not equipped to enforce law or observe due process protections. Though international organizations are Western creations, they too have few traditions or mechanisms to guarantee due process of law. There is no separation of powers at the UN, no clearly defined division of federal powers, no bill of rights with any history or prospects of effective enforcement, no body of common law or due process protections that are shared among a common political culture. As for the EU, its "democratic deficit" is legendary.

Rather than assuming that Anglo-American judicial standards will be replicated abroad to poor nations, it is much more likely that our own domestic standards will be debased by importing nebulous and unenforceable international measures that are far more political than they are judicial.

This is precisely what is happening. Our tradition of law enforcement depends on local jurisdiction, with guilt determined by a jury of one's peers. But nothing remotely similar is being practiced or proposed in the measures against trafficking. On the contrary, alleged "crimes" are not adjudicated at all but processed bureaucratically by civil servants, including State Department officials. Knowing that local juries are often an impossibility in poor countries (and they are becoming a thing of the past even the West), the US legislation provides that purported victims be "certified" as such by federal officials at, of all places, the domestic welfare offices of the Department of Health and Human Services (HHS).

The trafficking hysteria was partly the initiative of First Lady (later Secretary of State) Hillary Clinton, under whose influence Congress passed the Trafficking Victims Protection Act (TVPA) in 2000. As with the other new gender crimes, no public demand or outrage preceded the law or provided the impetus behind it, and no public debate was ever held in the media to establish the need for such a law. Yet the measure passed Congress by an overwhelming majority, another indication that little debate or scrutiny was involved.

To justify the measure, Congress invoked figures indicating 50,000 women and children are "trafficked" into the US annually. The only source for this CIA estimate was newspaper clippings; it was never documented or confirmed. The figure has been revised downward repeatedly, but even much lower figures have been strongly disputed. According to the *Washington Post* in 2007, "the administration has identified 1,362 victims of human trafficking brought into the United States since 2000." David Osborne of the Library of Congress believes, "The numbers were totally unreliable." A 2006 study by the Government Accountability Office (GAO) strongly criticized all the figures and refused to endorse the notion that trafficking is a serious problem at all:

> The accuracy of the estimates is in doubt because of methodological weaknesses, gaps in data, and numerical discrepancies. For example, the U.S. government's estimate was developed by one person who did

not document all of his work, so the estimate may not be replicable, casting doubt on its reliability. Moreover, the quality of existing country level data varies due to limited availability, reliability, and comparability. There is also a considerable discrepancy between the numbers of observed and estimated victims of human trafficking. The U.S. government has not yet established an effective mechanism for estimating the number of victims or for conducting ongoing analysis of trafficking related data that resides within various government agencies.[226]

In short, no "trafficking" problem has ever been proven.

A more recent analysis by the *Post* shows similarly politicized gimmicks. "The language regarding the crime of sex trafficking has become so fuzzy that even the nation's top law enforcement officer can speak before an international audience and utter wildly inflated statistics," the fact-checker concluded. "Neither DOJ nor the FBI can provide evidence that 'hundreds of sex traffickers' have been arrested . . . —unless one plays fast and loose with legal language."[227]

Even assuming that the government's figures are "true" (and aside from the hubris of Congress using legislation to declare statistical "findings," as if governments can legislate facts by majority vote), what precisely do they mean? Not only are these figures not verified; they are not verifiable, because again "trafficking" has no definition. "The TVPA does not specify movement across international boundaries as a condition of trafficking," the GAO points out; "it does not require the transportation of victims from one locale to another."[228] Even the State Department tells us, that "A victim need not be physically transported from one location to another in order for the crime to fall within these definitions."[229] So in what sense *is* this "trafficking"? Again, what is "trafficking"?

If this is prostitution, why not simply call it that? Prostitution is a specific act that everyone understands and that we can criminalize if we so choose, whereupon concrete definitions and rules of evidence can allow those accused to enjoy constitutional protections. "Trafficking" introduces vagueness into the law, a well-known prescription for railroading the innocent.

---

226. Jerry Markon, "Human Trafficking Evokes Outrage, Little Evidence," *Washington Post*, 23 September 2007, A01; *Human Trafficking: Better Data, Strategy, and Reporting Needed to Enhance U.S. Antitrafficking Efforts Abroad* (Washington: Government Accountability Office, 2006), 2–3.

227. Glenn Kessler, "Loretta Lynch's False Claim on Sex Trafficking Arrests," *Washington Post*, 24 November 2015 (https://www.washingtonpost.com/news/fact-checker/wp/2015/11/24/loretta-lynchs-false-claim-on-sex-trafficking-arrests/).

228. Ibid., 5.

229. *Trafficking in Persons Report*, 7.

Some do argue that all prostitution is trafficking, illustrating how the vague international standard is imported to supplant the concrete domestic one. New York's law "makes no distinction between human trafficking from far-off lands and traditional prostitution," so even US citizens working voluntarily within the confines of the United States can now be considered "trafficked." The law was spearheaded by New York governor Eliot Spitzer, who allegedly hired his own prostitutes and calls ordinary prostitution "modern-day slavery."[230] Making "trafficking" the charge for domestic prostitution creates a formula for further expanding federal and even international police power, since "trafficking" involves federal agents and international agencies. When it was called "prostitution," it was left to the local vice squad. Britain's Sexual Offences Act defines trafficking to include the organized transportation of a woman into prostitution even if she participates willingly.

The US federal government has spent enormous sums since 2000 to combat trafficking, with no less than ten federal agencies involved. The Justice Department alone created some forty-two task forces and made it a top priority for its Civil Rights Division (of all things), so following our now-familiar pattern trafficking is not simply a crime but a "civil rights" violation, politicizing the "crime" and encouraging people to seek official "victim" status in the hope of financial rewards. Yet it has never been proven that there are any victims or any identifiable problem. At a House of Representatives hearing prior to the federal law, Laura Lederer, a Harvard University "expert" on trafficking, seemed to have little expertise: "We have so very little information on this subject in this country . . . so very few facts," that she had to admit that she did not know if there was even a problem.[231]

The federal money is distributed to local police agencies for training schemes to "educate" officials in "how to spot trafficking," in the words of the *Post*. This language is familiar to us from similarly vague police re-education campaigns on bullying, domestic violence, rape, stalking, and child abuse—pressuring police to find crimes where no one else sees them and to view such incidents through the lens of politicized jargon. Sally Stoecker of Shared Hope International, which aims to "increase awareness" of sex trafficking, tells a training session of DC police (one of thousands of such sessions nationwide), "It's a huge crime, and it's continuing to grow." But she too has no evidence.

230. Jeffrey Tucker, "Spitzer Caught in His Own Reign of Terror," *LewRockwell*.com, 13 March 2008, http://www.lewrockwell.com/tucker/tucker94.html.

231. Markon, "Human Trafficking."

All this federalizes and politicizes police operations and gives police budgets a stake in creating new criminals through new and loosely defined crimes. The *Post* quotes Steven Wagner, who helped HHS distribute millions of dollars in grants to community groups to find and assist victims, as saying, "Those funds were wasted." All this is reminiscent of the federal largesse distributed for other ill-defined and politicized gender crimes, such as rape and domestic violence. "Many of the organizations that received grants didn't really have to do anything," said Wagner, who headed HHS's anti-trafficking program. "They were available to help victims. There weren't any victims."

Yet finding such victims to justify the spending has understandably become a relentless activity for those receiving the money. "We're giving money to [a public relations firm] so they can train people who can train people who can train people to serve victims," said one provider of "services," who receives government funding and spoke to the *Post* on condition of anonymity.

Statements from the US Justice Department are an open admission that the "problem" exists largely in the collective consciousness of advocates: "Despite growing awareness of the issue and an influx of resources from such influential bodies as the United Nations and other intergovernmental organizations, foundations, non-governmental organizations, and the US government," says the US government itself, "the field is still hampered by its inability to measure the size and scope of trafficking." In other words, there is no evidence of any problem aside from the numerous "awareness raising initiatives" of DOJ and its friends. This inability to prove any problem extends to law enforcement itself, where it could have dire consequences for anyone actually accused of this nebulous and invisible "crime." "Unfortunately, challenges also exist in gauging the effectiveness of the criminal justice system's response," DOJ continues. "Rates of identification, investigation, and prosecution are of limited value in determining the effectiveness of US responses to human trafficking because the data supporting prevalence estimates are unreliable."[232]

Over and over we find this in the literature: a terrible crime is being committed all around us, but we have no proof, no evidence, no documentation, no statistics, no cases, and no definition of what we are even talking about. But we need to be arresting more people. Much like the search for witches, we know they exist because so many people keep say-

232. Maureen Q. McGough, "Ending Modern-Day Slavery: Using Research to Inform US Anti-Human Trafficking Efforts," National Institute of Justice, 27 February 2013, http://www.nij.gov/nij/journals/271/anti-human-trafficking.htm.

ing they do. Perhaps the best treatise on trafficking is James Thurber's story, "The Day the Dam Broke."

DOJ cites an academic study that "found evidence of human trafficking in the majority of the cases." What was this "evidence"? "Among the indicators found were threatening to harm or actually physically or nonphysically harming the victim; demeaning and demoralizing the victim; dominating, intimidating, and controlling the victim; and disorienting and depriving the victim of alternatives." So "nonphysically harming" (whatever that means) and "depriving the victim of alternatives" are crimes and constitute evidence of a crime wave? Such weasel words indicate yet again that someone seems to be pulling the wool over our eyes. "Dominating, intimidating, and controlling the victim"? This sounds like someone is slipping another agenda, one of anti-capitalism or sexual liberation, into a program that is supposed to be about crime. "However, few suspects were actually charged with human trafficking offenses," DOJ concedes. "Even when they received specific human trafficking cases, prosecutors were more likely to prosecute using laws with which they, judges, and juries were more familiar, such as promoting prostitution, kidnapping, or fraud." So what is wrong with simply using laws and language that everyone understands because they refer to deeds that can be proven or disproven? If this is prostitution, why not simply call it that? If this really is "slavery," why not use existing statutes against kidnapping? Such laws exist, of course. "[T]hat was sort of the unwritten policy of the office. 'Why bother with this goofy human trafficking statute; just charge other crimes that you are more comfortable with and that you have used in the past.'" Precisely, and so that a jury can clearly understand why they are being asked to put someone in prison, which is what justice is supposed to be about, instead of officials telling us all to grab our pitchforks and start lynching villains for pseudo-crimes that none of us understands. (Perhaps inspired by their colleagues in the domestic violence business, DOJ wants "a specialized human trafficking unit.")[233] But perhaps traditional charges are too clear and inflexible to put away criminals who are conspiring to "deprive victims of alternatives." It is difficult to escape the conclusion that "trafficking" is one more concocted crime, cooked up specifically to avoid the specific provisions and protections of existing criminal statutes and railroad the defenseless.

This is confirmed by the political nature of what is ostensibly law enforcement. As with other new sexual crimes, "victims" are not designated by convictions of their victimizers in jury trials, as we tradition-

233. Ibid.

ally determine that a crime has been committed; instead, victims are officially "certified" by HHS, a welfare administration not normally mandated to operate as a police agency (let alone a jury). Why this peculiar, bureaucratic method of determining who is a crime victim? Because the officially certified "victims" (like their official certifiers) are then entitled to receive government money to relieve their distress. This explains why a social work agency like HHS has become concerned with law enforcement and provides yet another rationalization for social workers to operate as *de facto* police.

HHS openly acknowledges that it cannot find many "victims" but, fueled by federal money, it is indefatigable in trying. HHS deputy assistant secretary Brent Orrell said that certifications are increasing and that the agency is working hard to "help identify many more victims," adding, "We still have a long way to go." The Justice Department's own human trafficking task force has also mounted an aggressive effort to find victims. According to the *Post*: "at a meeting of the task force this year, then-coordinator Sharon Marcus-Kurn said that detectives had spent 'umpteen hours of overtime' repeatedly interviewing women found in Korean- and Hispanic-owned brothels. 'It's very difficult to find any underlying trafficking that is there,' Marcus-Kurn told the group." Once we understand how the sexualization of criminal justice operates, it becomes fairly clear that the victims do not exist. "Soon after [President George] Bush took office, a network of anti-trafficking non-profit agencies arose, spurred in part by an infusion of federal dollars."

At one point, HHS even hired a public relations firm to combat an alleged crime. "Legal experts said they hadn't heard of hiring a public relations firm to fight a crime problem," according to the *Post*. "Wagner, who took over HHS's anti-trafficking program in 2003, said that the strategy was 'extremely unusual' but that creative measures were needed." Creative measures? Why is a PR firm needed to combat crime? To convince the (alleged) criminals to stop their activities or turn themselves in? Or to alarm the public into believing in yet another new and ill-defined "crime" about which they previously had not heard, yet another rationalization to increase and centralize police power and relax due process protections, and to "re-educate" and indoctrinate police and other criminal justice officials with political ideology? Shared Hope International received federal money to "increase awareness of sex trafficking." Campaigns to "increase awareness" of crimes about which few were previously bothered are usually a sign that special interest groups are seeking power by inventing new problems, about which the public and police must be indoctrinated by public relations campaigns.

Administration officials and grant recipients respond by insisting that "even one case is too many." Here we have gone from 50,000 cases annually in the US alone to "one case" to justify 42 federal task forces. This "one case is too many" rationalization—another device familiar from federally funded gender crimes and child abuse programs that almost certainly create the problem they claim to be solving—is another clear admission that officials must drum up business to justify their spending by ever-looser definitions of the ostensible "crime."[234]

This appears to have been precisely what the 2000 US law did: created the crime and the criminals by expanding the definition. Whereas previously prosecutors were required to adhere to specific statutes to prove specific crimes by producing specific evidence, the new law provided a definition of the crime so open-ended as to be a catch-all for anything. No specific deed is required, no evidence, and no trial; "psychological" abuse is sufficient, a form of "abuse" that can be determined not by objective facts or rules of evidence, but by the subjective state-of-mind or "feelings" of the self-described and government-certified but judicially unproven "victim."

Again and again we are told that "precise figures are hard to come by" by people who insist that a serious problem exists. But no figures appear to be even remotely reliable (probably because no real definition is ever possible). The influential David Batstone, who claims academic credentials, states that "Twenty-seven million slaves exist in our world today." But while he claims this figure is "documented," he does not document it, adding of all his statistics, "the author holds no illusion of their 100% accuracy."[235] Illustrating the principle that everyone is conservative about matters that affect them personally, the leftist *Village Voice*, responding to allegations that its personal notices were being used for trafficking, demonstrated in 2011 that an influential study claiming to find astronomical increases in sex trafficking reported in sensationalized testimony before Congress and repeated unquestioningly in at least fourteen major news outlets was in fact fabricated. "The group behind the study admits as much. It's now clear they used fake data to deceive the media and lie to Congress. And it was all done to score free publicity and a wealth of public funding."[236]

Yet time and again (and much like rape and child abuse allegations), sensational government claims spread like wildfire through the credu-

---

234. Markon, "Human Trafficking."

235. David Batstone, *Not for Sale* (New York: HarperOne, 2007), 1 and note 1.

236. Nick Pinto, "Women's Funding Network Sex Trafficking Study Is Junk Science," *Village Voice*, 23 March 2011 (http://www.villagevoice.com/2011-03-23/news/women-s-fu nding-network-sex-trafficking-study-is-junk-science/).

lous media and are used to justify expanded police powers, only to be exposed as hoaxes. Britain's multi-billion pound Pentameter 2 campaign claimed to be the largest-ever police crackdown on human trafficking, according to Home Secretary and feminist Jacqui Smith, who called it "one of the worst crimes threatening our society." Yet investigations by the *Guardian* and *Daily Mail* found that the numbers were wildly inflated and that authorities could not find a single "trafficker" to convict. Belinda Brooks-Gordon of Birkbeck University, who has researched the sex industry in Britain for 15 years, says, "The way in which the 4,000 [victims] figure was reached is so bad that if it was handed in to me by a student, I would think it was a spoof."[237]

Spoof is an apt description for many claims, which are far from harmless. One sensational international campaign to "redeem slaves" turned out to be "a carefully orchestrated fraud."[238] In numerous instances, "the slaves weren't slaves at all, but people gathered locally and instructed to pretend they were returning from bondage."[239] "The slave redemption makes for powerful human drama," begins the account in the *Irish Times*.

> A line of women and children emerges from the African bush. A slave trader in front, wrapped in the white robes of an Arab. And before them, waiting with a bag of money at his feet, is a white, Christian, man. The procession halts under the shade of a tree. There is discussion, then money changes hands. Suddenly the trader gives a nod, the slaves walk free and there are cries of joy as families are re-united. Freedom at last. Who could fail to be stirred by this emotional sight? . . . The highly publicised redemptions have touched millions of hearts— and wallets—across the world but particularly in the US. Celebrities and politicians have chained themselves to railings in protest. Pop stars have given free concerts. Little girls have given their lunch money.

Yet the reality turned out to be very different, "nothing more than a careful deceit, stage-managed by corrupt officials":

> In reality, many of the "slaves" are fakes. Rebel officials round up local villagers to pose for the cameras. They recruit fake slavers—a light

237. Tom Rawstorne, "The Myth of Britain's Foreign Sex Slaves," *Daily Mail*, 13 November 2009 (http://www.dailymail.co.uk/news/article-1227418/SPECIAL-INVESTI-GATION-The-myth-Britains-foreign-sex-slaves.html#ixzz1OUvRJ4ET).

238. "Scam in Sudan," *The Independent on Sunday*, 24 February 2002. Unless indicated otherwise, quotations from newspaper reports come from the compilation by David Hoile, "'Slave Redemption' Fraud and Naivety in Sudan: The Final Word?" *Media Monitor Network*, 4 April 2002 (http://www.mediamonitors.net/espac17.html).

239. Markon, "Human Trafficking."

skinned soldier, or a passing trader, to "sell" them. The children are coached in stories of abduction and abuse for when the redeemer, or a journalist, asks questions. Interpreters may be instructed to twist their answers. The money, however, is very real. CSI [Christian Solidarity International] can spend more than $300,000 during a week of redemptions at various bush locations. After their plane takes off, the profits are divvied up—a small cut to the "slaves" and the "trader" but the lion's share to local administrators and SPLA [Sudan People's Liberation Army] figures.

As indicated, rather than freeing "slaves," Western money ended up further fueling the corruption that is endemic to poor societies like Sudan. A senior SPLA commander, Ayieny Aleu, claimed that "slave redemption" had become a "racket of mafia dimensions." He said one of his lighter-skinned relatives, another SPLA official, had been "forced several times to pretend as an Arab and simulate the sale of free children to CSI on camera." Yet, Aleu declared: "It was a hoax. This thing has been going on for no less than six years."

Indeed, the redemption money appears to have become a major source of funding for the rebel militia. The *Irish Times* reported that one SPLA commander has earned enough from the scam to acquire forty wives. "Other SPLA figures were said to have built houses or financed businesses with their cuts." As we have seen, Western aid in various forms often fuels corruption and killing by both corrupt governments and rebel groups, and money for "redemptions" simply fits this larger pattern. The militia is described by *The Economist* as "little more than an armed gang . . . killing, looting and raping. Its indifference, almost animosity, towards the people it was supposed to be 'liberating' was all too clear." *The New York Times* likewise reported that the SPLA "have behaved like an occupying army, killing, raping, and pillaging" and that it was led by one of Sudan's "pre-eminent war criminals." Such inflammatory allegations about "war criminals" (another possible contradiction in terms) should themselves be taken with a grain of salt, but the diversion of aid money to political purposes is endemic in these countries. Significantly, this hysteria appears to have fed its sister-hysteria, that over "child soldiers." According to the *Irish Times*: "The primary purpose . . . of luring and keeping thousands of boys away from their families and in separate boys-only camps was, in the judgment of Human Rights Watch, a military purpose. This resulted in the training and recruitment of thousands of underage soldiers who were thrust into battle in southern Sudan and briefly in Ethiopia."

More is at work here than gullibility and "good intentions" gone awry. More subtle than other examples, this too has all the ingredients of ideology, notably the refusal to accept facts when they contradict ideological fixations. "The warning signs have been there for years," according to the *Irish Times*:

> It seems almost incredible that tens of thousands of abducted civilians could cross a dangerous frontline undetected by government forces. Moreover, aid workers north of the line saw no evidence of large movements south, and their colleagues in the south saw no sudden demand for extra food or medicines by redeemed slaves. Put simply, the numbers didn't add up. And yet no questions were asked. The dollars rolled in and the redemptions continued.

Even those appalled at these revelations nevertheless remain stubbornly convinced that "real" slaves still need to be redeemed. Yet if so, why were they not redeemed instead of the fakes? Why did virtually *all* the "slaves" turn out to be fake?

Again, there can be no doubt that in circumstances where war and insurgency are combined with poverty and underdevelopment, some pretty awful practices will take place. No doubt they involved forced movements, capture, and indeed killing, as well as rape and prostitution—phenomena that are endemic to both war and poverty, especially in combination with one another. But enlisting ideologized and incomprehensible jargon to suggest lawbreaking by conveniently unknown people who have no opportunity to speak in their own defense is not "good intentions." It is the dangerous fruits of ideological self-righteousness and shows a callous disregard for the cost to other people that these cheap efforts take to achieve moral superiority. As a respected Sudanese opposition leader, newspaper publisher, and university lecturer wrote to Baroness Caroline Cox: "I sincerely hope that this type of game stops. . . . I sincerely hope that you do see the harm that could be caused and that you will refrain from this activity in the future."

This is not the first time feminist victimology has culminated in centralized power. "Historically, anti-trafficking conventions were derived from the discourses of white slavery—a racialized campaign to protect the chastity of white women."[240] This campaign (which by anyone else would be called "racist") was also spearheaded by feminists and other radicals, who understood the power of sensationalism when combined with the potential to provide employment. "Only when human sorrows are turned into a toy with glaring colours will baby people become interested—for a while at least," wrote the anarchist-feminist Emma Goldman with cynicism but possibly some accuracy. "The 'righteous'

---

240. Zheng, "Sex Trafficking," 5.

cry against the white slave traffic is such a toy. It serves to amuse the people for a little while, and it will help to create a few more fat political jobs—parasites who stalk about the world as inspectors, investigators, detectives, and so forth."[241]

Even today's promoters of trafficking allegations recognize that "Many contemporary historians share the view that the number of white slavery cases was actually very low."[242] Yet the sensation led directly to the massive and arguably unconstitutional centralization of police power in the US federal government. The first FBI director, Stanley Finch, took up his post in 1908 specifically tasked with defeating "white slave traffic," known before its politicization by the suffragists simply as prostitution. "Initially, the main problem was seen in terms of 'white slavery' and the fear that European women were being abducted and transported around the world where they were forced to prostitute themselves with non-white men."[243] Like rape hysteria, the problem thus originated in the racist culture of early feminism. "Finch had suffragettes to thank, in part, for his appointment," reports the *Washington Times*. Much of the manpower was also a response to feminist demands that "local white slave officers" be appointed throughout the country. Thus did the nonexistent "crisis" rationalize a massive and permanent increase in federal police power (arguably, much as it is now being used to justify an increase in international criminal jurisdiction among various national and international quasi-judicial bureaucracies). Though many of the white slave officers ("almost all of the officers were attorneys") proved unnecessary, they remained in the bureau and served as agents for other purposes.[244]

Here too, few journalists or academics dare to question the government line on trafficking. "There's huge political momentum," said one recipient of federal money quoted in the *Post*. "No one is going to stand up and oppose fighting modern-day slavery." In most cases the wheels of legislation turn slowly. If US Congress, dozens of US states, and other governments are rushing headlong into drastic action with very little

241. Quoted in Kristiina Kangaspunta, "A Short History of Trafficking in Persons," *Freedom from Fear website*, http://www.freedomfromfearmagazine.org/index.php?optio n=com_content&view=article&id=99:a-short-history-of-trafficking-in-persons&catid =37:issue-1&Itemid=159.

242. Ibid.

243. Sullivan, "Trafficking," 90.

244. "FBI Directors through the Years in a League of their Own," *Washington Times*, 25 July 2008, A19; Jessica Pliley, *Policing Sexuality: The Mann Act and the Making of the FBI* (Cambridge: Harvard University Press, 2014), 89.

information or understanding that a problem even exists, it may say more about the political clout of groups seeking government money and power than it does about any actual "crisis." Ronald Weitzer, a criminologist at George Washington University and an expert on trafficking, says that "this problem is being blown way out of proportion."[245]

What also emerges fairly clearly is that "trafficking" is another term to reformulate old-fashioned prostitution so that only the men are criminals. Whereas prostitution suggests three parties that may be restricted—the pimp, the john, and the prostitute—"trafficking" and "sex slavery" turn the prostitute into a victim and leaves only the men liable to restriction or prosecution.[246] Combining child labor with prostitution reinforces this and the parallel trend toward similarly criminalizing parents.

Yet as always with prostitution, the operators are mostly female. It is not surprising therefore that the UN Office on Drugs and Crime found that "most human traffic perpetrators are women." "Women commit crimes against women, and in many cases the victims become the perpetrators," Antonio Maria Costa, director of the UNODC said. "They become the matrons of the business and they make money."[247] This parallels what we saw in the case of child soldiers, where the "victims" are in fact those whom we have "liberated" from traditional constraints such as families, who then go on to continue their own liberation with destructive radical ideologies that rationalize the seduction and, yes, often the enslavement of others. Of course such niceties are quickly forgotten when it comes time to apply the handcuffs.

Whether all the allegedly "trafficked" women are, in fact, forced into the business is also highly questionable. From the inception of the campaign more than a century ago, "trafficking always involved prostitution, and women's consent was irrelevant."[248] It is widely known that, among the supposedly trafficked women of Eastern Europe "most women volunteer for the trip Westward because of the money they can make." Most of the women are well aware that they will be working as prostitutes, according to Assistant Chief Constable Andy Felton, a police

---

245. Markon, "Human Trafficking."

246. Elizabeth Nolan Brown, "In Seattle, Crime of 'Patronizing a Prostitute' Redefined as 'Sexual Exploitation,'" *Reason*, 14 January 2015, http://reason.com/blog/2015/01/14/seattle-change-to-prostitution-code#.buiylt:huDg.

247. "United Nations Discovers Most Human Traffic Perpetrators are Women," *Fox News*, 12 February 2010, http://www.foxnews.com/story/0,2933,491904,00.html. See also Louise Shelley, *Human Trafficking* (Cambridge: Cambridge University Press, 2010), ch. 3.

248. Sullivan, "Trafficking," 91.

officer who worked in Romania for three years.[249] Phelim McAleer likewise regards trafficking as simply a new term to describe ordinary prostitution, most of whose practitioners engage in the work voluntarily, despite the language of the International Office of Migration (IOM), which collects money to rescue and shelter "victims." "As anyone who works closely with the prostitutes and who isn't infected with victimitis knows, the IOM version of events is nonsense."[250]

Ironically, feminists themselves have begun calling attention to the inconsistencies in the trafficking alarm their sisters sounded. "The dominant trafficking discourse not only conflates labor trafficking with sex trafficking but also conflates voluntary prostitution with sex trafficking," Tiantian Zheng points out.[251] Feminists object to anti-trafficking measures because "they may have the effect of limiting women's mobility" to undertake "sex work."[252] In one study, "the women and children, and not men, were labeled as 'victims of trafficking,'" writes Zheng. "Yet interviews with the women have demonstrated that they made the decision to move for a better living and a new livelihood."[253] The latest feminist orthodoxy constitutes an open admission that most of the "sex trafficking" alarm is hysteria. Fearful that anti-trafficking campaigns endanger the rights of "sex workers," feminists now berate conservatives who have taken up the call. "The Bush administration has an obsession with prostitution, and, as a result, 'fighting trafficking in the United States has been a pervert [*sic*] such that under Bush it is largely a campaign to abolish prostitution.'"[254]

As elsewhere, a delicate political *pas de deux* seems to be taking place. Having created the trafficking hysteria, feminists then recoil from it when conservatives use it to reinforce controls on prostitution and illegal immigration. Since many feminists advocate legalized prostitution and unlimited immigration, the "trafficking" narrative was no longer politically acceptable. Thus feminist scholars must now show that the women are victims not of trafficking but of immigration restrictions and "capitalism": "Rather than victims of trafficking, these migrants are victims of border control practices, and global capitalist labor markets." One may accept or reject this argument, but the feminist literature provides a useful gloss on the trafficking paradigm, providing ample docu-

249. Phelim McAleer, "Happy Hookers of Eastern Europe," *Spectator*, 5 April 2003, (http://www.lewrockwell.com/spectator/spec51.html).

250. McAleer, "Happy Hookers."

251. Zheng, "Sex Trafficking," 2.

252. Sullivan, "Trafficking," 93, 99.

253. Zheng, "Sex Trafficking," 7–8.

254. Ibid., 3, quoting J. Brinkly.

mentation that the "trafficked" women are not victims in the least. Once they have reason to look for it, even the feminist scholars can begin to find the truth:

> [I]llegal female migrants exercised agency in appropriating the label of trafficking and representing themselves as victims in order to legally stay in the country. Their claim to being trafficked was not informed by their lived experiences, but by Canadian immigration laws, legal categories, and feminists who offered this frame to them. In reality, however, far from victims, they were agents who sought out and hired people to smuggle them into Canada and some perceived sex work as part of survival strategies. Once the claim to "victim of trafficking" failed, they stopped using it.

Now, in the latest development, it appears that the Christian groups that have taken up the feminists' "trafficking" narrative are discovering they have, so to speak, entered into a pact with the devil, as feminist groups are starting to use the campaign as a method for legalizing prostitution and abortion.[255]

Yet feminist opportunism again reflects the pattern we have seen with other gender crimes: liberalize, then criminalize. Encourage unimpeded freedom—especially sexual freedom—and then criminalize those—usually the men—who engage in it. One feminist scholar wants to remove all restrictions on "sex work" and migration: legalize prostitution, eliminate all immigration controls, and institute open borders. "We need to eliminate immigration controls and end exploitative practices under global capitalism," she writes.[256] Neither of these is going to happen; what is likely to happen is that "trafficking" will be invoked to rationalize the growth of prosecutorial power by targeting not powerful "exploiters" but those within easy reach, however marginal their offenses.

As with rape, whether a particular woman is coerced or not is something that can only be determined on an individual basis by examining evidence and following established rules of procedure (which often do not exist internationally). To generalize about various and diverse phenomena on a worldwide scale is meaningless. To do so with blanket accusations of criminality is reckless. As feminists understand keenly, once women are "liberated" from traditional constraints they are free to engage in unlimited sex for pleasure or profit or power and then disavow

---

255. Austin Ruse, "New Human Trafficking Foundation May Support Abortion and Prostitution," C-FAM internet site, 12 May 2017, https://c-fam.org/friday_fax/new-human-trafficking-foundation-may-support-abortion-prostitution/.

256. Zheng, "Sex Trafficking," 8–9.

all responsibility by claiming that they were "raped" or "trafficked" or "bullied" or "abused" by men, and it is impossible to prove otherwise. (Homosexualists are adopting similar ploys with "discrimination" and, likewise, "violence.") This is why sexual freedom and sexual radicalism are so open-endedly "empowering," and all the more so when the fool-proof method to escape responsibility for one's own acts is to bring criminal charges against others. No stable or free society can permit such sexual-legal chaos, which is why sexual liberation cannot possibly result in any outcome other than the arbitrary and blanket criminalization of heterosexual men and from there to the collapse of the rule of law altogether.

So does this leave the world helpless before what is undeniably a sordid and degrading business that, because of its international dimensions, is largely beyond the reach of effective law enforcement and justice? Must we simply ignore international prostitution, child labor, and other exploitation? Further, are we powerless against undeniable atrocities by international terrorist groups like ISIS, who, certainly do kidnap women and hold them in conditions that indeed constitute sexual slavery? For (as with rape, child abuse, and the rest) the point here is not that such things do not happen—they certainly do—but that they should not be conflated with streetwalkers in Hoboken and call for a wholly different response.

If individual governments or humanitarian groups have identified instances where specific individuals are truly victims of kidnapping, involuntary servitude, and forced labor that is beyond the reach of any effective legal remedy, and they have the means to rescue such individuals, then they are in conscience bound to do what they can, using any means at their disposal, to alleviate the suffering. Given the anarchy of the international environment, unilateral action undertaken by militaries, private groups, or individuals on a case-by-case basis, even if it requires physical violence, is almost certainly less threatening to the rule of law (and more likely to achieve the desired goal) than is sweeping "empowerment" of centralized governments and international organizations. But unilateral action would require risk, courage, and sacrifice, not empowerment. It is tempting to conclude with the unmentionable obvious: that it would require men to risk their lives to protect women and children, as they have always had to do—the same men who are now being systematically emasculated by the legalistic machinery that claims to empower women but in reality empowers governments and officials.

Islamism as a Sexual Ideology

Sexual radicalism is also polarizing the world and provoking conflict in more violent ways, first religiously and then politically. The threat to Western society from Islamist radicalism is not generally perceived in sexual terms, and its theoretical incompatibility—indeed, its direct antagonism—with the secular sexual ideologies of the West is obvious. Yet these two ideological systems might more instructively be seen less as enemies than as rivals. For all their differences, they share aspirations to political power based on their claims to control the terms of sexual and family relations.

"The centrality of gender relations in the political ideology of Islam" is now widely acknowledged by scholars.[257] Almost all the points of conflict between Islam and the West involve women and sex. "The issue of women is not marginal," write Ian Buruma and Avishai Margalit; "it lies at the heart of Islamic [radicalism]."[258] In the most complex and advanced Islamist country, Iran, "The *hejab* has been identified by the regime as the very cornerstone of its revolution," notes Haideh Moghissi. "It is described as basic to Islamic ideology."[259]

The role of women has long distinguished Islamic from Western, Christian civilization. A Turkish envoy in Vienna in the seventeenth century wrote of a "most extraordinary spectacle": "In this country and in general in the lands of the unbelievers, women have the main say." Historian Bernard Lewis writes that for centuries "The difference in the position of women was indeed one of the most striking contrasts between Christian and Muslim practice and is mentioned by almost all travelers in both directions." Lewis describes the status of women as "probably the most profound single difference between the two civilizations."

Western sexual activists often imply (invariably without providing evidence or explaining why) that the status of women in Islam is somehow connected with the Islamic world's failure to develop economically. There may indeed be some truth in this, though it is hardly as self-evident or simple as its advocates insist. Accepting that the family is society's most basic economic unit, the role of women might well influence

257. Parvin Paidar, *Women and the Political Process in Twentieth Century Iran*, quoted in Masoud Kazemzadeh, *Islamic Fundamentalism, Feminism, and Gender Inequality in Iran Under Khomeini* (Lanham, MD: University Press of America, 2002), 4.

258. Ian Buruma and Avishai Margalit, *Occidentalism: The West in the Eyes of Its Enemies* (New York: Penguin, 2004). The online version of this book does not appear to have page numbers.

259. Haideh Moghissi, ed., *Women and Islam* (London: Routledge, 2004), 77–78.

the family's role as the driver of economic prosperity in the larger society. By this hypothesis, the role of women in Islam may well impede the formation of economically viable and prosperous families. Economic historian David Landes offers a suggestive contrast to Islam in his portrait of Japanese women, their contribution to the household economy, and the implications this carries for economic development and prosperity.[260]

Yet it hardly follows, as sexual libertarians suggest, that programs promoting unlimited sexual liberation and government welfare contribute to economic development; quite the opposite, as we have seen.

Islam's treatment of women also does not proceed simply from some obscurantist refusal to modernize. Lewis points out that today's Muslim extremists have no hesitancy in adopting modern technological and economic methods. Yet Western sexual relations involve not modernization (which is desired) but Westernization (which is not). "The emancipation of women, more than any other single issue, is the touchstone of difference between modernization and Westernization," Lewis writes:

> Even the most extreme and most anti-Western fundamentalists nowadays accept the need to modernize and indeed to make the fullest use of modern technology, especially the technologies of war and propaganda. This is seen as modernization, and though the methods . . . come from the West, it is accepted as necessary. . . . The emancipation of women is Westernization; both for traditional conservatives and radical fundamentalists it is neither necessary nor useful but noxious, a betrayal of true Islamic values. . . . It must be ruthlessly excised.[261]

This issue is not incidental to the clash between the two civilizations; it is central. The standard Western explanations for Islamist resentment of the West are the alleged imperialist and capitalist exploitation of poorer countries (the left) or an irrational hatred of Western society "for our freedom" (the neo-conservative right). Though both are indeed invoked by Islamists, both explanations are inadequate. To begin with, Danesh D'Souza has demonstrated how much of Muslim fear and hatred of the West proceeds from the perception of our sexual depravity: "The main focus of Islamic disgust [over Abu Ghraib] was what Muslims perceived as extreme sexual perversion." In D'Souza's view, Muslim revulsion over the treatment of prisoners proceeded not from its brutality but from its debauchery. "What that female American soldier in uniform did to the Arab man, strip him of his manhood and pull

---

260. *The Wealth and Poverty of Nations* (New York: Norton, 1999), ch. 24.
261. Lewis, *What Went Wrong?*, 73.

him on a leash," comments one Muslim, "this is what America wants to do to the Muslim world."

This fear for "manhood" is echoed by terrorists like Osama bin Laden himself: "They want to skin us from our manhood." There can be no doubt that this directly fuels Muslim radicalism. "The West is . . . a society where the woman does as she pleases even if she is married, a society in which the number of illegitimate children approaches and sometimes surpasses the number of children from permitted unions," declares one radical sheikh. "These putrid ideas . . . are being pushed on us in the name of women's rights."[262]

Such perceptions are simply facts that the West refuses to face and whose consequences are having a debilitating effect on Western society itself. "The most basic right of a child is to have two parents, and this right is taken away from nearly half of the children in Western society," writes one Muslim scholar, also quite accurately.[263] Western fathers who are not permitted to see their children and incarcerated without trial on any number of pretexts might well validate this assessment and that of the Ayatollah Mottahari, who describes the Western welfare state and divorce machinery in incontestable terms:

> The replacement of the father by the government, which is the current trend in the West, will undermine maternal sentiments, alter the very nature of motherhood from an emotional tie into a form of waged employment with money as an intermediary between mother and her love; motherhood then is no longer a bond, but a paid employment. It is obvious that this process would lead to the destruction of the family.[264]

Here is yet another instance of the absence of opposition and even active collusion by conservatives who profess family values but whose own ideological agenda takes priority. "Conservatives completely missed the significance of Abu Ghraib," writes D'Souza. "In trying to defend the indefensible, conservatives became cheap apologists for liberal debauchery." Claiming to stand for traditional morality, conservatives driven by a political agenda end up defending sexual depravity. "They sometimes make it sound as though they would have no objec-

---

262. Danesh D'Souza, *The Enemy at Home: The Cultural Left and Its Responsibility for 9/11* (New York: Doubleday, 2007), 150, 152.

263. Ibid., 153.

264. Quoted in Abida Samiuddin, "Iranian Women and their Support for Islam," in *Muslim Feminist and Feminist Movement: Middle East—Asia*, vol. 1, ed. Abida Samiuddin and R. Khanam (Delhi: Global Vision, 2002), 312. Cp. Stephen Baskerville, "From Welfare State to Police State," *The Independent Review*, vol. 12, no. 3 (Winter 2008).

tion to Islam if only Muslim girls were free to wear miniskirts, join the army, and divorce their husbands," notes another observer.[265]

Yet D'Souza draws his material on this point not from some Islamic family values advocates but from the leading perpetrators of Islamist terror, such as bin Laden and Sayyid Qutb. If he means to suggest that Islamist militancy is a simple return to family values (much as the Western left tries to equate the Islamic State with Focus on the Family), he should be disabused. It is an extremist ideology that freely borrows from its kindred Western ideologies, revolutionary Fascism and Marxism. "While steeped in Islamic myth and forms, the events of 1979 represented first and foremost a political revolution," writes a scholar, referring to Islamism's most sophisticated creation so far:

> Khomeini's revolutionary role models were secular and, for the most part, Western. During the revolution and since, revolutionary political goals have always taken precedence over religious goals. . . . Iranian law contains many non-Islamic concepts: legal (if not *yet* actual) *equality between the sexes concerning property, employment, and family rights.*[266]

Indeed, unlikely as it may seem (and as the last line indicates), even feminism manages to make its peace with radical Islam, as we will see shortly.[267]

Islamism thus constitutes a complex and potent mixture of anti-Western grievances whose eclecticism divides Westerners themselves in their response and allows Islamists to increase in influence within Western societies. Muslim immigration into Europe and its dilution of Western culture is perhaps most politically alarming with the importation of Islamic law, sharia, as a parallel legal system. Law constitutes a nation's claim to sovereignty. Allowing alternative or parallel legal systems within a nation's borders seriously undermines its sovereignty and independence. It is a major step toward a "failed state." The fact that Islamic law recognizes no separation of religious from secular law further undermines Western values, as does the fact that Islam shows little respect for national borders and state sovereignty.

Yet it is also no accident—though it is ignored by scholars—that the

265. D'Souza, *Enemy at Home*, 151; F. Roger Devlin, *Sexual Utopia in Power* (San Francisco: Counter-Currents, 2015), 101.

266. Caroline Ziemke, "The National Myth and Strategic Personality of Iran: A Counterproliferation Perspective," in *The Coming Crisis: Nuclear Proliferation, US Interests, and World Order*, ed. Victor A. Utgoff (Cambridge, MA: Belfer Center for Science and International Affairs, 2000), 98–99 (emphases added).

267. Kay S. Hymowitz, "Why Feminism is AWOL on Islam," *City Journal*, Winter 2003.

main wedge inserting sharia law into Western society is family law. Laws covering divorce and child custody are precisely the ones where Muslims first and most frequently demand to observe *sharia*. *Sharia* councils and Muslim Arbitration Tribunals, recognized by the British government and the Archbishop of Canterbury, judge in civil, not criminal, cases. Significantly, they "judge cases relating to economy, divorce, domestic violence, inheritance, and forced marriage." According to one scholar: "In Norwegian court decisions, *especially in family cases*, I see that Muslims argue in the same way . . . as they would in sharia courts in Muslim countries."

Westerners, including conservatives who are the most alarmed about *sharia*, are obliging the Muslims by reflexively and blindly asserting the superiority of "liberal"—meaning sexually innovative and permissive—Western family law. As we have seen, Western family law is the arena and source of radical and flagrantly unjust innovations that few of its apologists themselves understand. "They think that women are at risk of being pressured by their family or others in their community to solve conflicts via the *sharia* council instead of British law, because women end up more badly than men in Islamic legislation." Therefore we must rescue these women without first bothering to ask where justice lies. And what precisely are the heinous injustices that sharia law inflicts on women? "Divorce isn't as easy for women to obtain."[268]

If this is the most serious charge the Norwegians can marshal against Islamic law, it is hardly surprising if potential recruits to Islamism are tempted to conclude that perhaps it is not so onerous after all. The point is that the refusal to confront the injustices of Western family law leaves Western society defenseless against a more rigorous Islamic system of justice and morality and opens the door to importing *sharia* law in a realm that it confronts and Western law does not. Blindly asserting the superiority of Western law in a matter where it is obviously seriously defective (or worse, citing its most serious defects as evidence of its superiority) is evading, not confronting, the problem of how to resist *sharia* and its appeal. Here sexual freedom and family deterioration weaken Western society not only socially but through sovereignty, defense, and security.

And yet to compound the ironies (and to offer further insight on the compatibility of Islamism with Western sexual ideology), it turns out that these restrictions that *sharia* allegedly places on women, especially in their Islamist form, may not be nearly so restrictive as we are led to

---

268. "Norway: Sharia Courts a Possibility," *EuropeNews*, 21 June 2010 (http://europe-news.dk/en/node/33097, emphasis added).

believe. Despite media obsessions with female attire, in the areas that truly matter (and the ones studiously ignored by the media) women have acquired enormous power in Islamic—and especially Islamist—society, especially in better-educated societies like Egypt and Iran, where their power is hardly inferior to their sisters in the West.

The areas that matter, once again, are family law—the critical one being, also as indicated above, divorce. In not only Egypt and Iran, but other Islamic societies like Pakistan and Bangladesh, women now have the power to divorce unilaterally and without grounds—in effect, "no-fault" divorce. In 2000, Egypt enacted a law providing for *talaq-i-tafwid*, or the ability of the wife to divorce unilaterally without giving reasons.[269] In fact, this is also the case in many Islamic countries. "Through *talaq-i-tafweez* the wife can initiate divorce without requiring any permission or agreement from the husband, and retains all her financial rights," we are told. "She does not have to prove any grounds for divorce."[270] Compared with this power, regulations on fashion are trivial.

This provides some perspective on what is for many the most perplexing paradox: the substantial role women play in radical Islamism, especially in its most sophisticated and successful episode, the 1979 Iranian Revolution. If Islamist radicalism so severely oppresses women, why does it attract so much enthusiastic support from such large numbers of them? "Many observers have wondered why women in the hundreds of thousands, including educated women, actively supported a movement which appeared to curtail their rights."[271] That they in fact did and do so is undeniable, especially (but not only) in the complex circumstances of Iran. "A distinctive feature of the Iranian Revolution was the participation of large groups of women," writes a feminist scholar.[272] "Women have acquired a very prominent position in the ideology as well as practice of the Islamic Revolution and the Islamic Republic." This is often explained away as part of the general opposition to the Shah rather than enthusiasm for a specifically Islamist regime, but this is much too easy. "In the case of women . . . the most militant advocates of Islamisation are among the highly educated graduates of

269. *The Islamic Marriage Contract: Case Studies in Islamic Family Law*, ed. Asifa Quraishi and Frank E. Vogel (Cambridge, MA: Harvard University Press, 2008), 242. I owe this reference to Alyssa Mundy.

270. Muslim Marriage Contract website: http://muslimmarriagecontract.org/contract.html#delegation_of_divorce (accessed 16 December 2013).

271. Ruth Roded, *Women in Islam and the Middle East* (London: I.B. Tauris, 1999), 255. It is unclear from the text who precisely is speaking.

272. Anne Betteridge, "To Veil or Not to Veil: A Matter of Protest or Policy" in *Women and Revolution in Iran*, ed. Guity Nashat (Boulder: Westview Press, 1983), 109.

universities."[273] These were consciously dedicated Islamist women, attired decidedly in veils and often armed. "Observers have all noted the presence and activism of women in the Islamist movement," writes Olivier Roy; "recall the demonstrations of armed and veiled women in Iran." Often too they were prominent spokeswomen for the movement. "Both Iran and Egypt boast an elite class of Islamist intellectual women who write and are published."[274]

Political correctness notwithstanding, these women are not coerced into this involvement. They are part of a movement consciously seeking political power, and they understand the most effective means of attaining it. Islamist sexual puritanism, like all radical puritanism, is a claim to moral superiority and therefore a challenge to existing political authority.[275] The creed of all radicals is that the morally virtuous are the most entitled to rule and the most effective in doing so. Sexual purity for Muslim radicals confers the authority to fight and to rule for God. This is true for women as well as men.

The revolutionaries themselves saw it as a method of empowering women, admittedly on their own terms and for their own purposes. Ayatollah Khomeini explained to journalist Oriana Fallaci, in terms worthy of a Western feminist, the kind of women who helped make "the Revolution":

> The women who contributed to the Revolution were, and are, women in Islamic dress, not elegant women all made up like you, who go around all uncovered, dragging behind them a tail of men. The coquettes who put on makeup and go in the street showing off their necks, their hair, their shapes, did not fight against the Shah. They never did anything good, not those. They do not know how to be useful, neither socially, nor politically, nor professionally.[276]

The fact that some later felt betrayed and turned against the regime tells nothing against validity of this logic; revolutions always alienate and devour their own children. The women knew what they were doing. They were consciously participating in the acquisition of power, and they understood very well that sexual puritanism was the most effective

---

273. Afsaneh Najmabadi, "Hazards of Modernity and Morality: Women, State, and Ideology in Contemporary Iran," in *Women, Islam, and the State*, ed. Deniz Kandiyoti (Philadelphia: Temple University Press, 1991), 63–64.

274. Olivier Roy, *Failure of Political Islam* (Cambridge, MA: Harvard University Press, 1998), 59.

275. Michael Walzer, *The Revolution of the Saints* (Cambridge, MA: Harvard University Press, 1965).

276. Quoted in Betteridge, "To Veil or Not to Veil," 122.

and, in the event, successful means of acquiring it. The required rhetorical and ideological casuistry is not difficult: "The values and standards of dependence on imperialism and capitalism make of woman the object of lust, a most desirable object that must beauty [*sic*] and expose herself."[277]

Militant Islamism is a political religion and ideology that freely borrows from other ideologies whatever serves its purpose, and as we have seen it has frequently borrowed ideas and methods from the Western left.[278] It is hardly surprising therefore that it can co-exist even with radical feminism. For Islamism is also a sexually driven ideology, no less so than feminism or homosexualism, because it understands that political power derives from controlling the terms of sexuality and the family. This explains the paradoxical *pas de deux* between the two ideological systems. After the hundreds of tomes and articles and media reports on the relationship between women, feminism, and Islam (now a major publishing industry in Western academia), this is the constant to which it all reduces. Islamists and feminists share the human craving for power. Everything else can be subject to debate: the veil, the chador, divorce law, welfare, the place of women, ideological purity. But the bottom line is power. If it can be achieved through the veil, the veil will be worn willingly and even enthusiastically. If not, the veil will readily be discarded. But the criterion for all such questions is what delivers power—or, as we hear *ad nauseam*, "empowerment."

Homosexualist militants too are becoming adept at the game. They enlist the sympathy and support of Western neo-conservatives by posing as the victims of Islamic "homophobia."[279] Meanwhile they team-up with Islamist militants as the common victims of the traditionally Christian West. It is no accident that Islamists and homosexualists have devised parallel language to express parallel grievances against "Islamophobia" and "homophobia" and that both groups demand government protection from "discrimination" and "harassment," which is defined as private individuals professing their political or religious beliefs.[280] These two groups alone successfully demand officially-enforced immunity from criticism and punishment of those they deem guilty of "hate speech" for criticizing them or their agenda.

277. Zahra Rahnavard, quoted in Samiuddin, "Iranian Women," 298.

278. Malise Ruthven, "'Born-again' Muslims: Cultural Schizophrenia," *Open Democracy*, 10 September 2009, http://www.opendemocracy.net/faith-islamicworld/article_103.jsp.

279. Jamie Glasov, "Did the Cultural Left Cause 9/11?" *FrontPageMag*.com, 25 January 2007, http://archive.frontpagemag.com/readArticle.aspx?ARTID=475.

280. See above, under "Sex and the International Regime."

Failure to understand and confront these dynamics allows the world's sexual ideologues—feminist, homosexualist, and Islamist—to make common cause against the West and divide the defenders of traditional Western values. It also leaves Western defenders indecisive and helpless in their responses, as they seek to respond to terrorism in a "gender sensitive manner."[281]

Even today, as young Western women enlist in the ranks of the fanatical Islamic State, it is clear that they seek both power for themselves and to attach themselves to power-seeking men—thus exploiting what feminists make possible: both male and female forms of power. Female recruits supervise the morals brigades, policing the public sexual morality of the occupied territories. "Al-Khanssaa patrols walk the streets of Raqqa seeking out inappropriate mixing of the sexes and anyone engaging in Western culture," according to Melanie Smith of the International Centre for the Study of Radicalisation at King's College, London.

And it is the women fleeing Western decadence who are the most zealous. "The British women are being given key roles in the brigade because they are considered by ISIL commanders to be the most committed of the foreign female jihadis to the cause," according to the *Daily Telegraph*, quoting Smith. "The British women are some of the most zealous in imposing the IS laws in the region." But they do not seek simply to exercise power themselves; they also want to be the brides of power-driven men:

> Many of the women heading for Syria had gone there to find a husband among the jihadi fighters. . . .
>
> Miss Smith says the jihadi social media is "buzzing" with marriage proposals, and many of the fighters have taken several wives. . . .
>
> Miss Smith said a famous Dutch jihadi, known as Yilmaz, who married this week has "broken the hearts" of scores of Western Muslim women who have all made marriage proposals in the last few months.
>
> A monitor of Yilmaz's internet accounts show that he received an astonishing 10,000 marriage requests during his time as a jihadi fighter up until his marriage.
>
> Miss Smith said: "It is clear that some of these women who have been travelling to Syria have since married jihadists and foreign fighters." Some, said Miss Smith, want to marry a martyr.[282]

---

281. Organization for Security and Cooperation in Europe website: http://www.osce.org/odihr/145681, 19 March 2015.

282. *Daily Telegraph*, "British Female Jihadis Sign Up to the Islamic State's All-Women Police Force," 7 September 2014 (http://www.telegraph.co.uk/news/uknews/terrorism-in-the-uk/11079386/British-female-jihadis-sign-up-to-the-Islamic-States-all-women-police-force.html).

Nina Shea perceives the significance through the West's stultifying ideological correctness: "She is no innocent, duped into a life of terror, or pushover for male domination," Shea writes of one of the leading morals policewomen. "She is living refutation of the theory that female empowerment alone is the path to Islamic moderation, as the State Department has long maintained.... For too long, American forces seemed to underestimate such women, taking them to be simply victims within a large undifferentiated class of oppressed women."[283]

As always, both sides of the dynamic involve power, both directly for themselves and indirectly through their new husbands. Thus they have the advantage of all worlds: exercising power as both terrorists and victims—and, like child soldiers, immune from criticism. Is the Dutch woman who joined jihadists because she wanted to marry a "real man" typical of young women confused by the relentless feminization and emasculation of Western society?[284] The headline is revealing of Western moral indirection and legal nihilism: "Dutch jihadi bride: 'Is she a victim or a suspect?'"

Sexualizing War

The military is the greatest bastion of masculinity in any society, for obvious reasons. "Nowhere is the assault on manhood and masculinity more explicit—or more dangerous—than in the American military," writes Kathleen Parker. "The military is the Maginot Line in the battle of the sexes, the final remaining bastion of institutionalized masculinity and the last place left in the civilized world where characteristically male traits—aggression, risk taking, courage, and strength—are respected and valued."[285]

For precisely these reasons, the armed forces are now a major battleground in radical sexual politics. Despite a huge government and media propaganda campaign promoting it and touting its unqualified "success," feminization is predictably eviscerating military effectiveness and power. "No sooner did many women begin to enter the armed forces during the 1970s than their presence started giving rise to endless, and continuing, trouble," writes one eminent military authority. "It is hardly possible to open a newspaper or switch on the TV without coming

283. Nina Shea, "Equal Opportunity Terrorism," *The Weekly Standard*, 19 October 2015 (http://www.weeklystandard.com/articles/equal-opportunity-terrorism_1042864.html).

284. *Daily Telegraph*, 23 November 2013 (http://www.telegraph.co.uk/news/worldne ws/islamic-state/11247941/Dutch-jihadi-bride-Is-she-a-victim-or-a-suspect.html).

285. Kathleen Parker, *Save the Males: Why Men Matter and Women Should Care* (New York: Random House, 2008), 158.

across some story of the damage that feminization is causing both in fiscal terms and from the point of view of fighting power."[286] Here more than anywhere can be seen not only the debilitating effects of feminization but the bizarre contradictions that must arise from demonizing masculinity and banishing masculine behavior while simultaneously pretending that no such thing exists. Military affairs are a world conveniently separate from the experience of people who agitate for feminization and denigrate masculinity. "What we are sacrificing in the push to satisfy civilian goals of absolute equality is the reality of what it takes to prevail against real enemies in war and to save real lives," writes Parker. "We have allowed ourselves to enter a pretend world where what is false is true—and we have turned a blind eye to the consequences in the name of equality."[287] Here, more starkly than elsewhere, can be seen how the radical sexual agenda—where euphemisms such as "equality" and "discrimination" trump all other values—undermines the structures of a stable, prosperous, and free society. It is perhaps not surprising that campaigns to feminize and sexualize the military are having widespread rebound effects throughout society. Because the military is the most powerful man-made physical force, its politicization always threatens civic freedom.

Masculinity and specifically masculine virtues are not simply integral to military effectiveness; they are virtually synonymous with it. To populate military units with women who lack physical strength and endurance, who are not required to demonstrate physical courage, who feel no need to overcome or hide their weaknesses, who elicit sexual attractions from soldiers and experience sexual attractions themselves, who become pregnant, and who demand special protections and privileges—this debilitates military effectiveness and strength in ways too obvious to need describing. The presence of homosexuals who do not accept traditional standards of masculine conduct, who claim the prerogative to assume quasi-feminine behavior when they choose, and who experience sexual attractions toward other soldiers, has comparable effects.

What does need describing is the political determination to push forward an impossible agenda of creating a sex-neutral and sexualized military—regardless of the distortions, deceptions, and mendacity required or the punishments inevitably meted out to silence those who speak the

---

286. Martin Van Creveld, *Men, Women, and War* (London: Cassell & Co., 2001), 193, 10.
287. Parker, *Save the Males*, 158.

truth about how impractical, counterproductive, and dangerous this project is to an effective fighting force and a free society.

The eminent military historian and theorist Martin Van Creveld summarizes the experiment in treating Western militaries "not as fight machines but as social laboratories for some feminist brave new world":

> This they do by compelling the forces to pretend, against all the evidence that soldiers and doctors can muster, that women are as fit for war as men: ... turn training into a mockery and humiliation for those men who are involved in it alongside women; absorb the extra costs involved in paying for everything from separate toilets to pregnancy care and from special uniforms to post-natal leave of absence; deny or cover up any damage done and loss suffered; and ignore or silence or discharge anybody who objects.[288]

Similar mendacity has recently been extended to homosexuals, who here as elsewhere have piggybacked onto the feminists' agenda. "Gay activists began ... arguing that if mixing men and women in the military didn't reduce readiness, how could mixing gays and straights?" Brian Mitchell points out. "It was no accident that the drive for gays in the military followed so closely the successful drive for women in combat, or that feminist champions ... lined up in support of gays. The advocates of both movements ... used the same arguments ... and both were determined to use the military to revolutionize American society." Perhaps even more than feminism, homosexualism has introduced ideology into the military mission. "For more than two centuries, the US military never had a public celebration of anybody's sex life—until the recent 'gay pride' event under the Obama administration," writes Thomas Sowell. "Here as elsewhere, the gay political agenda is not equality but privilege."[289]

Any experienced soldier can testify that a unique relationship is necessary and cultivated among fighting men, a relationship of cohesion and trust without which survival, let alone success, is not possible. "Combat is a team endeavor," explains John Luddy, a former Marine infantry officer: "To win in combat, individuals must be trained to subjugate their individual instinct for self-preservation to the needs of their unit. Since most people are not naturally inclined to do this, military training must break down an individual and recast him as part of a team. This is why recruits give up their first names and why they look,

---

288. Ibid., 11.

289. Brian Mitchell, *Women in the Military: Flirting with Disaster* (Washington: Regnery, 1998), 280–82; Thomas Sowell, "Random Thoughts," *Jewish World Review*, 25 July 2012, http://jewishworldreview.com/cols/sowell072512.php3#.UrmG0_RDuSo.

act, dress, and train alike."[290] Sexual dynamics undermine this fundamentally. As a senior Marine officer writes: "I can tell you, first hand, that females and males in forward deployed units do not mix well. Flirtations and relationships on ships and remotely deployed units do have an adverse effect on morale and unit cohesiveness. We deal with it every day here in Iraq."[291]

Combat effectiveness "requires a unique blend of skills, ethics, culture, and bonding to ensure an effective warfighting force."[292] The presence of both women and homosexuals undermines this. The notion that a commanding officer can be having sex with a woman or with several men in his unit without undermining cohesion, morale, discipline, respect, or authority is patently ludicrous. From a military standpoint, the very idea of admitting women and open homosexuals into fighting units borders on madness.

Yet this is precisely what has been imposed on the armed forces. So much has been written about the debilitating effects of women in combat that it requires little treatment here. They have far higher rates of attrition, much greater need for medical care, much higher rates of nonavailability, lower rates of deployability, and of course less strength, endurance, and overall physical ability.[293] In training, much less is expected of female recruits, standards are lowered both for them and for all recruits in a futile pretense at uniformity, and resentment is inspired by men toward women and one another.[294] In Air Force Academy training, "very few of the women could perform one pull-up or complete any of the other events," and so different standards were devised for them. Predictably:

> They fell out of group runs, lagged behind on road marches, failed to negotiate obstacles on the assault courses (later modified to make them easier), could not climb a rope, and sometimes broke down in tears when confronted with their own limitations. The rate at which the female cadets sought medical attention could hardly have allowed them to keep up the pace of training.[295]

290. Albert Mohler, "Homosexuality and the Military—What's Really at Stake?" Albert Mohler.com, 4 June 2010, http://www.albertmohler.com/2010/06/04/homosexuality-and-the-military-whats-really-at-stake/.

291. Elaine Donnelly, "Constructing the Co-Ed Military," *Duke Journal of Gender Law and Policy*, vol. 14 (2007), 943 (http://www.law.duke.edu/shell/cite.pl?14+Duke+J.+Gender+L.+&+Pol%27y+815).

292. Robert Maginnis, "Gay Review and Combat Effectiveness," *Human Events*, 4 March 2010 (http://www.humanevents.com/article.php?id=35839).

293. Mitchell, *Women in the Military*, 348.

294. Ibid., ch. 3.

295. Ibid., 43.

Women could not negotiate obstacle courses. "Nor could women throw a hand-grenade . . . to the minimum distance necessary so that they would not be blown to pieces." They suffer many times the number of injuries as men and visit doctors multiple times more frequently.[296]

Accounts of women in combat or other physically demanding tasks sound like the misadventures of the Keystone Kops. "Time previously devoted to marksmanship had to be dropped in favour of classes in contraception." Women are permitted to keep their hair and wear jewelry, and female officers may carry umbrellas "to protect their hair." Women are (or at least were) allowed to keep stuffed toy animals in their bunks. Orientation videos tell female recruits, "It's okay to cry."[297]

Drill sergeants and others responsible for maintaining disciplinary standards must instead be sensitive to the recruits' feelings and check their discipline, lest someone cry and lodge a complaint about "trainee abuse." "It changes the way you think," says one. "It's like you are protecting your own interests."[298] In other words, it politicizes military life and transforms the relationship between soldiers (as it has already transformed that between men and women) from one of camaraderie and solidarity into an unending contest for power.

Women require extensive accommodations in battlefield situations, alterations in military structure and organization, and expensive technological changes. Weapons and equipment are redesigned so women can use them, even when the results are inferior. Prior to deployments, women suddenly become pregnant in large numbers and are excused from duty. When combat actually commences, commanders are "flooded with requests from female soldiers for transfers to the rear." With little fear of punishment, women simply refuse to engage in training exercises and battlefield operations, desert their posts, break down in tears, and otherwise exhibit behavior that in men is (or used to be) called cowardice.[299]

In the Navy, "most female recruits preferred traditional jobs comfortably ashore to dirty work on the rolling waves," and they are duly accommodated. The Navy has been pressured to lengthen submarines in order to accommodate women. "In almost every instance the good of equal opportunity takes precedence over the good of the service." As a

---

296. Van Creveld, *Men, Women, and War*, 193–94.

297. Ibid., 195–6, 214; Parker, *Save the Males*, 175.

298. Mitchell, *Women in the Military*, xiii. See also Susan Keating, "Was It Fixed?" *People*, 25 September 2015, http://www.people.com/article/female-ranger-school-graduation-planned-advance.

299. Ibid., 145–47, 204–5, 78.

physiologist wrote in the *Navy Times*, "the Navy's recent enthusiasm for putting more and more women aboard ship makes little sense, unless the Navy doesn't mind sacrificing survivability (and possibly the lives of its sailors) for the sake of enhancing opportunities for women."[300]

Sex among soldiers and pregnancy present additional complications. Even pregnant women are not automatically discharged. They may abrogate their commitment and leave without penalty, or they can carry on pretending to be soldiers, though with so many exemptions and privileges that they become even more of a burden to their units than usual.[301]

Mitchell provides numerous testimonies from women who develop second thoughts when they discover the realities of combat. "I'm a woman and a mother before I'm a soldier," one said, in tears. "If this is a test, I'm gonna fail. A lot of other women are too, and I guess we're just going to have to accept that." Striking is the defensive tone of these women's testimony, as if they feel they must be ashamed of the realities of being women. "A mother should be left with her children," said another. "It doesn't fit with the whole scheme of the women's movement, but I think we have to reconsider what we're doing." One seems to detect a tone of disappointment at having to jettison some ideological principle that would otherwise hold the status of sacred orthodoxy and that they are made to feel they have betrayed. "I'd rather be home cooking and cleaning, all those things I've been complaining about for twenty-six years," said a third. "I don't think females should be over here. They can't handle it," said a fourth. "Those feminists back home who say we have a right to fight are not out here sitting in the heat carrying an M16 and a gas mask, spending sixteen hours on the road every day and sleeping in fear you're gonna get gassed." As Mitchell adds with understatement, "Their male comrades were understandably resentful."[302]

The contradiction is seen in the disparate attitudes of female officers and enlisted women and in the resentment of the latter. "The way enlisted women saw it, female officers did not grasp the physical hardship that combat entailed in the enlisted level; this was even more true for their supporters in the feminist lobbies, hardly any of whom had ever spent a day in the military," Van Creveld notes. "Thus it all boiled down to an attempt by well-educated, well-to-do, successful women to advance their own careers and political agendas ... at the expense of

300. Ibid., 130, 144, 147; Donnelly, "Constructing the Co-Ed Military," 856–69.
301. Mitchell, *Women in the Military*, 151–56.
302. Ibid., 203–4.

their poorly educated, less affluent, less successful 'sisters.'"[303] An official survey found that more than 92.5% of Army women said they did not want to be assigned to units such as the infantry, armor, artillery, and combat engineers.[304]

Sexualization also exposes soldiers, even more than other men, to the feminist honey trap (which partly explains its appeal). The presence of "cadets with beautiful, boyish hair . . . was an appeal that touched fantasies," according to one account. In an institution populated by young men, the main reason why feminization has proceeded so irresistibly is because women are so irresistible. "The men were charmed," writes Mitchell.

> They could never see the women as just cadets, and they could never treat women as they treated men. Men who remained critical of women in general could not be so critical of individual women they had come to know. The women were just too hard to hate. Some men could bluster threats and insults from a distance, but when they came face to face with the enemy, they quailed out of natural affection and decency.[305]

Writ large, this may explain why feminization, once undertaken, proceeds inexorably in any institution.

Beyond the sweet romance, the women also presented opportunities for casual sex and debauchery, which became rampant throughout the services after they were admitted. Women themselves are the main advocates for easing regulations against "fraternization" or romantic and sexual relationships between service personnel. "Instead of making servicewomen conform to the service, the services have conformed to the women."[306]

Given the political motivation driving all this from the start, neither the charm nor the pleasure could last. Even more than in civilian life, romance and indulgence predictably opened the door to accusations of gender crimes against the men, now almost a nightly news feature. The Navy's infamous Tailhook affair was only the most sensational example of how sexual indulgence, even when completely consensual, created the opportunity for feminist ideologues to launch not only accusations of pseudo-crimes against military men but also—with hardly anyone noticing the sleight-of-hand—simultaneous attacks on military values

303. Van Creveld, *Men, Women, and War*, 213.

304. Center for Military Readiness website (2015): http://cmrlink.org/data/sites/85/CMRDocuments/FactSheet-WDGC2015.pdf.

305. Mitchell, *Women in the Military*, 68–69.

306. Ibid., 161.

themselves. As elsewhere, rather than being presented as a breakdown of both standard military discipline and traditional sexual morality, "the event was judged by newer, feminist standards, which came down hard on the men but went easy on the women." The result offered a huge opportunity to replace standard discipline with ideological indoctrination. In meting out punishments, the Navy sent "a very important message" that it planned, not to restore the standard discipline and morality that had long existed to prevent precisely such indulgence and the unpleasantness that inevitably arises from it, but to impose feminist ideology on its personnel and purge all non-feminists from its ranks. "We get it," declared a spokesman: "We know that the larger issue is a culture problem which has allowed demeaning behavior and attitudes toward women to exist within the Navy Department.... Sexual harassment will not be tolerated, and those who don't get that message will be driven from our ranks."

Not simply for their sexual immorality, but for their ideologically incorrect "attitudes," the Navy launched what Mitchell calls a "witch hunt," a purge reminiscent of the Communist regimes, in which "aviators found themselves hounded like vicious criminals":

> Officers reported being threatened with punishment or dismissal or with having their names leaked to the media if they did not cooperate. One Marine officer claimed that he was threatened with an IRS audit and subsequently endured one. Some were offered immunity in exchange for incriminating testimony. Others were ordered to take polygraphs. Agents asked suspects probing questions about their sex lives such as whether they masturbated. They even attempted to intimidate officers' wives at home to get information.... In one case, a Defense Department agent tricked a civilian nurse ... into signing a statement alleging that Navy Lieutenant Cole V. Cowden ... had sexually assaulted her by pressing his face against her chest, even though the woman repeatedly said that she did not consider Cowden's actions an assault or herself a victim.[307]

In the ensuing purge no one was spared, including senior officers with distinguished careers and "men who were expert in performing their military missions, men whom the Navy had spent hundreds of millions of dollars to train, men with decades of experience, who had been tested in combat, and who had offered their lives in the service of their country."[308] And of course it was only the men.

---

307. Ibid., 259, 271–72.
308. Ibid., 278.

In the years following Tailhook the military was besieged with accusations of the same gender crimes now familiar in civilian life: rape, sexual assault, sexual harassment. When these produced too many acquittals, the rules were changed to ensure more convictions. "For all the talk about rape, there was very little evidence of it," writes Mitchell, though there was evidence of using accusations of it for political purposes. "Five women lined up and publicly accused Army investigators of trying to blackmail them into making *false* accusations of rape, and threatening to charge them with fraternization and sexual misconduct if they did not cooperate." One sergeant was convicted, even though "one woman testified that she not only had sex 'willingly' but that investigators pressured her into accusing" him falsely.[309]

All this follows the stock feminist formula for female "empowerment": relentless pressure to lower standards on sexual morality and encourage permissiveness and promiscuity followed by prosecutions of men for gender crimes—replacing morality with ideology. "The military's moral standards . . . were too high, according to the know-it-all nonveterans in the media and in Congress," writes Mitchell (who describes how the formula was eventually applied to homosexuals as well). "At the same time, the services were more obligated than ever to prosecute men for the slightest sexual infraction."[310]

Throughout the Western world during these years, "Hundreds of regulations aimed at defining, preventing, and punishing 'sexual harassment' were instituted," as Van Creveld recounts. "In one military after another, 'hot lines' were opened to enable female soldiers to inform on their male comrades behind the latter's backs." The result now is that "On both sides of the Atlantic . . . scarcely a week goes by without some unfortunate male officer or soldier being accused of 'sexual harassment' and being hounded out of the services." The *modus operandi* is familiar from civilian life: "Even if the alleged incident took place many years previously; even if it was the woman who made the initial advances and seduced him; even if his record of service is otherwise excellent; often even if he is found innocent of the charges."[311]

The leftist Palm Center now alleges an "epidemic of internal violence, of rape by US soldiers of their comrades." Their evidence? A female soldier making a spectacle of herself in a shopping mall says so, along with unsubstantiated "reports" of the kind we have encountered when feminists issue wild accusations of rape, domestic violence, and child

---

309. Ibid., 211, 213.
310. Ibid., 319–20.
311. Van Creveld, *Men, Women, and War,* 219, 10.

abuse.[312] As Elaine Donnelly of the Center for Military Readiness writes, "Professional victimologists routinely confuse one-sided allegations with substantiated crimes, excuse women of the consequences of their own high-risk behavior, demand punishment even when self-proclaimed victims do not report offenses, and are not satisfied with anything less than courts-martial and convictions, even when guilt is unproven."[313] Claims by the Pentagon and the Obama administration to quantify an epidemic of sexual assault have repeatedly been shown to be based on concocted statistics.[314]

This politicized hysteria over "violence against women" is especially ironic and self-contradictory because, of course, it directly contradicts the purpose of the military. The same activists who characterize verbal arguments and consensual sex as "violence" and urge ruthless prosecution of men not only ignore, but themselves are, the leading advocates for exposing women to real and deadly violence in war. "Many officials in Congress, the Pentagon, and the service academies are eager to establish ubiquitous 'victim advocate' offices, staffed by professionals who vow to protect military women from the slightest form of harassment, real or imagined," writes Donnelly. "The same officials simultaneously promote the deliberate exposure of military women to extreme abuse and violence in close, lethal combat, where females do not have an equal opportunity to survive or to help fellow soldiers survive." Here too, political ideology has acculturated us to a double standard reaching bizarre dimensions by immunizing us from the horror of unnecessary violent death: "Allegations of sexual abuse in the military inspire outrage, but news stories about unprecedented numbers of women killed and injured in the war are met with stoic and resigned acceptance," Donnelly adds. "Soldiers are beginning to doubt the judgment of their leaders, although they are rarely asked or permitted to express their concerns publicly. Ordering women into land combat also creates a moral and cultural contradiction: violence against women is all right, as long as it happens at the hands of the enemy." [315] Here as elsewhere, the

---

312. Palm Center internet site: www.palmcenter.org/blog/jeanne_scheper/Performa nce%20Brings%20Attention%20to%20Sexual%20Violence%20in%20the%20U.S.%20 Military.

313. Elaine Donnelly, "Pentagon Anti-Male Room?" *Washington Times*, 2 February 2006 (http://www.washtimes.com/functions/print.php?StoryID=20060201-090147-3512r).

314. Rowan Scarborough, "Doubts on Military's Sex Assault Stats as Numbers Far Exceed Those for the US," *Washington Times*, 6 April 2014 (http://www.washingtontim es.com/news/2014/apr/6/doubts-on-militarys-sex-assault-stats-as-numbers-f/?page=all #pagebreak).

315. Donnelly, "Constructing the Co-Ed Military," 931–32, 849–50.

illogic proceeds not from any failure to understand what is happening (let alone from any real concern for the women). Clearly driving both sides of the peculiar contradiction is the ideologues' pursuit of power.

This purpose is rendered stark by realizing how integral it is to the sexual debauchery in the first place—most strikingly when initiated, as it often is, by the women. Note Kayla Williams' choice of words to describe the sexual bonanza for women at being admitted to the company of so many captive and sex-starved men. "Their eyes, their hunger: yes, its shaming—but they also make you special," she writes. "I don't like to say it—it cuts you inside—but the attention, the admiration, the need: they make you powerful." Whether it is luring the men into sex, or springing the legal trap once they take the bait, the bottom line throughout, once again, is always power. Williams manages to swallow the politically incorrect truth because it is politically essential. "If you're a woman in the Army, it doesn't matter so much about your looks. What counts is that you are female." Sexual integration has predictably turned the Army into a brothel, and not only by the men. As if it were necessary, Williams describes how the competition for power plays out among the competitors. "And I know something else," she adds:

> How these same guys you want to piss on become *your* guys. Another girl enters your tent, and they look at her the way they looked at you, and what drove you crazy with anger suddenly drives you crazy with jealousy. They're yours. F—k, you left your husband to be with them, you walked out on him for them. These guys, they're your husband, they're your father, your brother, your lover—your life.[316]

In such circumstances, the contradictions make functional life impossible. "Men don't know how to act because some women want to be treated like women and others want to be 'one of the boys'—until they get hurt physically or emotionally," Donnelly comments. "It is difficult for a young man to know how to be 'an officer and a gentleman' when the word 'lady' is considered a four-letter word, and the Pentagon wants to expose unwilling women to more violence in land combat."[317]

Indeed, much of the "sexual assault" so skillfully exploited by leftists itself turns out to be the product of their agenda: with the admission of homosexuals into the military, a large majority of "sexual assault" is male-on-male, according to a Pentagon report. And male victims "report at much lower rates than female survivors," according to a Pentagon spokeswoman.[318]

316. Parker, *Save the Males*, 186.
317. Scarborough, "Doubts."

The military has long recruited from the ranks of low-income men. Its feminization is having the same effect on women, who now comprise the fastest-growing group of enlistees. The difference is that the women bring along their children and produce more of them. "Funds spent to sustain stable families have . . . attracted thousands of young custodial single parents [mothers]," writes Donnelly. "Many . . . live beneath the poverty line, and depend on food stamps as well as financial support and benefits from the DoD [Department of Defense]."[319]

The military already operates as a vast system of government provision. By necessity, material needs are provided not only for soldiers but also their families at public expense: food, clothing, housing, education, and healthcare. In this as in other respects the military is often at the forefront of trends that expand to the wider society, and provisions that begin with military necessity have often served as forerunners for civilian welfare systems.

This extensive government provision is necessary and justified for one specific and essential purpose. But this functional substitution of government for husbands and fathers who by necessity are occupied elsewhere presupposes stable families held together by traditional values such as faith, self-reliance, male protection and provision for women and children, and a traditional division of household labor in which mothers care for children while fathers are away serving their country. Populating the armed forces with socially dysfunctional and sexually promiscuous people such as single mothers and homosexuals can only distort this arrangement, expand the expense, and turn the military into a gigantic welfare agency. "In the military, generous education, housing, and medical benefits serve as an almost irresistible magnet for single parents with custody, the greater proportion of which are mothers," writes Donnelly. "Gender-based recruiting quotas increase numbers of deployable mothers even more, especially in the National Guard, which allows single parents with custody to sign up for deployable positions." The leap from attracting single mothers to facilitating more of them is one the welfare system made long ago, and the military is following suit. "In this and many other situations involving single- or dual-service parents, family subsidies that are needed to support stable families have had the unintended effect of creating more *unstable* families." Already

---

318. Rowan Scarborough, "Victims of Sex Assaults in Military are Mostly Men," *Washington Times*, 20 May 2013 (http://www.washingtontimes.com/news/2013/may/20/victims-of-sex-assaults-in-military-are-mostly-sil/?page=all).

319. Donnelly, "Constructing the Co-Ed Military," 937.

highly bureaucratic, the military will become less of a fighting force and more of a massive enabler of single motherhood and an extensive system of social welfare. "The military is rapidly expanding the number of child care facilities to accommodate the growing legions of dependent children," of single mothers and other servicewomen, Mitchell wrote over a decade ago, and since then the number has increased dramatically. "The cost of caring for everyone's children has already eaten up funds for other projects."[320]

Social practice in the military spills over on society in other ways. The US military operates the world's largest school system. What is practiced in military life is taught in military schools, and military schools influence other public school systems. An openly homosexual presence in the military not only normalizes homosexuality in social institutions but marginalizes and even criminalizes those who oppose it. "If you teach homosexuality is OK for the Marine Corps, then why is it not OK for the local schools?" asks Donnelly. "If you have a school curriculum in all of the military training reflecting support for the LGBT, that would get into the elementary schools where everyone would have to go along with this."[321]

For these reasons and more, recruiting women and homosexuals accelerates the trend of transforming the military from a fighting force into a bureaucracy and consumes financial resources as new functions must be found for female personnel to justify their presence. "For all the talk about equality, and in *every* organization for which data are available," writes Van Creveld, "they tend to drift back in 'traditional'—read safe and usually desk-bound—jobs."[322] The feminist demand for "equality" proceeds from a view of the military, not foremost as a force for defense and security but as a vehicle for "career opportunities." Accordingly, women are promoted much faster than men. Straining credulity, this politically driven fact is actually then presented as evidence of women's superior competence as soldiers.[323]

Sexualization is also responsible not only for the presence of women in the military but also for the absence of men. Recruitment of men has declined sharply as heterosexual men show little interest in a military dominated by women and homosexuals. According to surveys of youth by Joint Advertising, Market Research, and Studies, 12% of male and

---

320. Ibid., 936–37; Mitchell, *Women in the Military*, 159.

321. "Alarms Raised over Boot Camps as Social Experiments," *WorldNetDaily*, 22 July 2010, http://www.wnd.com/index.php?fa=PAGE.view&pageId=182037.

322. Van Creveld, *Men, Women, and War*, 234 (original emphasis).

323. Mitchell, *Women in the Military*, xv, 139.

20% of female respondents said they would be less likely to join the military if women become eligible for the combat arms.[324] Significantly, the only field where military recruitment is booming is among attorneys.[325]

Though military men (and everyone else) hesitate to make this argument, there is also the question of the authority over men who must risk their lives by women who are not required to do so. To command men to risk their lives requires the authority of a commander who is himself willing to incur the same or greater risks. To give such power to women who are not required to undertake equal dangers cannot but inspire resentment and contempt among soldiers, attitudes that will certainly erode cohesion and morale. The assignment of women to safer and more comfortable duties, though without any corresponding diminution of pay or advancement prospects inspires similar resentment among men who must accept a corresponding increase in more dangerous and uncomfortable assignments. "To pretend that the members of the two sexes risked their lives, or shed their blood, to roughly equal extent is to devalue the very meaning of heroism," write Van Creveld; "no wonder the supply of potential heroes, in other words men willing to enlist, is drying up." For all these reasons, "military women are often absolutely detested by the male majority," as Van Creveld writes. "As a result, the more determined and the more successful their quest for equality, the more their special privileges were taken away and the more exposed they felt to 'sexual harassment,' both real and imaginary."

But perhaps the greatest threat to military readiness is hardly even on the political radar screen of its staunchest defenders. As in civilian life, divorce courts are nothing less than a massive machine for systematically looting fathers, and military fathers are sitting ducks. It is hardly an exaggeration to say that military service has been transformed into a massive trap to tie the hands of men so that they are unable to defend themselves as women and divorce lawyers plunder and criminalize them. "Sometimes I just feel like a sucker," one veteran tells the Los Angeles *Daily Breeze*. "Veterans Day only reminds me that my government holds me and other vets in such contempt that it cannot lift a finger to stop a blatant fraud which victimizes tens of thousands of servicemen. Worse, the government actively enforces that fraud."[326]

324. Center for Military Readiness website (2015): http://cmrlink.org/data/sites/85/C MRDocuments/FactSheet-WDGC2015.pdf.

325. Karen Sloan, "Military JAG Corps Report Recruitment Surge," *National Law Journal*, 8 June 2009 (https://goo.gl/VMmFBD).

326. Jeffery Leving and Glenn Sacks, "Defrauded Veterans Have Mixed Emotions on Veterans Day," *Daily Breeze*, 11 November 2003 (http://www.glennsacks.com/veteran_ feels_mixed.htm).

While risking life and limb for their country, servicemen are now routinely divorced unilaterally and without any grounds, lose their children and everything else they possess, and even return home to face criminal sentences when they cannot pay the crushing child support imposed on them in their absence. Against this betrayal of fighting men, the military services and other institutions in the country for which they have risked their lives, such as pastors both in or out of the service, will provide no defense or assistance; on the contrary, they are much more likely to assist the women and the lawyers to ransack their former comrades-in-arms.

Military service provides a standard excuse to strip fathers of not only custody of their children but any association with them. While some mothers have been victimized, feminists have moved quickly to publicize cases where mothers lose their children as a result of deployment.[327] Astoundingly, it is now standard for a man's (but not a woman's) military service to be treated by the courts as him having "abandoned" his children. Meal allowances are counted as income for assessing child support levels, and disability benefits are confiscated not only for child support but also forcibly assessed attorneys' fees.[328]

Not surprisingly, given the easy windfall, military divorces have skyrocketed in recent years. "We've seen nothing like this before," says Colonel Glen Bloomstrom, a chaplain who invokes the standard clichés: "It indicates the amount of stress on couples, on families, as the Army conducts the global war on terrorism." It indicates nothing of the kind. "There most certainly is a relationship between current recruiting problems and an increase in military divorces," writes a retired Navy chaplain and authority on military marriage.[329]

Laws protecting active duty servicemen against legal actions are simply ignored by family courts. Deployed servicemen have virtually no protection against divorce proceedings initiated unilaterally and without any "fault" grounds on their part while they are serving their country that permanently separate them from their children. Child kidnapping laws likewise do not protect them from having their children relocated, even to foreign countries, while they cannot be present

327. Charles Toutant, "Military Parent's Overseas Deployment Has No Presumptive Effect on Custody," *New Jersey Law Journal*, 17 December 2009 (https://goo.gl/UpZutY).

328. *In re* Marriage of Pope-Clifton, No. 4–04–0307, 823 N.E.2d 607, 291 Ill. December 31, 2005 WL 293516 (4th Dist. February 7, 2005).

329. David Crary, "Army Divorce Increase with Deployments," *Denton Record*, 30 June 2005, A3; Gene Thomas Gomulka, "Marriage in the Military: Recruitment and Divorce," Miliary.com (2005, http://www.military.com/NewContent/0,13190,Gomulka_062005,00.html).

to defend their parental rights. When they return, they have no necessary right to see their children at all (and can be arrested for trying to do so), who often join the ranks of the permanently fatherless.

The *Lansing State Journal* reports on a National Guardsman who "would still have his son if he hadn't been deployed," according his lawyer. Invoking the stock legal buzzwords, the mother and her lawyer claim he lost custody not because of his deployment but because of his "parenting skills." Yet his alleged parental deficiencies (which no one mentioned before the divorce was filed), proceeded entirely from his duties as a soldier. The court stripped him of custody and the right to see his child because his divorcing wife was the "day-to-day caretaker and decision-maker in the child's life" during his deployment. According to the mother's lawyer, "He was engaging in behaviors that brought fear." In other words, he was helping his country fight a war.[330]

Even more astounding, vicariously divorced servicemen are criminally prosecuted for child-support arrearages that are almost impossible to avoid while they are on duty. Reservists are hit especially hard because their child-support burdens are based on their civilian pay and do not decrease when their income decreases. Because reservists are often mobilized with little notice, few get modifications before they depart, and modifications are almost never granted anyway. "As a result, many reservists fall hopelessly behind while serving, and can be subject to arrest for nonpayment of child support upon their return," write two columnists. "Even those returning servicemen who avoid jail or other sanctions may still spend years trying to pay off their child support debt—a debt created entirely by their willingness to serve their country."[331] At least one reservist was ordered to pay *increased* child support when his salary decreased by deployment, allowing the state to seize his entire salary, clean out his family's bank account, and leave his current family so destitute that they could not buy food.[332] "It is not exceptional to see military men paying over half of their pretax income as child support," according to David Usher of the American Coalition for Fathers and Children, Missouri Coalition.[333] They get no relief when they

330. Stacey Range, "Serve Your Country, Lose Your Child," *Lansing State Journal*, 25 August 2005 (http://66.221.222.84/forum/index.php?topic=1612.0;wap2).

331. Dianna Thompson and Glenn Sacks, "Families and the War," *Washington Times*, 21 November 2002.

332. James Beaty, "As He Prepares to Go to War, Soldier Faces DHS Red Tape," *McAlester News-Capital*, 13 October 2007 (http://mcalesternews.com/x963739190/As-he-prepares-to-go-to-war-soldier-faces-DHS-red-tape?keyword=leadpicturestory).

333. David Usher, "Divorce and Child Support are Eviscerating Military Recruitment," *NewsWithViews*, 4 June 2005, http://www.newswithviews.com/Usher/david.htm.

return because federal law prohibits debt reductions for any reason. Once arrearages reach $5,000, the soldier becomes a felon and subject to imprisonment. As one Army spouse writes to me, soldiers

> have been evicted from their homes, had vehicles repossessed and were forced to take out loans just to survive. One soldier in particular deployed to Iraq and although he was divorced from his spouse and child support had been set and he was current, she was able to successfully petition the court . . . to increase his support . . . even though he had joint custody of their children and the Army allowed for him to maintain quarters for them. This increased his support to over $3,000 per month for two children, and when he returned from war he was forced to file for bankruptcy.

But bankruptcy offers no protection against arrest.

Deployed soldiers are also targeted by women who falsely designate them as the fathers of newborns, because the state will garnish a soldier's wages even if he can prove that he is not the father.[334] "The military provides a steady, easily garnished income as well as medical care," says Carnell Smith of Citizens Against Paternity Fraud.[335] It is difficult to contest paternity while fighting a war thousands of miles away.

Wives are given other incentives to divorce and then loot military husbands. A serviceman must complete 20 years of active service to qualify for retirement pay. A woman married to the man for one day may claim a portion of that pension for life, without regard to fault or need, simply by divorcing him. There is also no limit on how many times a woman can do this.[336] Moreover, the soldiers she targets must start the payments at the earliest possible retirement date, prematurely forcing seasoned soldiers out of the service.[337]

In every other area of life, deployed servicemen are protected from civil court action by the Servicemembers Civil Relief Act. "They can't be evicted. Creditors can't seize their property. Civilian health benefits, if suspended during deployment, must be reinstated." But nothing pro-

334. Jeffery Leving and Glenn Sacks, "Servicemen Victimized by Child Support System," *WorldNetDaily*, 27 June 2007, http://www.wnd.com/2007/06/42280/.

335. Quoted in Jeffery Leving and Glenn Sacks, "Military Service Costs Some Men Their Children," *Honolulu Star-Bulletin*, 16 March 2004 (http://www.glennsacks.com/military_service_costs.htm).

336. Richard Crouch, "Malpractice Traps in Virginia Family Law and Procedure," website of Crouch & Crouch firm: http://patriot.net/~crouch/fln/malptrap.html.

337. Hans Bader, "Divorce Courts Harass Our Troops and Small Businesses," *Examiner*.com, 25 May 2009 (https://cei.org/blog/divorce-courts-harass-our-troops-and-small-businesses).

tects them from the feminists. "And yet service members' children can be—and are being—taken from them after they are deployed."[338]

The Army responds by wasting millions on therapeutic gimmicks in a futile effort to appease divorcing wives: counseling services, support groups, romantic getaways, even preposterous advice on how to pick spouses wisely. "Our hope is to change the culture," says Bloomstrom, obviously familiar with the weasel words fashionable among civilian-sector conservatives. "Initially there's a stigma about any program to do with relationships. We need to teach that there's nothing wrong with preventive maintenance for marriage."[339]

As elsewhere, the Army is burying its head in the sand. "I've been in the Army 20 years, and I've never seen the Army pay for programs like this," said one chaplain."[340] Presumably communications workshops and cultural understanding are not the approach they take to enemies in the field. But here the threat comes from not Islamic radicals but feminist radicals (often allies, as we have seen). What is new is not the stress of war; it is the muscle of the feminist lobby.

Those affected see through the obfuscation: "This is outrageous," said Kathy Moakler, deputy director of government relations of the National Military Family Association. "It's a scary precedent to set, charging the parent with abandonment because he was deployed."[341]

The effect on morale is predictable. Men do not risk their lives, fight, and die for a country that is an abstraction. They fight and die for their families and homes and freedom, all of which are being taken by feminist divorce courts. "Sometimes I wonder what I risked my life for," one soldier tells Glenn Sacks. "I went [to Afghanistan] to fight for freedom but what freedom and what rights mean anything if a man doesn't have the right to be a father to his own child?"[342] Gordon Dollar was a reservist for sixteen years in the National Guard and Naval Reserves. "I

338. Pauline Arrillaga, "Deployed Troops Battle for Child Custody," *Washington Post*, 5 May 2007 (http://www.washingtonpost.com/wp-dyn/content/article/2007/05/05/AR20 07050500673.html).

339. Pauline Jelinek, "Army Teaches Troops How to Pick a Spouse," Associated Press, 4 February 2006 (http://news.yahoo.com/s/ap/20060204/ap_on_re_us/marrying_a_jerk _5); "Military Divorce Rates Spurs Action," *Marine Corps New*, 11 January 2006 (http://www.marine-corps-news.com/2006/01/military_divorce_rates_spurs_a.htm).

340. Kimberly Hefling, "Army Seeks to Save War-Torn Marriages," *USA Today* (Associated Press), 29 December 2004 (http://usatoday30.usatoday.com/news/nation/2004-12 -29-army-marriage_x.htm?csp=34).

341. Range, "Serve Your Country."

342. Glenn Sacks, "The Betrayal of the Military Parent," *Los Angeles Daily News*, 4 May 2003 (http://glennsacks.com/blog/?page_id=4742).

told my unit that I'm getting out, and they can go recruit some judge's son/daughter to go die for the ridiculous laws they enforce," he tells Usher. "I regret that I ever served this nation." "I have friends that are very motivated and dedicated people, Frogmen/SEALS, Green Berets, and Rangers, and they were getting out too. In short, I think people who served this country are feeling betrayed by it, and see no point in serving it."[343] This is almost certainly driving the record number of military suicides recently reported,[344] though the "antiwar" lobby that reports it refuses to identify the causes.

But soldiers' freedom may not be the only freedom lost in the rush to sexualize the war machinery.

The military is not just another area of civil society like a school or church or bowling league. It is a unique organization that operates under qualitatively different rules from the rest of society—rules not permitted in the civilian life of free societies. Soldiers operate under a discipline that regulates and legitimates killing. This constitutes a standing threat to the very freedom that it exists to protect. Politicizing the military is always dangerous.

Military society by its nature is more authoritarian than civilian. That is why free societies are careful to maintain civilian control and a sharp separation of military rules from civil laws. Nevertheless, there is a constant danger that military standards will encroach on and undermine the freedoms and protections of civilians.

Ironically, this is now being engineered not by obvious militarists but by radicals who often hold military values in contempt. Under the guise of "civil rights," we are substituting radical political principles for military necessity as the main operational criterion. In fact, sexualizing the military, here again ironically justified in terms of "equal rights," would undermine all citizens' civil rights with draconian ("zero tolerance") prohibitions on disagreement with government policy. Military effectiveness requires that soldiers not be permitted to voice disagreement with their superiors' decisions. This accounts for the peculiar fact that this debate—even more than the others examined—prohibits the people most involved from participating in it. "In the military, more than in any other institution, it is possible to prevent men from saying what they really think of their female comrades by simply ordering them to shut their mouths." The nature of the military dictates that the soldiers, sailors, and airmen are not permitted to voice their opinions. The

343. Usher, "Divorce."

344. Jason Ditz, "US Army Suicides in 2009 a New Record," Antiwar.com, 15 January 2010, http://news.antiwar.com/2010/01/15/us-army-suicides-in-2009-a-new-record/.

debate over women and homosexuals in the military is one "the men in the field and fleet were prohibited from joining." Indeed, as Mitchell points out, they are not permitted to have beliefs or convictions, only undesirable "attitudes" that are targeted for eradication.[345]

What happens to soldiers—and there are many—who disagree with women and homosexuals in combat units? Are they to be punished? Court-martialed? Do their religious and political views—that in other citizens would be protected by the First Amendment and other guarantees for freedom of expression—constitute disobedience to orders? If so, this means using the severe standards of military discipline to enforce a political ideology and punish doctrinal heterodoxy, even when it is nothing more than traditional beliefs and has no bearing on military effectiveness. Further, as Donnelly explains, this censorship would actually be less tolerant of dissent than standard military discipline, which does allow appropriate avenues for soldiers to raise questions and point out problems:

> Some advocates suggest that the duty to follow orders is so absolute that dissent on social policies is unprofessional at best and mutinous at worst. If the same standard were applied to the Pentagon's decisions about weapon systems, officers would have to remain silent about poorly designed equipment that creates unnecessary risks or detracts from the effectiveness of military missions. Although the US Constitution properly assigns control of the military to civilians, political correctness within the Pentagon has become a formidable, vitiating force.[346]

This in turn sets a dangerous precedent for civilian life. Whereas in free societies civilians may criticize government policy and ideologies like feminism or homosexuality (for now), military personnel may be physically punished according to military justice for failing to conform their political or religious beliefs to what is in reality government ideology. "Because everyone must follow orders," writes Donnelly, "the armed forces are a prime venue for social engineering."[347]

As indicated, religious freedom is especially vulnerable. What of soldiers who find homosexuality or gender neutrality inconsistent with their religious beliefs and military chaplains who preach against it? Will they be disciplined? "The religious liberties of millions of uniformed Americans will be put at immediate risk by the normalization of homosexuality in the military," writes Albert Mohler, "and these are the very

345. Van Creveld, *Men, Women, and War*, 220; Mitchell, *Women in the Military*, 138.
346. Donnelly, "Constructing the Co-Ed Military," 821.
347. Ibid., 816.

people who are putting their lives on the line to preserve these liberties for others."[348] These are also the people we depend upon to fill the military ranks in the first place. The military is already facing a recruiting crisis (exacerbated by the obesity epidemic, as millions of potential recruits are raised by single mothers on diets of junk food). What happens when the core religious values of the men most likely and fit to serve are declared politically unacceptable and the military is deserted by precisely such men?

As with divorce and other coercion forcing people to accept practices they consider immoral, the standard feminist and homosexualist solution is government-mandated "education," or "sensitivity training"—a concept directly antithetical to military prowess because of its anti-male bias. "US Army recruits actually spend more time on this kind of training than in learning how to use their weapons," Van Creveld reports; "to say nothing of the implicit message that men are louts who do not know how to treat women properly."[349] Soldiers must think in terms of strength and courage, not "sensitivity." The complex ethics of killing in war have been debated for centuries (more in military academies than in universities or seminaries), but confronting the ethics of warfare is not the same as the backdoor expedient of making soldiers more feminine.

Politicizing military discipline in turn also means militarizing civilian life, since the intolerance cannot help but spread to the civilian sphere. Already, a kind of authoritarian ethic, essential to military effectiveness but antithetical to civilian freedom, tempts the civilian sexual elite as they discover the enormous coercive power that accrues to them by commandeering military discipline for political purposes. A survey found that half of Democrats favored punishing soldiers who disagree with a policy of homosexuals in the military.[350] The temptations of power can always degenerate into an authoritarian mindset, and no power is greater than that of an army.

It might seem appropriate here to engage with the arguments used by feminists and homosexuals against these objections. Yet strikingly, there essentially are no such arguments. Here again sexual advocates do not bother to answer the objections, because facts do not really enter into the debate. "No one, it seems, is courageous enough to approach the issue of women in the military as one would any other issue, analyzing it

348. Mohler, "Homosexuality and the Military."

349. Van Creveld, *Men, Women, and War*, 220.

350. Adam Cassandra, "Half of Democrats Favor Punishing Soldiers Who Oppose Homosexuality, Survey Finds," *CNSNews.com*, 10 August 2010, http://www.cnsnews.com/news/article/70876.

with cold rationality in the simple terms of costs versus benefits," writes Mitchell. "The problem, of course, with weighing the pluses and minuses of using women in the military is that there are too many minuses."[351] Instead of engaging in critical debates, advocates simply scream past the objections with self-righteous, headline-grabbing indignation over "inequality," "discrimination," and "harassment" in the military, as if these terms can simply be transferred to an institution that cannot possibly operate on the basis of equality, that must exercise rigorous discrimination, and where physical and psychological harassment is an essential part of the training.

The result is a litany of falsehoods, each necessitating the next, turning the military into a giant (and armed) propaganda machine: "It is a lie that military women are meeting the same standards as men," Mitchell insists. "Nowhere are women required to meet the same physical standards as men, and nowhere are women subjected to the military's sternest trials of mind and body." Mitchell's assessment more than a decade ago was already reminiscent of Soviet practice. "These are the lies that our officers force upon their subordinates with Soviet slavishness," he continues:

> Duty in the American military means doing as one is told. Obedience to civilian control is the supreme law. . . . The American military has no tradition of honorable dissent, of standing upon principle against official policy. . . . They follow orders even if it means acting contrary to conscience. . . . After more than two decades of political correctness, the men and women who have survived to become today's admirals and generals are . . . unprincipled opportunists who enthusiastically persecute the men under them to protect and advance their own careers, who will not put their stars on the table to see justice done and the defense of the nation assured.[352]

Thus we return to a central theme of this study: an ideological juggernaut that destroys every obstacle in its path—facts, scholarship, debate, criticism, civility, freedom. "The only reason to use women is not a military reason," Mitchell concludes. "It is a political reason driven by an ideology that is hostile to the military, according to which the advancement of women, under the euphemism of 'equal opportunity,' trumps the needs of the military and the cause of national defense."[353]

---

351. Mitchell, *Women in the Military*, 340. As with critics of other aspects of feminism, if Mitchell is aware of how his point about the defiance of facts could apply to other feminist campaigns, he does not express it.

352. Ibid., 342–44.

353. Ibid., 340–41.

And here again we can see, perhaps more starkly than elsewhere, the process by which radical ideology becomes official government policy, allowing the full force of the penal system to punish heterodoxy. West Point created "Institutional Plans to Overcome Sexism" the avowed purpose of which (ironically reflecting trends in civilian academies) was to suppress data about the adverse consequences of sexual integration: "avoid research activities which have sexist consequences." It also called for suppressing documents with "sexist" language such as "he." "At all of the academies, classes on sexism and sex-role socialization, taught solely from the feminist perspective, were mandatory," writes Mitchell. "Feminism was the official orthodoxy... and if cadets... were not among the faithful 'then they're in the wrong line of work,' warned General Goodpastor." Military cadets are "assumed to be ignorant, superstitious primitives," as Mitchell puts it. If they do not support feminism, "it was because they did not 'understand' it" and need further "education." Their "attitudes" must be expunged, using military discipline ("strong negative sanctions").[354]

Here more seriously than elsewhere, the result turns both the military and the rest of us into what Theodore Dalrymple calls "a society of emasculated liars"[355]—all part of the larger campaign to abolish masculinity itself. "They cannot get a handle on this problem [of "sexual harassment"] because of a military culture that is macho," says Karen Johnson of the National Organization for Women. What connection with reality does such a statement betray?

The Army itself has absorbed this thinking, becoming ashamed for "the encouragement of a 'macho' male image." "There is nothing inherent in what the Army does that must be done in a masculine way," argues a West Point study, apparently in all seriousness; "therefore, women must be offered the opportunity to be feminine and nothing should be done to deny women opportunities to be feminine." But male soldiers too must be more feminine, because the Army is a "caring" organization where the needs of combat have given way to those of the emotionally sensitive: "We want soldiers, of all ranks, feeling they belong to a 'family'.... Building the family requires a professional sensitivity toward and caring for one another.... We want these professional, caring relationships because they are necessary to build the vertical bonds which tie leader to led."[356]

354. Ibid., 69–70.
355. Parker, *Save the Males*, 189.
356. Ibid., 337–39.

Such political cowardice by the military leadership does not bode well for the physical courage needed elsewhere. Mitchell's entire book (like others) is largely a litany of craven cowardice by high-ranking officials both in the Pentagon and among politicians in the face of politicized and aggressive women. "From the top down," he writes, "the example to follow is one of cowardly, self-protective deceit." A senior Navy figure offered his own list of distinguished officers whose careers were destroyed by feminist justice (one "without being given so much as five minutes to explain his own actions . . . to the admiral who summarily dismissed him"), while their colleagues stand by in silence:

> When a whole generation of officers is asked to accept . . . the destruction of the careers of some of the finest aviators in the Navy based on hearsay, unsubstantiated allegations, in some cases after a full repudiation of anonymous charges . . . what admiral has had the courage to risk his own career by putting his stars on the table and defending the integrity of . . . his people?[357]

Here we arrive at the bottom line of the sexual revolution, not only in the military but throughout society. For if courageous men, who do not hesitate to lay their lives down for their fellows, their families, and their country are reduced to eunuchs when challenged by women, what hope do less determined and well-trained men have? And indeed, if there is one word that explains the lightning speed with which the Sexual Revolution has spread throughout the Western world and beyond, with almost no opposition, it is male cowardice. But it is a new kind of cowardice, not easy to understand, because it is occasioned not by physical danger but by emasculation and driven not by competing men but by women.

The result is a dynamic of fear and suspicion, reminiscent of Soviet experience, where the only certain way to escape punishment is to actively abet the punishment of others. Mitchell describes a "fear of being burned for not burning others" that fits all the witch hunts generated by the Sexual Revolution. "Only accusers survive," he concludes (as we have seen with child abuse, rape, domestic violence, universities, and more). "Everyone else is a suspect."[358]

All this is easily externalized from military staff to military targets, which have likewise been chosen by domestic political criteria. Military officials have begun targeting American citizens on American soil as

---

357. Ibid., 343, 205–6. As of 2015, little has changed: Mike Fredenburg, "Putting Women in Combat Is an Even Worse Idea Than You'd Think," *National Review*, 15 July 2015.

358. Ibid., 278.

"hate groups" because of their religious convictions. In military briefings, officials labeled groups of law-abiding citizens like the American Family Association (AFA) as hate groups because of their sexual morality. "Why is the military training their personnel about domestic organizations, about what's going on here inside the United States? Isn't the purpose of the military to fight wars overseas?" asks Tim Wildmon of AFA. "It's kind of troubling to think that the US Army is focusing on groups like the American Family Association." In effect, the military is taking sides in domestic political issues to the point of making religious convictions grounds for military intervention. "It's spooky and in fact dangerous to see the US military even involved in policing pro-family groups on American soil," says Bryan Fisher of AFA. "Their job is to fight al-Qaeda, not their own citizens."[359] American soldiers were reportedly told they could be punished for supporting such legal organizations.

As institutionalized sexual ideology works itself out to its logical, neo-Stalinist conclusion, feminists are increasingly using women's empowerment to rationalize military action itself for feminist ends.

Feminists have been a vocal component in the "peace movement" going back at least to the First World War, and they have long been a major force in demonizing the military. Integrating women into the military thus creates ambivalences and ironies within the sisterhood itself. "Thoughtful feminists did not miss the irony that a movement dedicated to womanly nonviolence and life-giving concerns had been largely, if not solely, responsible for trivializing war." The only plausible explanation for this paradox is that ideologues always prefer power to principles. This is confirmed by the connected paradox occasioned by the opportunistic observation that the military is a highly effective vehicle for social engineering: "Many feminists were caught between an automatic revulsion at anything military and the recognition that, like it or not, the military was doing what pacifistic feminism was not," Mitchell observes. "It was changing American society." According to Sue Berryman of the Rand Corporation, "The armed forces have done as much, if not more, to advance the social and economic role of women in our society than practically any other factor or organization."

No weapon is more powerful, after all, than the institution that has weapons. "It is the power of the military to direct society that united feminists in pursuing a greater role for military women," writes Mitchell (who notices, as we have, that "Power is a favorite word among all feminists."). "The issue of women in the military is really an issue of power

---

359. *OneNewsNow* internet site: https://goo.gl/teV6Ar.

—power, policy, and women in policy positions," says one prominent feminist. "Power is what the military has to offer all feminists—not just power for individual women over others in the military, but power for all women over all of society." Mitchell quotes one Army feminist: "Women have been deliberately and often legally excluded from society's legitimate, organized, planned, rewarded, technological force—the force applicable by the policy and the military." The same feminist "presents a sound, practical argument against women in combat but nevertheless endorses their involvement in combat because 'the implications of exempting women from combat thus seem to include the exclusion of women from full citizenship.'"[360]

There is some historic logic to this. In republican theory dating at least to the Italian Renaissance and very influential on theorists of the English and American revolutions, a militia was superior to either a professional army or, worse, mercenaries, because defense of the land was entrusted to citizens who were also defending their homes, families, and freedom. Citizenship and military service were thus inseparable, but that conception presupposed the household and the householder, who bore arms in defense of his home and family, as well as country. The militiaman also protected freedom by precluding the need for a professional "standing army" that potentially threatened free institutions.

The modified understanding of this historic relationship by today's sexual ideologues, superficially compatible, would in fact invert it by making the citizen an extension of the professional, increasingly bureaucratic soldier—not creating a citizen army but in effect militarizing citizenship. This is essentially what Communists did. Like feminists, they attacked "imperialism" and "militarism" and then proceeded to construct states far more militaristic than those they replaced by creating ideological and bureaucratic armies that required all "comrades" to obey political orders. The military thus becomes the vehicle to transform citizens into a cadre of ideological shock troops. Far from being citizens-in-arms, the soldiers become functionaries-in-arms.

The specter of a military government by sexual radicals is not fanciful. Today's military is already highly bureaucratic, and like all ideologues, feminists are very adept at commandeering and expanding bureaucracies. This in fact institutionalizes politically what in many ways has been the norm throughout history: not the few but well-publicized instances of women restraining men from war, but the far more common phenomenon of women egging men on to fight and die for them using sexual favors as the carrot and fear of shame and emascula-

---

360. Mitchell, *Women in the Military*, 192–93.

tion as the stick.[361] Women are also much more concerned than men about physical safety, and feminists are not now, as women have seldom been in the past, hesitant about expecting men to risk and sacrifice their lives to protect them.[362] "Peace is inextricably linked to equality between women and men and development," insists one UN document, without providing any explanation or logic for why. "Why precisely is inequality between the sexes a cause of war," ask two scholars, "unless one country attacks another at least partly to eliminate that form of inequality, which is what Americans did in Taliban-ruled Afghanistan?"[363] Like the pigs in Orwell's *Animal Farm*, feminists have found that power trumps principles and that the ultimate act of politics—war—is useful as a method of aggrandizing power. "When the war in Afghanistan began, the liberation of Afghan women was one of the most important justifications for military intervention," Wazhma Frogh points out in the *Washington Post*, and the words of the Bush administration bear her out.[364] Feminists seemed quite content to see the war in Afghanistan continue, even after every other military or political justification had evaporated, in what strategist William Lind calls the "war for women": "The important question ... is which stipulations the Obama White House regards as domestic political requirements. One leaps from the page: 'the equality of women.'"[365]

While feminists are embarrassed by this newfound source of power, it does not stop them from using it. "Women for Afghan Women deeply regrets having a position in favor of maintaining, even increasing troops," says one Western feminist group, whose regrets about the position they hold are evidently not deep enough to prevent them from holding it. "We are not advocates for war, and conditions did not have to reach this dire point, but we believe that withdrawing troops means abandoning 15 million women and children to madmen who will sacrifice them to their lust for power." This is not the first time that feminists have justified war and male deaths for the sake of gender equality.[366]

361. Van Creveld, *Men, Women, and War*, ch. 1.

362. See Kate Hymowitz, "Why Feminism is AWOL on Islam," *City Journal*, Winter 2003 (http://www.city-journal.org/html/13_1_why_feminism.html).

363. Nathanson and Young, *Legalizing Misandry*, 398.

364. Wazhma Frogh, "Risking a Rights Disaster," *Washington Post*, 18 October 2009; "Mrs. Bush Cites Women's Plight Under Taliban," *New York Times*, 17 November 2001 (http://www.nytimes.com/2001/11/18/us/a-nation-challenged-the-first-lady-mrs-bush-cites-women-s-plight-under-taliban.html).

365. William Lind, "War for Women," *The American Conservative*, online edition, 3 January 2011, http://www.theamericanconservative.com/articles/war-for-women/.

366. Van Creveld, *Men, Women, and War*, 23.

Esther Hyneman of this group, who apparently believes the US (and especially US men) can do nothing right, justifies her demand for prolonged endangerment and sacrifice of American male lives by the US failure to provide adequate psychotherapy. "The United States have done a terrible job there," Hyneman declares. "We've promoted the warlords, financed the warlords. We should have demanded that the warlords be bought before a court, a trial, a reconciliation process."[367] Even Code Pink, the leading feminist anti-war group, came to believe that war is peace, or at least a method for liberating women. "Without international troops . . . armed groups could return with a vengeance—and that would leave women most vulnerable."[368] Much as Western feminists were long the main lobby for increasing police and incarceration, so they are now emerging as the foremost domestic pressure group advocating war. "A growing number of Afghan women say the development process is far removed from their needs, and hampered by foreign donors' focus on short-term wins," or at least the *Christian Science Monitor* says it. War brings faster results. "Those who are against the progress of women are stronger than we are," says journalist and activist Jamila Mujahed, who also wants more troops. Here once again the ironies demonstrate that feminists cannot transcend—they can only politicize—the "stereotypes" they so stridently attack. What the media cannot bring themselves to admit is that feminists are insisting that women need men to protect and die for them. "In the current situation of terrorism, we cannot say troops should be withdrawn," Shinkai Karokhail, an Afghan woman activist. "International troop presence here is a guarantee for my safety."[369] Yet after risking and sacrificing their lives for the women, these troops will not be lauded as protectors. They will be demonized as killers. "American feminists are no doubt willing to see the war go on indefinitely in pursuit of their fantasy," writes Linn. "After all, most of the American dead are male soldiers and Marines, a type of man feminists particularly loathe."[370]

367. Michelle Goldberg, "A Feminist Case for War?" *The American Prospect*, 27 October 2009 (http://www.prospect.org/cs/articles?article=a_feminist_case_for_war). For the therapeutic dimension of such trials see John Laughland, *Travesty: The Trial of Slobodan Milosevic and the Corruption of International Justice* (London: Pluto, 2007).

368. Aunohita Mojumdar, "'Code Pink' Rethinks Its Call for Afghanistan Pullout," *Christian Science Monitor*, 6 October 2009 (http://www.csmonitor.com/World/Asia-South-Central/2009/1006/p06s10-wosc.html).

369. Gayle Tzemach, "Afghan Women Fear a Retreat to Dark Days," *Christian Science Monitor*, 18 December 2008 (http://www.csmonitor.com/World/2008/1218/p07s03wogn.html).

370. Lind, "War for Women."

Conclusion

"Sex is a river of fire that must be banked and cooled by a hundred restraints if it is not to consume in chaos both the individual and the group."
　　　　　　　　　　　　　　　　　　　　　　　—Will and Ariel Durant[1]

EVERY SOCIETY must regulate sex. It is not healthy for any society to be so saturated with sex that it dominates the political system. When sex becomes a society's political currency, then public life comes to be dominated by those willing to use sexuality as a weapon to acquire power.

In retrospect, the notion that a society could simply dispense with the mores and restrictions that have kept sex under control in this and every civilization for millennia, and instead adopt the sexual morality of Woodstock hippies, and that this could be done with no adverse social or political consequences, seems breathtakingly naïve. It is not possible to rearrange matters as fundamental as the relationships between men and women, sexuality, and family structure without far-reaching consequences that cannot possibly be foreseen. In the decades since we began this experiment, little effort has been made to step back and assess the wisdom of what we are doing. Rather than heed the warning signs, we seem determined to plough on regardless, willfully oblivious to the consequences.

Even today, few comprehend the full extent of those consequences or express any desire to do so. Even as the fallout becomes glaringly apparent, we seem intent to avert our eyes as we plunge headlong, like adolescents pleased with our own naughtiness, into ever more daring sexual experimentation to "push back the frontiers" and transgress yet another "last taboo." The scholars and intellectuals whose responsibility it is to provide us with a disinterested appraisal of our society's trends themselves seem so intoxicated with the new sexual freedom and the power it confers—of which they themselves are among the foremost partakers—that not only do they show virtually no concern for understanding and

---

1. *The Lessons of History* (New York: Simon and Schuster, 1968), 35–36.

377

elucidating the larger implications with any detachment; they punish and excommunicate those few among their ranks who try.

For their part, conservative and religious moralizers seem only able to shake their heads and lament the sad state of affairs, often before they try to disguise their own irrelevance by parroting the jargon and tagging along with the mob demanding punishment for those who fall afoul of the new sexual regime and its dogmas.

It is one thing to experiment with the boundaries of sex or "gender" roles, provided some escape is available when the boundaries are reached and the experiment threatens to get out of hand. When this foray into sexual liberalism began a half century ago, we saw it as an exploration. What would happen if we challenged "stereotypes"? Why do we need formalized rituals like marriage? What would happen if we ignore or deliberately proscribe the traditional roles of men and women and remove all stigmas on homosexuality and other alternative sexualities? Why should men and women have different responsibilities in the family and elsewhere? Why should we not indulge in recreational sex purely for pleasure and without limit? What harm could it all do?

No one seemed to have very definite answers to these questions. People who were uncomfortable with the experiment had trouble articulating precisely why. Objections were shouted down as "old fashioned," "repressed," "prudery," "bigotry," religious dogma, or "male privilege." (Though if anyone stopped to ask what connected all these disparate sneers, no one seemed very interested in providing answers. This should have clued us in that something was amiss.)

Even today, many people who do not sympathize with the radicals' demands have trouble expressing why or resisting the relentless "progress" (the self-serving faith of the politically and sexually energetic) that the radicals insist is taking us toward some utopia of sexual release. In any case, the radicals' program of sexual liberation allowed for so much pleasure, profit, and power for so many people, all under the intoxicating guise of righteous moral indignation, that voices of restraint were not only dismissed but ridiculed, threatened, ostracized, and silenced. When some began finding themselves in handcuffs and behind bars, often without understanding the rationalizations for how they got there, their objections were dismissed as rain on the parade.

Today we do have answers to those questions, however much they must struggle to be heard, and this book has been an attempt to air them. We are now seeing quite clearly the very concrete consequences: to children, to families, to the social order, to limited government, military readiness, religious freedom, civil liberties, and to those looted by government functionaries and accused of crimes so vague and ill-defined that they cannot possibly defend themselves and so despicable that no one else dares to defend them.

Moreover, much of it appears to be irreversible, so that even if we want to stop or reverse the experiment, it is not clear that we can do so. For one thing, it is dangerous for any public figure, scholar, or journalist even to raise any objection, for fear of joining those accused of "discrimination" or "oppression" or "hate" or "bigotry" or "violence" against some sexual "victim."

The fundamental premise of sexual ideology cannot be openly questioned, even though the vast majority of people certainly do not share it: that differences between men and women, and between healthy and confused sexualities, have no basis in reason or reality but are artificially or "socially constructed" by some nefarious power; and that both the differences and the power must be eradicated by seizing the coercive state machinery and using it to control the lives of people who are not criminals.[2] Accept this premise and its corollary, that unlimited "gender equality" and "non-discrimination" must be achieved at all costs, and the most intrusive interventions into private life are rationalized. If we cannot be permitted to distinguish or "discriminate" unavoidable differences between males and females in the course of our daily lives then no private life is possible. Heterosexuality is itself "discrimination" after all, as are private living arrangements and the natural procreation of children. It is no accident that these are currently targeted as obstacles to the "empowerment" of the discontented. Suzanne Venker is not far wrong when she suggests that feminists operate "by the notion that progress for women requires 'liberation'—not just from the home and all its supposed restrictions, but from being female." One radical transsexual seemed to understand the logic when she suggested that the only way to fully eliminate "discrimination" against women is to eliminate women.[3]

No stable public life is possible either. If we must pretend there is no difference between people who bear children and those who are dependent on others for their children, between people who have a legal requirement to risk their lives, kill, and die to protect their families and communities and those under no such obligation, between those who can be accused of serious crimes and those who can only accuse, then public policy likewise cannot help but become seriously distorted and perverted.

2. Steven Rhoads, *Taking Sex Differences Seriously* (San Francisco: Encounter, 2005).

3. Suzanne Venker, *The War on Men* (Washington: WND Books, 2013), 88–90; Kate Bornstein, *Gender Outlaw: On Men, Women, and the Rest of Us* (New York: Routledge, 1994), 115, quoted in Dale O'Leary, *The Gender Agenda* (Lafayette, LA: Vital Issues Press, 1997), 88–90.

And this is precisely what we now see, as our society increasingly resembles what the East European dissidents used to call "Absurdistan" —a society where reality is forced to conform to ideology:

- where wild fantasies like a multiplicity of "genders" are taken seriously;

- where able-bodied young men push strollers and change nappies while pregnant women pretend to be soldiers and face death in combat, and where combat units are expected to function effectively while their members are having sex with one another;

- where the young male population is routinely inducted into prison rather than into families or education or employment, and where this is cheered by the media;[4]

- where tens of millions of children grow up under court-ordered and government-enforced fatherlessness, while legally unimpeachable fathers face jail for unauthorized association with their own children;

- where rationalizations are found for evicting law-abiding citizens from their own homes, forcibly separating them from their own children, and seizing their property;

- where governments concoct "child abuse" accusations to rationalize military operations against their own citizens on their own soil;

- where people legally falsify official documents to pretend they are a different sex;[5] where people are held up for public opprobrium simply for recognizing a person's true sex;[6] where parents try to disguise from

4. Jessica Abrahams, "Are Men Natural Born Criminals?" *Daily Telegraph*, 15 January 2015, http://www.telegraph.co.uk/women/womens-life/11342408/Are-men-natural-born -criminals-Prison-numbers-dont-lie.html. As Abrahams summarizes "feminist criminology," the principal method for men to avoid prison is to be more like women: "most criminologists point to . . . social and cultural stereotypes [that] dictate that men are about strength and having power over other people, and being able to show off, and being bread-winners."

5. "Lydia Foy Settles Transgender Birth Cert Case against State," *Irish Times* (http:// www.irishtimes.com/news/crime-and-law/courts/lydia-foy-settles-transgender-birth-ce rt-case-against-state-1.1979314), 28 October 2014. Not only does the article use the feminine gender to refer to a man; it provides no indication that legitimate reasons may exist for preventing the falsification of a birth certificate. On the contrary, "Foy sought a birth certificate in her acquired female gender and damages for breach of her rights," and the court ruled that "the State's failure to legislate to recognise transgender persons in their preferred gender breached the European Convention on Human Rights."

6. Brendan O'Neill, "Call Me Caitlyn or Else: The Rise of Authoritarian Transgender Politics," *Spectator*, 2 June 2015 (http://blogs.spectator.co.uk/brendan-oneill/2015/06/call -me-caitlyn-or-else-the-rise-of-authoritarian-transgender-politics/).

their children the knowledge of what sex they are;[7] where doctors mutilate the bodies of healthy people, including young children, in a futile pretense of changing their sex; where employers and individuals can be looted with massive fines for failing to use a government-mandated pronoun;[8]

• where government officials redefine words so that females are fathers and males are wives;[9]

• where adult child molesters can sue the children they have drugged and raped and collect income from them; where men are forced to pay support for children that do not exist; where middle-aged men can sue their own aged parents for "child support" for themselves,[10] and where men are jailed without trial not for failing to pay financial support for their children financially, but for paying too much;[11]

• where mobs of naked women attacking churches and disrupting religious services are treated as serious political advocates, and where grown men are taken seriously as public policy advocates by publicly removing their clothes and exhibiting themselves in feathers or women's underwear;[12]

and where we are expected to pretend that all this is normal behavior and anyone who questions these bizarre practices is accused of "bigotry" or "hate" or obstructing political "progress" or even "violence." This is a society in which political ideology has run amok and one flirting with collective madness.

But as with an earlier generation's exemplars of Absurdistan, the absurdity is only an indicator of more serious consequences:

• a massive epidemic of abused children that is almost entirely the product of the experiment in single motherhood;

---

7. David Wilkes, "Boy or Girl?" *Daily Mail*, 20 January 2012, http://www.dailymail. co.uk/news/article-2089474/Beck-Laxton-Kieran-Cooper-reveal-sex-gender-neutral-chi ld-Sasha.html.

8. "NYC Will Fine Employers. . . ." *LifeSite News*, 23 December 2015, https://www.life sitenews.com/news/nyc-will-fine-employers-up-to-250000-for-referring-to-transsexual s-by-their.

9. John Bingham, "Men can be 'Wives' and Women 'Husbands' as Government Overrules the Dictionary," *Daily Telegraph*, 27 June 2013, http://www.telegraph.co.uk/news/ politics/10147246/Men-can-be-wives-and-women-husbands-as-Government-overrules-the-dictionary.html.

10. Stephen Baskerville, "Absurdistan in America," *LewRockwell*.com, 24 September 2003, and "The Doofus Department," *LewRockwell*.com, 27 December 2004.

11. "Father Sentenced to 6 Months in Jail for Paying Too Much Child Support," Fox26, 9 January 2014, http://www.policestateusa.com/2014/clifford-hall-child-support/.

12. See https://www.youtube.com/watch?v=fOCD_T9Qqpc.

- heroic men and women needlessly endangered because women are thrust into combat situations and men must fight alongside them;

- men facing decades in prison for "rapes" and other redefined "crimes" that everyone knows never happened;

- children bred from the beginning of their lives in anti-social and deviant behavior, such as violent crime and substance abuse, because their perfectly fit fathers have been ordered by judges not to associate with them;

- history's most affluent and successful societies voluntarily bankrupting themselves to create and pay the costs and consequences of tens of millions of dysfunctional single-mother homes, when fit fathers are able and willing to provide for them;

- clergy and other citizens prosecuted as "human rights" violators for expressing their religious and political convictions or for the conduct of their private lives.

And all this proceeds not simply from a stubborn refusal to accept reality, but from a drive for power and a corollary resentment of those whose power is envied. Feminism and politicized homosexuality do not represent simply personal "preferences." They share a palpable hostility toward heterosexual masculinity, which plays itself out in both their personal sexuality and their aggressive political agendas in a way that makes the two inseparable. "Feminism isn't about equal rights, nor is it about providing women with choices," writes Venker. "The mission is clear. Feminism is a war on men."[13]

But the war conscripts ordinary, apolitical women as foot soldiers by creating new, dysfunctional rules and then exploiting the emotional discontents that inevitably ensue. "It's impossible . . . to understand anything about women in this country today, unless you understand that a) they're angry, and b) their anger is directed at men," writes Michelle Langley, who is referring to ordinary women unable to cope with the impossible expectations raised by the new rules of courtship. "Women today aren't seeking equality," she adds. "They want retribution— revenge."[14] Similar resentfulness now appears among homosexuals.

What confronts us is no longer merely an indulgent pastime of over-affluent, opinionated students and hormone-driven and self-righteous adolescents. It is increasingly driven by disturbed and self-destructive people, whose sexual confusion and open-ended resentment against

13. Venker, *War on Men*, 75–76.
14. *Women's Infidelity*, quoted in F. Roger Devlin, *Sexual Utopia in Power* (San Francisco: Counter-Currents, 2015), 47.

their unnamed "oppressors" has been indulged beyond the boundaries of common sense in ways that cannot possibly be healthy for themselves or the rest of us.

For sexual radicals today, political activism is not the necessary and limited means to rectify some specific, concrete injustice imposed by the state, as the individualist and "civil rights" rhetoric would like us to believe or as superficial moralists like to delude themselves. As their literature makes very clear, it is an open-ended, existential revolt for its own sake. As any adolescent can attest, sex is not only difficult to resist physically; it is also a highly satisfying weapon for expressing rebellion against authority, beginning with parents and especially fathers. It is no accident that sexual and political awareness emerge at roughly the same age, and that, if left uninstructed and unrestricted, both quickly become vehicles for revolt against parents and every other authority.[15] What is new is that this rebelliousness is now expressed ideologically, organized programmatically, advocated politically by ostensibly grown-up men and women, many with a vested professional interest in the power and earnings it confers, including the state gendarmerie.

Increasingly it is the political agenda of resentful people to wield the coercive state machinery and marshal it to punish others for personal hurts. A testament to this resentment is the politicized exhibitionism of half-naked Femen protests, "Slut Walks," "Gay Pride" parades; the attack on an Argentine cathedral by a mob of topless women;[16] and the self-righteous thrill with which these young radicals invoke political agendas as a moralistic fig leaf to rationalize removing their clothing and displaying their hyper-sexualized bodies in public—often thereby posing as the victims of ill-defined crimes for which conveniently unspecified others become liable to arrest and incarceration.

Feminist political theorists insist that the relationship between men and women is one of "power."[17] There is some truth to this, and taking them at their word, we have emphasized their own obsession with "empowerment." Yet this dynamic is more complex than the simple competition for power between men and women that the radicals themselves have tried to make it.

For most people, in most of the world, for most of history, there was no contest for power between men and women because men wielded

---

15. This is very clear in today's pop music videos, where the dominant theme is not simply rebellion against sexual mores but that the sexual is an instrument of rebellion against other authorities.

16. See https://www.youtube.com/watch?v=wPUvUYU7Qzw&feature=youtu.be.

17. Carol Pateman, *The Sexual Contract* (Stanford: Stanford University Press, 1988).

power, preferably limited, and conferred its benefits to women and children through marriage. Because power is sexually attractive to women but not to men, little objection was heard. It was not that men *had* power: men and masculinity *are* power. Political theory (along with the criminal justice system) has long been dedicated to controlling the power specifically of men. The family household was a unit of protection and provision because it channeled the strength and drive of men to protect and provide for women and children, while preserving the family as a refuge from the larger competition for power. Controlling the potential abuse of that power was the task of the extended family, local community, and church, with the state as a last resort.

With the decline or programmatic weakening of these institutions and deliberate design to pit men and women in competition with one another, the radicals have initiated an open-ended and unstable contest for power that (much like sexual desire) can never be satiated. Once men and women are placed in competition with one another, then male strength and drive cannot help but stimulate in some women the most dangerous emotion in politics and the one that feeds all deadly political ideologies, whatever their content: resentment. Women who uncritically internalize the simplistic claim that they can "do anything a man can do" will naturally become resentful when they discover that they must make different choices than men must make. Apparently "a 1993 Gallup poll reported that 40% of women were often or very often resentful of men."[18] The complex relationships of homosexuals and homosexual politics to masculinity are also suffused with resentment, as we have seen.

Women and homosexuals do not (as groups) need power in order to protect and provide for families. To the extent that they become heads of "families" their authority is in collusion, rather than competition, with the state, who becomes the real protector and provider—in contrast to families headed by heterosexual men. They are free therefore to crave power, like they can crave sex, purely for pleasure—both of which desires the political literature expresses very forthrightly. But the lust for power, like the lust for sex, can never be permanently satisfied. Both can only be limited and controlled. The radicals have already thrown off the controls on sex, and it is the argument of this book that they are likewise now throwing off the controls on political power.

The soft response to gender resentment is to make men more like women. But no society can remain free that dispenses with masculine

---

18. Christine Rosen, "What (Most) Women Want," *Claremont Review of Books*, 16 May 2005, http://www.claremont.org/crb/article/what-most-women-want/.

principles and relies exclusively on feminine ones. Masculine strength is the only counterweight to the power of the state, and it is only stable within the context of family households. A free society needs people who are required to show courage, risk their lives, and sacrifice them if necessary for our security and freedom—not just people who will do so, but people who must, on pain of social ostracism. It requires people who cannot evade responsibility and danger by claiming weakness or sensitivity or special exemptions based on what they declare "deeply offensive." And it needs such people in private households, apart from the state security. Otherwise the state will wield a monopoly of these qualities, which makes it total.

Men (and men alone) are required to risk their lives for our security and freedom. Women and homosexuals may indeed exhibit these qualities, but women are not required to do so, and homosexuals have opted out of the requirement. No stigma attaches to a woman for cowardice, and a homosexual has largely declared himself immune from such a stigma. A heterosexual man will be ostracized from civilized society. Pretend as we might, there is no alternative to this.

The only way these groups can be "empowered" vis-à-vis heterosexual men, whose justification for existing is their strength and courage, is by enlisting the police. This is why the open-ended attack on all things masculine cannot possibly end anywhere but in the limitless expansion of what one scholar calls the carceral state.[19]

The alternative is to understand and accommodate the sexual dynamic whereby women partake of masculine power not by trying to commandeer it but by cooperating with it. It is a central problem of every civilization to regulate this dynamic for its own stability, prosperity, and freedom. Traditionally, the principal mechanism for this regulation is marriage. This why the married, two-parent heterosexual family is the only family configuration that checks and diminishes government power and why every other claim to be a legitimate "family" increases state power open-endedly.

The rules governing the universal institution of marriage are furnished by the much more variable institution of religion. "Religion is central to sexual regulation in almost all societies," writes Dennis Altman. "Indeed, it may well be that the primary social function of religion is to control sexuality." This is simplistic. (For one thing, another critical social function of religion, not incidentally, it to control resentment.) Nevertheless, the point is essential.

---

19. Marie Gottschalk, *The Prison and the Gallows: The Politics of Mass Incarceration in America* (Cambridge: Cambridge University Press, 2006).

While marriage is universal among civilized societies, not all marriage arrangements are identical, because not all religions regulate sexuality in the same way or with identical consequences. The differences in the terms by which they do so result in enormous variations in the societies' social stability, economic prosperity, and civic freedom.

This can be seen very clearly by comparing the outcomes of different religious cultures. But it is perhaps most stark in our own recent, ostensibly "secular" deviations. Our modern illusion that we can simply ignore sex (or dispense with religion) and leave it unregulated is not only foolish but impossible and leaves us vulnerable not only to social anomie, but also to those who will step in and regulate it for their own purposes, imposing criminal penalties and rationalizing their repression with various alternative, politicized theologies. "Ironically, those countries which rejected religion in the name of Communism tended to adopt their own version of sexual puritanism," Altman observes, "which often matched those of the religions they assailed."[20] Today's sexual revolutionaries are refining the Bolsheviks' experiment.

And as the Bolsheviks demonstrated, the endpoint of all ideological warfare, including gender warfare, is the gulag. It is an old principle of political thought that deposed kings are never permitted to live out their lives in private peace; they are always imprisoned and usually killed, because they pose a standing threat to the regime that overthrew them. Swelling prison populations demonstrate that modern ex-patriarchs are subject to a similar dynamic. The only really secure place for superfluous men who have been stripped of paternal authority is prison. This is demonstrated unmistakably by the experience, since the inception of the welfare state, of the African-American male (historically the first and still most likely target of false rape and other accusations) and recent immigrant males in Europe, who constitute the canary in the mineshaft. It is also quite clearly the trajectory of feminist and homosexualist politics, which has now devised so many rationaliza-

---

20. Dennis Altman, *Global Sex* (Chicago: University of Chicago Press, 2002), 6. A major achievement of Lenin and Bolshevism was to discipline the cadres' puerile bohemianism, and part of their organizational effectiveness was in channeling the libido into party activity. "Drown your sexual energy in public work," urged Nicolai Semashko, the first People's Commissar for Health. "If you want to solve the sexual problem, be a public worker." Geoff Eley, *Forging Democracy: The History of the Left in Europe, 1850–2000* (Oxford: Oxford University Press, 2002), 188. When bohemianism crept back into early Soviet family policy in the form of easy divorce laws, it caused social havoc and had to be abandoned. Even the Soviets had to impose limits. Altman adds: "Whether it be Catholicism, Hinduism, Islam, or Communism, religions tend to claim a particular right to regulate and restrict sexuality, a right which is often recognized by state authorities."

tions for incarcerating heterosexual men that hardly a male in the Western world has not been threatened by at least one.

However we might try to disguise it with qualifications and euphemisms, the logical conclusion of radical androgyny clear: heterosexual sexuality and its offspring are crimes; the principal criminals are men; heterosexual women are their accomplices; the penal apparatus is a legitimate instrument to control and punish their natural sexuality; and alternative moralities like religion constitute impediments to the radicals' power to legislate the society's sexual rules.[21] This may not always be the conscious intention, but it is the clear logic and the inescapable result. It is also now the working assumption of huge and increasing cadres of state functionaries and recipients of government largesse, because it is the only justification for their employment and earnings.

The power to define crime and sin is the claim to rule, and desecrating and discarding the old taboos is merely the prelude to issuing new ones. The radical paradigm cannot admit non-political transgressions like "sin" or "immorality," much less "adultery" and "fornication," nor that relationships between men and women should be regulated by social conventions that recognize the differences between men and women. Instead of these apolitical complementarities we now find politicized competitions, and the terms refereeing the lopsided competition are increasingly the only ones the state functionaries understand how to mediate: that of criminal and victim.

A similar polarity increasingly characterizes the inescapable power differential between parent and child, as attempts to criminalize parental discipline make clear. "Women and children share a similar victim status in that both groups are dependent upon another group of people from whom rapists or abusers are drawn," according to one prominent feminist. "Just as women have traditionally been dependent on men, children are dependent upon adults."[22] Note the sleight-of-hand that equates being a "dependent" with being the "victim" of a maybe-crime like "abuse" or a real one like "rape." Being protected and provided for now breeds resentment that constitutes victimization. More recently, sexual radicals have endeavored to establish a similar criminal relationship between homosexuals and religious believers.

"All politics is on one level sexual politics," writes George Gilder. At least sexual politics is the logical culmination of all *radical* politics, which is the politics that has defined modern history. More than any

---

21. See for example, http://witchwind.wordpress.com/2013/12/15/piv-is-always-rape-ok/.

22. Quoted in Kay Hymowitz, *Ready or Not* (New York: Free Press, 1999), 43.

previous ideological experiment, politicized sexuality demands that we all examine our own reflexes and habits in a world where radical assumptions have now permeated well beyond the manifestos of committed ideologues. It demands that we challenge not just this or that doctrine, but the very dominance of our public life by ideologies, activists, advocates, organizations, opinion-mongers, functionaries, and a professional political class for whom wielding governmental power is an all-consuming identity, and instead try to recover a civic life within the control of citizens, householders, parents, local communities, houses of worship, and values that transcend the calculations of political power. Communist-era dissidents called this "anti-politics" and "nonpolitical politics": a world where, contrary to communists, feminists, and all totalitarians, the personal is not political.

Index

STEPHEN BASKERVILLE is Professor of Government at Patrick Henry College, and Research Fellow at the Howard Center for Family, Religion, and Society, and the Independent Institute. He writes on comparative and international politics and on political ideologies, with an emphasis on religion, family policy, and sexuality. His writings have appeared in such publications as the *Washington Post, Washington Times, Independent Review, Salisbury Review, The American Conservative, Chronicles, Touchstone, Human Events, Women's Quarterly, Catholic World Report, Crisis, Insight, World Net Daily, The Family in America, Family Policy Review, American Spectator, The Spectator, The American Enterprise*, and *National Review*, among others. He has appeared on national and international radio and television programs, including The O'Reilly Factor, Hardball with Chris Matthews, The Dennis Prager Show, The Michael Medved Show, CNN, Think Tank with Ben Wattenberg, and others.

Made in the USA
San Bernardino, CA
31 January 2018